D0768637
WITHDRAWN
UTSA LIBRARIES

The Globalization of Martyrdom

The Globalization of Martyrdom

Al Qaeda, Salafi Jihad, and the Diffusion of Suicide Attacks

ASSAF MOGHADAM

The Johns Hopkins University Press
Baltimore

Printed in the United States of America on acid-free paper
2 4 6 8 9 7 5 3 1

The Johns Hopkins University Press
2715 North Charles Street
Baltimore, Maryland 21218-4363
www.press.jhu.edu

Library of Congress Cataloging-in-Publication Data
Moghadam, Assaf, 1974–
The globalization of martyrdom : Al Qaeda, Salafi Jihad, and the diffusion of suicide attacks / Assaf Moghadam.
p. cm.
Includes bibliographical references and index.
ISBN-13: 978-0-8018-9055-0 (hardcover : alk. paper)
ISBN-10: 0-8018-9055-1 (hardcover : alk. paper)
1. Terrorism. 2. Suicide—Political aspects. 3. Suicide bombings. 4. Qaida (Organization). 5. Jihad. 6. Terrorism—Religious aspects—Islam. I. Title.
HV6431.M633 2008
363.325—dc22 2008010830

A catalog record for this book is available from the British Library.

The Johns Hopkins University Press uses environmentally friendly book materials, including recycled text paper that is composed of at least 30 percent post-consumer waste, whenever possible. All of our book papers are acid-free, and our jackets and covers are printed on paper with recycled content.

For Yaara

CONTENTS

ACKNOWLEDGMENTS

This book is an outgrowth of work that began when I was a doctoral student at The Fletcher School at Tufts University. My first thanks go to my mentors and teachers, above all, to Richard Shultz, my academic adviser and a staunch supporter since my first day at Fletcher. I am greatly indebted to him for encouraging me to pursue this project from the very outset and for providing his input along the way. Robert Pfaltzgraff, who has a vast knowledge in security studies, has been a true inspiration and a constant reminder of how much more I still have to learn. Jessica Stern has long been an adviser and mentor. She epitomizes intellectual curiosity, honesty, and excellence in research, and I have attempted—I hope with some degree of success—to emulate her academic philosophy.

For their inspiration, advice, and immense impact on my thinking on terrorism, I wish to thank Martha Crenshaw, Bruce Hoffman, and my first teacher on the subject of terrorism, Ehud Sprinzak, may his memory be blessed. I am enormously indebted to Reuven Paz, whose encyclopedic knowledge of radical Islamism has guided my understanding for nearly a decade. My friends and colleagues Ami Pedahzur and Arie Perliger have not only supported and inspired me over the years with their commitment to academic excellence but have also generously provided me with the dataset on suicide terrorism used in this book. For their work on this dataset, my thanks also go to the researchers at the National Security Studies Center at the University of Haifa. The SITE Institute, and especially its director, Rita Katz, have generously provided me with biographies of suicide bombers and given me a unique chance to peruse dozens of jihadist videos.

Several institutions generously provided research support, without which I would not have been able to complete my research and writing. Essential support came from the Fletcher School, especially its International Security Studies Program. The ISSP's Roberta Breen and Freda Kilgallen deserve special thanks for their support over a period of seven years. The Bradley Foundation and the Scaife Foundation have provided generous research funding, as did the Fletcher School's Jebsen Center for Counterterrorism Studies for research in Jordan. I thank especially its director, Russ Howard, for his support and Jeannine Lenehan for administrative assistance.

I was privileged to spend the research and writing phases of this book as a fellow at some of the world's leading research institutions. At the Belfer Center for Science and International Affairs at Harvard, I would like to thank Steven E. Miller for his guidance, intellectual input, and steady support, as well as Susan Lynch, the late Peggy Scannell, and Sharon Wilke for making my time at Belfer so enjoyable.

At the Olin Institute for Strategic Studies at Harvard, where I spent a year as a fellow in National Security, I would like to thank Stephen Peter Rosen, Ann Townes, and Paige Duhamel for providing me with the opportunity to complete my dissertation in an exceptionally supportive and stimulating environment.

A postdoctoral fellowship at the Belfer Center's Initiative on Religion in International Affairs has enabled me to complete my book manuscript. I would like to express my gratitude to Monica Duffy Toft for selecting me as a fellow and for her steady support over the years.

Naturally, my gratitude goes to the Combating Terrorism Center at West Point for enabling me to complete the final parts of my manuscript in the fall of 2007. I would like to thank Colonel Michael Meese and Colonel Cindy Jebb for their support, and I am especially grateful to General (Ret.) John P. Abizaid, the CTC's Distinguished Chair, and to Colonel Joe Felter, both of whom have inspired me with their leadership, dedication, service, and integrity.

I am indebted to a great many people for their advice, ideas, patience, support, and inspiration. At the Fletcher School, I would like to acknowledge in particular Alejandra Bolaños, Andrea Dew, Itamara Lochard, Ronnie Olesker, Anna Seleny, and Rockford Weitz for their invaluable comments during the various stages of the dissertation. While at Harvard, I have benefited tremendously from the comments of Dima Adamsky, Michael Boyle, Lindsay Cohn, David Cunningham, Kelly Greenhill, Michael Hays, Michael Horowitz, Piki Ish-Shalom, Andy Kennedy, Adria Lawrence, Terence Lee, Sean Lynn-Jones, Jeff Mankoff, John Park, Margaret Sloane, Jessica Stanton, Julie Taylor, James Walsh, and Thomas Wright. I would like to thank in particular Ersel Aydinli, Nick Biziouras, Olivier Brighenti, Omar McDoom, and Sebastian Rosato for their advice, support, and friendship.

I am also grateful to several other colleagues and friends who have made enormous contributions to the field that have helped shape my understanding of terrorism or the Middle East. I would like to mention in particular Rogelio Alonso, Nichole Argo, Peter Bergen, Anat Berko, Mia Bloom, Patrick Clawson, David Cook, Paul Cruickshank, Boaz Ganor, Mohammed Hafez, Andrew Hess, Samuel Huntington, Farhad Khosrokhavar, Martin Kramer, Matt Levitt, Gavriel Mairone, Benjamin Orbach, David C. Rapoport, Marc Sageman, Robert Satloff, Yoram Schweitzer, Anne Speckhard, Heiko Stoiber, Lorenzo Vidino, Leonard Weinberg, and Brian G. Williams.

I would be remiss not to acknowledge the highly competent editorial and marketing team of my publisher, the Johns Hopkins University Press. I would like to thank in particular Henry Tom, the executive editor of Social Sciences, for his interest in this project and for overseeing it from start to finish; Brian MacDonald for his outstanding copyediting of the manuscript; and Brendan Coyne for his marketing efforts.

This book would not have been written were it not for the encouragement, support, and love of my parents, Lida and Abraham, to whom I owe more than to anyone.

Finally, I want to thank my wonderful wife, partner, and best friend, Yaara, for her patience, trust, encouragement, support, and love. She is truly the luck of my life.

ACRONYMS

AQAP	Al Qaeda in the Arabian Peninsula
AQI	Al Qaeda in Iraq
AQIM	Al Qaeda in the Islamic Maghreb
ASG	Ansar al-Sunna Group
CIA	Central Intelligence Agency
EIJ	Egyptian Islamic Jihad
GI	Islamic Group (Gamaa al-Islamiyya)
GIA	Armed Islamic Group (Groupe Islamique Armé)
GICM	Moroccan Islamic Combatant Group (Groupe Islamique Combattant Marocain)
GIMF	Global Islamic Media Front
GSPC	Salafist Group for the Call and Combat (Groupe Salafiste pour la Prédication et le Combat)
IDF	Israel Defense Forces
IED	Improvised Explosive Device
IMU	Islamic Movement of Uzbekistan
ISAF	International Security Assistance Force (Afghanistan)
ISI	Islamic State of Iraq
JI	Jemaah Islamiyah
KSM	Khalid Sheikh Muhammad
LET	Lashkar-e-Taiba
LIFG	Libyan Islamic Fighting Group
LTTE	Liberation Tigers of Tamil Eelam
NATO	North Atlantic Treaty Organization
NGO	nongovernmental organization
PFLP	Popular Front for the Liberation of Palestine
PIJ	Palestinian Islamic Jihad

PKK	Kurdistan Workers Party (Partiya Karkerên Kurdistan)
SMs	Suicide Missions
UN	United Nations
UNAMA	United Nations Assistance Mission in Afghanistan

The Globalization of Martyrdom

Introduction

I will always remember the events of September 4, 1997, when three suicide bombers detonated themselves nearly simultaneously on Jerusalem's main pedestrian mall. Suicide bombings in Jerusalem had long since become a sad but common feature of everyday life in Israel. This attack had a more personal impact, for one of the three bombers set off his nail-studded explosive device steps away from the building on 5 Ben Yehuda Street where two friends and I shared an apartment on the top floor. We were lucky, for our lease had expired just four days prior, and we had already vacated the apartment.

When I visited the area a day or two after the bombings, I hardly recognized my old neighborhood. Ben Yehuda was usually teeming with a mix of young and old Jerusalemites socializing on the city's famed shopping street, grabbing a falafel or sipping coffee at one of the many coffee shops lining the street. The aftermath of the bombing offered a drastically different picture of Jerusalem's city center. Although first responders had long erased most of the bloody traces of the bombings, the damage to many shops and restaurants was still evident. What struck me, however, was the silence that prevailed in a street whose noise level on a typical day could easily compete with that of an average Western nightclub. The silence was deafening. It was the silence of grief.

In 1997 Israel was not the sole country to grieve the victims of terrorism, but it was one of only four countries where a sustained campaign of suicide attacks had taken place. Only a handful of other countries had experienced the devastating consequences of this tactic until then. The first wave of suicide bombings, which hit Israel in the mid-1990s, was not Israel's first encounter, though. In the previous decade, its army had suffered many casualties from suicide attacks in Lebanon, where the Shia militant group Hizballah had also used suicide operations against U.S. and French forces. In July 1987 the Liberation Tigers of Tamil Eelam (LTTE) had adopted this modus operandi in Sri Lanka, where it fought the Sinhalese-dominated government in order to establish a national homeland for the Tamils. Within a decade after its first suicide attack, the LTTE would firmly establish itself as the most proficient and innovative employer of suicide attacks. In 1996 another group vying for self-determination, the Kurdistan Workers Party (PKK), began adopting suicide missions in its attacks against Turkey. Over the course of more than three years, the group would stage more than a dozen of these attacks, focused mainly on the Turkish army.

Why Another Book on Suicide Attacks?

Fast forward to 2008, when more than thirty countries located on every continent save for Australia and Antarctica have experienced the devastating consequences of suicide attacks. Suicide bombings not only occur in a growing number of countries but are planned and executed by more and more organizations, which kill a greater number of people every year. More suicide bombings have occurred in Iraq since 2003 than in all other countries in the preceding twenty-five years combined. Suicide bombings have killed important political figures, like Pakistan's Benazir Bhutto,[1] and wounded others, like former Sri Lankan president Chandrika Kumaratunga. Suicide missions are increasingly targeted at Muslims and are employed today as part of a strategy not only to gain a national homeland but also to help depose regimes that are regarded as un-Islamic. Suicide missions have emerged in many new countries with no prior history of suicide attacks, such as Afghanistan, Somalia, and Uzbekistan. Perhaps most important for the West, suicide attacks are no longer a distant threat. They have hit Western countries on their home turf, in places like New York, London, and Madrid.[2]

The unprecedented numerical rise, geographic spread, growing lethality, and marked increase in the number of groups employing suicide missions every year has amounted to nothing less than a full-scale globalization of this tactic. The main aim of this book is to examine the causes and nature of this "globalization of martyrdom." Its central argument is that there are two interrelated reasons for the globalization of suicide missions: the rise of Al Qaeda as a global terrorist actor; and the growing appeal of the Salafi Jihad, the guiding ideology of Al Qaeda and its affiliated and associated movements.

Suicide attacks are important to study because they are one of the most lethal tactics used by terrorist and insurgent organizations today. According to one researcher, suicide attacks account for only 5 percent of all terrorist attacks but are responsible for roughly half of all fatalities from terrorist incidents.[3] The mere extent to which this highly lethal tactic has proliferated in the twenty-first century alone justifies scholarly attention to this phenomenon. In addition, suicide attacks are a timely subject of study because of their potential to create turbulence in international affairs at large. The quadruple suicide attacks of September 11, 2001, and the war in Iraq—where suicide operations have become the signature mode of attack—have highlighted how suicide attacks may not only lead to considerable losses of human life and physical infrastructure but can also influence the course of global events.

Existing studies on suicide terrorism have produced a number of key insights into the nature and causes of this tactic. Terrorism researchers have noted, for instance, that suicide attacks have been employed by organizations acting on behalf of a national or religious community that strives for a degree of regional autonomy, and often self-determination. Researchers have also shown that suicide terrorism has often occurred in regions ravaged by decades, and often centuries, of violent conflict between two communities that differ in their ethnic or religious background. Existing research suggests—and rightly so—that suicide terrorism is not merely a religious phenomenon, because secular organizations have also used this tactic to achieve their goals. Finally, some researchers have argued that suicide attacks have often taken the form of systematic campaigns of terrorism designed to break the will of a seemingly stronger enemy in an asymmetric battle.

In my view, only some of these findings apply to the contemporary phenomenon of suicide attacks. Most existing explanations are more convincing in explaining suicide attacks that have been used in the context of the Hizballah-Israel, Israeli-Palestinian, Tamil-Sinhalese, and Turkish-Kurdish conflicts. All these conflicts, however, are characterized by their localized nature. Upon closer inspection, the theories that illuminate the use of this tactic in these localized conflicts seem less capable of explaining suicide attacks perpetrated by cells affiliated with or inspired by Al Qaeda. Perhaps most importantly, such explanations have all but ignored the importance of ideology in the global diffusion of suicide attacks.

I propose that Al Qaeda and its Salafi-Jihadist ideology are directly responsible for the rise in the number of suicide attacks, the rise in the number of countries in which suicide attacks have occurred, and the rise in the number of organizations that employ suicide attacks, as well as for a growing percentage of suicide attacks against civilian populations. Al Qaeda's and the Salafi Jihad's influence on the phenomenon of suicide attacks is so profound that we can identify an entirely new pattern of attacks, namely "globalized suicide attacks." Not only is this pattern distinct from the traditional, localized pattern of suicide attacks—a pattern epitomized by Palestinian groups, the LTTE, Hizballah, and the PKK—but it has also gradually sidelined the traditional pattern of suicide attacks. Globalized suicide attacks, which are planned and executed by Al Qaeda and its associated movements, are the most vital threat to the security of the United States and its allies today. Thus, it behooves us to analyze their causes, nature, and consequences.

For this discussion, I draw upon qualitative and quantitative analyses, using a number of data sources. The data for the numbers and figures found in chapter 1 come from the Suicide Terrorism Database of the National Security Studies Center of the University of Haifa, one of the most reliable and extensive datasets on suicide terrorism.[4] The database lists a total of 1,269 suicide attacks from 1981 until April 5, 2007, the cutoff date for the data used here. The case study discussions of chapters 5, 6, and 7 are updated as of December 31, 2007, and may contain data on suicide terrorism that are at variance with the data presented in chapter 1 because of the inclusion of more recent data that supersede the numbers in the dataset. In each case where the numbers vary with the dataset's figures, I cite the alternative source of the data.

I also study biographical data of suicide attackers found in primary and secondary sources. I am acutely aware that the amount of biographical information available about suicide attackers is limited and that this information may not be an accurate reflection of the actual motivations of the suicide bombers. This problem is a persistent one that all terrorism researchers face and cannot be solved in this book. Any findings pertaining to the individual motivations of suicide attackers must therefore be considered suggestive rather than conclusive.

I have also scrutinized official statements attributed to organizations that have engaged in suicide attacks, including official mission statements, semiofficial pronouncements, and interviews with leading group members and other statements attributed to key leaders. To back up these official statements, I have also consulted Web sites, press reports, terrorism databases, and anecdotal sources.

The book's first four chapters discuss the nature and causes of the globalization of suicide attacks of the past decade. Chapter 1 provides empirical evidence for the globalization of suicide attacks and introduces the main argument of this book, namely that the globalization of suicide attacks is a result of the rise of Al Qaeda and Salafi-Jihadist ideology. Chapter 2 discusses the evolution of Al Qaeda and the importance the group has afforded to suicide attacks. Chapter 3 examines Salafi-Jihadist ideology, its origins, and its relationship with martyrdom and self-sacrifice. Chapter 4 lays out the globalization of Al Qaeda and its transition into the vanguard of a global jihadist movement.

The next three chapters comprise more than a dozen case studies of countries that have been targeted by "globalized" suicide attacks. Chapter 5 surveys suicide attacks in Afghanistan, Algeria, Chechnya, Egypt, Indonesia, Jordan, Morocco, Pakistan, Saudi Arabia, Turkey, and Uzbekistan. Chapter 6 offers an in-depth examination of the United Kingdom that focuses on the 7/7 bombings. Chapter 7 examines suicide attacks in Iraq, the main contemporary theater of suicide attacks. The final chapter draws together the findings of this book and considers its research and policy implications.

The remainder of this introductory chapter reviews the definition of suicide missions used in this book and it also presents a historical and theoretical examination of suicide attacks.

Defining Suicide Missions

One of the terms more commonly used to describe the modus operandi of suicide missions is *suicide terrorism*—a term that, upon closer examination, is not without problems.[5] The most obvious is that no agreed upon definition of suicide terrorism is possible as long as the word terrorism itself is subject to various different interpretations.[6] Terrorism—a pejorative word most organizations refuse to be labeled by—remains a concept that lacks a universally accepted definition, as terrorism scholars have so frequently noted.[7] The same is true for suicide terrorism, a subcategory of terrorism.[8]

Another problem is that, historically, suicide missions as a modus operandi have been used not only during campaigns of terrorism but also during conventional military forays against standing armies. Most definitions of terrorism, however, strictly distinguish acts of terrorism from conventional warfare because the former are generally understood to emanate from nonstate actors.[9] For example, although the Japanese kamikaze pilots were clearly involved in a campaign involving suicide missions, kamikaze attacks during World War II are not usually considered acts of terrorism because the suicide pilots were acting at the behest of a state at war.

Even when an attack does emanate from a nonstate actor, such an attack should still not be labeled a terrorist attack if it is targeted against members of an army, because attacks are ordinarily labeled terrorist attacks only when they are aimed at noncombatants.[10] Bombings, shootings, kidnappings, and similar methods are generally labeled guerrilla warfare, insurgency, or low-intensity conflict if they are directed against uniformed men and women on active duty.

The terms *suicide mission* (SM), *suicide attack*, *suicide operation*, or *human bomb* are far better choices than suicide terrorism, and are the preferred terms in this book. Unlike the value-laden word terrorism, the terms suicide attacks, suicide operations, or suicide missions are value-neutral and emphasize the mode of attack—namely, one that involves the death of its perpetrator—rather than the type of attack, in this case terrorism, and thus, by association, one's opinion over the legitimacy of the attack.

Unlike ordinary suicide, which is "done by oneself and to oneself,"[11] suicide terrorism requires not only a willingness to die but also a willingness to kill.[12] It is generally assumed that the acts of dying and killing occur simultaneously, although a broader definition of SMs is more flexible and allows for a certain time lag between the act of killing and the act of dying. There is a consensus, however, that in an SM, the act of killing and the act of dying occur as part of the same mission. Hence, a terrorist responsible for detonating an explosive device in a market, killing innocent bystanders, will not be considered a suicide terrorist even if he later commits suicide in prison. The notorious West German terrorists Ulrike Meinhof and Andreas Baader, both of whom committed suicide in prison in the second half of the 1970s, are therefore not considered suicide terrorists. Nor do we consider Bobby Sands and nine other members of the Irish Republican Army (IRA) who starved themselves to death in prison in 1981 to be suicide terrorists. Instead, these are examples of terrorists who committed suicide.

Suicide missions are traditionally defined as attacks whose success is contingent upon the death of the perpetrator.[13] According to this definition, suicide operations such as the 9/11 attacks or the London bombings of July 7, 2005, are clear instances of SMs. Instances such as the February 1994 killing spree by Baruch Goldstein, who shot twenty-nine Muslim civilians during prayer at a holy site in Hebron, are not considered SMs under this "narrow" definition. Although Goldstein probably had no delusion that he would survive the attack, his death was not necessary for the attack to occur—his ability to enter the holy shrine and to fire his weapon before being overrun was the only precondition for success. In this book, SMs are hence understood in a narrow sense: as a violent modus operandi designed to inflict harm on individuals and/or physical infrastructure, whereby the success of the act is strictly dependent on the death of the perpetrator or perpetrators.

The term suicide should not be understood as a value judgment, and it must be acknowledged that many suicide attackers believe not that they are committing suicide in the ordinary sense but that they are sacrificing themselves for a cause larger than themselves. Nor is it my intention to suggest that suicide attackers are akin to ordinary suicides, who, as studies have shown, usually suffer from a personal crisis or a "kind of Darwinian inability to live at all or live well enough to survive."[14]

A Historical Sketch

The onset of the modern phenomenon of suicide attacks is usually placed in the early 1980s, but precursors of this modus operandi have existed for more than three millennia. Before providing a brief history of SMs beginning with the biblical figure of Samson, I revisit the historical prominence of two related phenomena: the relationship between suicide on the one hand and politics and conflict on the other; and the concept of the cult of the fallen hero, a ubiquitous feature of a multitude of communities and nations throughout history. The overview demonstrates that SMs and related phenomena are neither a recent development nor necessarily religious in character, and certainly not an exclusive feature of Islam.

The Role of Suicide in Politics

Suicide by a public figure is not simply a flight from personal distress; it can also be a political statement and a political act. One of the most prominent examples of a politically motivated suicide is that of Cato, who criticized Julius Caesar and protested his corruption at a time when the Roman Republic was in a period of decline. During the ensuing civil war that shook the Roman Republic, Cato was the most vocal of Caesar's critics. Caesar oftentimes pardoned his critics and showed mercy to his opponents, and he planned to do the same with Cato. In a stunning act of defiance, however, Cato committed suicide rather than provide Caesar the opportunity to grant him clemency and thus humiliate him. Cato's death managed to consolidate the resistance to Caesar and likely contributed to his assassination less than two years later.[15]

Ritual suicide with a political undertone has also been a prominent feature of Japanese culture. Two forms of ritual suicide (*seppuku*) were practiced by the samurai, namely *setsujoku* and *kanshi*. Whereas *setsujoku* denotes a suicide committed in order to prevent one's capture by the enemy, *kanshi* was carried out in protest against a superior, when one firmly believed that the superior's course of action was mistaken.[16] Sacrifice of one's life in battle was a core tenet of *bushido*, a code of honor by which every *bushi* (warrior) was expected to abide and an element of *kokutai*, Japan's philosophical concept of achieving fame and honor for one's country.[17]

Suicide as political protest has perhaps assumed its most notorious form in the act of self-immolation. Perhaps the best-known example in recent years is that of Thich Quang Duc, a Buddhist monk who on June 11, 1963, set himself afire to protest Vietnamese president Ngo Dinh Diem's favoritism toward the country's Catholic minority.[18] Other acts of protest marked by a willingness to risk one's life include hunger strikes, often used by nonviolent actors such as the Suffragettes but also by terrorist groups such as the IRA, which orchestrated in 1981 a mass suicide involving ten imprisoned terrorists, led by Bobby Sands, in protest of their treatment.

The Cult of the Fallen in History

Suicide attackers do not usually claim to act out of despair, or for personal, fatalistic reasons. Instead, they usually claim to act as martyrs for altruistic reasons—that is, for the sake of their larger community, their country, or religion.[19] The veneration surrounding martyrs and their sacrifice has taken on the form of a cult of martyrdom in many cases, such as the mass sacrifice of Iranians during the Iran-Iraq War and the numerous suicide bombers in both the Lebanese and Palestinian societies.

The cult of martyrdom practiced by many contemporary supporters of suicide missions has a long history filled with countless narratives recording the veneration of the fallen, from ancient Greece to modern twentieth-century dictatorships. Under King Leonidas, for example, Spartan heroes fought to the death at the Battle of Thermopylae because their acts were sanctioned by the gods. The cult of the dead was similarly present in the Nordic sagas, which tell how heroes who had fallen in battle were taken to Asgard, the realm of the gods.[20] The sacrifice of the Prophet Muhammad's grandson Hussein at the plain of Karbala in today's Iraq is a significant act of martyrdom that has been the central emotive drama for Shia Muslims, as will be described later.

Arnold von Winkelried, the legendary Swiss hero of the Battle of Sempach in 1386, provides another example of self-sacrifice in battle. By throwing himself into the enemy's lances, Winkelried forced the Habsburgs to focus on him while opening a passage for his fellow fighters. This breach in the lines of the Habsburgs enabled the victory of the Old Swiss Confederacy.

Another legend from the Middle Ages is contained in the Chanson de Roland, which tells the story of a heroic rearguard action at Roncevalles by the emperor's army. According to the legend, Roland, the nephew of Charlemagne, his friend Olivier, and thirty knights faced the superior army of the Saracens but were too proud to sound the horn that would call for help until it was too late. According to the Chanson, Roland, Olivier, and their comrades died not only for France but, more importantly, in defense of their religion against the pagans. The church rewarded them by honoring them as martyrs.[21]

During the modern age, the poet Theodor Koerner wrote on the eve of a battle against Napoleon that "happiness lies only in sacrificial death,"[22] while across the Atlantic Ocean, during the Texas Revolution, a small garrison of 188 Texan rebels struggled against a Mexican army of at least 3,000 people at the 1836 Battle of the Alamo. The thirteen-day siege culminated on March 6, when the mission was captured and nearly all the defenders had died. Despite this loss, the sacrifice of the rebels provided a setback to the Mexican forces in their ensuing battles.

The call to sacrifice oneself for the nation was particularly prevalent during the modern fascist dictatorships. In early Spanish fascism, for example, the head of the *falange*, José Antonio Primo de Rivera, preached a spirit of self-sacrifice, urging the students of Salamanca University in October 1936, "Down with the intellectuals, *viva la muerte*!"[23] Examples of the cult of the fallen heroes in Nazi Germany abound as well. They include the skull-and-bones insignia worn by SS troops and the veneration of fallen comrades in songs like the "Horst-Wessel-Lied," which assured the National Socialists that those comrades who had been shot down by communists continued to march along with the Nazis in spirit even after death.[24]

Suicide Missions and Their Precursors from Biblical Times to 1981

The foregoing examples demonstrate that the history of politics, conflicts, and wars is filled with acts of suicide perpetrated for political reasons. They also show that history is replete with examples of how the fallen heroes of communities and nations the world over have been respected and venerated, at times with a near-religious devotion. These examples, however, are hardly acts of SMs as defined in this book—namely, acts of violence that require the death of the perpetrator/s in order to be successful. Suicide attacks are defined as missions in which the perpetrators exhibit not only a willingness to die for political reasons but also a willingness to kill. The combination of death and killing lies at the core of suicide operations, and, like suicide for political reasons, the combination of death and killing has historical antecedents, too.

The modern phenomenon of SMs is often dated to the early 1980s, when a series of suicide attacks in Lebanon struck the Iraqi and American embassies as well as other U.S., French, and Israeli military targets. Antecedents of this tactic, however, can be found as early as biblical times. In that period, suicide attacks were rarely used as part of a terrorist campaign in the modern sense of the word. Instead, prototypes of the modern tactic of suicide terrorism were carried out by various actors, including individuals, groups, sects, and armies associated with nation-states such as Japan, Vietnam, or Iran.

The first recorded SM dates back more than 3,000 years to the biblical figure of Samson. The book of Judges of the Old Testament tells the story of Samson's betrayal by Delilah, to whom he had revealed the secret of his strength. Delilah delivered that secret to the Philistines, who promptly imprisoned Samson and tortured him by gouging his eyes. When the Philistines brought a sacrifice unto their god Dagon, they called in Samson to entertain them, placing him near the central pillars of their Gazan temple. Samson used his humiliation as an opportunity to exact revenge on his captors:

> And Samson said unto the lad that held him by the hand, Suffer me that I may feel the pillars whereupon the house standeth, that I may lean upon them. Now the house was full of men and women; and all the lords of the Philistines were there; and there were upon the roof about three thousand men and women, that beheld while Samson made sport. And Samson called unto the Lord, and said, O Lord God, remember me, I pray thee, and strengthen me, I pray thee, only this once, O God, that I may be at once avenged of the Philistines for my two eyes. And Samson took hold of the two middle pillars upon which the house stood, and on which it was borne up, of the one with his right hand, and of the other with his left. And Samson said, Let me die with the Philistines. And he bowed himself with all his might; and the house fell upon the lords, and upon all the people that were therein. So the dead which he slew at his death were more than they which he slew in his life.[25]

Samson's attack neatly fits the definition of SMs adopted in this book—and, indeed, by most scholars of suicide operations—because his death was a precondition for the success of his vengeful act. Had Samson not died himself, he could not have killed the assembled Philistines. His utterance of the sentence "Let me die with the Philistines" embodies the very essence of the tactic of suicide operations, namely the confluence of the willingness to kill and to die.

Since these biblical times, nearly all religions have employed SMs as a tactic at one point or another. The best-known precursors of the modern-day suicide attackers are the medieval Assassins who were active mainly between the eleventh and thirteenth centuries. A radical offshoot belonging to the Ismaili-Nizari branch of Shiism, the Assassins were devoted to spreading the Ismaili version of Shia Islam across parts of the Middle East, and thus to tear down Islam's competing Sunni order. From the Assassins' base, the castle of Alamut in the Alburz Mountains south of the Caspian Sea, their leader, Hassan-i Sabbah, established a group of devoted followers who were tasked to help him in this endeavor by advancing far into modern-day Iran, Iraq, Syria, and other regions. The Assassins' strategy was to seize fortresses and use them as bases from which to conduct campaigns of terror. When they succeeded in the late eleventh century in taking a number of strategic castles in the eastern Alburz and near Isfahan in today's Iran, the Assassins were able to threaten the Turkish Seljuk Empire in Persia and Syria.

The Assassins regarded themselves as messengers of God. Their preferred tactic was to kill the leader of their enemies, which included all those who resisted the Assassins' attempts to convert the "nonbelievers." Their preferred targets were members of the Sunni establishment, including princes, officers, ministers, religious dignitaries, and city prefects. They generally abstained from attacking fellow Shia, even those who belonged to the majority (Twelver) branch of Shiism, and refrained from attacking native Christians and Jews.[26]

Their weapon of choice was the dagger, which they used to kill their enemies in broad daylight, even in the presence of bodyguards. In 1192 the Assassins staged their biggest coup by killing Conrad of Montferrat, the Crusader king of Jerusalem, in Tyre. The act sent shockwaves throughout the Crusader ranks, who believed that the Assassins' leader, known as The Old Man from the Mountain, possessed supernatural powers and was a megalomaniac, believing in no God but himself. The Crusaders also perpetuated the belief that the Assassins were enticed by the Old Man's promises of eternal pleasures, rendering them more willing to die than to live.[27]

Indeed, the Assassins rarely attempted to escape from the scene after killing their victims and seemed fearless in the face of their own death. According to Bernard Lewis,

> the killing by the Assassin of his victim was not only an act of piety; it also had a ritual, almost sacramental quality. It is significant that in all their murders, in both Persia and Syria, the Assassins always used a dagger; never poison, never missiles, though there must have been occasions when these would have been easier and safer. The Assassin is almost always caught, and usually indeed makes no attempt to escape; there is even a suggestion that to survive a mission was shameful.[28]

Lewis ascribes this willingness for self-sacrifice—so reminiscent of the desire for martyrdom found among present-day suicide attackers—to the Ismaili, and larger Shia, ideology:

> The reformed Ismaili religion, with its memories of passion and martyrdom, its promise of divine and human fulfillment, was a cause that gave dignity and courage to those that embraced it, and inspired a devotion unsurpassed in human history. It was the loyalty of the Assassins, who risked and even courted death for their Master, that first attracted the attention of Europe, and made their name a by-word for faith and self-sacrifice before it became a synonym for murder.[29]

This seemingly fanatical courage of the Assassins inspired the myth that they had been drugged with hashish, a belief that gave the Assassins (*hashashiyoun* or *hashishiyyin* in Arabic) their name.[30] Most modern scholars of the Assassins, however, believe the story about the use of hashish in drugging these early suicide attackers to be untrue. Lewis suggests that the most likely reason for the creation of this myth was their enemies' contempt for the Assassins' beliefs, behavior, and methods; thus, the charge was an attempt to discredit them, rather than an accurate depiction of their conduct.[31] The Assassins were eventually wiped out during the Mongol invasion of the thirteenth century, which wreaked havoc not only on these early Muslim terrorists but also on large swaths of the Middle East.

In more modern times, antecedents of suicide missions were employed over the course of several centuries in three Muslim communities in the Malabar coast of southwestern India, Aceh in northern Sumatra, and Mindanao and Sulu in the southern Philippines.[32] Stephen Dale ascribes the use of attacks by individuals willing to die in large part to the systematic exploitation of the local Muslim population and economy by Western nation-states, coupled with the early religious zeal with which the Spanish and Portuguese attempted to convert the Muslim populations to Christianity following the arrival of Vasco da Gama in the Indian Ocean in 1498. By the sixteenth century, influential Muslims began calling for a jihad against the Western presence. One such call was issued by Zayn al-din al-Mabari, who, after pointing out to Muslims in Malabar that they had come under attack by the Portuguese, urged them to heed Islamic law and undertake a jihad, emphasizing that those killed in the course of this struggle would be venerated as martyrs among the Muslim community. The resistance against the colonialists in Aceh and the Philippines was similarly justified in religious terms,[33] and the fallen heroes were glorified in ways reminiscent of the contemporary culture of martyrdom prevalent among Palestinians, Sri Lankans, or Salafi-Jihadists. In the case of the Malabar Muslims, this cult included not only the performance of certain rituals before the attacks but also the postmortem celebration of the fallen heroes in literature, as well as depictions of the pleasures awaiting the *shuhada* (martyrs) in paradise.

Dale reports that what he calls "suicidal attacks" in Islamic Asia began to appear in Malabar in the first half of the eighteenth century. One of the earliest descriptions is dated 1742, when agents of the English East India Company in Malabar reported that a small number of Muslims "who have selected themselves to Murder any Christian when if they Die in the Attempt they are persuaded it is very meritorious and have Adorations paid to their memory by many Enthusiasticks of their faith."[34] It is, however, not apparent from this report whether those attackers actually killed themselves along with their targets, or whether they were simply willing to (or expecting to) die in the attack. It is more likely that these attackers were more akin to what the Spaniards called *juramentado* (those who took the oath), in reference to those who were fighting *fi sabil Allah* (in the way of God). The mode of attack of the *juramentados* entailed, first, the taking of initiation rites and prayers, after which the fighters "rushed at the enemy, trying to kill as many of them as possible, until they themselves were killed. Scores of Spanish soldiers thus perished and there is no record of a *juramentado* who had returned home alive."[35] "Invariably," according to one historian, the *shahid* "was killed since he kept going on looking for Spanish soldiers right up to the fort itself."[36] Those who changed their mind were ridiculed as "half-martyrs," which led many to conduct renewed attacks.

These "suicidal attacks" in Islamic Asia, which were used until the mid-twentieth century, are more likely precursors to modern SMs, as defined in this study. That should not detract from the firm willingness to die that the Muslim attackers of Malabar, Aceh, and the Philippines had professed throughout the centuries—a willingness that Dale attributes to "desperation and an admission of military impotence."[37]

A form of SMs more akin to today's human bombs was used by anarchist terrorists in the late nineteenth and early twentieth centuries.[38] Of those attacks by anarchists that seemed to be SMs, the best known is the assassination of Tsar Alexander II by the anarchist terrorist group Narodnaya Volya (The People's Will) on March 1, 1881. It was the ninth attempt on the tsar's life and succeeded because one of the four Russian revolutionaries who equipped themselves with bombs on that day decided to detonate the bomb in such close proximity to the tsar that it would ensure not only his target's death but also his own. Another clear case of an SM is the October 1904 self-detonation at a police headquarters in Belostok by anarchist Nisan Farber. According to historian Anna Geifman, Farber's dedication was not unusual. "With the headless determination of true fanatics," she writes, "anarchists made their way into police headquarters in various parts of the country and blew themselves up with dynamite, along with everyone present."[39]

Prior to the contemporary proliferation of suicide attacks, perhaps the most prominent use of this modus operandi was by the Japanese kamikaze suicide pilots, who staged more than 3,000 suicide sorties during World War II, specifically between October 1944 and August 1945. Japanese SMs during World War II were not limited to their best-known form of aerial attacks, which were staged by the Shinpu (Divine Wind) Special Attack Corps established by Admiral Onishi in October 1944, although these were by far the most dominant and destructive type of SMs. Aerial suicide attacks were first used in a systematic manner near the Philippines between October 1944 and January 1945, followed by more numerous waves of attacks off Okinawa, Kyushu, and Iwo Jima between February and August 1945.[40]

Apart from airplane attacks, the Japanese also designed and used—albeit with varying degrees of success and frequency—the *oka* (cherry blossom), a rocket-powered piloted bomb; the *kaiten* (turning heaven), a pair of connected manned torpedoes equipped with a conning tower and periscope; and suicide motorboats (*maru-re* and *shinyo*) designed for the defense of Japan's coastline.[41]

When compared to other tactics, SMs not only had a disproportionately more effective military impact but also claimed a heavy psychological toll on the intended targets. Nevertheless, in the ultimate analysis the kamikaze planes achieved only limited success as they were unable to prevent Japan's unconditional surrender.

The use of SMs by Japan during World War II helps dispel some popular misconceptions about this modus operandi. First, state sponsorship demonstrates that this tactic is not exclusive to terrorist organizations. Second, and perhaps more important, along with the example of Samson and the Russian revolutionaries, the kamikaze missions provide early evidence that, historically speaking, the use of SMs has not been justified exclusively by religion. Although almost all Japanese are nominally both Buddhist and Shinto, and many cherish Confucian values such as filial piety, submission to authority, and diligence, Japanese suicide attackers seemed to be motivated more by a desire to protect their country and their families rather than merely by a keen devotion to their emperor.[42] In addition, it should be kept in mind that suicide in Japan is morally justifiable, as has been argued earlier, especially as an honorable way out of an impossible situation.

Other countries besides Japan also engaged in SMs during World War II. Two U.S. airmen crashed their planes onto Japanese ships—one during the Battle of the Coral Sea in May 1942, the other during the Battle of Midway in June 1942.[43] Russian and German troops also adopted this tactic during desperate times. Russian commanders, for example, instructed their fighter pilots to crash their planes into enemy aircraft after Hitler's invasion of the Soviet Union. Similarly, the German Luftwaffe established a special experimental unit during World War II known as Sturmstaffel 1 (Storm Squadron I) or, more popularly, as *Rammjäger* (ram fighters). The task of the squadron was to test new methods in which to attack Allied bomber formations. The *Rammjäger* plane was designed to thread itself into enemy formations with the intent of breaking them up, and ramming the enemy fighter planes as a last resort. As one scholar notes, however, it is not entirely clear precisely what "ramming" entailed. New tactics of close combat enabled the German air force to shoot down enemy planes without the need to come into physical contact with them.[44] It is possible, however, that accidental collisions occurred. Furthermore, Hitler seemed reluctant to order SMs until a later stage of the war, when, in an attempt to obstruct the Red Army's advance onto Berlin, he instructed Luftwaffe planes to crash into bridges. The pilots apparently signed a statement to the effect that they were aware that their mission would result in their death.[45]

Ironically, the Nazi leader himself escaped assassination by suicide attack in 1944. In that year, British spy Eddie Chapman offered to kill Hitler by perpetrating an attack that Chapman knew would cost him his life. Chapman volunteered for an SM, saying that he had an opportunity to approach the German leader with a hidden bomb. He justified his willingness to sacrifice himself with the hope that history would judge him as a hero. The MI5, however, rejected Chapman's offer in part due to his murky past. The British leadership also believed Hitler's war strategy at this stage of the war to be so irrational that the Führer was perceived to be of more value alive than dead.[46]

In the post–World War II period, precursors of modern-day SMs have also emerged in Vietnam, especially in the second half of the 1960s, when two types of Viet Cong units carried out suicide attacks. The first were the "suicide cells" (or "suicide teams"), established in November 1967 as part of the Tet Offensive. These SMs were aimed to weaken the Saigon government by capturing and holding cities whose civilian population—many of whom were suspected of collaborating with the South—would be exposed to a campaign of terror. According to captured Viet Cong documents, suicide teams of between ten to twenty members were established in places like Binh Dinh Province. These teams were then further divided into cells consisting of three persons. The tasks for these cells, which included both males and female teenagers over the age of fifteen, consisted not only of killing "wicked tyrants" (i.e., local notables) with grenades and daggers but also of inspiring members of other villages to join the side of the Viet Cong.[47]

The second type of SMs in the context of the Vietnam War involved sapper units affiliated with the Viet Cong and the North Vietnamese. The sapper units were active beyond the villages, in larger cities such as Saigon, where they conducted not only SMs but a variety of high-risk operations against American and Army of the Republic of Vietnam forces. Unlike the younger, expendable cannon fodder that composed the suicide cells, the sappers were professionals, highly trained in the use of explosives and assault. They were sent on SMs against high-prestige or high-visibility targets during the Tet Offensive. Units of some 250 men and women attacked the U.S. Embassy compound and the South Vietnamese Joint General Staff headquarters in Saigon, the navy headquarters, the Presidential Palace, and similar targets.[48]

Some records may leave doubts over whether the suicide cells and the sapper units conducted SMs as they are commonly understood today. It is more likely that in the majority of cases, the suicide teams dispatched by the North Vietnamese and their allies were what German soldiers describe as *Himmelfahrtskommandos*—units dispatched on missions that are so risky that they will result in almost certain death. That said, based on a study by Weinberg, at least a number of these attacks seem to have been "conventional" SMs, that is, operations in which the death of the perpetrators was a precondition for the success of the attack. In the aftermath of Tet, sappers oftentimes attempted to penetrate and destroy U.S. command centers and other military installations by detonating explosive devices that they carried on their bodies. An interview Weinberg conducted with a former U.S. Army officer substantiates this account. According to the officer, who witnessed attacks on U.S. Army bases south of Khe Sanh near the Laotian border,

> We were told at the time that the Sappers mode of operation was to place charges to blow up barbed-wire obstructions and to throw satchel charges (bags of plastic explosives) into bunkers and artillery firing pits. We were also told that they were prepared to detonate the charges on themselves if it came to that. . . . My experience . . . in Northern I Corps (Quang Tri Province) [was that] suicide acts by sappers were not the norm but a fallback strategy when there was no other way.[49]

Unlike many contemporary SMs, missions employed by the South Vietnamese Viet Cong and their North Vietnamese allies against U.S. military and civilian forces and the Saigon government were conducted mainly for secular causes.[50]

The Onset of Suicide Terrorism after 1981

In 1981 the history of suicide attacks underwent a dramatic shift. From Lebanon, where the radical Shia Hizballah adopted the tactic, it spread rapidly to violent groups in many other countries and increasingly adopted the form of suicide *terrorism*—a trend that continues to this very day. The roots of the contemporary phenomenon of SMs, and particularly of religiously inspired SMs, are found in post-1979 Iran, from where the tactic had spread to Lebanon in the first place.

During the Islamic revolution and in its aftermath, the Iranian regime actively disseminated the notion that "martyrdom" in the name of God was not only a noble but also a desirable deed. More than any other regime before it, the Iranian mullahs, led by Ayatollah Ruhollah Khomeini, provided the religious and ideological justification for the use of violence in the name of Islam. Jihad and self-sacrifice were the core tenets within this framework as martyrdom was expected, and even demanded, to fulfill the goal of spreading the ideas of the revolution—and especially jihad—outside of Iran. In order to overcome Islam's traditional sanctioning of suicide and permit operations in which the individual would engage in activities that would certainly result in his or her death in the name of jihad, Khomeini downgraded the *taqiya*, the right to be exempted from religious duties in times of crisis in order to avoid bodily harm. By giving specific meaning and substance to martyrdom, he placed it in the context of traditional Shia motifs of sacrifice.[51]

The relationship between Shiism and martyrdom dates back to the early years of Islam.[52] Shiism, a word derived from *shia,* meaning "party" or "faction" in Arabic, was used to describe the "party of Ali." Following the Prophet Muhammad's death in 632, Ali, the Prophet's cousin and son-in-law, had been repeatedly blocked from assuming the post of *caliph* (literally, successor), he who was to succeed the prophet in leading the Muslim community of believers, known as the *umma*. When Ali was murdered by a Kharajite in 661, his death was regarded as a shameful killing of the closest remaining male relative of Muhammad—someone who not only had been the first convert to Islam but was also believed to possess many of the exceptional qualities of the prophet. It is for that reason that the fate of Ali, "a man betrayed by his friends as well as his enemies, became a symbol of the inherent injustice in life," as one scholar has observed.[53]

The incident that proved most formative for the emergence of Shiism, however, was the martyrdom of Ali's son Hussein on a desolate plain in Karbala in today's Iraq in 680. Shortly before Hussein's death, Muslims based around Kufah, a stronghold of loyalists of Ali and his descendants, had urged Hussein to contend for the accession to the caliphate of the new Umayyad leader, Yazid I, by virtue of Hussein's descent from the Prophet. Hussein heeded the request, and set out from Medina to Kufah to organize a Shia revolt. Near Karbala, Hussein, a small band of followers, and the women and children from his household who had accompanied him were confronted by Umayyad troops, besieged, and finally massacred on Ashura, the tenth day of the month of Muharram. Hussein is said to have died while carrying his son in his arms.

Ever since that fateful Ashura, the martyrdom of Hussein at Karbala has become a central component of Shia identity and has imbued this community's awareness with an "emotive drama of martyrdom," as Kramer noted.[54] The martyrdom of Hussein has since become "the prototype of every struggle for justice, every suffering," Richard remarked. "That is where the heart of Shiism lies, in this agony which is at one and the same time a revolt and a sign of hope."[55]

An additional example for the centrality of martyrdom among the Shia is found in the fact that early Islamic anecdotes often refer to Hussein's childhood, during which he is described playing with his Prophet grandfather, while joyfully riding through Mecca on the shoulders of his father Ali. Kermani juxtaposes this benevolent and cheerful picture with Hussein's brutal murder and the subsequent desecration of his body, and he describes the humiliating effect that the martyrdom had on the Shia:

> The humiliation of the murdered son-in-law of the Prophet perpetrated—out of all people—by the leader of the Umayyads, the most fervent opponents of the Prophet, constitutes more than a shame to those defeated [by the Umayyads]: It represents the restoration of the pre-Islamic rule of the nobility that Islam seemed to have done away with. The fact that in the following year Yazid ordered a three-day massacre in Medina, and a year later the destruction of the Kaba, completes the picture of the usurpation. . . . To Shiis, the betrayal of everything that Muhammad represented by divine decree . . . is the original event out of which they interpret the entire subsequent and failed history of an Islam stolen by the Sunnis.[56]

In Damascus, the capital of the Umayyad Empire, where Yazid gloated over Hussein's severed head, a number of shrines commemorate the Battle of Karbala. The best-known shrine is Mashhad Ras al-Hussein, the Shrine of Hussein's Head, located in the northeast corner of the Great Umayyad Mosque. To this day, Shia pilgrims visit this and other shrines associated with the Battle of Karbala.[57]

The martyrdom of Hussein and the subsequent killings of all but one rightful imam neatly fit the perception of suffering and repression that has accompanied the Shia ever since the seventh century. In the course of their history, the Shia have often been a minority persecuted by the Sunni rulers, although there were periods of Shia rule in the Islamic heartland, notably the Fatimid and Safavid empires. By and large, however, the Shia have suffered persecution throughout their history and were at best tolerated by the ruling Sunni establishment.[58]

Even in modern times, martyrdom for the sake of God has been extolled as the greatest possible service to God by leading Shia thinkers such as Ali Shariati, Ayatollah Sayyid Mahmud Taleqani, and Ayatollah Murtaza Mutahhari.[59]

In the wake of the Islamic Revolution, the idea of the merits of martyrdom was horridly brought to the fore during the initial period of the Iran-Iraq War, which raged from 1980 to 1988. From 1981 to 1984, the regime called upon Iranian youth to volunteer for what one journalist described as "the most disturbing and gruesome parade of mass self-sacrifice in living memory"[60]—the so-called human wave attacks. Each attack consisted of up to 20,000 children as young as twelve or thirteen who were sent into the line of fire and across minefields, with no backup. Exploding the mines with their own bodies, these children were used to clear the way for the soldiers who followed them. In return for their almost certain death, the children were provided with a plastic key that they wore around their neck. If they would die as martyrs, they were told, that key would open the gate to paradise.

The youths were part of a popular paramilitary organization called Bassidj (Mobilization), formed shortly after the overthrow of the shah as a state-supported and state-funded force independent of the traditional army. The recruits of the Bassidj were not only schoolchildren but also men between the ages of eighteen and thirty, along with a minority of old men. Most were from the urban lower classes. All were volunteers who were willing to sacrifice themselves for the sake of the revolution. At its peak, the Bassidj consisted of some 400,000 members "who distinguished themselves by their devotion and lack of fear in the face of death."[61]

Iranian children were recruited as part of a movement launched in 1981 that bore the slogan "Offer one of your children to the Imam," which reportedly attracted more than a million volunteers within two weeks.[62] Recruiters went to the schools, where the schoolchildren were subjected to systematic manipulation. Participation in the war, they were told, would turn them into modern heroes and martyrs. Those children selected as "Volunteers for Martyrdom" swore an oath: "In the name of Allah the Avenger and in the name of Imam Khomeini I swear on the Holy Book to perform my sacred duty as a Child of Imam and a Soldier of Islam in our Holy War to restore to this world the Light of Divine Justice. May Allah be my Guide on the Path of Jihad and of *qital* [armed struggle]."[63]

To recruit the pupils, the revolutionary regime produced propaganda films with heavenly messengers dressed in white, urging children to join paradise. The glorification of death was omnipresent and reminiscent of the culture of martyrdom that in subsequent years and decades would be commonplace in Lebanon, the West Bank, the Gaza Strip, and other locations.

It is no coincidence that the cynical call for martyrdom that helped prolong a war that cost more than a million Iranians and Iraqis their lives made its next appearance in Lebanon. The first act of suicide terrorism of the modern era occurred in December 1981 in the capital of Beirut, where 27 people died and more than 100 were wounded when a member of the Iranian-backed Shia group Al Dawa (The Call) drove a bomb-laden car into the Iraqi Embassy in Beirut.

Sixteen months later, SMs hit Western targets. On April 18, 1983, a suicide bomber drove a van loaded with 400 pounds of explosives into the U.S. Embassy in Beirut, killing 63 people and wounding another 120. On October 23 of that year, another suicide attacker drove a car through the gates of the Beirut International Airport and into the U.S. Marine Barracks that was located on the compound; 241 American servicemen died in the attack that collapsed the four-story building. Two minutes later, another truck exploded in the compound that housed French forces, killing 58 people, most of them French troops. By February 1984 President Reagan withdrew U.S. troops from Lebanon, and SMs appeared to be a tactic that worked. The modern phenomenon of SMs had made its successful debut, and no other organization became more proficient in the use of SMs in the early 1980s than Hizballah—the group that years later would be held responsible for the 1983 attacks.

Hizballah was established sometime between 1982 and 1983 with the assistance of between several hundred to a thousand Pasdaran, the Iranian Revolutionary Guards who arrived in Lebanon with Syrian authorization in the summer of 1982, aiming to establish an outpost for the Islamic Revolution. Following the attacks on U.S. and French targets, most SMs in Lebanon were directed at the Israel Defense Forces (IDF) and their allies, the South Lebanon Army (SLA). In total, Hizballah perpetrated at least thirteen confirmed SMs between 1983 and 2000. The actual number of suicide operations executed by Hizballah, however, is likely higher, because during that period fourteen unclaimed SMs were staged, the majority of them most likely perpetrated by Hizballah.[64] The Hizballah is also believed to be responsible for two SMs in Argentina, namely the March 17, 1992, suicide car bombing of the Israeli Embassy in Buenos Aires, which killed 29 people and injured more than 250; and the July 18, 1994, suicide car bombing of the Jewish Community Center building (known as AMIA) in Buenos Aires, which killed more than 80 people and wounded some 300, an attack that was likely ordered by Iran.[65]

A number of secular terrorist organizations in Lebanon soon emulated Hizballah's innovative tactic in an effort to outbid Hizballah.[66] Between 1985 and 1987, these secular organizations—many of them pro-Syrian—even surpassed Hizballah in their use of SMs. They carried out twenty-two attacks, which included eleven attacks by the Syrian National Party, six SMs by the Syrian Baath Party, one by the Arab Socialist Union, and two each by the Lebanese Communist Party and the Nasserist/Socialist Organization.[67] The Syrian National Party also dispatched the first women suicide bombers. On March 10, 1985, eighteen-year-old Sumayah Saad drove a car loaded with dynamite into an Israeli military position in southern Lebanon, killing twelve Israeli soldiers and wounding fourteen others. Two weeks later, seventeen-year-old Sanah Muheidli drove a TNT-laden car into an IDF convoy, killing two soldiers and wounding two more. The two women were posthumously awarded the honorific Brides of Blood (Arous ad-Damm).[68]

The cult of martyrdom that helped Hizballah and other organizations in Lebanon recruit and indoctrinate volunteers for self-sacrificial operations was also copied from revolutionary Iran. Thus, the phrase *al-amalyiat al-istishhadiyya* (martyr operation) was used as a euphemism instead of the word *intihar*, which describes ordinary suicide due to personal distress. Similarly, the martyr (*shahid*, lit. witness) was described as a "happy martyr" (*shahid as-said*) or "he who gives himself over to martyrdom" (*istishhaadi*). Another cult practice, later adopted by Palestinian organizations, was the celebration of the death of the martyr as a wedding (to virgins in paradise)—a tradition that goes back to the events in Karbala revolving around the martyrdom of Muhammad's grandson Hussein.[69] In addition, radio stations and, since 1990, television stations announced and celebrated SMs and the names of the perpetrators. As many Palestinian, Iraqi, and other suicide bombers would do in subsequent years, Lebanese *shuhada* recorded a farewell video. These videos were frequently broadcast alongside the footage of the attack itself. Martyrs' funds were established, and the deeds of the martyrs were praised in mosques.[70]

The Hizballah leadership explained the attacks as a response to foreign occupation, and struggled to justify these attacks on moral grounds. The group's spiritual leader, Sheikh Muhammad Hussein Fadlallah, was unwilling to endorse this mode of operations with a religious decree (*fatwa*). Yet, invoking the argument that Muslims needed to defend themselves against militarily superior enemies—Israel and the United States—Fadlallah legitimized SMs in order to neutralize this imbalance with "special means of their own."[71]

Overall, SMs in Lebanon as a tactic succeeded in substantially raising the costs of military presence for foreign states. In the case of the French and the United States, SMs had their clearest successes, as the tactic was the main factor in hastening the withdrawal of Western troops. SMs may also have contributed to Israel's withdrawal from Lebanon to its self-proclaimed "security zone," although SMs did not contribute to Israel's full withdrawal from Lebanon in 2000, which came at a time when SMs were no longer used in Lebanon.

The success of the tactic in Lebanon soon prompted other groups to adopt SMs, among them the Liberation Tigers of Tamil Eelam (LTTE). Its leader, Vellupillai Prabhakaran, was greatly impressed by Hizballah's successful use of SMs as a tool to fight an asymmetric battle.[72] Beginning in July 1987, the LTTE's charismatic leader decided to adopt suicide tactics in order to offset the militarily more powerful Sri Lankan state, which is dominated by ethnic Sinhalese. Between 1987 and 2001, the LTTE planned and executed an estimated 200 SMs[73]—more than any other group at the time.

The LTTE has managed to stage a number of high-profile SMs against civilian targets such as the airport in Colombo; the Temple of the Tooth, which houses Sri Lanka's most sacred Buddhist relic; and Colombo's World Trade Center. An estimated one-quarter of the LTTE's SMs have been political assassinations,[74] oftentimes executed by female suicide bombers. Such attacks included the killing of Indian prime minister Rajiv Gandhi on May 21, 1991. On December 18, 1999, the LTTE dispatched another female "Black Tiger," as the group's suicide squad is known, to attack Sri Lankan president Chandrika Kumaratunga, who survived the attack but lost an eye in the explosion. For those attacks targeted against civilians, however, the LTTE usually shunned responsibility in an attempt to present itself in a more legitimate cloak.

Nevertheless, unlike most other organizations that have used SMs primarily as a terrorist tactic, the extensive and sophisticated use of suicide attacks by the Black Tigers should be seen as part and parcel of its insurgency strategy. Targeting civilians and creating fear in their midst—in other words, conducting a campaign of terror—did not seem to be the LTTE's principal goal.[75]

The LTTE appears to have reached the decision to adopt SMs primarily out of tactical considerations. To be sure, the LTTE is practicing a culture of martyrdom similar to that of the Hizballah and Palestinian organizations. Drawing on the Hindu tradition of heroic self-sacrifice, asceticism, and obligation, which are firmly entrenched within Tamil society, the Sri Lankan version of the culture of martyrdom features such practices as the building of holy shrines for the fallen heroes; the addition of five occasions to its calendar when martyrs are venerated; and the establishment of a cult around the use of the cyanide capsule, which is issued to every LTTE fighter.[76] Nevertheless, as a recent study on the LTTE has concluded, "it is not the act itself—killing by suicide—that is the Black Tigers' original or even main aim, but the military impact of the act."[77] This is particularly evident in the LTTE's use of the elite Black Tigers suicide squad as a special weapon to help penetrate military installations that would otherwise be difficult to pierce. In addition, SMs by the LTTE seem to have surged at times when military victories against the superior Sri Lankan army appeared particularly pressing in order to reach a "balance of deterrence."[78]

A more prominent SM battlefield in recent years than the Sri Lankan example is the Israeli-Palestinian conflict. The first Palestinian organization that staged an SM was Hamas, which contemplated the use of this tactic as early as 1989[79] but did not execute the first mission until April 16, 1993, at a restaurant near the Mehola Junction in the Jordan Valley.

In the first period of their use against Israel, from 1993 to 1998, two organizations—Hamas and Palestinian Islamic Jihad (PIJ)—planned and executed SMs on 28 occasions.[80] In the next wave of attacks that occurred during the Second Intifada that started in September 2000, SMs became even more widely used. Between September 2000 and December 2005, 156 male and 8 female suicide bombers conducted a total of 147 SMs in Israel, the West Bank, and Gaza. During that period, the Israeli security establishment prevented an additional 450 attacks.[81] The 147 attacks that were not foiled killed 527 people and wounded some 3,350 more, the overwhelming majority of whom were Israelis.[82]

During the Second Intifada, four organizations employed SMs. Hamas and PIJ were now joined by Fatah's Al-Aqsa Martyrs Brigades and the Popular Front for the Liberation of Palestine (PFLP), who together ran the ideological gamut from religious to nationalist to Marxist organizations.[83] Among these organizations, Fatah's adoption of SMs was the most surprising because its members had previously abstained from "martyrdom operations." Fatah adopted suicide bombings at a time when the popularity of its leadership, including that of Yassir Arafat, had sunk to a low, while that of Islamist organizations had increased. The reason for its adoption of SMs seems to be a clear example of organizational outbidding.[84] Pedahzur explains that, "as events of the intifada escalated, Fatah set up the Al-Aqsa Martyrs Brigades which relied on the Tanzim infrastructure—a network of local organizations uniting the younger members of Fatah among them. The goal of the Al-Aqsa Martyrs Brigades was to serve as a counterweight to the suicide arms of Hamas and Palestinian Islamic Jihad, the brigades of Izz-a-Din al-Kassam and the Al-Quds Brigades."[85] The Al-Aqsa Martyrs Brigades' first attack occurred in Hadera on January 17, 2002. Within six months, Fatah's suicide attack brigades became the most active perpetrator of SMs.[86] Fatah also sent out the first female Palestinian suicide bomber. On January 27, 2002, twenty-seven-year-old Wafa Idris, a Fatah activist from the al-Amari refugee camp near Ramallah, carried a bomb that detonated in central Jerusalem, killing an eighty-one-year-old Israeli and injuring more than a hundred.

Unlike the LTTE, whose SM targets are divided almost equally between attacks against military and civilian targets,[87] three-fourths of SMs by Palestinian organizations during the Second Intifada were directed at nonmilitary targets. Of all the victims of SMs by Palestinian organizations, 81 percent were civilians, most of whom were killed in buses or at bus stops, as well as in entertainment venues such as discotheques, restaurants, or shopping malls.[88]

In the first wave of Palestinian SMs, between 1993 and 1998, the perpetrators turned out to have been in their early twenties, single, male, unemployed, and from lower socioeconomic strata.[89] Most bombers had completed high school and had sometimes enrolled in college. The average age of the Palestinian suicide bomber in late August 2001 was twenty-one.[90] Moreover, many suicide bombers were deeply pious. After 2000, however, establishing a common profile among Palestinian "martyrs" became increasingly problematic. A growing number of Palestinian suicide bombers were from middle or upper-middle classes, such as Izzedine al-Mazri, who killed sixteen people at a Sbarro Pizzeria at a busy intersection in central Jerusalem on August 9, 2001, and was the son of a wealthy businessman.[91] Others were older and married with children, such as forty-eight-year-old Muhammad Shaker Habeishi, who on September 9, 2001, detonated a bomb at the train station in the northern Israeli town of Nahariya, killing himself and three other Israelis. Habeishi had run for mayor in the Galilee village of Abu Sinan about a year before the attack. A father of eight, he became the first Arab Israeli to commit an act of suicide terrorism.[92] Daoud Abu Sway, who died in a busy intersection in central Jerusalem on December 5, 2001, in what seemed to be a premature explosion of a device strapped to his body, was a father of eight. Like Habeishi, he was in his forties.[93]

In the Israeli-Palestinian arena, SMs peaked in 2002, when sixty attacks were staged, and has dropped consistently in numbers ever since, owing in large part to Israeli counterintelligence successes, including the building of a network of informants and collaborators.[94] The climax of SMs in that year was accompanied by an intense cult surrounding martyrdom among Palestinians that made the cult of self-sacrifice in Lebanon during the 1980s and early 1990s pale in comparison.

Suicide missions have also been used in the context of the Turkish-Kurdish conflict between 1996 and 1999, when the Kurdistan Workers Party (PKK) executed fifteen SMs and planned another seven attacks that failed.[95] The PKK can be usefully compared to the LTTE. Like the Tamil Tigers, the PKK was led by a highly charismatic leader, Abdullah Ocalan. Additionally, the cadres of both organizations include many women, who perpetrated more than two-thirds of the PKK's suicide attacks (eleven out of fifteen). Attacks by the PKK peaked in 1999, following Ocalan's capture in Kenya. They came to a temporary halt when in August 1999 the PKK's imprisoned leader announced a "peace initiative" and denounced violence, after which the Turkish authorities commuted his death sentence to life imprisonment.

The PKK's SM campaign differed from that of Hizballah and the Palestinian organizations in several respects. First, PKK attacks caused by far the fewest casualties. Second, suicide attackers affiliated with the PKK sought little publicity after their attacks and left no wills, statements, or video recordings in their wake. Third, suicide attackers by the PKK seemed to have been members of the organization, rather than walk-ins, as has often been the case with the Hizballah and Palestinian organizations.[96]

The PKK adopted SMs following a military escalation on the part of Turkey that included incursions into Kurdish regions in Iraq as part of Operation Steel. The first attacks by the PKK took place shortly after the Turkish military claimed to have killed more than 500 PKK members.[97] The PKK may also have adopted SMs to expand its support base at a time when large parts of the Kurdish population were sympathetic to religious parties. According to Bloom, the PKK's relations with a number of religious terror organizations were marked by ideological rivalry over the Kurdish population in the southeast of the country.[98] Pedahzur believes that the adoption of SMs "can be interpreted as an attempt by Ocalan and his people . . . to signal to the Kurdish population that their organization was not significantly different from those same religious organizations that had gained the support of the Kurdish population," but he ultimately believes that the key reason for the use of suicide missions was strategic.[99]

The Advent of Al Qaeda and the Globalization of Suicide Attacks

On August 7, 1998, a set of explosions, only minutes apart, rocked the U.S. embassies in Nairobi, Kenya, and Dar-es-Salaam, Tanzania. The embassy bombings were a milestone not only in the confrontation between Al Qaeda and the United States but also in the history of suicide attacks. They revealed the growing influence of Salafi-Jihadist ideology among individuals and groups involved in suicide attacks. Indeed, since 1998, Salafi-Jihadist groups have become not only the most dominant perpetrators of SMs but also the most lethal ones.

In the course of the 1980s and 1990s, suicide bombings had become a common tactic in some parts of the world, but it was not until the 1998 embassy bombings that this modus operandi turned into a truly global phenomenon—as measured in the exponential rise in the number of suicide attacks, the number of organizations perpetrating suicide missions, and the rapidly rising number of countries targeted since 1998 (see chapter 1).

The influence of Al Qaeda and its guiding ideology—the Salafi Jihad—defines the vast majority of groups perpetrating most suicide attacks today in countries such as Iraq, Afghanistan, Pakistan, Somalia, the United Kingdom, and even the United States. This book argues that suicide attacks by Salafi-Jihadist groups constitute an entirely new pattern of suicide attacks—the globalization of martyrdom—that is more dominant than the traditional pattern of suicide attacks carried out by groups such as the LTTE, the PKK, Palestinian groups, and Hizballah.

The Causes and Characteristics of Suicide Missions

A proper explanation of suicide attacks requires several levels of analysis. It must strive to explain why individuals are willing to die in order to kill; why organizations plan and execute suicide operations; and what role the larger environment plays in enabling individuals and organizations to do so.[100] The multicausal approach adopted in this book rests upon earlier theoretical studies that have identified a need to understand the causes of terrorism in general from a number of different perspectives. Thus, Martha Crenshaw, in a classic study on the causes of terrorism, highlights the need to distinguish between three levels of causations—situational variables (such as broad political, economic, or social conditions), the strategy of the terrorist organization, and "the problem of individual participation"—that together render the likelihood of terrorism higher in some situations than in others.[101]

Individual motives must be distinguished from causes on the organizational level for several reasons. The first is that individuals motivated to carry out an SM are very unlikely to possess the resources, level of operational intelligence, and logistical capacity required to organize a suicide bombing. They require an organization to assist them.

Second, organizations rarely supply suicide bombers from among their own ranks but instead opt to recruit individuals from outside of the group.[102] It is uncommon for organizations, cells, or other terrorist entities to send the top leadership and members on the lieutenant levels on suicide missions, and there is no evidence that a leader of a group that has adopted SMs has volunteered to detonate himself in the course of an attack.

Most importantly, a distinct organizational level of analysis is required because terrorist groups have goals and motives that differ from those of individuals. These organizational goals include the need to maintain themselves, to seek power, to act in line with the group's own ideological prescriptions, to compete with other organizations for social support, to weaken their opponents politically, or to undermine the security or political legitimacy of their enemy.

The third level of analysis refers to the context within which the individual and the organization function. Understanding how individuals and organizations are affected by the larger environment surrounding them—an environment shaped by various political, historical, cultural, societal, religious, and economic factors—is the sine qua non to explaining terrorism in general, and suicide missions in particular. Individuals and groups do not act in a vacuum. What, then, are the results of the growing number of studies on the causes and nature of suicide attacks conducted to date?

The Individual: Commitment, Revenge, Crisis, and Benefits

In the past decade, a number of studies have set out to examine the motivation of suicide bombers.[103] In the course of their research, analysts from a variety of disciplines have been able to reject a number of previously held beliefs about suicide bombers. They have concluded, for instance, that suicide bombers cannot be compared to ordinary suicides. While ordinary suicides are usually drawn to their deaths due to a personal crisis, suicide bombers, by and large, tend to act for what they believe to be altruistic reasons—a distinction dating back to the French sociologist Emile Durkheim.[104]

Terrorism scholars have also been able to dispel the often held belief that "all suicide bombers are alike." Thus, while a number of earlier studies of suicide attackers have argued that suicide bombers have a common profile, more recent studies based on additional data have concluded that these attackers do not share many similar characteristics. Although most bombers are young, male, and Muslim, nearly all religions have produced suicide attackers at one time or another. "Human bombs" hence can be rich or poor, young or old, male or female, married or single, employed or unemployed, religious or secular.

Although many researchers have examined the role that psychological factors play in the genesis of suicide bombers, they have failed to produce evidence that conclusively links psychopathology with the resort to terrorism. While clearly highly alienated from society, most experts agree, terrorists are sane and relatively "normal" in the sense that they do not exhibit signs of suffering from a salient psychopathology.[105] For that reason, mental illness as a factor in suicide terrorism has been dismissed.[106]

In terms of the motivations, some suicide bombers have suffered from a personal crisis, which is likely to have played a role in the decision to become a human bomb. Yet, although personal crisis appears to be particularly common among women suicide bombers, such as the Chechen Black Widows,[107] it is not a universal—and hence not a necessary—motivation for an individual to become a suicide attacker.

Many studies suggest that some suicide attackers are seeking revenge, and that this motive is reinforced by the individual's perception of humiliation.[108] Kimhi and Even, for instance, identified the individual seeking retribution for suffering as one of four prototypes of Palestinian suicide bombers.[109] The perception of humiliation is also a strong motivator for suicide bombers who kill themselves in the name of Al Qaeda.

Several researchers also suggest that suicide attackers tend to act out of a deep sense of commitment to a larger cause, to their social network, or to a terrorist organization and its ideology.[110] According to Pedahzur, this sense of commitment applies particularly to those suicide bombers who have been members of organizations, as opposed to individuals recruited for the particular task of a suicide mission.[111] Strong commitment can be the result of psychological pressure exerted by the group's leadership, which can help present self-sacrificial attacks as a way for an ordinary individual to defend his country and his people. Suicide bombings can be highly empowering in that regard. Hafez, for example, argues that militant groups call upon suicide bombers to "perform their duty to their own values, family, friends, community, or religion. Failure to act, consequently, creates dissonance because it is perceived as a betrayal of one's ideals, loved ones, country, God, or sense of manhood."[112] Suicide attacks may thus be conceived as a way for individuals to overcome and reverse their perceived sense of humiliation, shame, and injustice to achieve honor, respect, and redemption.[113]

The expectation of posthumous benefits is also likely to heighten some bombers' willingness to become martyrs. Such benefits can include the suicide attacker's elevated social status after death, rewards for the family, and the attainment of heavenly pleasures in the afterlife. The expectation of personal benefits in the afterlife that seems to motivate many Muslim suicide bombers, such as a guaranteed place in heaven, the eventual reunification with one's family, or sexual pleasures, does not necessarily apply to nonreligious cases of suicide attacks. In the case of the nationalist Black Tigers, for example, there is no expectation of compensation after death.

Finally, some students of suicide attacks have argued that suicide bombers may act partly out of financial incentives,[114] a motivation that has affected some nonsuicidal terrorists in their decision to join or remain in terrorist organizations.[115] Monetary rewards for the families of suicide bombers have been common among Palestinian suicide bombers as well as those of Hizballah.

In sum, studies examining individual motivations of suicide terrorism have established that suicide bombers can be motivated by a range of factors that often include a strong commitment and the seeking of revenge, and sometimes a sense of personal crisis and the expectation that death will be rewarded in some form. It is likely that a combination of motivations influences a single suicide attacker, as opposed to a single motivation alone.[116] To date, however, no study has been able to identify either necessary or sufficient conditions for an individual's resort to suicide terrorism. These studies have instead indicated merely which factors likely heighten the risk of a given individual to become a suicide bomber. Thus, no studies have established why some highly committed individuals become suicide bombers while others do not, or why revenge leads to suicide terrorism in some cases and not in others. Although studies focusing on the individual level of analysis have made important contributions to the understanding of why individuals may be motivated to sacrifice their lives for a larger cause, they also leave many questions unanswered.

The Organization: The Role of Strategy and Tactics

Partly in response to these limitations, some researchers on suicide attacks have focused on the role of the organization in the genesis of suicide attacks.[117] Analyzing organizations is crucial because since 1981 suicide attacks have been mostly acts of terrorism, which in turn are rarely carried out by individuals acting on their own; rather, they are the acts of individuals who are members of organizations, groups, or cells attached to a larger network.[118] Studies at the organizational level typically build on the theoretical work of Crenshaw, who argued that terrorism can be understood as the result of a deliberate choice by terrorist organizations that believe that violence is the best means to advance their political goals.[119] Based on this explanatory framework, terrorist organizations select SMs as a means to realize various rational interests, ranging from the basic need to survive to sophisticated strategic and tactical considerations.

The strategy of suicide terrorism is designed either to weaken an external opponent or to strengthen the organization itself. Internally, SMs may be adopted because they are believed to enhance the group's perceived need to survive.[120] A minimum degree of violent presence is necessary for all terrorist groups to remain effective. Failure to maintain such a degree of violence will eventually lead—or will be perceived to lead—to the group's irrelevance and eventual disappearance as a political force.

Another use of SMs as a strategy designed to strengthen the group adopting this tactic can occur if groups believe that adopting this tactic can widen their support among the domestic population—a plausible, yet increasingly problematic theory.

Others have argued that groups employ SMs because they are a proven strategy to weaken the group's opponent. Pape, for example, argues that the high degree of lethality renders the use of suicide attacks a rational or "logical" choice for organizations and states under certain circumstances, asserting that "the main reason that suicide terrorism is growing is that terrorists have learned that it works."[121]

The value of SMs as an efficient tactic especially when smaller groups face militarily superior forces is hard to deny. Clearly, their value in "leveling the playing field" for groups that perceive themselves to be militarily disadvantaged is a key reason why groups decide to employ this tactic. Thus, in his book *Knights under the Prophet's Banner*, Al Qaeda deputy leader Ayman al-Zawahiri acknowledges that "the method of martyrdom operations is the most successful way of inflicting damage against the opponent and the least costly to the mujahideen in terms of casualties."[122] Nevertheless, SMs are hardly employed for military purposes alone. More likely, organizations utilize this tactic for a combination of military effectiveness and political purpose. The frequent videotaping of suicide bombers prior to their mission underscores the fact that terrorist organizations attempt to elicit maximum propaganda benefits. Similarly, suicide bombings are often timed to derail political events contrary to the cause of the terrorist group—be it the Israeli-Palestinian peace process or elections in Iraq.[123]

Brym and Araj have cogently argued that characterizing SMs as strategically rational oversimplifies the complexity of motivations on the organizational level. They found that suicide bombings involve mixed rationales for groups. The campaigns are rarely timed to maximize strategic advantages of the group because other considerations, such as revenge or retaliation, or the existence of certain opportunities to strike, prevail over purely strategic considerations. Consequently, they argue, the timing of the attacks "may not maximize the strategic gains of the attackers and on some occasions may even minimize such gains."[124] They have identified a number of different possible rationales for suicide attacks. These include the desire to achieve a short-term tactical, a longer-term strategic, or even a religious goal; and the desire for retaliation, as either a response to an attack on members of the group or an attack on the community that the group claims to represent. SMs often follow specific precipitants. In the Israeli-Palestinian context, they found such precipitants to be the assassination of organizational leaders, the killing of Palestinians, other anti-Palestinian actions, and significant domestic political (such as elections) or religious events.[125]

Beyond strategic benefits, terrorist groups are drawn to suicide attacks because of a number of well-known tactical benefits that they offer. First, even more than ordinary terrorist attacks, suicide operations are likely to draw attention to a group's cause, aided in large part by the extraordinarily high attention such operations enjoy in the media. In this regard, SMs can be thought of as a form of "strategic signaling," whereby terrorist attacks are used to communicate a group's character and goals to the target audience. As pointed out by Hoffman and McCormick, for instance, the LTTE used SMs to signal an image of elitism, professionalism, invincibility, and fanatical single-mindedness to the Sri Lankan government.[126]

Second, SMs, even more than ordinary terrorist attacks, serve the organization's attempt to create extreme fear in the larger population—a key feature, in fact, of all terrorist attacks. This occurs in part due to the group's demonstration of the inefficacy of the targeted government and in part due to the demoralization of the public and of law enforcement agencies. Not only does a suicide attack create a disproportionately intense amount of fear among the targeted population, but its effect may be particularly traumatizing and long-lasting,[127] thus serving, as Stephen Holmes puts it, as an "intensifier of enemy despair."[128] Adding to the frustration of the targeted population is the inability of the targeted community to exact revenge on the perpetrators, arguably rendering the recovery from these attacks more difficult than from ordinary terrorism.

Third, suicide attacks may serve as an internal morale booster for the terrorist group. The use of this tactic indicates the complete dedication of the suicide attackers to their cause. It can create heroes among the group's members whom broader segments of the population may want to emulate, thus raising the level of popularity of the group. It can also lead to a sense of moral superiority of the groups' members over their adversaries, which may result in a group's perception that it will eventually prevail over its enemies.[129]

Finally, terrorist organizations adopt SMs because of a number of unique operational benefits. They are a cost-efficient tool, with suicide vests costing as little as $50 to $150. They are also high-precision weapons of sorts, and have therefore often been called the "ultimate smart bomb." The explosive devices, which are usually strapped on to the perpetrator's body, can be detonated at the time and place of the attacker's choosing, thus maximizing the lethality of the improvised explosive device (IED). Other tactical benefits of suicide attacks are that their use obviates the need for the complicated task of planning an escape route. Furthermore, the suicide bomber's ensured death nullifies the risk of his or her capture. The risk that the bomber will be intercepted, interrogated, and compelled to disclose incriminating information about the organization is minuscule.[130]

In sum, organizations employ suicide attacks for a number of strategic and tactical benefits. These reasons have little, if anything, to do with the motivations that lead individuals to become suicide bombers. Similar to the individual-level studies, however, organizational approaches have limitations. They fail to explain why, if the benefits of SMs are so numerous, many organizations avoid their use. Nor do they provide a satisfying answer to the question of when a terrorist group decides to adopt a suicide attack.

The Environment: The Culture of Martyrdom and the Role of Occupation

To overcome the limitations of organizational approaches, many students of suicide missions have examined the role that societal and other structural factors may play in the emergence of suicide attacks. Some believe that individuals and organizations are more likely to volunteer for, plan, and execute suicide missions if there is widespread social support for this tactic. Others have instead pointed at structural factors as the cause, blaming economic factors, such as poverty or unemployment, or political factors, such as foreign occupation, for the emergence of suicide attacks.

The explanation that suicide bombings are enabled by a widespread public support for this tactic seems to be sustained by the examples of Lebanon and Israel, where a cult of martyrdom has been apparent—manifesting itself in venerations of suicide bombers, the prominent use of euphemistic labels for SMs and their perpetrators, and the penetration of the suicide bomber into popular culture, such as movies, comics, or plays.

In terms of the effects of economic variables on suicide terrorism, the relationship between economic destitution and terrorism is a particularly complex one. Most researchers believe that economic distress is one among a number of factors that may play a role in the decision to become a suicide bomber. Few scholars, however, argue that economic distress is the sole, or even main, factor motivating suicide attackers. Indeed, a number of recent studies have shown that there is little direct connection between poverty or poor education and terrorism.[131] On the other hand, poverty may exert indirect influence on the rise of terrorism: first, poor countries are more likely to serve or be exploited as safe havens by terrorists; second, poor countries are more likely to undergo ethnic and religious conflict, which in turn may breed homegrown terrorism or may attract foreign elements; third, poverty may indirectly affect the rise of terrorism in that the usually more well-to-do leadership levels of terrorist organizations can more easily exploit the grievances of economically disadvantaged classes.[132]

As far as political factors are concerned, several authors, most notably Robert Pape, place the blame of SMs mainly on the existence of foreign occupation[133]—a point that has been challenged by others.[134] While occupation is certainly likely to contribute to the emergence of SMs by creating what one scholar calls "collective frustration,"[135] it is an indisputable fact that not all societies under occupation have produced suicide bombers, and not all suicide missions have taken place in societies under occupation.[136]

The occupation theory is one of two influential theories that are examined in more depth in the final section of this chapter. Although both theories have advanced our knowledge to some degree, their limitations are particularly striking in explaining suicide attacks by Al Qaeda and other Salafi-Jihadist groups.

The Limitations of Existing Theories
A Critique of the Occupation Theory

In his book *Dying to Win*,[137] Robert Pape argues that the "bottom line is that suicide terrorism is mainly a response to foreign occupation,"[138] which he defines as "one in which a foreign power has the ability to control the local government independent of the wishes of the local community."[139] He argues that every suicide campaign between 1980 and 2003 had as a major objective the coercion of a foreign government to take its forces out of what the terrorist organization regards as its homeland.

Upon closer inspection, however, there are three reasons why occupation itself does not account for many contemporary SMs. First, these attacks increasingly occur in countries where there is no discernible occupation. Whereas occupation is likely to have influenced suicide attacks by Palestinian groups and Hizballah against Israel, by the LTTE against the Sri Lankan government, and by the PKK against Turkey, occupation—at least as defined by Pape—is more problematic in explaining the current phenomenon of SMs in places like Bangladesh, Indonesia, Jordan, Morocco, Saudi Arabia, the United Kingdom, the United States, or Uzbekistan. Second, in those countries such as in Iraq, where there is an occupation, the attacks are oftentimes not directed at the occupiers themselves, who, one would think, would be the most obvious target. Many of the suicide bombings in Iraq have not targeted the occupiers—that is, the coalition forces—but have been aimed instead at Shias, Kurds, and Sufis, in an apparent effort to stir ethnic tensions in the country and delegitimize the Iraqi government in the eyes of Iraqis. Some Iraqi suicide bombers have gone as far as targeting civilians in neighboring countries not directly involved in the occupation of Iraq, as has happened in the attacks on three hotels in Amman, Jordan, on November 9, 2005. Third, even if they do target the occupation forces, many SMs are not carried out by those individuals who, theoretically, should be most affected by the occupation. In Iraq, for instance, most attacks that do target occupation forces are carried out not by Iraqis but by Saudi, Syrian, Kuwaiti, North African, and other foreign jihadis.[140] Similarly, the SMs conducted against the United States homeland on September 11, 2001, may be explained as "a response to occupation," but the perpetrators were from Egypt, Saudi Arabia, and the United Arab Emirates rather than from countries under physical U.S. occupation. Pape may be correct in suggesting that occupation matters, but he overstates its importance while playing down other factors. This is particularly striking in his discussion of Al Qaeda.

In the case of Al Qaeda, Pape overstates the importance of occupation, while understating the role that religion and ideology—however distorted they may be from true Islam—play in the eyes of the group. "For al-Qaeda, religion matters," Pape writes, "but mainly in the context of national resistance to foreign occupation."[141] Pape's argument, however, is hardly supported by evidence. A closer reading of statements issued by Al Qaeda leaders suggests that religion plays a more central role in Al Qaeda's ideology and mission than Pape would ascribe to it. "Osama bin Laden and Al Qaeda are engaged in a defensive jihad against the crusader-Zionist alliance" because they believe that the United States has made a "clear declaration of war on God, his messenger, and Muslims," to quote bin

Laden.[142] In a statement aired on the satellite television channel Al-Jazeera in November 2001, bin Laden stated that "this war is fundamentally religious. . . . Under no circumstances should we forget this enmity between us and the infidels. For, the enmity is based on creed."[143] In another message dated October 2002, bin Laden went so far as to urge Americans to convert to Islam: "A message to the American people: Peace be upon those who follow the right path. . . . I urge you to become Muslims, for Islam calls for the principle of 'there is no God but Allah.' "[144]

Al Qaeda's desire to end foreign occupation is only the first step in its grand vision—shared by other Salafi-Jihadist groups it inspired—to reverse the decline of Islam and recapture the grandeur of this religion's past. Meanwhile, the Salafi-Jihadist mission lies in restoring Islam's golden age. According to the group's rationale, that redemption of Islam hinges upon Muslims' return to the ancient religious faith and practices of the Prophet Muhammad and his companions.[145]

Pape is, without a doubt, correct in pointing out that occupation is a key grievance reiterated by Al Qaeda's leaders on numerous occasions. However, it is Al Qaeda's particular perception of occupation, rather than American "boots on the ground" or the ability of a foreign power "to control the local government independent of the wishes of the local community" that matters in this regard. To Al Qaeda, occupation is a much more loosely defined concept: it is part of a laundry list of historically accrued injustices currently manifested in the military, religious, political, economic, and cultural influence that the "Crusader-Zionist alliance" is perceived to exert on the larger Muslim world, thereby humiliating it.

Dying to Win also fails to explain why most SMs are perpetrated by groups claiming to act in the name of religion, while attacks by secular organizations have declined in recent years. Pape correctly notes that "modern suicide terrorism is not limited to Islamic fundamentalism,"[146] but he fails to acknowledge that, nevertheless, most SMs are perpetrated by radical Islamist groups. Citing data from the Rand Terrorism Incident Database, Bruce Hoffman notes that 78 percent of all SMs since 1968 have occurred since the 9/11 attacks. Of these, 81 percent have been executed by Islamic groups. Moreover, thirty-one of the thirty-five groups that have employed suicide operations are Islamic.[147] These figures require an explanation not provided by Pape.

Meanwhile, attacks by the non-Islamic LTTE—the organization cited so often by Pape to substantiate his claim that SMs have little connection to religion—have decreased drastically. Since the 9/11 attacks, the Tamil Tigers have perpetrated about a dozen SMs. However relevant the LTTE had been in the pre–September 11 era, the group's significance in the post-9/11 era pales in comparison to groups that claim to act in the name of religion.[148]

"Overall," Pape calculates, "Islamic fundamentalism is associated with about half of the suicide terrorist attacks that have occurred from 1980 to 2003."[149] Not included in Pape's count, however, is the high tally of SMs that have occurred in Iraq since the U.S. invasion in March 2003. The vast majority of SMs in Iraq, in turn, have been conducted by Salafi-Jihadist groups—groups that conduct a self-declared "holy war" in the name of a distorted view of Islam.[150] If one were to add that number to Pape's count, the picture of non-Islamic versus Islamic suicide attacks would look radically different.

A Critique of the Outbidding Theory

Another prominent scholar on suicide missions, Mia Bloom, posits that groups may adopt suicide bombings because they are trying to compete against—that is, outbid—other groups for the support of the local population, thereby increasing their "market share" among that community. This theory thus rests on the assumption that sustained campaigns of SMs depend on the support of the local population. "In the war for public support," Bloom writes, "when the bombings resonate positively with the population that insurgent groups purport to represent, they help the organization mobilize support. If suicide bombing does not resonate among the larger population the tactic will fail."[151]

The outbidding theory appears to be a plausible explanation for the adoption of SMs by several organizations, including the Popular Front for the Liberation of Palestine (PFLP),[152] the Fatah Al-Aqsa Martyrs Brigades,[153] and Amal in Lebanon, which seemed to attempt to outbid Hizballah by using SMs.[154]

The outbidding theory falls short of providing a satisfactory explanation for the adoption of SMs in many other cases, however, including some of the cases noted in *Dying to Kill*. The theory, for instance, cannot explain why the LTTE has adopted SMs only in 1987, at a time when the internal rivalry between radical Tamil organizations had already reached its pinnacle with the May 1986 massacre of the Tamil Eelam Liberation Organization (TELO) and the killing of its leader.[155] By that time, the LTTE had eliminated not only the TELO but all of its other rivals, too.

The outbidding theory is also problematic because it rests on the assumption that groups are vying for the support of a local population. This, however, seems to contradict Bloom's finding that SMs in Sri Lanka are not condoned among the Tamil population. Based on her interviews and polls of "hundreds of Tamils all over Sri Lanka," she found that "there was virtually no support for attacking civilians, regardless of whether they were in Sinhalese territory or in the Tamil regions."[156] Despite this limited support from the general population, the LTTE continued with its relentless SM campaign (including attacks against civilians), apparently undeterred.

Even if we do assume that groups that have traditionally employed SMs have attempted to win sympathies among the domestic population, it is becoming increasingly obvious that this explanation is wedded to a paradigm of traditional conflicts, in which a large segment of a given population supports the actions of suicide bombers as a legitimate form of resistance designed to achieve self-determination, or at least some degree of autonomy. The market-share theory is not compatible with the global jihad waged by transnational groups that entertain goals that are far less defined and are often of a grandiose and implacable nature. For that reason, the notion that suicide attackers are vying for domestic popular support is most problematic with regard to Al Qaeda and the global jihad movement—perhaps the most obvious example of the weakness of the market-share theory. Because the goal of Al Qaeda and the global jihad movement is by definition transnational rather than national, Salafi-Jihadist groups accordingly appeal to a transnational rather than to a domestic population. Many groups that today conduct SMs are no longer vying for the support of a domestic population because they do not necessarily act on behalf of the local population but on behalf of a larger cause that exceeds the goals of more "traditional" suicide attackers in such places as Sri Lanka or Palestine.

The London bombers of July 2005, for example, have targeted their own fellow British citizens. Similarly, a growing number of SMs conducted in Iraq today target Iraqis rather than the occupying forces. One can hardly argue that Iraqi suicide attackers are trying to gain the sympathy of the very people in whose midst they are exploding themselves.

The outbidding theory is also incompatible with Al Qaeda's self-definition. As will be seen in chapter 2, Al Qaeda's goal from the very outset was not to become the leader of the Islamic movement as much as to serve as a vanguard that would serve to spark international waves of jihad, which would eventually be fought by a reawakened, globally active jihadist movement. Al Qaeda therefore regards coordination among various groups—as opposed to competition—as imperative in order to create a phalanx among Muslims. Cooperation and support of other groups creates a multiplier effect in the eyes of Al Qaeda that would strengthen the forces of "true" Muslims against those of the infidels and apostates.

CHAPTER ONE

The Global Proliferation of Suicide Missions

Since the late 1990s, there has been a rise in the number of suicide attacks, the number of countries targeted by suicide attacks, and the number of organizations that plan and execute suicide attacks. What has caused this unprecedented globalization of suicide attacks? In an attempt to answer this question, I first provide statistical evidence for the global rise of suicide attacks, relying on a database of the nearly 1,300 SMs perpetrated between 1981 and April 2007. Then, I consider Al Qaeda's rise as a global terrorist actor and the growing influence of its guiding ideology, the Salafi Jihad. Finally, I discuss the theoretical implications of these findings by arguing that SMs by Salafi-Jihadist groups are so different from traditional SMs that scholars may draw a distinction between traditional, localized suicide attacks and the more dominant contemporary pattern of globalized suicide attacks.

The Statistical Evidence
Suicide Attacks and Their Sponsors

According to most indicators, the use of suicide missions has been on a steady rise since the first modern suicide operation in 1981.[1] Based on a suicide terrorism database maintained and updated by the University of Haifa,[2] a total of 1,269 suicide attacks have been perpetrated between 1981 and April 5, 2007 (figure 1.1). Throughout the 1980s and until 1993, the number of suicide attacks remained relatively small, never exceeding seven attacks per year, with the single exception of 1985, when a total of 22 SMs were carried out. Beginning in 1994, the number of SMs began to increase noticeably, peaking temporarily in 1995, when 27 attacks were carried out. The number of attacks dropped slightly in the second half of the 1990s, never reaching the number of attacks of 1995. The year 2000 brought a new record of suicide attacks, with 37 attacks carried out in that year, and signaled the beginning of an upward trend in the number of SMs that would span most of the 2000s. Thus, between 2000 and 2005, the number of attacks rose steadily each year, from 53 in 2001 to 73 in 2002, 81 in 2003, 115 in 2004, and 298 in 2005. The number of attacks declined to 279 in 2006, although trends in the course of 2007, with 175 SMs carried out by April 5, suggest that the decline in 2006 is a statistical outlier.[3]

In the first decade after the first SM, from 1981 to 1990, an average of 1.5 organizations perpetrated suicide attacks every year. Between 1991 and 2000, three times as many organizations (an average of 4.5) conducted suicide operations on average per year. In the third decade, from 2001 to April 2007, an average of 12.3 organizations planned and executed suicide attacks every year (figure 1.2). For reasons that are not entirely clear, the trend in 2006 and 2007 has slightly reversed itself.

Casualties of Suicide Attacks

Suicide attacks have claimed an enormous human toll. The 1,269 SMs recorded between 1981 and April 5, 2007, have caused more than 50,000 casualties. In that period, 16,172 people were killed in SMs while at least 35,008 were wounded (figure 1.3) The first major peak in the number killed occurred in 2001, and reflects the nearly 3,000 people killed in the attacks of September 11, 2001. The second spike is in 2005. As opposed to 2001, no single incident is responsible for this spike. Instead, the year 2005 witnessed a general upsurge in particularly lethal suicide attacks. For example, 39 SMs during 2005 caused the death of 30 or more people. Of these, 16 attacks had a toll of 50 or more killed, and 4 attacks—all of them in Iraq—killed at least 100 people.[4]

The overall trend in the number of injured is largely comparable to the number of people killed, although in two years—1996 and 1998—the number of people wounded in SMs is particularly high (figure 1.3). The 1996 figure includes a suicide car bombing perpetrated on January 31, 1996, by a member of the Liberation Tigers of Tamil Eelam (LTTE). In that attack, which took place near a bank in Colombo, 19 people died and an estimated 1,400 people were wounded. The 1998 figure includes the suicide bombing of the U.S. Embassy in Nairobi, Kenya, on August 7, 1998. That attack killed 213 people and wounded an estimated 4,000. The sharp increase beginning in 2003 is due—as in the case of the number of people killed—largely to the ongoing war in Iraq.

Based on the same database, the average SM between 1981 and April 5, 2007,

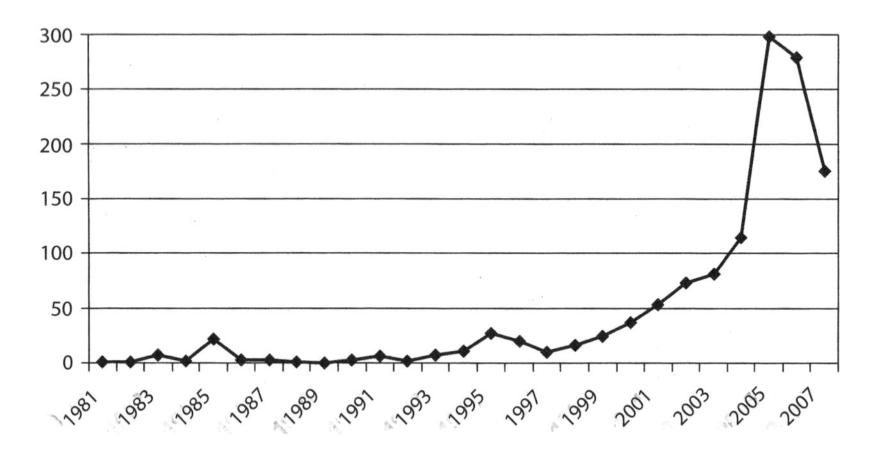

Fig. 1.1. Suicide Missions by Year, 1981–April 5, 2007

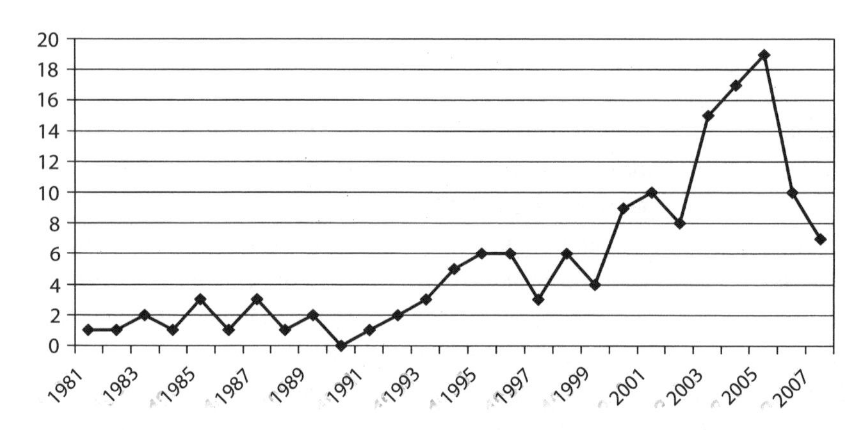

Fig. 1.2. Number of Organizations per Year, 1981–April 5, 2007

killed 12.7 people and injured 27.4. These numbers, however, should be approached with caution because the range was exceedingly wide, and because information about casualty rates of SMs (and especially of the number of wounded) is often incomplete or entirely missing. The median of the number of people killed is 4, while the median of the number of people wounded is 9. Because there are no indications, based on the data, that SMs have become increasingly lethal over time, these figures may suggest that suicide terrorism tactics and methods have not necessarily improved significantly over the past quarter of a century.[5]

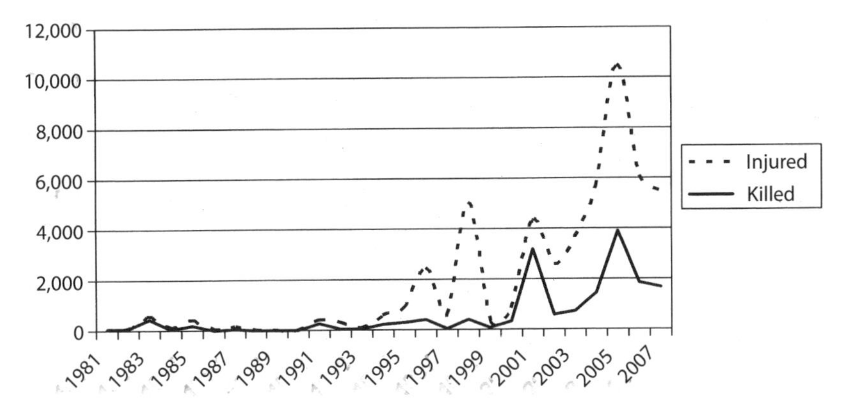

Fig. 1.3. Number of Casualties per Year, 1981–April 5, 2007

Trends in the Countries and People Targeted

Between 1981 and 2007, the number of countries in which SMs have occurred has generally been rising. The most noticeable change occurred in the mid-1990s. Until 1994 SMs were usually conducted in up to three countries. The average number of countries witnessing SMs per year between 1981 and 1994 was a relatively low 1.7. Lebanon and Sri Lanka were the most frequently targeted countries in that period. Beginning in 1995, the average number of countries in which suicide attacks took place rose by a factor of more than four. On average, in each year between 1995 and 2007, 7.5 countries were locations of suicide attacks. In 2005 alone, SMs were executed in 15 countries—the highest number of countries recorded (figure 1.4).

Suicide missions have occurred in at least 31 countries (figure 1.5). Of these, 628 attacks—nearly half of all suicide attacks between 1981 and April 5, 2007 (49.1 percent)—occurred in Iraq. In that time period, according to the suicide terrorism database, 182 (14.2 percent) SMs took place in Israel (including the West Bank and Gaza Strip); 140 (11 percent) in Afghanistan; 99 (7.8 percent) in Sri Lanka; 41 (3.2 percent) in Lebanon; and 33 (2.6 percent) each in Russia and Pakistan. A total of 121 attacks have occurred in other countries, namely Algeria, Argentina, Bangladesh, China, Croatia, Egypt, Finland, India, Indonesia, Jordan, Kenya, Kuwait, Morocco, Panama, Qatar, Saudi Arabia, Somalia, Tanzania, Tunisia, Turkey, the United Kingdom, the United States, Uzbekistan, and Yemen.

The 1,269 SMs recorded for the period between 1981 and April 2007 have been aimed at a variety of targets (figure 1.6). Civilians were the most frequent target,

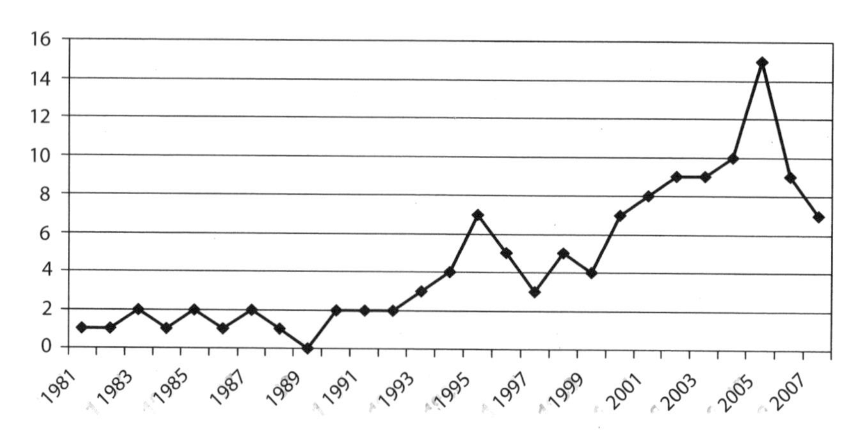

Fig. 1.4. Number of Countries Targeted, 1981–April 5, 2007

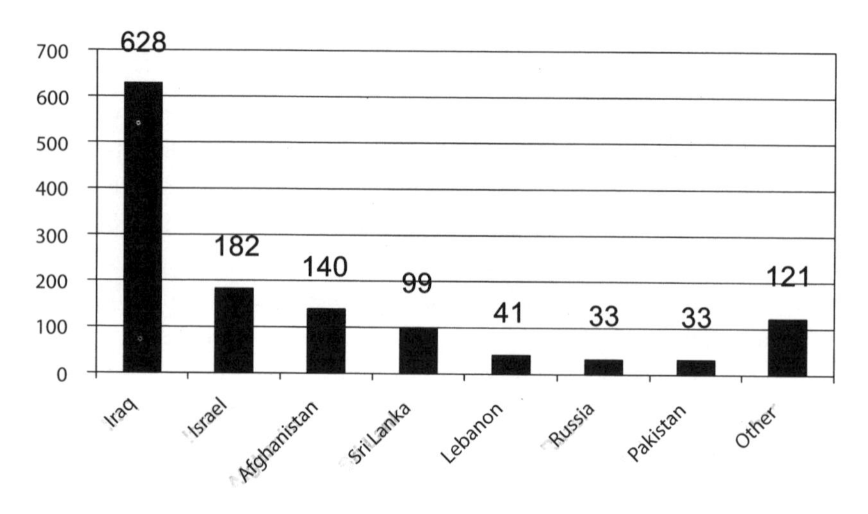

Fig. 1.5. Number of Suicide Missions by Country, 1981–April 5, 2007

the focus of one-third of all SMs. About 29 percent of all SMs were employed against military targets, while an additional 18 percent were aimed at individuals and institutions connected to law enforcement. A political and diplomatic focus accounted for 9 and 3 percent, respectively.

Among civilian targets, buses and bus stops (18 percent) and religious sites (12 percent) are preferred by suicide bombers, accounting for roughly one-third of all civilian targets. Shopping, recreational, and entertainment sites such as shopping malls and markets (14 percent), restaurants (8 percent), hotels (5 percent),

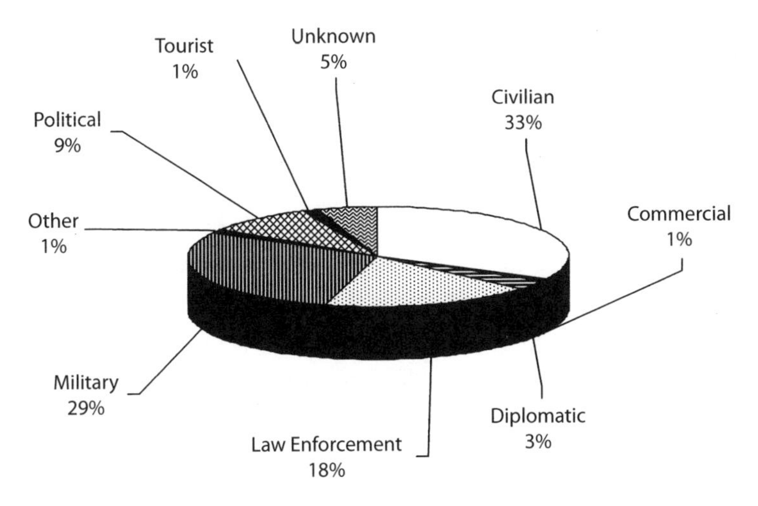

Fig. 1.6. Target Profiles, 1981–April 5, 2007

and nightclubs and theaters (3 percent) account for an additional one-third of attacks against civilians. Attacks against hospitals (3 percent) and funerals (2 percent) underscore the cruelty apparent in the target selection of many suicide bombers and their handlers.

The Role of Al Qaeda and the Salafi Jihad

Al Qaeda and Suicide Attacks

The cause of this unprecedented rise in the number of suicide attacks, the number of organizations involved in suicide bombings, and their increasing lethality lies in two related and mutually reinforcing phenomena: the rise of Al Qaeda and its guiding ideology, Salafi Jihad. The idea of Al Qaeda was conceived around 1988. Its establishment is connected to the nine-year-long Afghan-Soviet War in the 1980s and is partly due to the desire to organize the records of foreign Muslim fighters (mostly Arabs) who joined the battle against the Soviet army. These fighters became known as "Afghan Arabs."

In order to strengthen the claim that the rise of Al Qaeda in part accounts for the globalization of SMs, two separate issues must be explained: first, the importance Al Qaeda places on SMs as the primary method of terrorist operations; and, second, why and how Al Qaeda became a global entity in both outlook and practice.

Suicide attacks are Al Qaeda's preferred mode of attack because they symbolize the group's tenaciousness, they help inspire many young Muslims, and they create more fear and terror among the enemy than any other weapon. No other group appears to have invested the time, effort, and money that Al Qaeda has in preparing its cadres for suicide attacks, and no other group has imbued the collective psyche of its fighters to the same extent with a cult of martyrdom and the spirit of self-sacrifice. As expressed by its leading strategists, Al Qaeda is acutely aware of the tactical advantages SMs offer, and these advantages are particularly important given the power and might of its chosen enemies. With regard to the global scope of Al Qaeda's operations, three key reasons have affected its decision to "go global": the core doctrine of Al Qaeda, the global spread of the Afghan Arabs after 1988, and a strategic decision to focus on Western targets in the second half of the 1990s.

The original idea of Al Qaeda—as envisioned by Abdullah Azzam, the co-founder of Al Qaeda and bin Laden's mentor—was to establish this group as a vanguard of a new global Islamic insurgency devoted to the defense of the *umma* wherever its well-being would be imperiled. This Muslim legion would be self-perpetuating, as it would generate new waves of Islamic warriors who would fight and defeat infidel and apostate countries the world over. As Rohan Gunaratna points out, Al Qaeda's doctrine and activities had never been guided by territorial jurisdiction—"its theatre of support, as well as its operations, is global . . . its forces are being harnessed by contemporary Islamist groups, constantly looking for new bases and new targets worldwide."[6]

The second reason for the globalization of Al Qaeda's SMs is the physical diffusion of the Afghan Arabs following the retreat of the Soviet forces from Afghanistan. During the 1990s and until the attacks of 9/11, many of the Afghan Arabs and subsequent generations of mujahideen training in jihadist camps fulfilled Azzam's dream by participating in local jihads in countries like Jordan, Egypt, or Saudi Arabia, as well as in Europe. Serving as the very vanguard that Azzam had envisioned, most of these Afghan alumni chose violence as their preferred tactic.[7]

Finally, Al Qaeda's decision to go global was based on a deliberate shift in strategy. Between 1995 and 1996, after heated internal discussions, Al Qaeda decided not to attack the "near enemy," that is, the local Arab regimes it regarded as apostate, but to target the "far enemy"—Western "infidel" countries, above all the United States.[8] This shift in strategy became most evident when, in 1996, Al Qaeda declared war on the United States, and when, two years later, it announced the formation of a global alliance to defeat the "Crusader-Zionist" enemy. Al Qaeda's first major SM, the bombings in 1998 at the U.S. embassies in Nairobi and Dar-es-Salaam, embodied that strategic shift.

Salafi Jihad and Suicide Attacks

The Salafi Jihad is the guiding ideology of Al Qaeda and its associated groups and networks. It is a radical offshoot movement with roots in a broader Islamist trend known as Salafism, but it also incorporates elements of Saudi Wahhabism and the Qutbist faction of the Muslim Brotherhood. Salafis adopt a strict implementation of Islamic religious law, and their doctrine centers around a far more literal understanding of the concept of *tawhid* (the unity of God) than does that of ordinary Muslims. For Salafis, the unity of God—a concept that all Muslims believe in—extends to the belief that all man-made laws must be rejected as an interference with the word and will of God. Salafis reject the division of religion and state and believe that only the *salaf*—the Prophet himself and his ancient companions—led a life-style that was in accordance with God's will and hence pleasing to him. Only by emulating that life-style can Muslims reverse the decline of Islam.

Whereas ordinary Salafis believe that God's word should be spread by *dawa* alone—the nonviolent call to Islam by proselytizing—Salafi-Jihadists advocate waging violent jihad. This advocacy of violence leads to four main points of contention between the two groups: unlike Salafis, Salafi-Jihadists give priority to jihad, elevating it to the same level as the five pillars of Islam; they engage in *takfir*, the process of labeling fellow Muslims as infidels (*kufr*), thus justifying violence against them; they condone the targeting of civilians; and they support the use of suicide operations.[9]

Salafi-Jihadists believe that suicide operations against infidels and apostates—shorthand for non-Muslim infidels and nominally Muslim traitors—are the ultimate form of devotion to God and the best way to wage jihad. They present jihad and self-sacrifice as the antithesis to everything that the West stands for, and hence repeat the mantra that "the West loves life, while true Muslims love death."

Salafi-Jihadist preachers such as Abu Hamza al-Masri or Omar Bakri Muhammad help inspire thousands of Muslim youth to develop a cultlike relationship to martyrdom in mosques. Other preachers are mainly active on the Internet, where they often provide legitimation for what they term martyrdom operations. Because Islam forbids the taking of one's own life, Salafi-Jihadists draw a conceptual distinction between suicide and martyrdom, arguing that ordinary suicides kill themselves for personal reasons, such as distress or depression, whereas true martyrs die primarily for the sake of God, but also for the greater good of the Muslim community at large.

Salafi Jihad as Religious Ideology

Is the Salafi Jihad better understood as a religion or as an ideology? Although its beliefs seem more akin to modern political ideologies than to a religion, the Salafi Jihad, unlike most modern ideologies, is not secular because it invokes religion and claims to act on its behalf. Specifically, Salafi-Jihadists define themselves and their enemies in religious terms; describe their main mission and strategy as acts of religious devotion; and justify violence by (selectively) invoking religious texts. The Salafi Jihad is therefore best described as a religious ideology.

Ideologies have several core functions, of which the first is to raise awareness of certain issues to a particular group of people. Ideologies explain to their adherents why social, political, or economic conditions are as they are. Because individuals oftentimes seek explanations in times of crisis, ideologies are particularly appealing when a given group of people perceives itself to be in a predicament.

The second function is a diagnostic one, whereby the ideology attributes blame for the present predicament of the ingroup upon some outgroup. The latter group of people is identified with a certain behavior that, according to the narrative offered by the ideology, undermines the well-being of the ingroup.

A third function of ideology lies in the creation of a group identity. At the same time that an outside group is blamed for the predicament of the group represented by the ideology, the ideology identifies and highlights the common characteristics of those individuals who adhere to, or are potential adherents of, the ideology.

The fourth and final function of ideologies is a programmatic one. The ideology puts forward a particular program of action said to relieve the ingroup of its predicament and urges its adherents to implement that course of action.[10]

Ideologies are links between thoughts, beliefs, and myths, on the one hand, and action, on the other hand. They can be instruments of preservation, whereby they may help a given group preserve its political power. More commonly, however, ideologies are used as instruments of competition and conflict, whereby a group can utilize ideology as a means of opposition and contestation. Once a group internalizes ideology, it can provide a "cognitive map" that filters the way social realities are perceived, rendering that reality easier to grasp, more coherent, and thus more meaningful. Ideologies offer some measure of security and relief in the face of ambiguity and particularly in times of crisis.

Ideology may help create significant divides between adherents and non-adherents. Individuals who are especially convinced by an ideology can exhibit "a remarkable ability to ignore, deny, or reinterpret information which is incompatible with tenets of their belief system."[11] "Ideologues," meanwhile, "tend to be explicit in their cognitive claims, exclusionary in their membership, authoritarian in their leadership, rigorous in their ethical mandates, and insistent on the rightness of their causes."[12]

To the ingroup, ideology confers identification with a particular cause, and thus a sense of purpose. That shared sense of purpose can form a common identity among the members, while at the same time heighten opposition and feelings of separation from individuals who do not share these beliefs.

The Salafi Jihad is more akin to ideology than to religion because, like other ideologies, but unlike religion, it is an outgrowth of modernity—a by-product of the industrialization that has swept through Europe beginning in the nineteenth century. It is intimately linked to the dislocating and turbulent effects of globalization, as rapid changes in the social, political, and economic realms of life are uprooting established notions of identity provided by traditional social structures.

It is also an ideology because its functions are essentially congruent with those of other ideologies. The Salafi-Jihadists' first goal is to raise awareness among Muslims that their religion has been on the wane. Since Islam was at its peak during the first centuries of its existence, Salafi-Jihadists urge Muslims to understand that the tide has turned and that Muslims are in a constant state of decline in religious, political, military, economic, and cultural terms.

Second, and in line with the diagnostic function of modern ideologies, the Salafi Jihad identifies the alleged source of the Muslims' conundrum in the persistent attacks and humiliation of Muslims on the part of an alliance of what it terms Crusaders, Zionists, and apostates.

The third function of the Salafi Jihad also parallels that of all ideologies, in that it helps build an identity. Like other ideologies such as fascism or communism, Salafi Jihad gives individuals a new sense of self-definition by offering individuals confused by modernization a membership to a supranational entity. Salafi-Jihadists attempt to instill into Muslims the notion that the only identity that truly matters is that of membership in the *umma*, the global community of Muslims that provides comfort, dignity, security, and honor to the downtrodden Muslims.

Finally, like all ideologies, Salafi-Jihadists present a program of action, namely jihad, understood in military terms. Jihad will reverse the tide of history and redeem adherents and potential adherents of Salafi Jihad (i.e., Muslims) from their misery. Martyrdom, meanwhile, is the ultimate way in which jihad can be waged.

Like other ideologies, the Salafi Jihad sharply distinguishes between its adherents and those who reject its doctrines. Westerners are commonly described as infidels, while moderate Muslims and Arabs are labeled apostates. To the most extreme Salafi-Jihadists, Muslims who reject the tenets of Salafi Jihad are tantamount to infidels, thus deserving of death.

Like leaders of other ideologies, Osama bin Laden and other leaders of Salafi-Jihadist groups ignore, deny, or reinterpret information that counters or could potentially weaken their argument. For instance, Salafi-Jihadists ignored Western support to a Muslim country like Indonesia in the aftermath of the tsunami. They interpret their violence on other Muslims as religiously sanctioned, ignoring sections of Muslim holy texts that prohibit internecine fighting or the killing of civilians. They single-handedly blame the West for every misfortune that has befallen Muslims.

As an ideology, the Salafi Jihad has much in common with radical leftist ideologies of twentieth-century Europe. Like the radical left, for example, the Salafi Jihad describes its action in part as a revolt against injustice, and it rejects bourgeois values, imperialism, and materialism. The goal of both the leftist movements and Salafi-Jihadists is essentially an elusive quest to help bring about a more just society—violence is seen here as a justified means to an end. Both Salafi-Jihadists and radical leftist revolutionaries believe that the scope of their activities, and the importance of their actions are global in nature, as are their goals. As Stephen Holmes observes, for Salafi-Jihadists the caliphate "is the religious equivalent of Marx' Communist utopia."[13] Parallels between the radical left in Europe and the Salafi Jihad can also be found in the individuals recruited to these respective ideologies. In both cases, young recruits tend to feel alienated by the more settled life-style of their parents, with which they are unable to connect.

But how do ideologies differ from religions, and why is the Salafi Jihad not a religion? Religions differ from ideologies in an important respect that has relevance to the discussion of Salafi Jihad: the primary focus of ideologies is the group, whereas that of religions is the individual. As Bruce Lawrence has pointed out, "religion focuses on maximizing individual benefit through group participation, while ideology is intent on maximizing group benefit through individual participation."[14] As a result of the ideology's preoccupation with the group as a whole, it demands great loyalty and commitment on the part of the individual member. Ideologies, like religions, demand verbal assent from their members, but more than that, they demand complete control over the thoughts, words, and deeds of their adherents.[15]

Although the Salafi Jihad therefore differs from religions, it also differs from ordinary ideologies in an important respect—it tends to use religious words, symbols, and values to sustain itself. Ideologies are usually devoid of religious symbols. Ian Adams, for instance, writes that "what separates [religion from ideology] is that while the central feature of a religious understanding is its concept of the divine, the central feature of an ideological understanding is its conception of human nature."[16]

The Salafi Jihad, however, invokes religion in three ways. First, it describes itself and its enemies in religious terms. Salafi-Jihadists label themselves in such religious terms as the Army of Muhammad, the lions of Islam, and jihadist. At the same time, they describe their enemies in religious terms such as Crusaders, apostates, infidels, or Zionists (the last term usually used synonymously with the term Jews). Second, Salafi-Jihadists describe their strategy and mission as a religious one. Their struggle is a jihad, which they themselves define in military terms and not as an internal war against human temptations. Their main tactic is not suicide attacks, but martyrdom operations—a term whose origin is ironically associated with Shia Islam, which itself is deemed apostate by Salafi-Jihadists. Finally, they justify acts of violence with references drawn selectively from the Quran.

The Salafi Jihad is not alone in invoking religious texts, symbols, or values for mostly political goals. Other fundamentalist movements too invoke religion. Fundamentalism, writes Lawrence, "is a religious ideology since the beliefs of its adherents, their practices, their challenges, their aspirations, all are framed in discourse that authorizes action through scriptural, creedal, and moral referents."[17] The Salafi Jihad is the most recent incarnation of a fundamentalist, religious ideology.

Evidence for the Link between Salafi Jihad and Suicide Attacks

Although statistical evidence for the growth of the Salafi Jihad in the world is scant, ample anecdotal evidence of the growing appeal of this ideology—to both men and women[18] in general,[19] and to people in Europe,[20] the Middle East,[21] Central Asia,[22] Southeast Asia,[23] and Africa[24] in particular—does exist.

In this book, I demonstrate the rise of Salafi Jihad by examining the groups that have employed suicide missions. To demonstrate the close links between Al Qaeda and Salafi Jihad, on the one hand, and the internationalization of SMs, on the other hand, I proceeded to code all forty-three groups that have employed SMs between 1981 and April 5, 2007, based on their guiding ideology or doctrine.

Groups have been coded as Salafi-Jihadist,[25] mainstream Islamist,[26] nationalist-separatist, Shia,[27] Marxist hybrid,[28] and unknown.

The list of groups that have employed SMs is based on a dataset of the universe of SMs as recorded by the National Security Studies Center at the University of Haifa.[29] In order to be coded as Salafi-Jihadist, a group must be a Sunni Islamic group to which at least one of the following must apply in addition:

1. Membership of and/or adherence to Al Qaeda is reflected in the group's name.
2. The group has "internalized the worldview of Al Qaeda and global jihad."[30]
3. The group is devoted to and actively practices violence to overthrow an existing Islamic regime or regimes with the aim to create a transnational caliphate in its stead.[31]
4. The group has engaged in the practice of *takfir*—the labeling of some other Muslims as *kufr*, or heretics.[32]

Several sources have been used to ascertain the ideological or doctrinal orientation of groups that employ suicide terrorism:

- The Terrorism Knowledge Base of the Memorial Institute for the Prevention of Terrorism (MIPT)[33]
- The 2005 Country Reports on Terrorism, published by the U.S. Department of State's Office of the Coordinator for Counterterrorism
- A two-part book series titled *Beyond Al Qaeda* published by the Rand Corporation,[34] which details information on the ideological affiliation of jihadist groups (assessments made in these two studies are based on the consensus agreement of eight of Rand's terrorism experts)
- Anecdotal information, when the first three sources do not provide sufficient information to establish the ideological identity of groups

The results of this categorization are summarized in the appendix, which lists nineteen (44 percent) Salafi-Jihadist groups out of the forty-three groups that have conducted SMs in the quarter century since 1981. Salafi-Jihadist groups have carried out some 15 percent of all SMs between 1981 and April 2007—more than any other group (figure 1.7). Nationalist-separatist groups are second, with 13 percent of all suicide attacks. Of the 1,269 suicide attacks that have been conducted between 1981 and April 5, 2007, 681 (54 percent) have been perpetrated by organizations whose identity has not yet been ascertained. Of these 681 attacks by unknown perpetrators, however, 521 (76.5 percent) have occurred in Iraq and 98 (14.4 percent) in Afghanistan—both countries in which the vast majority of organizations conducting suicide bombings are known to be Salafi-Jihadist.[35]

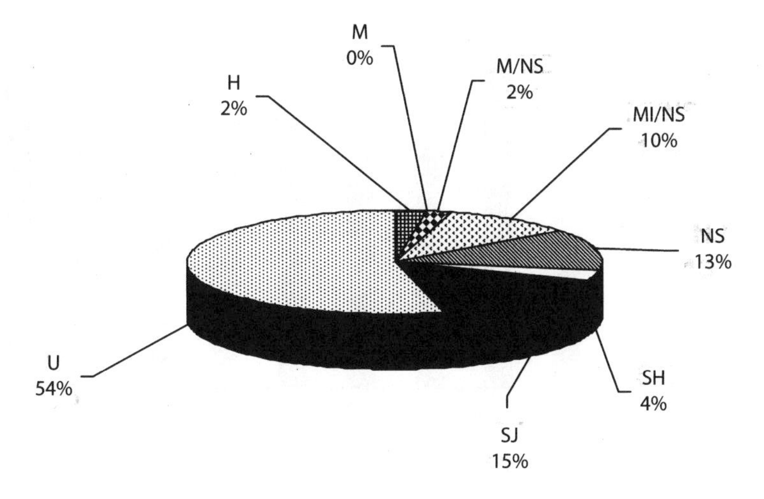

Fig. 1.7. Percentage of Attacks by Ideology, 1981–April 5, 2007. H = hybrid; M = Marxist; M/NS = Marxist/nationalist-separatist; MI/NS = mainstream Islamist and nationalist-separatist; NS = nationalist-separatist; SH = Shia; SJ = Salafi-Jihadist; U = unknown

In Iraq, for example, the bulk of SMs are known to have been perpetrated by Salafi-Jihadist groups such as Al Qaeda in Iraq and the Ansar al-Sunna Group,[36] whereas in Afghanistan the Taliban—a longtime Al Qaeda ally—is the main perpetrator of suicide attacks.[37] This additional information about these attacks strongly suggests that the vast majority of SMs in the unknown category are attacks by Salafi-Jihadist groups. The percentage of Salafi-Jihadist suicide attacks out of the total number of attacks is therefore considerably higher than even figure 1.7 would suggest.

More importantly, Salafi-Jihadist groups have assumed the leadership among groups that employ this modus operandi in a number of respects, including in terms of numbers of organizations, numbers of attacks, and even in the average and overall lethality of SMs (figure 1.8). In 1997, for example, none of the groups that perpetrated SMs were Salafi-Jihadist. A year later, 17 percent of the groups that conducted SMs adhered to Salafi-Jihadist ideology, followed by 25 percent in 1999 and 67 percent in 2000. Since 2000, there has been a trend toward growing dominance of Salafi-Jihadist organizations among all groups employing SMs. In 2006 and 2007 that percentage peaked at 70 percent and 67 percent, respectively.

The growing dominance of Salafi-Jihadist groups among groups employing SMs is paralleled by the relative decline in importance of groups adhering to other ideologies (figure 1.9). During the 1980s, Shia groups were the dominant perpetrators of SMs, followed by groups with a nationalist-separatist agenda.

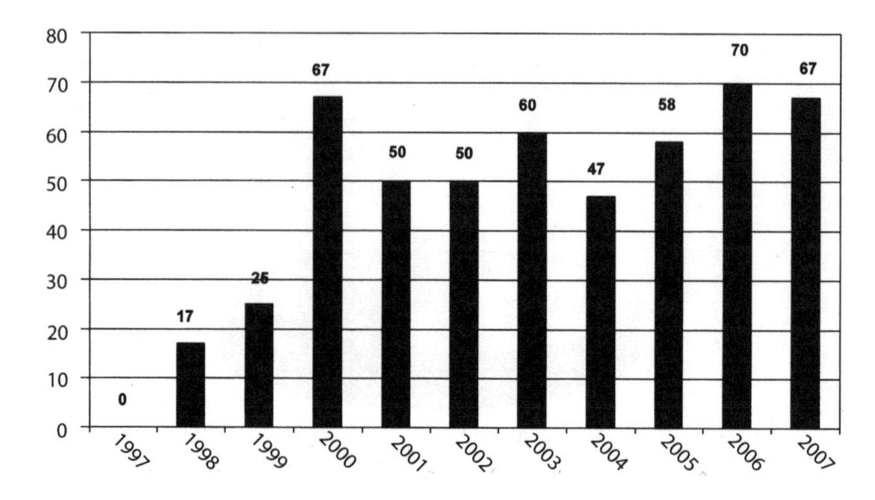

Fig. 1.8. Percentage of Rise in Salafi-Jihadist Groups, 1981–April 5, 2007

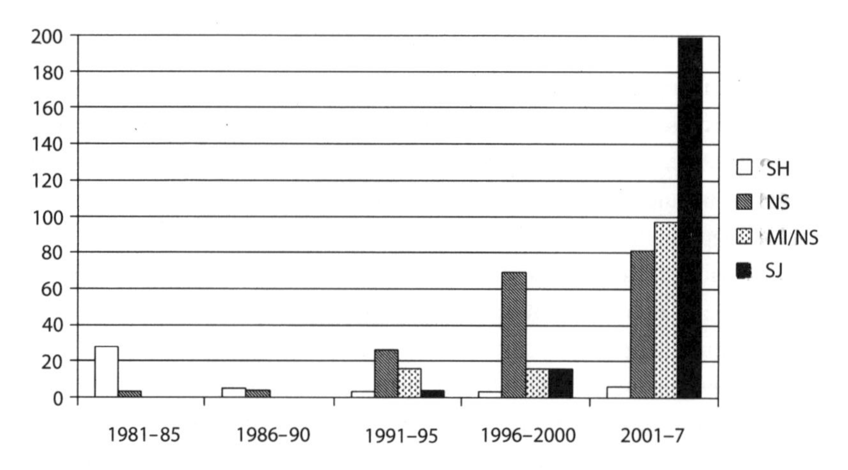

Fig. 1.9. Attacks by Ideology, 1981–April 5, 2007. SH = Shia; NS = nationalist-separatist (including Marxist/nationalist-separatist category); MI/NS = mainstream Islamist and nationalist-separatist; SJ = Salafi-Jihadist (including hybrid category, groups that are only partially Salafi-Jihadist)

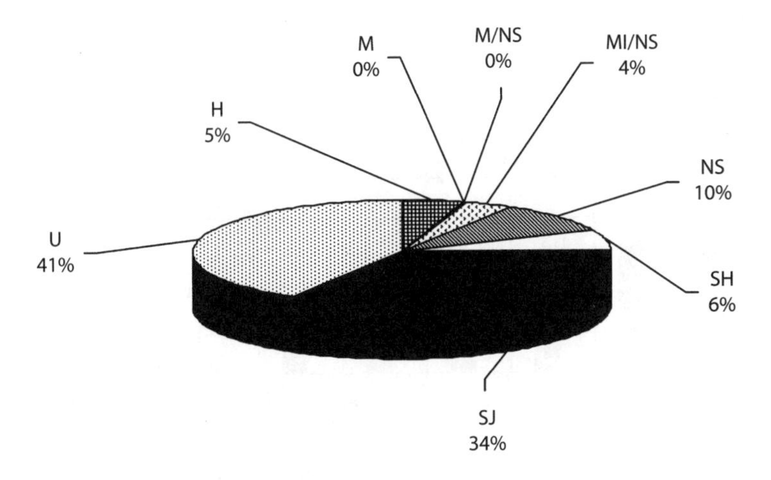

Fig. 1.10. Percentage of Fatalities by Ideology, 1981–April 2007. H = hybrid; M = Marxist; M/NS = Marxist/nationalist-separatist; MI/NS = mainstream Islamist and nationalist-separatist; NS = nationalist-separatist; SH = Shia; SJ = Salafi-Jihadist; U = unknown

During the 1990s nationalist-separatist groups were by far the most frequent users of SMs, followed by groups with a combination of mainstream Islamist and nationalist-separatist agenda. Since the turn of the millennium, as is evident from figure 1.9, suicide attacks by Salafi-Jihadist groups are far more common than are attacks by all other groups.

The steep rise in the number of attacks by Salafi-Jihadist groups is even more worrisome when one considers that attacks by Salafi-Jihadist groups carry a much higher lethality than attacks by non-Salafi-Jihadist groups. Although Salafi-Jihadist groups are responsible for only 15 percent of attacks in the time frame of 1981 to April 2007, Salafi-Jihadist groups are responsible for at least a third (34 percent) of all fatalities caused by suicide attacks in that period. Even if only half of the fatalities in the "unknown" category have been caused by Salafi-Jihadist groups—an extremely conservative estimate, given that the majority of attacks falling in this category have been perpetrated by Salafi-Jihadists—it can be concluded that substantially more than half of all fatalities of SMs in the past quarter century have been caused by Salafi-Jihadist groups (figure 1.10).

This high degree of lethality makes the rise of Salafi Jihad particularly dangerous. The lethality ratio of groups that have employed SMs demonstrates that hybrid groups (i.e., those adhering partially to Salafi-Jihadist ideology) are the most lethal outfits, killing an average of 19 people per attack and wounding more

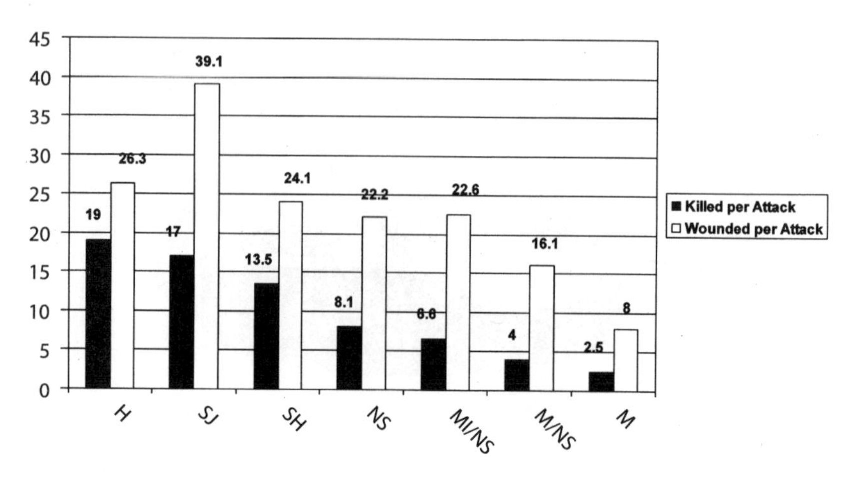

Fig. 1.11. Potency by Ideology, 1981–April 5, 2007. H = hybrid; SJ = Salafi-Jihadist; SH = Shia; NS = nationalist-separatist; MI/NS = mainstream Islamist and nationalist-separatist; M/NS = Marxist/nationalist-separatist; M = Marxist

than 26 (figure 1.11). They are followed by Salafi-Jihadist groups, with 17 fatalities per attack and wounded per attack in excess of 39. Shia groups also prove to be highly potent, with 13.5 killed and more than 24 wounded individuals per attack. They are followed in potency by nationalist-separatist groups (8.1 killed and 22.2 wounded), mainstream Islamists/nationalist-separatists (6.6 and 22.6), Marxists/nationalist-separatists (4 and 16.1), and Marxist groups, the least potent category of groups (2.5 and 8).

From Localized to Globalized Patterns of Suicide Attacks

The final section of this chapter is a theoretical reflection of the nature of SMs that builds upon the preceding discussion. The goal is to offer a conceptual framework that reflects the changes in the nature and employment of some SMs in the wake of the rise of Al Qaeda and Salafi-Jihadist ideology. Specifically, I argue that the advent of Salafi Jihad has altered the nature and employment of some SMs in five key areas in a way that allows us to distinguish between two broad patterns of SMs—a traditional pattern of localized SMs and the predominant, contemporary pattern of globalized SMs. The five areas of divergence are the types of conflicts in which SMs are used; the types of groups employing SMs; the geographic scope of these actors; their target definition; and the types of goals these actors pursue.

Localized Suicide Attacks

The overwhelming majority of SMs in the first two decades after 1981 have occurred in relatively localized settings. Localized suicide attacks tend to have several characteristics.

CONFLICT TYPE

SMs have traditionally occurred in the context of a relatively localized conflict that is identified as such by two belligerent parties. Examples of these conflicts are those between Israel and Hizballah, Israelis and the Palestinians, Tamils and Sinhalese, and Turks and Kurds. These conflicts have generally raged for many years, often decades, and are usually long-standing conflicts between groups of a different ethnic background and/or religion.[38]

IDEOLOGY

SMs that fall into the traditional, localized pattern have been planned and executed by groups that have been both religious and secular, Marxist, ethnonationalist, or nationalist. Religion alone is therefore unable to account for the genesis of the traditional pattern of SMs. Examples of religious groups that have employed localized-pattern SMs include Hamas, Palestinian Islamic Jihad (PIJ), and Hizballah. Examples of groups that are secular or nationalist in character include the LTTE, the PFLP, Fatah's Al-Aqsa Martyrs Brigades, the PKK, and the Syrian Socialist Nationalist Party.

GEOGRAPHIC SCOPE OF ACTORS

Traditionally, most SMs have been planned and executed by subnational terrorist or insurgent actors such as Hizballah, the LTTE, Hamas, PIJ, or the PKK. Palestinian organizations employing SMs, for example, have largely conducted the operational planning of suicide missions locally—although they may have been receptive to the strategic message and direction of an exile leadership.[39] The subnational nature of these groups that execute this pattern of SMs implies that these organizations have recruited and trained suicide bombers mostly in or near the conflict area proper and have rarely sought them abroad. Unlike modern suicide bombers, who oftentimes migrate to blow themselves up in a foreign country, "traditional" suicide bombers appear to be largely residents of the area of conflict. Most recruits of the PKK, for example, stem from large, poor families residing in Turkey.[40] In the case of attacks by Palestinian organizations, more than 99 percent of the bombers between 1993 and 2005 have been residents of the area of conflict—the West Bank, Gaza, and Israel proper. The only exceptions were two Britons involved in the attacks on Mike's Place bar in Tel Aviv on April 30, 2003.[41] As far as the LTTE is concerned, experts on the group believe that it is unlikely that it has drawn Black Tiger recruits from outside Sri Lanka because they are chosen from within the existing ranks of the regular LTTE army, where motivation to serve is high.[42] According to Stephen Hopgood, for example, "the emphasis on commitment to the cause both for regular cadres and Black Tigers makes non-Sri Lankan or Indian Tamil recruits highly unlikely. The LTTE seems to have no recruitment problems for Black Tigers, so looking outside would only be necessary if some ethnic or linguistic feature of the operative's identity was necessary to accomplish the mission."[43]

TARGETS

Hamas, LTTE, PKK, and Hizballah—groups that have conducted localized SMs—have mostly targeted people and assets of the enemy state in the conflict area proper, or in close proximity thereof, while by and large refraining from targeting assets of their foes in other locations. The PKK, for instance, has conducted all of its SMs in Turkey. Hamas and other Palestinian organizations have never executed an SM against Israeli or Jewish targets outside of Israel, the West Bank, and Gaza. Hizballah's SMs against Israel were staged mostly against IDF troops inside Lebanon—with the exception of two suicide attacks on Israeli and Jewish targets in Argentina, for which the group has declined to assume responsibility.[44] The LTTE has staged the vast majority of its estimated 200 attacks in Sri Lanka proper—a notable exception being the killing of Indian prime minister Rajiv Gandhi in the Indian city of Madras in May 1991.[45] Experts on the LTTE consulted by the author are unaware of additional SMs carried out by the LTTE outside of Sri Lanka.[46] To quote Hopgood again, "the LTTE is very careful to make it clear its target is the Sri Lankan state, and its collaborators, rather than all Sri Lankans. It is conscious of its public image and escalating to attack on foreign soil would be counterproductive both to legitimacy and diaspora fundraising."[47]

GOALS

The subnational terrorist or insurgent movements that characterize localized patterns of SMs generally aim to advance limited and well-defined political goals for the community they purport to represent. Such political goals may include an end to foreign occupation or military presence, increased regional autonomy, and self-determination. The struggle for an independent homeland, whether it is Tamil Eelam, Kurdistan, or Palestine, lies at the center of the conflicts in the course of which SMs have traditionally been adopted.

Globalized Suicide Attacks

The localized pattern of suicide missions contrasts sharply with a different general pattern of globalized SMs epitomized by Al Qaeda and its affiliates. The globalized pattern of SMs bears a number of distinct characteristics.

CONFLICT TYPE

The new pattern of globalized SMs may occur in the context of clearly identifiable conflicts such as Iraq, but those conflicts may not necessarily be historical and/or long-standing. SMs in Iraq, for example, occurred less than a week following the beginning of the U.S. led invasion of Iraq in March 2003[48]—hardly long enough to produce the types of deep-seated grievances that have presumably affected Palestinian, Tamil, or Kurdish suicide bombers in localized contexts. Nor are the targets of many of today's globalized SMs always aware that they are involved in a conflict with a bitter enemy who seeks their death along with its own. Unlike traditional SMs, globalized SMs frequently occur in areas that—by any objective standards—are not identified by all parties as zones of conflict. The 9/11 attacks, for instance, did not take place in a region where a large ethnic group is vying for an independent state while battling an occupation army. The same is true for the SMs at Khobar Towers, Saudi Arabia, in June 1996; the U.S. embassy bombings in Kenya and Tanzania in August 1998; the attack on the USS *Cole* in October 2000; and other examples of globalized SMs in Djerba (April 2002), Bali (October 2002 and October 2005), Mombasa (November 2002), Saudi Arabia (May 2003), Casablanca (May 2003), Istanbul (November 2003), London (July 2005), and Amman (November 2005), to cite a few examples.

IDEOLOGY

Whereas traditionally both religious and secular groups have perpetrated SMs, Salafi-Jihadist groups have overwhelmingly planned and executed the new globalized SMs, as has been demonstrated earlier in the chapter.

GEOGRAPHIC SCOPE OF ACTORS

Unlike localized SMs, which are executed mainly by subnational actors, many of today's globalized SMs are planned and executed by cells and groups that are connected to a transnational terrorist or insurgent network or movement. The transnational nature of the groups that execute this pattern of SMs implies that the planning of the SM and its execution may occur in entirely separate places. Whereas localized SMs are generally planned in or near the area of conflict—where these attacks are also executed—globalized attacks may be planned in one country and executed in another. This is true, for example, for the 9/11 attacks, which were not planned in Washington and New York; the April 2002 attack on a synagogue in Djerba, which was planned in Pakistan;[49] or the 7/7 London bombings.

Additionally, unlike the pattern in localized SMs, organizations conducting globalized SMs no longer recruit and train the suicide bombers exclusively in the country where the attack will eventually be executed. Instead, the suicide attackers are increasingly implanted from other countries. This is true, again, in the case of the 9/11 attacks and the bombings in Amman and is especially evident in the preponderance of foreigners who volunteer for SMs in Iraq and Afghanistan.[50] The November 2005 bombings in Amman, for example, were executed by three Iraqis,[51] while many suicide bombers in Afghanistan appear to be non-Afghanis.[52]

TARGETS

Organizations and cells staging globalized SMs no longer limit their attacks to an identifiable zone of conflict, as has been the case in traditional, localized SMs. In fact, due in large part to the nature of Salafi Jihad, which speaks on behalf of a worldwide community of Muslim believers, many of today's suicide attackers regard much of the world as a legitimate target. Hence, even though Al Qaeda has declared the United States as its main enemy, it does not limit its SMs to the U.S. homeland. Instead, it will strike U.S. interests wherever an opportunity may arise. In addition, it may also strike targets of real or perceived allies of the United States.

GOALS

The goals of the organizations that are responsible for the traditional pattern of SMs are often extreme—Hamas, for instance, calls for the destruction of Israel—but they nevertheless tend to be clearly pronounced, relatively well defined, and geographically narrow in scope. The globalization of SMs, on the other hand, is characterized by organizations whose goals are more elusive. It is not entirely clear, for instance, whether the SMs in Amman in November 2005 were intended to punish the Hashemite monarchy for its pro-Western stance, including its relations with Israel; to target foreign diplomats; to hurt Israeli and Jewish interests in the kingdom; to create instability in the kingdom and spark an anti-Hashemite backlash; or to extend the jihad in Iraq to the broader Middle East. Similarly, Western analysts are often at odds over what exactly Al Qaeda's goals and motivations are, although there is an overall consensus that Al Qaeda's demands are maximalist.[53]

The Interaction between the Local and the Global

The local and global patterns are broad and parsimonious descriptions (table 1.1), but they nevertheless help illustrate a general trend in which most suicide attacks today are closer to the pattern of globalized than to localized attacks. In reality, most SMs will bear characteristics of both patterns and thus fall somewhere in between. The argument made here, however, is that since 2001 globalized SMs have become the dominant pattern of SMs. The high lethality and global spread of Salafi Jihad render this significant change in pattern of SMs particularly important.

As much as globalized SMs dominate the picture of SMs in the past six to seven years, it would be premature to argue that globalized SMs are replacing localized SMs altogether. Indeed, part of the reason for the decline of localized SMs may simply be that countries have learned to cope with organizations that are located close to or within their borders—not that the motivations of groups employing localized SMs have diminished. This issue requires further analysis that is beyond the scope of this book.

What can be established is that, although globalized SMs are rising compared to localized attacks, localized and globalized SMs continue to coexist. Indeed, there is little reason to believe that all localized groups will assume globalized characteristics. Adopting a globalized stance may be harmful to a localized organization, particularly if it decides to target third countries. Drawing the ire of third countries (such as the United States) could be perceived as a potential existential threat to the localized organization.

The cases of Hamas and Hizballah, two localized organizations, are particularly telling. Although they are radical Islamist organizations, these groups are primarily local in outlook and goals. Although their members have staged a small number of attacks outside of their traditional area of operations, these groups adopt a strong nationalist agenda that separates them starkly from the global jihadist aspirations entertained by Al Qaeda. As a result, the Al Qaeda leadership strongly criticizes these groups for failing to wage jihad on a global

TABLE 1.1. *Localized versus Globalized Patterns of Suicide Missions*

	Localized	Globalized
Conflict	Identifiable, long-standing	Less identifiable, short-term
Ideology	Religious, ethnonationalist, secular	Salafi-Jihadist
Actors	Subnational	Transnational
Target Definition	Narrow	Broad
Goals	Limited	Unlimited
Examples	Hizballah, LTTE, PKK, Hamas, PIJ, PFLP, Fatah	Al Qaeda, Al Qaeda affiliates, Al Qaeda associates

scale. In an audiotape released on December 14, 2007, for example, Zawahiri criticized a Hizballah leader for representing a narrow, nationalist perception "unknown to Islam." In a statement that laid bare the distinction between Salafi-Jihadist and radical Islamist groups—the globalized and localized variants of Islamism, respectively—Zawahiri next criticized Hamas:

> I call upon you to declare, in the clearest possible manner, that you . . . aspire to implement sharia, that you reject the rule of the masses and any other rule except that of the Koran and the Sunna, that you strive to establish the Caliphate, that you will fight until the word of Allah [reigns] supreme . . . that you aspire to liberate every inch of Islamic land from Andalusia to Chechnya, and that you will join efforts with the rest of the mujahideen . . . [in the struggle against] the Crusader-Zionist enemy.[54]

While some localized groups can be expected to remain localized, many other previously localized groups have gone global, for example, by officially affiliating themselves with Al Qaeda. The Algerian Salafist Group for the Call and Combat, better known by its French acronym, GSPC, is a case in point. Around 2001 the group began operating outside of Algeria by establishing a number of cells in various European countries, after having been previously focused solely on Algeria. On the second anniversary of 9/11 in September 2003, the group made it clear that it now included the United States among its enemies when it stated that "We strongly and fully support Osama bin Laden's jihad against the heretic America."[55] Three years later to the day, Ayman al-Zawahiri announced the official merger of the GSPC with Al Qaeda.[56]

Examples of such previously localized groups who have, over time, become globalized also include the Islamic Movement of Uzbekistan (IMU; now known as the Islamic Movement of Turkestan). Once focused mainly on Central Asia, the IMU now champions Al Qaeda's internationalist goals, including the establishment of an Islamic caliphate.[57] The same trajectory from the local to the global applies to the Libyan Islamic Fighting Group (LIFG). Formerly focused on Libya, the LIFG has substantial ties to Al Qaeda. LIFG member Abu Anas al-Libi, for example, was a key planner of the U.S. Embassy bombings in Kenya. According to the State Department, non-Libyan members of LIFG are also suspected of involvement in the planning and facilitation of the May 2003 SMs in Casablanca.[58] In 2007 the group formally joined Al Qaeda and pledged allegiance to bin Laden.

Similarly, the Moroccan Islamic Combatant Group (GICM), once dedicated merely to the creation of an Islamist state in Morocco, now actively supports the objectives of Al Qaeda against Western countries. Lashkar-e-Taiba (LET), a group once solely dedicated to the ouster of Indian forces from Kashmir, recently shifted its focus to Iraq. In one of the group's publications, it calls on jihadists to go to Iraq and take revenge for the torture at Abu Ghraib prison and the alleged mistreatment of Iraqi Muslim women. "The Americans are dishonoring our mothers and sisters. . . . Therefore, jihad against America has now become mandatory" read a notice on the LET's Web site.[59] Sipah-e-Sahaba and its more militant offshoot, Lashkar-e-Jhangvi, two radically anti-Shia Salafi-Jihadist terrorist outfits previously focused on Kashmir as well, have increasingly adopted the goals of global jihad.

Perhaps the best-known group to have turned from a local to a global outfit is Jemaah Islamiyah (JI), an Indonesia-based group that is bent on establishing an Islamic caliphate throughout all of Southeast Asia. Parts of JI grew increasingly close to Al Qaeda after 9/11, when Al Qaeda began to exploit local causes of groups like JI while imposing its globalized, Salafi-Jihadist ideology on them.

CHAPTER TWO

Al Qaeda and the Primacy of Suicide Attacks

Al Qaeda: Roots and Evolution

Al Qaeda was established toward the end of a war waged by self-described Islamic holy warriors (*mujahideen*) in Afghanistan against the Soviet Union, which had invaded Afghanistan in December 1979. Shortly after the occupation, transnational Islamic religious networks used religious scholars (*ulema*) to issue a series of religious decrees (*fatwas*), which described the Soviet invasion as an attack by infidels against the *dar al-Islam*, the abode of Islam. That judgment rendered the jihad in Afghanistan a defensive jihad—one that each and every Muslim had a duty to support. The networks issuing the fatwas were mostly funded by Saudi Arabia, and they were influenced by Wahhabism—a puritanical tradition of Islam close to Salafism that originated on the Arabian Peninsula—and by the Muslim Brotherhood, the world's largest Islamist movement.[1] During the nine years of the war, about 3,000 foreign fighters joined the Afghan mujahideen in their efforts to repel the Soviet army and oust their puppet government in Kabul. Because most of the foreign fighters were Arabs, these foreign jihadists became known as Afghan Arabs. The story of Al Qaeda is intimately linked to the Afghan Arabs.

Upon arriving in the region, the Afghan Arabs' first station was Peshawar, a Pakistani city on the eastern end of the strategic Khyber Pass linking Pakistan with Afghanistan. In Peshawar, the recruiters of the Afghan Arabs established training centers amid millions of Afghan refugees.

The arrival of most of the Afghan Arabs was organized by Dr. Abdullah Azzam, a charismatic Islamic teacher, ideologue, and mystic of Palestinian background, and by Osama bin Laden, a wealthy and well-connected Saudi-born son of a construction magnate.[2] In 1984, when still relatively few Arabs fought in the

Afghan jihad, bin Laden suggested to Azzam that they formalize their responsibility over the foreign Arabs who were streaming into Afghanistan. Bin Laden pledged to offer a ticket, residence, and living expenses for every Arab volunteer and his family who was willing to join his and Azzam's new militia. Henceforth, the two decided, they would take on the foreign jihadists and train them for battle in camps built especially for that purpose in and around Peshawar. To implement their plan, bin Laden and Azzam soon established the Makhtab al-Khidamat, or Services Bureau, an Islamic nongovernmental organization (NGO) with recruitment branches in several countries. The Makhtab al-Khidamat was headquartered in Peshawar, in a house rented by bin Laden that received Arabs, helped recruit them for jihad, and also served as the headquarters for Azzam's magazine.

The Afghan Arabs were hoping to participate in the jihad against the Soviets, but their contribution to the victory of the Afghans over the Soviets was negligible. Of the roughly 3,000 fighters during the Soviet occupation, no more than a few hundred actually participated in combat activities. The majority never left Peshawar. Those who did often suffered from a lack of organization and were a burden to the Afghan mujahideen leaders, who sometimes sent them back to Peshawar as soon as they arrived.[3] Despite these failures, bin Laden had a vision to use the Afghan Arabs as a nucleus from which to create an international Arab fighting force that would come to the aid of Muslims wherever they were in need. To that end, bin Laden financed his first all-Arab training camp in 1986 at Jaji.

When the Soviet Union announced the withdrawal of all of its forces in 1988, Azzam and bin Laden had to decide what to do next with the jihad. Both agreed that they should establish a base, or a social movement, to carry out a future jihad. In April 1988 Azzam published an article called "The Solid Base" (*al-qaida al-sulbah*) in *Al-Jihad*, the Afghan Arabs' main magazine, which he founded and edited. In this article, Azzam laid out his basic idea of Al Qaeda to serve as a vanguard for the type of Islamic society envisioned by Azzam. In his words, "Every principle needs a vanguard [*taliah*] to carry it forward. . . . This vanguard constitutes the 'solid base' [*al-qaida al-sulbah*] for the expected society."[4] He laid out his strategy for establishing the true Islamic society:

> The Islamic society cannot be established without an Islamic movement that goes through the fire of tests. Its members need to mature in the fire of trials. This movement will represent the spark that ignites the potential of the nation [*umma*]. It will carry out a long Jihad in which the Islamic movement will provide the leadership, and the spiritual guidance. . . . It is the duty of the children of the Islamic world to firmly stand by this solid base, with their wealth and their lives.

The creation of a secret organization called Al Qaeda occurred sometime in 1988. On August 11, during a meeting called by Azzam to discuss the future of the jihad, a vote was taken to form a new organization designed to keep the jihad alive until after the Soviets' departure—although a secret Al Qaeda had already existed for several months. This is the first time that most of bin Laden's and Azzam's associates present heard the name Al Qaeda. It was decided at the meeting that future members of Al Qaeda would be composed of the best recruits among the foreign mujahideen. However, a clear mission statement for Al Qaeda was still lacking at this point.[5]

On August 20, 1988, during a follow-up meeting, the group around bin Laden and Azzam decided to establish a group called Al Qaeda al-Askariya (the military base), which had two components. A first component was to be embedded with Afghan mujahideen until the withdrawal of the last Soviet soldier. A second component consisted of fighters who were to enter a "testing camp." The best graduates of this camp would be chosen to become members of the new entity known as Al Qaeda. Within less than a year, Al Qaeda would be able to convene its first recruitment meeting in the Farouk camp, near Khost.[6]

For Azzam, the success of jihad in Afghanistan was perceived as a clear sign that God was on the side of the Muslims, and it was to be only the first step in a global endeavor to resurrect the spirit of Muslims through holy war. It was incumbent upon each and every Muslim to contribute his part to the continued success of the Islamic project in every region of the world that at one point has been under Muslim control and was now under the reign of the "infidels." "This duty will not end with victory in Afghanistan," he proclaimed. "Jihad will remain an individual obligation until all other lands that were Muslim are returned to us so that Islam will reign again: before us in Palestine, Bokhara, Lebanon, Chad, Eritrea, Somalia, the Philippines, Burma, southern Yemen, Tashkent and Andalusia."[7]

In the years after the mujahideen's victory over the Soviet army, Azzam's dream gradually came to fruition. Although some Afghan Arabs stayed in Afghanistan or Pakistani tribal zones, most returned to their home countries, where they received a lukewarm reception at best. Many participated in local jihads against entrenched regimes in countries like Jordan, Egypt, or Saudi Arabia. Others moved to third countries, including some in Western Europe. Turning Azzam's dream into a reality, many of the Afghan Arabs radicalized and mobilized Muslims wherever they lived. They regarded themselves as the vanguard that Azzam had foreseen, and many of them would choose violence as their preferred tactic.

With his idea of Al Qaeda, Azzam was hoping to seize upon the momentum of the Afghan victory over the Soviet Union. His goal was to create an Islamic army akin to an international rapid-reaction force that would come to the rescue of Muslims wherever and whenever they were in need. This Muslim legion would create another generation of fighters who would perpetually take on the infidels until Western countries and their apostate Arab and Muslim allies would be defeated. Bin Laden followed Azzam's suggestion of building up this Islamic vanguard and, in 1988, began to plan the establishment of that international Islamic force, which was formed around the Afghan Arabs.[8]

In his attempts to woo the wealthy bin Laden, Azzam increasingly clashed with Ayman al-Zawahiri, the leader of the Egyptian Islamic Jihad (EIJ). Zawahiri and his Egyptian followers exerted a growing influence on bin Laden during the last years of the Afghan-Soviet War. Their main point of contention was on the issue of *takfir*—the branding of other Muslims as *kufr*, or infidels. Azzam had always opposed the waging of *takfir*, which spread in the community of the Afghan Arabs, arguing that it would lead to permanent infighting among Arabs just at a time when Arab unity was needed above all else. Azzam and Zawahiri also differed regarding their priorities. For the Palestinian Azzam, the liberation of Jerusalem had always ranked high. For Zawahiri, on the other hand, starting a revolution in Arab countries—and above all in his native Egypt—has always been the top priority. Azzam's death in 1989 not only resolved this debate in favor of Zawahiri but also helped elevate the status of the Egyptian and his fellow countrymen within Al Qaeda.

In 1992 bin Laden, the now uncontested emir of Al Qaeda, completed his move to Sudan, where he set up a large and elaborate system of businesses and enterprises, along with a global network of bank accounts and NGOs that would serve him well in his future occupation as the world's most notorious terrorist. About 500 individuals were working with bin Laden during the Sudan years, but fewer than 100 of them were formally members of Al Qaeda.[9] While in Sudan, bin Laden also forged contacts with other militant Islamic organizations—some of which had been set up by alumni of the Afghan war—and he began establishing an extensive network of terrorist and insurgent organizations in places like Egypt, Algeria, Yemen, Lebanon, Morocco, Tunisia, Somalia, London, the Balkans, and the Caucasus. He also consolidated links with various groups in Kashmir, and with Jemaah Islamiyah in Indonesia.

When bin Laden returned to Afghanistan on May 18, 1996, the country was ruled by a new regime, the Taliban, whose leader, Mullah Omar, granted the Al Qaeda leader a safe haven. Although financially bankrupt at the time, bin Laden quickly reassumed full control over the Arab Afghans who had remained in Afghanistan and those who had flocked into the country after the Soviet withdrawal. He received support from Zawahiri, who rejoined bin Laden in Kandahar in May 1997. Over the next years, bin Laden allied himself, and his recently expanded Al Qaeda, with the Taliban—a cooperation that would eventually help the Taliban defeat its main challenger, Ahmed Shah Massoud's Northern Alliance.

After his return to Afghanistan in 1996, and especially after issuing a fatwa in which he called for the killing of Americans in February 1998, bin Laden formalized his new focus on the United States as his main enemy. The fatwa encouraged new generations of jihadist fighters to flock to Afghanistan. Bin Laden used Al Qaeda's rising fame to consolidate links to other terrorist groups, and the global network spearheaded by Al Qaeda steadily increased in size with groups of terrorists joining the network from the Maghreb, core Arab states, and Southeast Asia. According to U.S. intelligence, between 1996 and until the attacks of September 11, 2001, between 10,000 and 20,000 fighters, supported by Osama bin Laden, underwent training in camps in Afghanistan.[10] These camps were oftentimes aligned with groups that swore allegiance to one of the various factions of the Afghan civil war that followed the defeat of the Soviet Union. Other camps belonged to groups fighting in places like Kashmir, such as Hizb-ul-Mujahideen or Lashkar-e-Taiba. Bin Laden's support of a large number of training camps in Afghanistan affiliated with these various groups enabled Al Qaeda to screen and vet candidates it wanted to retain for its own organization. Al Qaeda, however, was picky, and only a select few who went through Al Qaeda–sponsored or Al Qaeda–operated training camps were asked to join the group. Many of these had special language or technical skills. Probably no more than a few hundred of these actually became members of Al Qaeda by swearing allegiance (*bayah*) to Osama bin Laden.[11]

Prior to bin Laden's move to Sudan in 1992, most Al Qaeda camps gathered recruits for training in insurgency rather than terrorism. Terrorist training picked up during the Sudan period, however, and was led by Ali Mohammed, a former member of the Egyptian army. Between 1996 and 2001, most men were trained as fighters, too, training in the use of Kalashnikov rifles. Only a small fraction was selected to continue with the special training in terrorism. Hence, terrorists in Al Qaeda camps represented just a small subset of all fighters that arrived.[12]

The training that mujahideen received in about a dozen training camps in Afghanistan after 1996 was, according to U.S. military officials, "on par with the world's best guerrilla forces,"[13] and at times emulated some of the training methods of the U.S. Army, Army Rangers, and the Marine Corps. The veterans of these training camps would also train other fighters, thus creating future generations of mujahideen. One notebook that was found in an Al Qaeda camp ended with an Arabic passage: "We ask you, dear brother, to spread around this document on all the mujahideen. Do not keep what you know a secret, if you please."[14] To that end, Al Qaeda produced several training manuals, including, most importantly, the 7,000-page, multivolume *Encyclopedia of the Afghan Jihad*, which covered issues such as weapons production, operational planning and security, first aid, handguns, topography, and land surveys.

In addition to the basic infantry training, the recruits received heavy doses of Islamic indoctrination, which Al Qaeda considered at least as important as physical training.[15] Particular emphasis was placed on instilling such values as "perseverance, patience, steadfastness, and adherence to firm principles," as Zawahiri indicated.[16] Camp guidelines found at safe houses in Afghanistan, for instance, listed several rules, such as the command to follow Islamic principles and pray five times a day.[17]

Those students who had special abilities or particular language skills were identified in basic camps and often sent to advanced courses that prepared them for more difficult missions, including terrorist missions.[18] One advanced class that taught bomb making was prefaced by the trainer with the words:

> God Almighty has ordered us to terrorize his enemies. In compliance with God's order and his Prophet's order, in an attempt to get out of the humiliation in which we have found ourselves, we shall propose to those who are keen on justice, fighting against those who oppose them and those who diminish them until they receive fresh orders from God. To those alone, we present: "Rudimentary Methods in the Manufacturing of Explosive Materials Effective for Demolition Purposes."[19]

Those who trained in Al Qaeda's training camps in the period between 1996 and 2001 differed from the Afghan Arabs who had fought the Soviets in several respects. Many of the Afghan Arabs were middle-class professionals from Egypt and Saudi Arabia, including doctors, teachers, and accountants, who often traveled to Afghanistan along with their families. They even included some Shias. The new, second generation of jihadists was composed entirely of Sunnis. They were younger, had a less homogeneous background, and included many volunteers from Europe and Algeria. They hoped to acquire the skills necessary to participate in combat in places like Bosnia and Chechnya.[20]

From its founding, Al Qaeda was designed as a secret organization almost virtual in character. Those who joined Al Qaeda received aliases, and were introduced to other fighters solely by these aliases, thus maintaining strict compartmentalization.[21] Until October 2001, when Al Qaeda's organizational infrastructure was substantially eroded by the American-led response to the 9/11 attacks, Al Qaeda's leadership appears to have been structured, in relative terms, like a hierarchy, and its day-to-day operations were subject to the constraints and necessities reminiscent of other bureaucratic organizations. Fighters, for example, had to sign an employment contract with Al Qaeda.[22] There was a strict separation between the leadership and the rank and file. Most members swore *bayah*, a fealty, to bin Laden, although others did not.[23] Al Qaeda's structure featured the emir-general, Osama bin Laden, at the top. Immediately following him was the *shura majlis*, or consultative council, which consisted of very experienced members. Four operational committees, which were directly below the *shura majlis* and reported to it, handled Al Qaeda's daily operations. They were the military committee, which was responsible for training, procuring, recruitment, transportation, military operations, tactics, and special operations; the finance and business committee; the fatwa and Islamic study committee; and the media and publicity committee.[24]

Many of Al Qaeda's senior positions were filled by Egyptians, a trend that existed years before the formal merger of the EIJ with Al Qaeda in June 2001. Egyptians were also in charge of many of the key departments within the network, including recruitment, training, and communications.[25]

Strategy and Goals of Al Qaeda

Al Qaeda is an Islamic revivalist program that aims to restore Islam's strength, as it manifested itself in the early centuries of its existence—centuries marked by a dramatic and incredibly rapid physical expansion of the *dar al-Islam*, the territory ruled by Muslims. Its ultimate goal is the establishment of the caliphate, the traditional, supranational Islamic form of government. Precedents of this form of government are found in the Umayyad and Abbasid empires in the early centuries of Islam, as well as, more recently, in the Ottoman Empire, whose formal existence spanned over 600 years, from 1299 to 1923. The style of the caliphate envisioned by Al Qaeda, however, would resemble more that of the Taliban than that of the historical empires, because it would be guided by the doctrinaire, puritanical, and relentlessly stringent form of practice of Islam currently advocated by Al Qaeda and like-minded groups.

Al Qaeda's strategy to achieve its aim is jihad, which is understood by this group as a violent, holy struggle that is at once sanctioned by God, fought for his sake, and pleasing to him. Al Qaeda aspires to achieve three partial goals on the

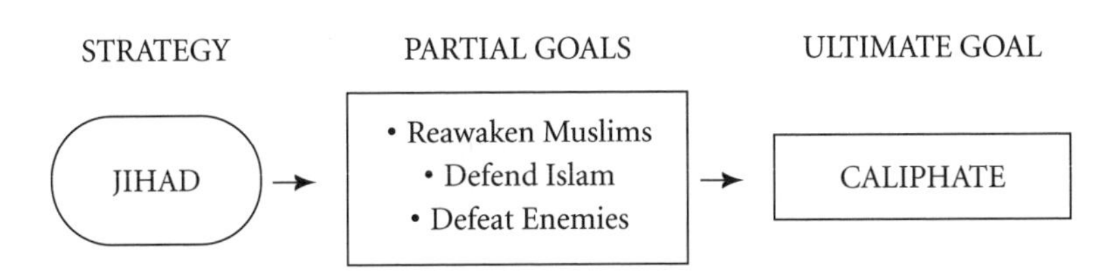

Fig. 2.1. Al Qaeda's Strategy and Goals

way to the desired caliphate: the reawakening of Muslims, the defense of Islam, and the defeat of the enemy (figure 2.1).

The Strategy of Jihad

From the very onset of Al Qaeda, jihad has been at the nexus of the group's strategy to bring about its vision of redemption for Muslims by ending the perceived attack on Islam by the West. It was Abdullah Azzam who elevated the role of jihad at the early phase of Al Qaeda. He saw it as a way of overcoming the strong sense of nationalism that had influenced local movements in Palestine and elsewhere. He believed that the entire *umma* of believers would identify with the jihad in Afghanistan, which in his eyes was clearly legitimate, because the Soviet invasion had been a clear case of an attack against Islam.

A look at Al Qaeda's bylaws leaves no doubt about the central role that jihad plays in ushering in the caliphate.[26] Al Qaeda defines itself as a "religious group of the nation of Mohammad [who] . . . are adopting Jihad as a method for change so that the 'Word of God' becomes supreme, and . . . are working to provoke Jihad, prepare for it, and exercise it by whatever means possible."[27] Osama bin Laden has since repeated the duty of jihad in nearly every statement of his. In the 1998 "Fatwa against Jews and Crusaders" issued by the World Islamic Front, bin Laden made it clear that Al Qaeda's understanding of jihad entailed the use of violence. Bin Laden quoted verses from the Quran that purportedly call upon believers: "But when the forbidden months are past, then fight and slay the pagans wherever ye find them, seize them, beleaguer them, and lie in wait for them in every stratagem (of war)."[28]

Like other Salafi-Jihadist groups, Al Qaeda elevated jihad to a key tenet of Islam, on par with the five established pillars of Islam. As bin Laden said in an interview in 2001, "jihad is the sixth undeclared element of Islam. Every anti-Islamic element is afraid of it. Al Qaeda wants to keep this element alive and active and make it part of the daily lives of Muslims. It wants to give it the status of worship."[29]

To Al Qaeda, the waging of this jihad is an individual duty from which no Muslim is exempted, because America's actions present a casus belli for Muslims. In the words of the 1998 fatwa, "all these crimes and sins committed by the Americans are a clear declaration of war on Allah, his messenger, and Muslims. And *ulema* have throughout Islamic history unanimously agreed that the jihad is an individual duty if the enemy destroys the Muslim countries. . . . Nothing is more sacred than belief except repulsing an enemy who is attacking religion and life."[30]

Jihad is also the unifying concept under which Al Qaeda hopes to unite all true Muslims to wage the global struggle against the so-called Crusader-Zionist alliance. According to bin Laden, the battle is not merely "between al-Qaeda and the U.S. This is a battle of Muslims against the global Crusaders."[31] In his book, Zawahiri describes the properties of the fundamentalist coalition of jihadist movements needed in order to repel the Western-led attack as a coalition that is

> rallying under the banner of jihad for the sake of God and operating outside the scope of the new world order. It is free of the servitude for the dominating western empire. It promises destruction and ruin for the new Crusades against the lands of Islam. It is ready for revenge against the heads of the world's gathering of infidels, the United States, Russia, and Israel. It is anxious to seek retribution for the blood of the martyrs, the grief of the mothers, the deprivation of the orphans, the suffering of the detainees, and the sores of the tortured people throughout the land of Islam, from Eastern Turkestan to Andalusia.[32]

The Reawakening of Muslims: The Creation of the Global Umma

A first step on the way to the creation of the caliphate, and in itself a fundamental goal of Al Qaeda, is for the group to reawaken and reinvigorate Muslims from their perceived slumber, to inject them with confidence, and instill in them the spirit of jihad. Osama bin Laden laid out Al Qaeda's role as a vanguard to that end in the "Declaration of War against the Americans Occupying the Land of the Two Holy Places." In this declaration, which was published in August 1996 in the London-based newspaper *Al-Quds al-Arabi*, bin Laden states, "[u]tmost effort should be made to prepare and instigate the Ummah against the enemy, the American-Israeli alliance occupying the country of the two Holy Places and the route of the Apostle (Allah's Blessings and Salutations may be on him) to the Furthest Mosque (Al-Aqsa Mosque). Also to remind the Muslims not to be engaged in an internal war among themselves, as that will have [grave] consequences."[33]

Mobilizing the Muslim masses is important because the war against the West is portrayed as one of cosmic proportions—a protracted and monumental battle of good versus evil. As Zawahiri puts it, "an important point that must be underlined is that this battle, which we must wage to defend our creed, Muslim nation, sanctities, honor, values, wealth, and power, is a battle facing every Muslim, young or old."[34]

According to Saif al-Adel, Al Qaeda's Egyptian operations commander who is presumed to be under Iranian house arrest, one of the goals in forming Al Qaeda was to establish the vanguard of a rebirth of the Islamic nation, "to lead humankind and save it from the darkness of injustice and aggression of the wicked [Zionist-Anglo-Saxon-Protestant] coalition." He added that Al Qaeda's objective is "the emergence of a sincere and virtuous leadership that rallies the nation's capabilities and motivates the weak and deceived in this world against this octopus that is represented by this wicked coalition."[35]

Al Qaeda's bylaws confirm Adel's description, and spell out Al Qaeda's role in this global Islamic awakening:[36]

1. Spread the feeling of Jihad throughout the Muslim nation.
2. Prepare and qualify the needed personnel for the Muslim world by training and practical fighting participation.
3. Support, aid, and help the Jihad movements around the world as possible.
4. Coordinate among the Jihad movements around the Islamic world in order to create a united global Jihad movement.

Reawakening Muslims from their hibernation is also a requirement for the goal of creating unity among Muslims, the precondition for the establishment of a true global community of believers. The unity of Muslims is based on the belief held among all Salafi-Jihadists that nation-state borders are irrelevant, because Muslims are but one extended family. According to bin Laden, for example, "geographical boundaries have no importance. . . . It is incumbent on all Muslims to ignore these borders and boundaries, which the kuffar [i.e., the infidels] have laid down between Muslim lands, the Jews and the Christians, for the sole purpose of dividing us."[37] In other words, as a high-level Al Qaeda operative, Mahfuz ibn al-Walid (better known as Abu Hafs al-Muritani) put it, "the land of Islam is one single abode."[38]

The reawakening of Muslims requires that Al Qaeda pay particular attention to Muslim popular support. It is hence not surprising that in his book Zawahiri writes at length about the jihadist movement's need to "come closer to the masses." Zawahiri suggests that the movement establish an entire wing dedicated to "work with the masses, preach, provide services for the Muslim people, and share their concerns through all available avenues for charity and educational work." Zawahiri could not be clearer about Al Qaeda's dependence on popular support when he writes:

> We must win the people's confidence, respect, and affection. The people will not love us unless they felt that we love them, care about them, and are ready to defend them. In short, in waging the battle the jihad movement must be in the middle, or ahead, of the nation. It must be extremely careful not to get isolated from its nation or engage the government in the battle of the elite against the authority. . . . The jihad movement must be eager to make room for the Muslim nation to participate with it in the jihad for the sake of empowerment (*al-tamkin*). The Muslim nation will not participate with it unless the slogans of the mujahidin are understood by the masses of the Muslim nation.[39]

Defending Islam against Attack

A second partial goal on the way toward the redemption of Muslims is the need to defend Islam against the perceived attack by an Islamophobic conspiracy led by an alliance between Crusaders, Zionists, and apostate regimes in Arab and Muslim countries. Indeed, Al Qaeda's entire narrative is built on the assertion that the group is merely acting in self-defense. Thus, in an interview with John Miller, bin Laden said, "And my word to American journalists is not to ask why we did that [attack U.S. targets] but ask what their government has done that forced us to defend ourselves."[40]

Defending Islam is, first and foremost, presented as a religious duty for all Muslims. For Al Qaeda, however, the call on Muslims to rise up and defend their religion is, no less importantly, an integral part of its project to reawaken Muslims from their hibernation and take their destinies into their own hands.

Al Qaeda presents a long list of Western infractions against Islam. It claims that these infractions have caused the killing and suffering of millions of Muslims, including the deaths of innocent children and the dishonoring of women. These infractions revolve first and foremost around the occupation of Muslim lands by the United States and Israel, and previously by other Western countries such as France and Britain. Bin Laden said, for example, that the September 11 attacks occurred after he had witnessed "the iniquity and tyranny of the American-Israeli coalition against our people in Palestine and Lebanon," which gave birth to his "resolve to punish the aggressors" and give America "a taste of what we have tasted and to deter it from killing our children and women. . . . Should a man be blamed for protecting his own? And is defending oneself and punishing the wicked an eye for an eye—is that reprehensible terrorism?"[41]

The notion of occupation is extended to the "apostate" regimes such as Jordan and Saudi Arabia, which bin Laden accuses of collaboration with the West and hence of treason to Islam—an infringement that is punishable by death. Even the United Nations is deemed to be "part of the Crusader kingdom, over which reigns the Caesar in Washington, who pays the salaries of Kofi Annan and his ilk," as Zawahiri declared in December 2005 in an interview published by Al Qaeda's media production arm, As-Sahab.[42] No less important, bin Laden accuses the West and its collaborators in the Middle East of having utterly humiliated the Muslim nation at large and robbed it of its honor. Al Qaeda therefore demands that West treat Muslims with respect, as Ayman al-Zawahiri noted in a statement in January 2006: "The reality you refuse to admit is that the Islamic nation will not allow you to treat it as you treat slaves and animals. Unless you deal with the Islamic nation on the basis of understanding and respect, you will continue to face one disaster after another. Your disasters will not end unless you leave our homelands, stop stealing our wealth, and stop corrupting leaders in our countries."[43]

Al Qaeda leaders also charge the United States with depriving the Middle East of its riches. In his book, Zawahiri accuses the United States of invading Afghanistan because of the large quantities of petroleum lying under the Caspian Sea. Similarly, Zawahiri finds unforgivable America's "sin" of support of Israel, which he describes as "in fact a huge US military base."[44]

Foreign occupation, however, is not the only way in which the West is allegedly attacking Islam. For Al Qaeda, and even for many less violence-prone Islamists, Western countries are involved in a conspiracy to incite non-Muslims against the followers of Muhammad. When in September 2005, *Jyllands-Posten*, a Danish newspaper, published a number of distasteful cartoons, some of which depicted the Prophet Muhammad in ways offensive to Muslims, bin Laden linked this incident with other perceived Western aggressions, saying that "the crime [of the caricatures] should be placed within the framework of the general aggressive trend [of America and the West] against our nation [*umma*] for the past several years and decades."[45]

Underlying Zawahiri's and bin Laden's opposition to U.S. and Western involvement in Islamic countries is a firm belief that the United States is bent on preventing Islam from playing a dominant role throughout the Middle East and beyond. Zawahiri believes that U.S. policies, its aid of Israel, and its opportunistic and devilish alliance with local Arab regimes are all designed to stem the rise of Islam, and thus constitute an attack on Islam's destiny, the faith chosen by God as the ultimate truth. In the words of Zawahiri,

> The United States, and the global Jewish government that is behind it, have realized that (government by) Islam is the popular demand of the nations of this region, which is considered the heart of the Islamic world. They have realized that it is impossible to compromise on these issues. Hence the United States has decided to dictate its wishes by force, repression, forgery, and misinformation. Finally it has added direct military intervention to all the foregoing methods.[46]

Zawahiri believes that the United States has taken its drive to stem the spread of Islam to the entire globe, and U.S. presence on any Islamic territory is framed as part of the American grand plan to defeat Islam. The United States is accused of "leading the battle" against Muslims "in Chechnya, the Caucasus, and also in Somalia where 13,000 Somali nationals were killed in the course of what the United States alleged was its campaign to distribute foodstuffs in Somalia." Zawahiri adds that "in the name of food aid, the United States perpetrated hideous acts against the Somalis, acts that came to light only later. Detainees were tortured and their honor violated at the hands of the international coalition forces that allegedly came to rescue Somalia."[47]

The Defeat of the Enemy

A third partial goal on the way to the caliphate is closely related to the perceived attack against Islam, and indeed a direct response to it—namely, the need to attack the aggressors and defeat them. Violence against the aggressors is necessary because the history of humiliations upon humiliations of Muslims have "proved" that the United States and its allies do not understand any other language than the language of force. As Zawahiri puts it,

> We must acknowledge that the West, led by the United States, which is under the influence of the Jews, does not know the language of ethics, morality, and legitimate rights. They only know the language of interests backed by brute military force. Therefore, if we wish to have a dialogue with them and make them aware of our rights, we must talk to them in the language that they understand.[48]

The aggressors consist of a powerful composition of Christians and Jews—the "Crusader-Zionist alliance"—which is supported by an array of Arab regimes in the Middle East, whose support and subservience to this alliance have rendered them "apostates," that is, non-Muslims for all purposes. The aggressions committed by this unholy alliance must be avenged, and the enemies defeated in order for Islam to reign supreme.

This aggressive stance is partly dictated by Al Qaeda's intrinsic urge to avenge Muslim suffering. In a statement in early 2006 Zawahiri, Al Qaeda's deputy, elevates the need for vengeance almost to the status of worship: "Allah has made Qisas [retribution] an observed law. So it is our right to attack whoever attacks us, and destroy the towns and villages of those who destroy ours, and destroy the economy of those who plunder our wealth, and kill the civilians of the country that kills our civilians."[49]

At the top of Al Qaeda's list of enemies is the United States, the "head of the snake," in the words of Saif al-Adel.[50] Al Qaeda's leaders portray America as inhuman and evil and find proof for this in countless U.S. policies, from the firebombing of Tokyo and the nuclear attack on Hiroshima and Nagasaki, to its sanctions on Libya, Iran, Syria, and Sudan, its occupation of Iraq, and its support of Israel.[51]

Al Qaeda is not interested merely in routing the United States out of Muslim lands but wants to defeat the United States entirely, while humiliating it in the process. One way to humiliate the aggressor is to taunt him, making extensive use of the media. "Who could have believed that the 'Capital of the World' and the giant of the New World Order could be turned in a few moments into a frightened, breathless, helpless dwarf!" wrote Mahfuz ibn al-Walid (aka Abu Hafs al-Muritani), one of the closest aides of bin Laden, with hardly disguised *Schadenfreude*.[52] In a similar vein, and with a healthy dose of sarcasm, another commentator, Yahya Ali al-Ghamdi, wrote in the Al Qaeda periodical *Muaskar al-Battar* that "fear of Islam has now gratifyingly settled upon Westerners, so that the term Muslim is now equated with terrorism, for which [we] Praise God."[53]

Al Qaeda has a precise plan of how it wants to achieve this aim, namely by eroding U.S. military power by spreading its military and intelligence forces thinner and in more costly manners.[54] Bin Laden's contempt for the United States finds an expression in his desire to hit the United States where it hurts. He hopes to punish the Americans economically and frequently boasts about his achievements. In his late October 2004 speech, for instance, he bragged that "each of Al-Qaida's dollars defeated one million American dollars, thanks to Allah's grace."[55] Ayman al-Zawahiri's call, in late December 2005, to attack Gulf oil facilities was similarly designed to punish Western economic interests, while also hurting the despised apostate regimes in the Persian Gulf.[56]

Al Qaeda also envisions a defeat—and, indeed, the wholesale annihilation of—

Israel. As Saif al-Adel made it crystal clear in his exchange with Jordanian journalist Fuad Husayn, "the liberation of the [Islamic] nation is contingent on dealing a strike to the Israelis and annihilating their state. There will be no change or liberation unless Israel is undermined and eliminated."[57]

According to Al Qaeda's narrative, Islam has also been betrayed internally by Muslim leaders, criminal despots who betrayed God and his prophet. Those who cooperate with the United States are labeled traitors and hypocrites, because they sell out their Muslim subjects due to a combination of weakness, greed, and godlessness. These apostates have betrayed the entire Muslim *umma* by gradually relinquishing their sovereignty to the West, thus having brought shame and humiliation upon Muslims.[58]

Few countries are more loathed by bin Laden than Saudi Arabia, which famously rejected bin Laden's offer of sending his mujahideen to Saudi Arabia in the early 1990s to repel Saddam Hussein from Kuwait. Saudi Arabia's decision to invite American forces to protect the lands that housed Islam's holiest shrines added insult to bin Laden's injury. Statements made by bin Laden in an audiotape released on December 16, 2004, serve as a good example of bin Laden's contempt as well as of *takfir*, the process in which an individual or a state is labeled an infidel:

> The acts of disobedience [against Allah] committed by the [Saudi] regime are very grave. They are worse than merely grave offenses and mortal sins; they are so serious that those who commit such things are no longer Muslims. . . . The government of Riyadh joined a world alliance with the Crusader heresy under the leadership of Bush against Islam and its people, as has happened in Afghanistan, and likewise the conspiracies in Iraq, which have begun and not yet ended.[59]

According to Zawahiri, the West has also aligned itself with Russia in the fight against Islam, and this Crusader-Zionist conspiracy has adopted a number of tools to fight Islam. He enumerates these tools in a list that sheds light on the extent to which Al Qaeda's worldview is influenced by conspiracy theories, according to which literally every international institution is part of the Western scheme to subjugate Islam. According to Zawahiri, the list includes, apart from the previously mentioned Middle Eastern apostate regimes, the United Nations,[60] multinational corporations, the "international communications and data exchange systems," the "international news agencies and satellite media channels," and the "international relief agencies, which are being used as a cover for espionage, proselytizing, coup planning, and the transfer of weapons."[61]

The Caliphate

Al Qaeda's goal of reestablishing a caliphate is a recurrent theme among many of its leaders and ideological supporters. Bin Laden has called on Muslims to find a leader who would unite them to create a "pious caliphate" to be governed by Islamic law and adhere to Islamic principles of financial and social conduct.[62] In a speech by bin Laden from July 2003 that was posted on a number of Islamic Internet forums, bin Laden decried the abolition of the last caliphate by Turkey in 1924 as a historic crime and claimed the reinstatement of the caliphate as one of Al Qaeda's central goals:

> Since the fall of the Islamic Caliphate state, regimes that do not rule according to the Koran have arisen. If truth be told, these regimes are fighting against the law of Allah. Despite the proliferation of universities, schools, books, preachers, imams, mosques, and [people who recite the] Koran, Islam is in retreat, unfortunately, because the people are not walking in the path of Muhammad. . . . I say that I am convinced that thanks to Allah, this nation has sufficient forces to establish the Islamic state and the Islamic Caliphate, but we must tell these forces that this is their obligation.[63]

In his book, Ayman al-Zawahiri concedes that the establishment of the caliphate may be farfetched, but it nevertheless is the ultimate aspiration of the group:

> The mujahid Islamic movement will not triumph against the world coalition unless it possesses a fundamentalist base in the heart of the Islamic world. All the means and plans that we have reviewed for mobilizing the nation will remain up in the air without a tangible gain or benefit unless they lead to the establishment of the state of caliphate in the heart of the Islamic world. . . . The establishment of a Muslim state in the heart of the Islamic world is not an easy goal or an objective that is close at hand. But it constitutes the hope of the Muslim nation to reinstate its fallen caliphate and regain its glory.[64]

In the context of Al Qaeda's goal of creating a caliphate, Iraq has played a growing role since 2003. While Afghanistan under the Taliban rule continues to serve as the best model for what type of regime Al Qaeda envisions, Iraq has presented Al Qaeda with an opportunity to establish such an Islamic state that will serve as the core for a future caliphate in "the heart of the Muslim world"—and in an Arab country no less. Moreover, Iraq's importance is amplified by the fact that it had once served as a seat of the Abbasid Caliphate, as bin Laden has emphasized.[65]

Al Qaeda and the Centrality of Suicide Attacks

In Al Qaeda's arsenal of tactics, suicide attacks play a pivotal role. No other tactic symbolizes Al Qaeda's tenaciousness and ability to inspire a large number of Muslims worldwide as much as "martyrdom operations," to use the group's euphemistic labeling. Al Qaeda has all but perfected the tactic it uses in order to generate—by its own admission—as much fear, terror, and confusion among the enemy as possible. Al Qaeda has institutionalized SMs to an extent not seen in other groups by instilling the spirit of self-sacrifice in the collective psyche of virtually all of its fighters, thus creating a cult of martyrdom that far exceeds the Palestinian and Lebanese cult of death in both scope and depth. The deadly result is a terrorist and insurgent tactic that the group has managed to successfully employ by air, land, and sea.

Abdullah Azzam, Al Qaeda's cofounder, was the first theoretician who succeeded in turning martyrdom and self-sacrifice into a formative ethos of Al Qaeda. It is largely thanks to him that self-sacrifice has become a moral code for Al Qaeda with which it justifies SMs against its enemies.[66] More than any other single jihadist, Azzam persuaded volunteers for jihad in Afghanistan that those who die for the sake of God (*fi sabil Allah*) will be rewarded in paradise. Azzam, however, understood martyrdom not merely, or even primarily, as suicide operations, but instead as any death occurring while "true" Muslims wage jihad. Such martyrdom would wash away the jihadist's sin and bestow him with glory.

A tireless traveler, Azzam instigated Muslims to seek jihad and martyrdom in many mosques and Islamic centers around the world, including the United States. His lectures and tracts were also distributed in books, videos, and audiotapes to Arabic-language bookstores and mosques around the globe. Many of his most popular books included lists of martyrdom-related eyewitness accounts, purportedly experienced by mujahideen during the jihad against the Soviets. Azzam spun stories of miracles that Arab fighters experienced in battle. He was particularly fond of telling stories of fighters who were rolled over by tanks but miraculously survived, or of mujahideen who were pierced with bullets but yet managed to remain unharmed.[67] He told stories of bodies of martyrs who still smelled fresh although the fighters had perished more than a year ago. The mujahideen, Azzam said, were aided by angels on horseback, while bombs dropped by the Red Army were intercepted by birds.[68]

Azzam's book *Lovers of the Paradise Maidens*, for example, contained the stories of more than 150 mujahideen who died fighting in the name of God.[69] A compilation of works by Azzam available on the Internet, *Virtues of Martyrdom in the Path of Allah*, outlines twenty-seven characteristics of the martyr. Point No. 6 outlined the benefits of the *shahid*, or martyr:

> Special Favours for the Shaheed: The Shaheed is granted seven special favours from Allah. He is forgiven (his sins) at the first drop of his blood. He sees his place in Paradise. He is dressed in the clothes of Iman. He is married to the Hoor al-'Ain (beautiful women of Paradise). He is saved from the punishment of the grave. He will be protected from the great fear of the Day of Judgement. A crown of honour will be placed on his head, one jewel of which is better than the whole world and what it contains. He is married to seventy-two of the Hoor al-'Ain, and he will be able to intercede for seventy members of his family.[70]

The fighters were so deeply affected by Azzam's pageant that the death-obsessed Afghan Arabs became a "curious sideshow to the real fighting in Afghanistan," Lawrence Wright observed. "When a fighter fell, his comrades would congratulate him and weep because they were not also slain in battle. These scenes struck other Muslims as bizarre. The Afghans were fighting for their country, not for Paradise or an idealized Islamic community."[71]

Al Qaeda's adoption of suicide attacks was also influenced heavily by the EIJ and its leader, Zawahiri. Years before Zawahiri and the EIJ formally joined Al Qaeda, the Egyptian organization had employed SMs as a terrorist tactic. In August 1993 a suicide bomber drove an explosives-laden motorcycle toward the car of Egypt's interior minister, Hassan al-Alfi, but he survived the attack. Suicide attacks until 1993 were a tactic that was heretofore associated mostly with Shia organizations, notably Hizballah. Although Hamas had perpetrated a suicide bombing earlier in 1993 at Mehola Junction in the West Bank, SMs by Sunni groups were still relatively rare. Like other suicide bombers in subsequent years, the EIJ also recorded the suicide bomber's will and later distributed the tapes. On November 19, 1995, the EIJ staged another suicide bombing at the Egyptian Embassy in Islamabad, Pakistan, involving two assailants, including one suicide bomber. Sixteen people were killed in this attack, which foreshadowed future SMs by Al Qaeda against embassies using several attackers.

Former jihadists confirmed in interviews with Fawaz Gerges that Zawahiri's advocacy of suicide bombings fundamentally impacted bin Laden's adoption of this tactic. The spectacular nature of Al Qaeda's suicide attacks, they told him, were adopted from the EIJ, which had always used extremely lethal and psychologically damaging attacks to differentiate itself from its jihadist rival in Egypt, the Gamaa al-Islamiyya.[72]

When he was subsequently pressed to explain the use of suicide bombers—a tactic that was still taboo, especially when used against fellow Muslims—Zawahiri explained that these martyrs represented a "generation of mujahideen that has decided to sacrifice itself and its property in the cause of God. That is because the way of death and martyrdom is a weapon that tyrants and their helpers, who worship their salaries instead of God, do not have."[73] Zawahiri made a claim that many other supporters of suicide attacks would repeat: the suicide attacker does not kill himself for personal reasons but sacrifices himself for God. He is therefore not committing suicide but martyrdom. It was a game of words, but it provided enough justification for hundreds of future suicide bombers to emulate these early *shuhada*.

In August 1996 bin Laden formally declared war against the United States.[74] The declaration features a lengthy call upon Muslim youth to sacrifice themselves, praising their courage and "love of death." Intending to provide religious justifications for martyrdom operations, bin Laden ties the longing for martyrdom to a number of verses from the Quran, *hadith* (sayings attributed to Muhammad), and other poems. According to bin Laden:

> Our youths believe in paradise after death. They believe that taking part in fighting will not bring their day nearer, and staying behind will not postpone their day either. Exalted be to Allah who said: "And a soul will not die but with the permission of Allah, the term is fixed" (Aal Imraan: 3:145). . . . Our youths took note of the meaning of the poetic verse: "If death is a predetermined must, then it is a shame to die cowardly," and the other poet saying: "Who do not die by the sword will die by other reason; many causes are there but one death." These youths believe in what has been told by Allah and His messenger—Allah's Blessings and Salutations may be on him—about the greatness of the reward for the Mujahideen and Martyrs; Allah, the most exalted said: ". . . those who are slain in the way of Allah, He will by no means allow their deeds to perish. He will guide them and improve their condition, and cause them to enter the garden [of] paradise, which He has made known to them" (Muhammad: 47:4–6).

Bin Laden then highlights a number of sayings that together describe the rewards of the martyr in Paradise:

> Allah, the Exalted, also said: "And do not speak of those who are slain in Allah's way as dead; nay, they are alive, but you do not perceive" (Bagarah; 2:154). His

> messenger—Allah's Blessings and Salutations may be on him—said: "For those who strive in His cause Allah prepared hundred degrees in paradise . . ." (Saheeh Al-Jame' As-Sagheer). He . . . also said: "The best of the martyrs are those who do NOT turn their faces away from the battle till they are killed. They are in the high level of Jannah (paradise). Their Lord laughs to them (in pleasure) and when your Lord laughs to a slave of His, He will not hold him to . . . account" (Narrated by Ahmad with correct and trustworthy reference). And: "A martyr will not feel the pain of death except like how you feel when you are pinched" (Saheeh Al-Jame' As-Sagheer). He also said: "A martyr's privileges are guaranteed by Allah; forgiveness with the first gush of his blood, he will be shown his seat in paradise, he will be decorated with the jewels of belief (Imaan), married off to the beautiful ones, protected from the test in the grave, assured security in the day of judgement, crowned with the crown of dignity, a ruby of which is better than this whole world (Duniah) and its entire content, wedded to seventy two of the pure Houries (beautiful ones of Paradise) and his intercession on the behalf of seventy of his relatives will be accepted."

He continues by praising the courage of the youthful martyrs who are willing to sacrifice themselves, suggesting that, through death, young Muslims will prevail in the struggle against the Crusaders:

> Those youths know that their rewards in fighting you, the USA, is double than their rewards in fighting someone else not from the people of the book. They have no intention except to enter paradise by killing you. An infidel, and enemy of God like you, cannot be in the same hell with his righteous executioner. . . . Our youths chant and recite the word of Allah, the most exalted: "Fight them; Allah will punish them by your hands and bring them to disgrace, and assist you against them and heal the heart of a believing people" (At-Taubah: 9:14) and the words of the prophet. . .: "I swear by Him, who has my soul in His hand, that no man get killed fighting them today, patiently attacking and not retreating, surely Allah will let him into paradise." And his (Allah's Blessings and Salutations may be on him) saying to them: "Get up to a paradise as wide as heaven and earth." The youths also recite the Almighty words of: "So when you meet in battle those who disbelieve, then smite the necks . . ." (Muhammad; 47:19). Those youths will not ask you [i.e., U.S. secretary of defense William Perry] for explanations, they will tell you singing there is nothing between us [that] need[s] to be explained, there is only killing and neck smiting. . . . The youths you called cowards are competing among themselves for fighting and killing you. Reciting what one of them said: "The crusader army

became dust when we detonated al-Khobar. With courageous youth of Islam fearing no danger. If (they are) threatened: The tyrants will kill you, they reply my death is a victory."

Al Qaeda's emphasis on SMs was naturally reflected in its Afghan training camps. A document found in an Al Qaeda safe house in Afghanistan titled "Goals and Objectives of Jihad," for example, ranked the goal of "attaining martyrdom in the cause of God" second only to "establishing the rule of God on earth." Another document listed two "illegitimate" excuses for leaving jihad as "love of the world" and "hatred of death."[75]

Khalid Sheikh Muhammad (KSM), the operational planner of the 9/11 attacks, told his interrogators that the most important quality for any Al Qaeda operative was a willingness to sacrifice himself. He stated that operatives used for an SM were not, for the most part, placed under any pressure to volunteer for such an operation. Instead, when a recruit arrived at the training camp in Afghanistan, he would fill out an application with standard questions. Every mujahideen who arrived was asked if he would be prepared to serve as a suicide operative. Those who answered in the affirmative were subsequently interviewed by operations chief Muhammad Atef.[76]

As was confirmed by another Al Qaeda operative, the willingness to participate in a martyrdom operation was the preeminent criterion in selecting the members of the 9/11 attacks—in addition to "demonstrable patience," due to the long time lag that could occur between the planning and execution of the attack.[77]

Given the importance of this tactic, Al Qaeda designed special programs by which it trained volunteers for martyrdom operations, most of whom, according to KSM, were Saudis and Yemenis.[78] For major operations, such as the 9/11 attacks, bin Laden would pick the recruits himself. KSM told his investigators that bin Laden selected recruits for the "planes operation," as the 9/11 plots were known internally, in as little as ten minutes. When the trainee was chosen, bin Laden would ask him to swear loyalty for a suicide operation. After the selection and oath swearing, the operative would be sent to KSM, who would train him and arrange for the shooting of a martyrdom video—a function supervised by KSM as the head of Al Qaeda's media committee.[79]

A key aspect of the training and subsequent execution of the SM was the empowerment of the martyrs, which would occur, inter alia, by forming teams of suicide attackers. As Schweitzer and Ferber point out, the linking up of suicide attackers in pairs reinforced the dynamic of mutual support and identification through "twinship," a process that helps reduce the sense of isolation embedded in the idea of suicide and the need to keep the attack secret.[80] From an operational point of view, the use of pairs of suicide bombers also increased the chance of success of these operations. In the case of a malfunction of the explosive device or the interception of one of the bombers, another bomber would be able to continue the plot. Empowerment also occurs because the individual cells are autonomous. There is a delegation of power that occurs, which enhances a sense of self-worth and confidence among the group. This, Schweitzer and Ferber add, "transforms the act of suicide into a psycho-spiritual act to be carried out in the name of the supreme goal, independent of the organization under whose auspices the members are working."[81]

In word, if not necessarily in deed, the devotion to martyrdom extends to Al Qaeda's leaders, as is evident from statements of its leadership, including bin Laden. In August 1998 the Al Qaeda head declared, "I am fighting so I can die a martyr and go to heaven to meet God. Our fight is now against America. I regret having lived this long. I have nothing to lose." He reiterated this statement in December 1998, saying, "I am not afraid of death. Rather, martyrdom is my passion because martyrdom would lead to the birth of 1,000s of Osamas."[82] In October 2003, months after the U.S. invasion of Iraq, he delivered a similar message to the Iraqi people on Al-Jazeera, saying "I wish I could raid and be slain, and then raid and be slain, and then raid and be slain."[83]

Bin Laden helped spread this veneration of martyrdom into the minds of Al Qaeda's trainees as well as the potential global recruits by releasing videotape and statements on the Internet, thus reaching a much broader audience. In 2004, for instance, bin Laden urged his followers to "become diligent in carrying out martyrdom operations; these operations, praise be to God, have become a great source of terror for the enemy. . . . These are the most important operations."[84]

Bin Laden's deputy Zawahiri, too, regularly elevates martyrdom as the most honorable act for Muslims. A videotape in which Zawahiri applauded the martyrdom of London bombers Shehzad Tanweer and Mohammed Siddique Khan demonstrated how the tribute of the bombers served in no small measure to inspire other potential jihadis:

> In order to remove this injustice, Shehzad began training with all his might and devotion. Together with the martyr Siddiq [*sic*] Khan, he received practical and intensive training in how to produce and use explosives, in the camps of Qaeda Al-Jihad. The recruits who join these camps do not have to achieve high averages or to pass entrance exams. All they need is to be zealous for their religion and nation, and to love Jihad and martyrdom for the sake of Allah."[85]

Like other groups that have engaged in SMs as part of their repertoire, Al Qaeda is well aware of its tactical benefits. Thus, in the fall of 1993, an Al Qaeda delegation reportedly went to the Bekaa Valley in Lebanon where it allegedly received training by Hizballah in explosives, intelligence, and security. Bin Laden, according to the report, was particularly interested in learning how to use truck bombs of the kind that had been used in the SM by Hizballah against the U.S. Marine Barracks in Beirut in 1983.[86]

During Al Qaeda's years in the Sudan, the group's then chief of operations, Muhammad Atef (aka Abu Hafs al-Masri), reportedly conducted a study concluding that traditional terrorist hijacking operations did not suit the needs of Al Qaeda. Al Qaeda leaders believed that hijackings did not inflict mass casualties but merely helped negotiate the release of prisoners. As a result, the study considered the feasibility of hijacking planes and blowing them up in flight—a concept that had been tried in the so-called Bojinka plot.[87]

The use of SMs is a logical outcome of Al Qaeda's desire of maximizing pain and suffering among its enemies in a struggle that it regards as protracted. In his 2001 book *Knights under the Prophet's Banner*, Zawahiri writes that "if our goal is comprehensive change and if our path, as the Koran and our history have shown us, is a long road of jihad and sacrifices, we must not despair of repeated strikes and recurring calamities."[88] There is a particular need on the part of the jihadist movement to offset the power of the Muslims' enemies, Zawahiri adds, whose numbers and capabilities have risen tremendously, as did "the quality of their weapons, their destructive powers, their disregard for all taboos, and disrespect for the customs of wars and conflict."[89] To match this asymmetry, Zawahiri suggests the following steps:

1. The need to inflict the maximum casualties against the opponent, for this is the language understood by the west, no matter how much time and effort such operations take.
2. The need to concentrate on the method of martyrdom operations as the most successful way of inflicting damage against the opponent and the least costly to the mujahidin in terms of casualties.
3. The targets as well as the type and method of weapons used must be chosen to have an impact on the structure of the enemy and deter it enough to stop its brutality, arrogance, and disregard for all taboos and customs. It must restore the struggle to its real size.
4. To reemphasize what we have already explained, we reiterate that focusing on the domestic enemy alone will not be feasible at this stage.[90]

He thus portrayed martyrdom operations as the weapon of the weak in an asymmetric battle against a materially superior enemy. In this battle, the mujahideen, who do not possess the weaponry and technological sophistication of the West, nevertheless defeat the West with their willpower, selflessness, and ingenuity, illustrated in their ability to beat the West at its own game by turning the West's technologies against itself. As Mahfuz ibn al-Walid put it when describing the September 11 hijackers, "the attackers did not come armed with any weapon from outside, nor did they manufacture any weapon on the inside; they came . . . armed only with their resolve and their spirit of sacrifice, and with that they managed to turn pacific, recreational, peaceful American technology into the strongest tool of military destruction with all the annihilation and the demolition they wrought."[91]

It is no wonder then, Walid adds, that the West is stumbling in confusion in the face of this tactic against which there is virtually no remedy:

> When a man can put himself at the top of the list of victims of an operation he is about to carry out, when he dissolves himself and his soul and his "ego" in the target he is aiming for, he paralyses the most sophisticated means of the adversary's defense and throws all his calculations and plans for defense and security—even retaliation—into confusion. As more than one leading American figure has said: no one can prevent or stand in the way of one who wishes for death.[92]

SMs thus weaken the morale of the enemy, throwing him off balance. His spirit is further undermined when several SMs are carried out simultaneously, as occurred in the 1998 suicide attacks against the U.S. embassies in Nairobi and Dar-es-Salaam, and the September 11 attacks, among other SMs. At the same time that the enemy is humiliated and his morale lowered, the self-confidence of the mujahideen and, by extension, that of the entire Muslim *umma* is given a boost. The *9/11 Commission Report*, for instance, suggests that bin Laden believed that an attack against the United States would benefit Al Qaeda by attracting more suicide operatives, eliciting greater donations, and increasing the number of sympathizers who are willing to provide logistical assistance.[93]

Hence, a positive side effect of SMs is that the stature of Al Qaeda in the eyes of the *umma* is raised, as members of the Islamic community are eager to join a movement that seems to be at the front lines of a battle between good and evil. SMs magnify, and indeed exaggerate, the power of Al Qaeda, leading many Islamists to want to join the winning side of history in this epic battle.

Suicide Attacks by Al Qaeda

Since August 1998 and until November 2002, Al Qaeda was intimately involved in the planning or execution of at least six successful suicide operations:[94] the August 1998 U.S. Embassy bombings in Kenya and Tanzania; the October 2000 attack on the USS *Cole*; the assassination of Ahmed Shah Massoud on September 9, 2001; the 9/11 attacks; the bombing of a synagogue in Djerba in April 2002; and an attack in Kenya in November 2002.[95] Hundreds of additional SMs supported or inspired by Al Qaeda (discussed in chapters 5 to 7) would subsequently be conducted in a host of countries.

U.S. Embassy Bombings, Kenya and Tanzania, August 7, 1998

The nearly simultaneous bombings of two United States embassies, in Nairobi, Kenya, and Dar-es-Salaam, Tanzania, on August 7, 1998, marked Al Qaeda's wholesale adoption of terrorist attacks, and specifically suicide operations, as its preferred tactic. Before 1998, Al Qaeda was involved in terrorism mainly through training, funding, and the supply of weapons. The embassy attacks in 1998 marked the beginning of Al Qaeda's involvement in the planning, direction, and execution of SMs, as well as its shift to a global strategy in which the "far enemy," especially the United States, would be targeted.

The attack in Nairobi occurred at 10:35 am. The blast completely destroyed the embassy and killed 213 people, mostly Kenyans, while wounding 4,000 others. In the Dar-es-Salaam bombings, which occurred four minutes later, 11 people were killed and 85 people were wounded.

U.S. officials suspected Al Qaeda immediately of implication in the bombings —they had been investigating cells linked to bin Laden for more than a year and received specific warning of possible attacks on the Nairobi embassy.[96] Bin Laden also praised the fighters as those who "risked their lives to earn the pleasure of God" and described them as "real men, the true personification of the word men. They managed to rid the Islamic nation of disgrace. We highly respect them and hold them in the highest esteem."[97]

Concrete evidence of Al Qaeda's involvement was obtained when a former sergeant in the U.S. Army, Ali Mohammed, directly linked Osama bin Laden to the bombings. He said that in 1993, bin Laden asked him to conduct surveillance of American, British, French, and Israeli targets in Nairobi, one of which was the local U.S. Embassy. He told an Egyptian court that he took pictures, drew diagrams, and wrote a report. Bin Laden personally reviewed the plan and personally pointed to a spot where he believed the suicide truck should be placed.

The cells were prepared in advance, with the help of Al Qaeda field commanders, who helped the mostly local cell members with the preparations, including the purchase of explosives, vehicles, and the gathering of field intelligence.[98] The suicide attackers, a Saudi in Kenya and an Egyptian in Tanzania, arrived close to the end of the process, and the field operatives left their respective countries prior to the attacks.[99] In Kenya, the infrastructure built for the attack was retained after the bombing, to be used four years later in the SM against a hotel frequented by Israelis.[100]

The embassy bombings were clearly a milestone for Al Qaeda. Occurring on the eighth anniversary of the arrival of U.S. troops in Saudi Arabia—and perhaps in order to avenge that perceived occupation—the attacks foreshadowed future spectacular SMs by Al Qaeda. The attacks also impressed jihadis to join the ranks of Al Qaeda. According to KSM, for example, these bombings convinced him that bin Laden was truly committed to attacking the United States.[101] Most importantly, however, the attacks were a milestone for Al Qaeda because they were the first attack on the "far enemy."

Attack on the USS Cole*, October 12, 2000*

On October 12, 2000, two Al Qaeda operatives steered a bomb-laden fiberglass boat into an American destroyer, the USS *Cole*, while making friendly gestures to the crew. The blast of the bombing ripped a hole in the side of the ship, which was harbored at the Yemeni port of Aden, killing seventeen crew members and wounding forty. The plot turned out to be a full-fledged Al Qaeda operation supervised directly by bin Laden, who chose the target, location, and the suicide bombers and provided the money.[102]

Al Qaeda's local supervisor of the USS *Cole* attack was Abd al Rahim al-Nashiri, a Saudi national who lived in Yemen. Nashiri was closely linked to Al Qaeda's terrorist network—his cousin, Jihad Ali (known as Azzam), was one of the suicide bombers of the attack on the U.S. Embassy in Nairobi.

Nashiri was reportedly recruited to his career as a terrorist by bin Laden, who urged him to attack the United States. In late 1998, after swearing his oath of allegiance to bin Laden, Nashiri proposed an SM against an American vessel. Bin Laden approved of the plan, sent operatives to Yemen, and later provided money to fund the operation. Nashiri reported directly to bin Laden—apparently the only other person who was aware of the details of the operation.[103]

When Nashiri had difficulty finding U.S. naval vessels along the western coast of Yemen, bin Laden suggested the Port of Aden, located on the southern coast of the peninsula. This resulted in an attempted attack on an American destroyer, the USS *The Sullivans*, on January 3, 2000. The attack failed, however, when the explosives-laden boat sank prior to impact.

On October 12 of the same year, the second attempt to ram a U.S. vessel, the USS *Cole*, succeeded. Following the attack, Nashiri was promoted to Al Qaeda's operations chief in and around the Arabian Peninsula. He was also responsible for the attack on October 6, 2002, on the French tanker *Limburg* in the Gulf of Aden.[104]

As the group and its affiliates would frequently do in the future, Al Qaeda recorded the attack on the USS *Cole* on video in order to reap maximum propaganda effect from the bombing. The videotape was distributed, along with images of Al Qaeda training camps and training methods, in a recruiting video that also highlighted Muslim suffering in Palestine, Kashmir, Indonesia, and Chechnya.

Assassination of Ahmed Shah Massoud, September 9, 2001

On September 9, 2001, two Al Qaeda members carrying Belgian passports approached Ahmed Shah Massoud, the leader of the Northern Alliance, the leading faction fighting the Taliban in the aftermath of the Soviet withdrawal. The pair had already spent nine days at the camp, patiently waiting for Massoud to free up some time. When Massoud was finally available for the interview, one operative detonated an explosives charge he carried either in the camera or on his waist. Ahmed Shah Massoud died of his wounds within a few minutes. One of the attackers and a second Northern Alliance official died in the blast, and two others were wounded.

Bin Laden had likely planned the killing of Massoud as a gift to Taliban leader Mullah Omar because the Tajik fighter represented the key obstacle to the Taliban's complete rule over Afghanistan. Timed only two days before the 9/11 attacks, the assassination was also meant to cripple the Northern Alliance. Al Qaeda must surely have anticipated a fierce U.S. response to the 9/11 attacks, and neutralizing Massoud would deny the Americans the support of the most competent of the Taliban's enemies.

The Attacks of September 11, 2001

The attacks on the American homeland on September 11, 2001, have been the subject of intense examination and analysis, most notably in the *9/11 Commission Report*.[105] The attacks were devised by KSM, who told his interrogators that the 1993 World Trade Center bombing, which was carried out by his nephew, Ramzi Youssef, taught him that the use of bombs and explosives could be problematic. Bent on staging a more sophisticated type of attack, he and Youssef began to think of using aircraft as weapons while they were working on the so-called Bojinka plot—a plan to detonate about a dozen airliners using explosives over the Pacific over a period of two days in January 1995.[106] KSM wanted the attacks of 9/11 to make a significant political and financial impact. While Washington was an obvious target, he was also eager to target the American economy, and hence chose New York, the economic capital of the United States.[107]

In March or April 1999, bin Laden supported KSM's proposal and would subsequently provide the entire funding for the plot, which was henceforth referred to as the "planes operation."[108] Bin Laden initially selected four suicide attackers: Khalid al-Mihdhar, Nawaf al Hazmi, Khallad (Tawfiq bin Attash), and Abu Bara al Yemeni, and more hijackers were later added. The hijackers received special training in the fall of 1999 while attending an elite training course at Al Qaeda's Mes Aynak camp in Afghanistan. Saif al-Adel provided a rigorous advanced commando training course that stressed personal fitness, firearms, close quarters combat, and especially mental training.

After the training in Afghanistan, three of the attackers moved to Pakistan, where KSM taught them basic English words and phrases, how to use the Internet, and how to communicate surreptitiously using code words. The four future hijackers, who, according to testimony by KSM, were aware that they had been sent on a suicide operation, then went to Kuala Lumpur.

Osama bin Laden, Muhammad Atef, and KSM had originally planned to use existing Al Qaeda members for the planes operation. In late 1999, however, four aspiring jihadis arrived from Germany and presented the operational planners of the 9/11 attacks with a more attractive alternative. They had two great advantages that would come in handy—fluency in English and familiarity with the Western life-style.[109]

The 9/11 Commission found no evidence of a link of the four jihadis from Germany—Mohammed Atta, Ramzi Binalshibh, Marwan al-Shehhi, and Ziad

Jarrah—to Al Qaeda before 1999, despite their prior attempts to link up to the jihad in Chechnya.

According to Binalshibh, it was a chance meeting on a train in Germany with a stranger, Khalid al Masri, that led the group to travel to Afghanistan and connect with Al Qaeda. Masri put the group in touch with Mohamedou Ould Slahi, a key Al Qaeda operative in the German city of Duisburg.[110] Slahi would urge the future 9/11 suicide hijackers to go to Pakistan, and then to Afghanistan. They heeded his words, and in late 1999 the quartet met bin Laden and swore allegiance to him. The team was quickly recruited to the planes operation, and initial roles were allotted. Binalshibh was the liaison between KSM and the team in the field. Atta was in charge in the field as the lead hijacker, and Hazmi was made his deputy.[111] As the *9/11 Commission Report* notes, the speed with which the German cell became members of Al Qaeda was remarkable, and indicated bin Laden's apparent unhappiness with the previous team designated for the operation.[112]

The radicalization of the 9/11 suicide hijackers is a testimony to the importance of friendship and kinship ties in the formation of jihadist cells in Western Europe.[113] The 9/11 team, for instance, included two sets of brothers (the Hazmi and Shehri brothers) and three cousins. More important perhaps is the crucial importance of friendship ties, which is extremely salient in the case of the 9/11 attacks and reminiscent of the friendship ties that characterized the radicalization and self-indoctrination of the July 7, 2005, London bombers, as will be seen in chapter 6. Given the importance of self-radicalization in small groups in SMs of Al Qaeda, it is worthwhile to recount the formation of the Hamburg cell in some detail.

The "Hamburg cell," as it became known, was the result of a convergence of nine individuals who came together in a student community of upper-middle-class expatriate Muslims. The nucleus of the group formed around Mohammed Belfas, who had immigrated to Germany after having lived in Indonesia, Yemen, and Egypt. Belfas conducted a study group at Hamburg's Al Quds Mosque in which several cell members participated. Mounir Motassadeq and Abdelghani Mzoudi, two fellow students who would later stand trial for providing support to the Hamburg cell, knew each other from Marrakech, where they had been friends. Motassadeq helped conceal the Hamburg cell's trip to Afghanistan in late 1999. Both Motassadeq and Mzoudi witnessed the execution of Atta's will.

Motassadeq's apartment became a center in the student dormitories where militant Muslim students gathered, ate, and discussed religion and politics. Binalshibh, a student from Yemen, who was sociable, extroverted, polite, and adventuresome, joined next. In the student community, it was well known that Binalshibh believed that jihad is the highest duty for every Muslim and that the highest honor is to die during the jihad.[114]

Binalshibh met Atta at a mosque in Hamburg in 1995, and the two became close friends. Said Bahaji, who was of German Moroccan origin, joined the group as well. Originally secular, Bahaji was quick to adopt Salafi-Jihadist ideology after joining the clique.[115] In late 1997 Ziad Jarrah, who came to Germany a year earlier, joined the clique when he met Binalshibh at Al Quds Mosque. Jarrah, who was Lebanese, did not display radical beliefs when he first moved to Germany. Instead, he had a reputation as a party person and drank beer. Signs of his radicalization were first seen in late 1996.[116]

A year later, Marwan al-Shehhi joined the group. Al-Shehhi was from the United Arab Emirates and would grow very close to Atta. At some point, Binalshibh became Belfas's roommate. Jarrah, meanwhile, met Zakarya Essabar, a Moroccan student who came to Germany in 1997, at a Volkswagen plant. Essabar was a Moroccan citizen who turned extremist very suddenly. Shortly before the 9/11 attacks, he traveled to Afghanistan to inform the Al Qaeda leadership about the exact date of the attacks.

In November 1998 Atta, Binalshibh, and Bahaji moved together into an apartment on Marienstrasse and referred to it as Beit al-Ansar. They strictly observed religious practices, prayed five times a day, and maintained strict Islamic diets. Their conversations revolved around the perceived state of Muslims and general damage done by Jews. They also watched battlefield videos and sang songs about martyrdom.[117]

German security services who monitored the clique heard the group talk a lot about the need to fight a jihad to defeat "world Jewry." Discussions about paradise were becoming more frequent, and the group as a whole became more religious over time. At Bahaji's wedding, for example, the group loudly proclaimed their devotion to God and jihad. Ultimately, by 1999, the cell, which had become cultlike, decided to join the jihad.[118]

The 9/11 attacks would not have been possible were it not for the inclusion of "muscle hijackers," whose job it was to assist the lead hijackers in taking over the plane and preventing mutinies. According to Saudi intelligence who interviewed the muscle hijackers, twelve of whom were Saudis, they came from a variety of educational and societal backgrounds and were between twenty and twenty-eight years old, mostly unemployed with no more than a high school education, and single. Four of them came from a cluster of three towns in the isolated and underdeveloped Al Bahah region and shared the same tribal affiliation. They may have known each other since 1999. Five others came from Asir Province, a poor region of southwestern Saudi Arabia bordering Yemen. Two of the muscle hijackers were brothers.[119]

Several of the muscle hijackers had planned to go to Chechnya but, when denied, returned to Afghanistan, where they came under the indoctrination of bin Laden and volunteered for SMs.[120] In late 2000 and early 2001, the muscle hijackers received training at the Al Matar complex in Afghanistan. The training included hijackings, explosive-handling, disarming air marshals, body building, and basic English. Their trainer even had them butcher a sheep and a camel with a knife for training. The muscle hijackers did not learn the details of the plan until they reached the United States in April 2001.[121]

Apart from the importance of friendship ties in the radicalization of jihadis, including suicide attackers, another important lesson to be drawn from the 9/11 attacks is the key importance of a "hub" such as KSM in the overall planning and execution of attacks. Like other hubs—actors at the center of a network with a large number of ties to other "nodes" within the network—KSM had specific skills that made him indispensable for the success of the attack, as well as that of his career as a professional terrorist. KSM was a Kuwaiti of Baluchi origins who was raised religious. At age sixteen he joined the Muslim Brotherhood, and he participated in the Afghan war against the Soviet Union. No less important for his success as a terrorist was his high education—he has a degree in mechanical engineering—his technical aptness, and his managerial skills.

When KSM went to Afghanistan to join the jihad against the Soviets, he was introduced to the legendary Abdul Rasul Sayyaf, who became his mentor and provided him with military training. After the war in Afghanistan, he also fought in Bosnia in 1992 and then moved to Qatar.

He supported Ramzi Youssef financially when the latter attempted to bring down the World Trade Center in 1993. It was after Youssef gained notoriety for his attempt that KSM decided that he too had to attack the United States.[122] KSM's ego also prevented him from pledging allegiance to Osama bin Laden in 1996. It was at that meeting when KSM first introduced the planes operation plot. KSM would later formally join Al Qaeda, but back in 1996 he had an urge to remain independent.

Suicide Bombing of a Synagogue in Djerba, Tunisia, April 11, 2002

On April 11, 2002, Nizar Nawar, a twenty-four-year-old unemployed Tunisian, drove a truck filled with liquid propane through the security barriers of the Al-Ghriba Synagogue on the Tunisian island of Djerba. The truck detonated in front of the synagogue, killing twenty-one people and injuring thirty more. Fourteen victims were from Germany, six were Tunisians, and one was French. Nawar was instructed by KSM and called him three hours before the attacks.[123] He also received remote instructions from other handlers via the Internet.[124]

Throughout his boyhood and adulthood, Nawar drifted through several places of residence. He was raised by his mother in Ben Gardane, a town in southern Tunisia. His father was a laborer who in 1971 moved to Lyon, France, and visited Tunisia infrequently. An uncle of Nawar said that throughout most of his life Nawar was not religious, drank alcohol, and frequented bars at tourist hotels. Unlike Islamists, he used to wear shorts. In 1999 he went to South Korea, where he worked in a restaurant, according to his family.[125]

Suicide Attack in Kenya, November 28, 2002

On November 28, 2002, a series of attacks shook Kenya. The first attack was an attempted downing of an Israeli Arkia charter airliner during takeoff from the Mombasa airport. Some twenty minutes later, a car filled with tanks of gas and about 500 pounds of explosives drove into the Paradise Hotel, which was frequented by Israeli tourists, where it detonated. Fifteen people—twelve Kenyans and three Israelis—were killed in the blasts and about eighty others were wounded. Al Qaeda took responsibility for the attack, using the name Qaedat al-Jihad, which it had formally adopted after its merger with the EIJ.

According to Schweitzer and Ferber, the attackers relied on an existing network of an Al Qaeda operative by the name of Fazul Harun, which was established before the 1998 Nairobi attacks. The cell members had trained in Afghanistan and communicated with one another through e-mail and cell phones. Most of the operatives were logistical collaborators for the Al Qaeda leadership, which directed the operation and provided the funding.[126]

CHAPTER THREE

Salafi Jihad and the Veneration of Martyrdom

Salafism and Salafi Jihad

Reformist Salafism

The Salafi Jihad is a faction within a larger stream of Islam known as the Salafi movement, which can be described as "a dogmatic relation to the fundamentals of the religion,"[1] or, in other words, "a methodology to understand and realize Islam."[2] It is also heavily influenced by the Qutbist faction of the Muslim Brotherhood movement and the Saudi version of Salafism known as Wahhabism.

The term *salafiyya* was popularized in the late nineteenth and early twentieth centuries in Egypt, where a pan-Islamic reform movement developed around the Islamic scholars Muhammad Abdu (1849–1905) and Rashid Rida (1865–1935). Abdu and Rida were concerned with reforming Islam in the wake of its general decline vis-à-vis the West and, as such, were walking in the footsteps of Jamal ad-Din al-Afghani (1839–97), a political activist who strove to reform Islam and adapt it to the challenge of colonization and westernization. Abdu and Rida's concerns grew out of the same intellectual debate that revolved around the reconciliation of Islamic heritage with modernity. They blamed the weakness of the *ulema*, social injustice, and blind imitation of the past (*taqlid*) for Islam's relative stagnation. Their Salafism also came in response to burgeoning pan-Arab nationalism—a force that competed with Salafism in trying to reconcile Islam with modernity. Islamic intellectuals like Abdu and Rida were opposed to pan-Arab nationalism due to its secular roots, and because many of its main ideological champions were Christians.[3]

Salafis such as Abdu and Rida were more liberal than many contemporary Salafis and believed that Islam could be prepared for modern times through reforms in education, economics, government, and other areas. These reformist

Salafis admired Europe's technological innovations and social advancements and sought to reconcile modernity with Islam.[4]

Although they share the same name, contemporary Salafis do not trace their ideological lineage to the reformist Salafis. Most Salafis today believe that, by incorporating rationalist reasoning, the reformist Salafis such as Afghani, Abdu, Rida and their followers deviated from true Islam, which must be guided by God's word only.[5]

Salafism

Many different Salafi groups exist today, each regarding itself as the only true heirs of the program of Allah, as conveyed by his messenger, Muhammad, and as practiced by him, his companions, and other righteous predecessors—known as al-Salaf al-Salih. Traditionally, Salafis favor the strict implementation of Islamic religious law, the Sharia, and thus reject all other schools of thought as innovation (*bida*). In terms of the religious and legal interpretations of Islam, most Salafis accept only the Quran and the Sunna (the sayings attributed to the prophet) as valid religious and legal interpretations of Islam, while rejecting less rigid forms of interpretation such as the use of analogies (*qiyas*) and consensus (*ijma*) as "innovations" that are in dissonance with God's word. Because they advocate a return to what they regard as the basics of religion, they are at times called fundamentalists or neofundamentalists.[6] They are at times also referred to as Wahhabis, although most scholars regard Wahhabism as a branch of Salafism,[7] and Wahhabis themselves tend to call themselves Muwahideen (monotheists) or Salafis.[8]

Most branches of Salafism reject any form of adaptation or compromise with other religions and do not believe in discussions or other contacts with Christians and Jews. Nor do most mainstream Salafists believe in the need to harm Christians and Jews, arguing that as long as these "people of the book" (*dhimmi*) remain nonbelligerent infidels, they shall be treated with leniency.

At the center of Salafi creed is the concept of *tawhid* (unity of God), which Salafis understand literally. All Muslims believe in the unity of God, but Salafis have a more radical understanding of the concept. Because God is one, Salafis believe that Muslims must abide only by God's laws, thus extending the unity of God to a unity of worship of Allah. The practical implication of this approach is that Salafis reject man-made laws as an interference with the word and will of God. They denounce the division of religion and state (which would suggest that man-made laws are supreme to those of Islam) and worship only God. They do not invoke any other entity and reject the veneration and idolatry of dead or live individuals, including the Prophet Muhammad. Wahhabis demolished the shrine of the Prophet Muhammad for that reason.

In order to abide by and protect *tawhid*, Salafis believe that Muslims must strictly follow the Quran. According to Salafis, all truth is found in this holy book, and that truth is universally applicable at all times. Salafis therefore reject the argument that times have changed and Quranic verses must be reinterpreted accordingly. In everyday life, the centrality of the Quran means that Salafis will first reference the Quran for any insights into solving a mundane problem. It is for that reason that Salafi-Jihadists like Osama bin Laden usually begin by citing Quranic verses during their statements.

Salafis also believe that Muslims must strictly emulate the model of the prophet Muhammad, who, as the Muslim exemplar, embodied the perfection of *tawhid*.[9] Salafis believe that only the *salaf*—the Prophet Muhammad and his companions—led a life-style that was in accordance with God's will and hence pleasing to him. As a result, they imitate Muhammad's life-style and that of his companions on even the most mundane issues. An example of this emulation is found in the letter written in all likelihood by lead 9/11 hijacker Muhammad Atta to the other 9/11 suicide pilots. In the letter, which investigators found in Atta's luggage, the lead hijacker calls upon his co-conspirators to tie their clothes around them "in the same way our good predecessors had done before you," to be courageous "as our predecessors [were] when they came to the battle," and even to press their teeth together "as the predecessors used to do."[10]

Because their only goal is to please God, Salafis do not engage in the study of history and philosophy, and they reject the application of Western laws of logic and reasoning. Rationalism is considered as opening a gateway to human desire, distortion, and deviancy, because Salafis consider the Quran and hadith to be self-explanatory. Using rationalism in effect would challenge the attributes of God because all knowledge comes from and is contained within Islam.[11]

Salafis also reject local cultural variations of Islam. The expansion of Islam to new territories led to the adoption of various local cultural elements into Islamic tradition. Salafis reject these cultural variations as innovation (*bida*) that do not reflect genuine Islam. Salafism is hence understood in part as a movement designed to purify Islam from these foreign and modern influences—a process that Roy has termed the "deculturation" of Islam.[12]

Through the education of Muslim men of the true meaning of Islam, Salafis aspire to create the genuine Muslim individual and to unite these genuine Muslims in a global Islamic community of believers, the *umma*. Abiding by the true tenets of Islam and widening the community of real believers are considered acts that are pleasing to God and that lead to the purification of self (*tazkia*)—an important goal in Salafi thought.[13]

Salafis make a particular diagnosis of the current state of Islam, as well as of the reasons for this state and possible remedies. They believe that Islam is in decline because it has abandoned the righteous path of Muhammad and his companions. The *umma*'s past strength, they believe, derived from its faith and practices, which were in accordance with God's will. Muslims can recapture the glory of Islam only if they return to the authentic faith and original practices of the *salaf*.[14]

Contemporary Salafi Factions: The Purists and the Politicos

The ideological forerunners of contemporary Salafis are found not in the reformers of the late nineteenth and early twentieth centuries, but in earlier figures such as Hanbali, Taymiyyah, and Wahhab, who were doctrinal purists. The doctrinal purists have influenced all major contemporary factions within the Salafi movement—the purists, the politicos, and the Salafi-Jihadists.[15]

The first contemporary faction among the larger Salafi movement is the purist faction, which believes in the spreading of Islam via proselytizing rather than using violence. Examples of purist Salafis are found in the *tablighi jamaat*, a group of missionary Salafis established in the late 1920s in India. Purists are also in control of the state religious establishment in Saudi Arabia, where they exert much influence over Saudi policy and advance purist interpretations of Islam. The purists' main aim is to promote the Salafi creed and fight against practices they deem as being deviant from true Islam. The purists reject political activity, which they believe leads to corruption. They frown upon basic political activities, such as the forming of political parties or voting in elections, because of democracy's negation of the sanctity of God-given law. Purist Salafis regard themselves not as a political movement but as a vanguard on a mission to protect *tawhid* and resist corruptive and innovative influences on Islam, be they Western influences or "deviant" local cultural variations.

Purists criticize the other major Salafi factions on several grounds. They accuse them of failing to emulate the model of the Prophet Muhammad and of being guided by the principles of rationalist thought in their attempts to effect political change. The purists believe that, by adopting political or military strategies to achieve their goals, other Salafi factions are guided not by the sources of Islam but by the principles of utility maximization. Purists thus frame other

Salafi branches as driven by human evaluations rather than the principles of the Muslim holy texts. The major concern of the purists is with the strategy of the other factions of Salafism rather than with their belief.[16]

The second main Salafi faction is that of the politicos, a faction that dates back historically to the emergence of the Muslim Brotherhood, an Islamist movement created in 1928 by Hassan al-Banna. The Brotherhood's strategy aimed to create a popular movement that would rely on reforming Islam to create a social revolution. To the Muslim Brothers, all the necessary answers to life's pressing problems were provided by Islam itself. As a total system, Islam would be able to steer the Muslim *umma* in the course of that revolution, which could use the Quran rather than the constitution as its main guide. During the 1930s and 1940s the Brotherhood's idea of generating a broad Islamic political and social movement began to dominate the Islamic discourse revolving around the desire to rebuild the caliphate. In the process, it increasingly prevailed over those voices that advocated a nationalist strategy based on reforming Arab states independently. The new strategy entailed the indoctrination of younger generations, but also the decision to find a modus vivendi with the existing political order of Arab states.

Beginning in the 1950s, a new phase began for the Muslim Brotherhood when the movement clashed with Arab governments in places like Jordan, Egypt, and later Syria—countries that had come under the influence of Gamal abd-el Nasser's hybrid form of socialism and pan-Arabism. Sayyed Qutb was the predominant ideologue against the Baathist and Nasserite form of Arab socialism. In his writings, which focused on social injustice, Qutb's ideas marginalized the remnants of the reformist Salafism that had still influenced Banna.

Following the violent crackdown on the Brotherhood under Nasser, the remnants of the movement found refuge in Saudi Arabia under King Faisal, where the new arrivals quickly established themselves in a country that was dominated by purist Salafis known to Westerners mostly as Wahhabis. Wahhabism, a Saudi variant of Salafism, originated on the Arabian Peninsula in the course of the eighteenth century. The term derives from Muhammad ibn Abd al-Wahhab, who preached a puritan form of Islam opposed to any form of "superstitions." In 1745 Wahhab allied himself with an *amir* (leader), Muhammad ibn Saud, thus creating the antecedent of the Saudi monarchy that rules to this very day.

The remnants of the Muslim Brotherhood quickly established a foothold in Saudi Islamic universities in the 1960s, especially the University of Medina, where it was able to spread its doctrine to students from all over the world. Although the Brotherhood's politically oriented doctrine directly negated the purist character of Saudi Salafism, it was successful mainly due to the attraction in Saudi

Arabia to the teachings of the more Salafist-oriented Qutbist faction of the Muslim Brotherhood, whose presence in Saudi Arabia was led by Sayyed Qutb's brother Muhammad.

By the 1970s the Saudi education system was filled with Muslim Brothers and other politically minded Salafis, who managed to transmit their beliefs to their students and thus across the larger Muslim world. Their students, many of whom graduated during the 1980s and adopted political Salafist doctrines, included such individuals as Safar al-Hawali, Salman al-Awdah, Abdullah Azzam, and Abu Muhammad al-Maqdisi, all of whom would influence the future course of Salafism.[17]

In the 1980s and early 1990s, several historical events, including the Iran-Iraq War and the Palestinian Intifada, promoted the rise of the politico faction of the Salafi movement. Most important among them, however, was the U.S. presence in Saudi Arabia, which spurred a movement in the kingdom known as Al-Sahwa al-Islamiyya, or Islamic Awakening. Led by Hawali and Awdeh, the Sahwa vocally criticized the entrenched purist Salafi faction, which issued a fatwa permitting the presence of U.S. troops in Saudi Arabia. The Sahwa criticized the purists for isolating themselves from politics and thus lacking the necessary knowledge of current affairs needed to issue informed religious decrees. At the same time, the politicos presented themselves as better able to tackle the "real" challenges facing Muslims, such as the repression of Muslims by the United States, Israel, the Soviet Union, India, and "apostate" Arab regimes.

By criticizing the purists, the younger generation of Salafi scholars not only distanced itself from the older, purist generation of Salafis, who opted to stay out of politics and were more concerned with religious questions, but also contributed to a permanent factionalization of Salafis.[18]

Salafi Jihad

In the mid-1990s, the Saudi regime cracked down on the younger generation of politico Salafi scholars. The imprisonment of Hawali, Awdeh, and others in 1994 allowed Salafi-Jihadists, the third major Salafist faction, to gradually fill the vacuum in the following years. Many of the repressed young Saudi Salafis left Saudi Arabia for London, where they encountered radical Algerian Salafis and Palestinian scholars such as Abu Qatada al-Falestini and adopted a militant form of Salafism, the Salafi Jihad.[19]

Salafi-Jihadist ideology came to existence during the Afghan war, where it formed as a doctrine that borrowed elements from Salafi doctrine, the puritan tenets of Saudi Wahhabism, and the branch of the Muslim Brotherhood associated with Sayyed Qutb.[20] Because of its eclectic sources of inspiration, however, the Salafi Jihad cannot be considered a homogeneous subset of Salafism. Like Salafism, the Salafi Jihad, too, is a broader trend whose adherents can be placed on a spectrum. On the one end are ideologically purist Salafis who, unlike nonjihadist Salafis, justify the use of violence. On the other end are the more pragmatic, strategically oriented jihadists, some of whom have little patience for the doctrinal purists on the opposite end of the spectrum.[21]

Most Salafi-Jihadists see themselves as true fundamentalists, understanding the Quran in the most literal sense. They merged the Salafists' traditionalist perspective of the Quran with a deep belief in jihad, which in their mind assumed a place on par with the five pillars of Islam—the five daily prayers (*salat*), the pilgrimage to Mecca (*hajj*), alms giving to the needy (*zakat*), the declaration of faith (*shahadah*), and the fast of Ramadan (*sawm*).

Salafi-Jihadists believe that Muslims must actively wage jihad (defined in its aggressive form) against all infidels and apostates until an Islamic state can be declared on as large a territory as possible. They have set their eyes not only on local regimes in the Middle East, whom they accuse of collaboration with the West, but also on the far enemy—the United States and its Western allies.

The division between Salafism and Salafi Jihad manifests itself in four major ways.[22] The first and most important point of disagreement between Salafis and Salafi-Jihadists is over the issue of jihad. By and large, mainstream Salafis believe that *dawa*, the nonviolent call to Islam, should be given priority over jihad, whereas Salafi-Jihadists regard jihad as a priority. External jihad in Islam comes in two forms, offensive and defensive. The offensive jihad is used in order to expand Islam to the *dar al-harb* (domain of war). According to most interpretations, however, an offensive jihad can be waged only under the leadership of a caliph. The more widely accepted form of jihad is that of the defensive jihad (*jihad al-dafaa*), which resembles Christian and Jewish doctrines of a just war. According to the doctrine of defensive jihad, a holy war must be waged if an outside force invades Muslim territory. If such aggression occurs, then it is the individual duty (*fard ayn*) of every Muslim to come to the aid of his Muslim brethren, because an attack on one Muslim territory is an attack on the entire *umma*. The argument that a defensive jihad exists is connected to the irreversibility of the Islamic claim over land that at some point has come under Islamic rule. A land once controlled by Muslim law cannot be controlled by any other law, just like a Muslim is theoretically unable to convert to another religion. If the land returns to non-Muslim control—and even if the land is reclaimed by the original sovereign—that land will be deemed occupied until it has fallen back under Muslim rule. In this Muslim reconquest, it is incumbent upon every Muslim to return this land to Islamic rule.[23]

Salafi-Jihadists saw the Soviet invasion of Afghanistan as a clear act of war against Muslims that warranted a defensive jihad. This interpretation, however, was less automatic in the eyes of most Islamic scholars at the time, who argued that jihad focuses on the inner struggle against one's vices. In the subsequent years, Abdullah Azzam, more than any other Islamist scholar, embarked on a campaign to spread the notion of the need to wage a defensive jihad, urging Muslims across the globe that it was their duty to help their Afghan coreligionists.

Salafi-Jihadists justify their radical definition of jihad as a military struggle between Muslims and infidels by citing the duty to emulate the Prophet Muhammad, who spent much of the final years of his life engaged in military jihad against the unbeliever. They also selectively cite Quranic verses that appear to emphasize the merits or need to wage a military struggle, such as Sura 8:39, which states, "fight them until there is not more fitnah and the religion will be for Allah alone." They also cite Sura 8:13 and 8:17: "I will cast terror into the hearts of those who have disbelieved, so strike them over the necks, and smite all their fingers and toes. You killed them not, but Allah killed them." Sura 2:191 similarly states: "And kill them (all opponents of Muhammad) wherever you find them, and turn them out from where they have turned you out. And Al-Fitnah (polytheism) is worse than killing." According to another oft-cited verse, Sura 2:216, "Jihad (Holy fighting in Allah's cause) is ordained for you (Muslims) though you dislike it, and it may be that you dislike a thing which is good for you and that you like a thing which is bad for you." Sura 9:23 calls upon Muslims: "Oh you who believe! Fight those of the disbelievers who are close to you and let them find harshness in you; and know that Allah is with those who are Al-Muttaqun (i.e., the Pious)."

A second issue that differentiates Salafi-Jihadists from mainstream Salafis is the issue of *takfir*, a term that describes the labeling of fellow Muslims as infidels (*kufr*), thus justifying violence against them. The practice of *takfir* was used by the medieval Kharajites,[24] and later propagated by Shukri Mustafa, who led the group Takfir wal Hijrah in the 1970s, a group that declared virtually all Egyptians who did not abide by its own doctrines as heretics.[25]

The vast majority of all Muslims do not condone *takfir* and refer to several hadith attributed to Muhammad in which he said that if a Muslim wrongly declares a fellow Muslim a *kufr*, then he himself turns into a *kufr*.[26] Mainstream Salafi trends argue that a Muslim leader can become an infidel only if he knowingly implements laws that are contrary to Islam and declares them as superior to Islam. The issue of *takfir* is controversial even among Salafi-Jihadists themselves.

Whereas some of the more radical Salafi-Jihadists argue that a person deserves excommunication if he has demonstrated unbelief in word or action and has been warned or offered a chance to repent, others believe that that person is not a *kufr* unless he has justified his sins in public. Because of their wont to engage in *takfir*, the more radical Salafi-Jihadists are sometimes referred to as *takfiris*.

Takfir has become an issue of great importance and even greater debate within the Salafist and Salafi-Jihadist movement. Al Qaeda and associated groups and networks regularly label Arab and Muslim leaders as infidels, thus engaging in *takfir*. Because those who are labeled *kufr* are no longer considered Muslims, the *takfiri* logic goes, it is permissible to fight them and kill them. In practice, *takfir* has been an enabler of internecine Muslim violence on a large scale, as evidenced in the various terrorist plots hatched by Salafi-Jihadist groups against pro-Western Arab and Muslim regimes or the frequent attacks against the Shia in places like Iraq, Pakistan, or Afghanistan.

A third issue that distinguishes Salafi-Jihadists from mainstream Salafists is the justification of targeting civilians. Most Muslims, including nonviolent Salafis, cite a number of sources from the Quran and hadith against the killing of civilians, although mainstream Salafis recognize that innocent civilians may be killed in the course of war, which is an acceptable consequence if the war is just.[27] They cite a number of Quranic verses and Hanbali rulings in support of their claim, including verse 16:126, "And if you take your turn, then punish with the like of that with which you were afflicted."

According to Wiktorowicz, the acceptance by Salafi-Jihadists of targeting civilians appears to be a recent phenomenon that emerged in the course of the Algerian war. He points out that some earlier theoretical exponents of violent Salafism, such as Wahhab and Sayyed Qutb, never argued that civilians could be targeted. On the contrary, the Quran and Sunna contain many verses calling for the protection of the sanctity of life and the need to limit attacks against noncombatants. Groups such as Al Qaeda, he adds, have therefore "broken new ground over the past decade or so to develop an expanded understanding about permissible targets in war."[28]

Arguments justifying the killing of noncombatants are often accompanied by intense dehumanization of the specific groups in question. Thus, Jews, Shia, or Arab rulers are oftentimes described as apes or dogs—animals that are considered impure in Islam. Another technique is by redefining ordinarily protected groups in terms that deprive them of their protected status. Thus, Salafi-Jihadists may redefine democrats as adherents of a polytheistic religion.[29]

Other justifications for violence against civilians are that the latter are surrogates or representatives of the enemy and are thus legitimate targets. Although even nonviolent jihadis agree with this, Salafi-Jihadists have considerably lowered the threshold at which a person counts as a supporter of the enemy. Recently, some have argued that, because Westerners elect the governments that represent them, they are fair game. "War is a common responsibility among people and governments," bin Laden said in this regard. "The war is continuing and the people are renewing their loyalty to their rulers and politicians and sending their sons to the armies to fight us. They also continue their material and moral support, while our countries are burning, our homes are being bombed, and our people are being killed."[30]

Sometimes the killing of civilians is justified by arguing that these civilians will inflict harm on Muslims at a later stage. Israeli children, for instance, are often cited as legitimate targets because they will grow up and join the Israeli army one day, where they would kill Muslims. Here, as in many other cases, Salafi-Jihadists have adopted justifications first used in the context of the Israeli-Palestinian conflict.[31]

Among the most prolific justifications for the killing of enemy civilians is the argument that, because the West targets Muslim civilians, it is permissible to strike back in kind. Suleiman Abu Gheith, Al Qaeda's chief spokesperson, says, for example, that given the extent of U.S. killing of Muslims, Muslims are permitted to kill 4 million Americans to reach parity.[32]

Finally, Salafi-Jihadists sometimes justify the killing of civilians by merely stating that the end justifies the means. According to Abu Musab al-Zarqawi, for example, "the shedding of Muslim blood . . . is allowed in order to avoid the greater evil of disrupting jihad."[33] In these cases, the jihadists usually emphasize that if Muslims who are killed are innocent, they are martyrs and will go to heaven anyway.

Salafi Jihad and the Ideological Justification of Martyrdom Operations

The fourth major distinction between Salafism and Salafi Jihad relates to the permissibility of suicide attacks. Early Islamic texts contain frequent references to the willingness of the mujahed to go into battle, despite his low chances of returning alive, and several verses in the Quran emphasize the overall positive attitude toward death in battle. Verse 9:38, for example, calls upon Muslims, "Oh ye who believe! What is the matter with you, that, when ye are asked to go forth in the cause of Allah, ye cling heavily to the earth? Do ye prefer the life of this world to the Hereafter? But little is the comfort of this life, as compared with the

Hereafter." In addition, verse 3:143 of the Quran states, "Certainly you desired death before you met it."

Other verses cite the early companions of the Prophet Muhammad, who ran into the phalanxes of the infidels, knowing full well that they were going to die in the process. Here, Salafi-Jihadists rely on a paradigm termed "plunging into the ranks" (*al-inghimas fi al-saf*), which dates back to the Prophet Muhammad. When Muhammad told of the benefits awaiting the martyrs in paradise, it is said that Muslims plunged headlong into the enemy forces, thus achieving martyrdom.[34]

Salafi-Jihadists today continue to rely on selected verses from the Quran to show that, traditionally, the Quran venerates the martyr. They cite verse 9:111, which states "Allah hath purchased of the believers their persons and their goods; for theirs (in return) is the garden (of Paradise): they fight in His cause, and slay and are slain." They also cite verse 2:154: "And call not those who are slain in the way of Allah "dead." Nay, they are living, only ye perceive not."

As far as the modern phenomenon of suicide attacks is concerned, the consensus reached among Salafi-Jihadists that this tactic is the ultimate form of devotion to God was made possible by the earlier legitimacy most religious scholars afforded to "martyrdom operations" against Israelis.[35] During the late 1980s and 1990s, and continuing today,[36] radical clerics and scholars shared a wide consensus that suicide attacks were always acceptable against Israelis. As Paz notes, the Arab and Islamic world "gave moral sanctioning to the Palestinian ethos of death," while the voices of those clerics who deplored suicide attacks were marginalized.

Ironically, legitimizing the tactic against Israelis gradually opened the door toward justifying the use of this tactic against other groups, including eventually against Muslims. Nowadays, many Salafi-Jihadist ideologues permit suicide attacks in Iraq and oftentimes limit their critique on the target selection rather than on the modus operandi.

While Salafi-Jihadists have adopted this legitimacy, it is nevertheless interesting, as Wiktorowicz notes, that Salafi-Jihadists care little about constructing theological justifications of SMs. Instead, their writings and speeches praise the virtues of martyrdom, which nearly all Islamic scholars agree on.[37]

Salafi-Jihadists present the willingness to perpetrate a martyrdom operation as the ultimate manifestation of complete submission to God's will in the holy struggle against the infidels and apostates. Equally important, however, this particular tactic also marks the difference between the mujahideen and his enemy. Salafi-Jihadists are often heard arguing that, while the West loves life, they love death. As Suleiman Abu Gheith declared, "those youths that destroyed

Americans with their planes, they did a good deed. There are thousands more young followers who look forward to death like Americans look forward to living."[38] Salafi-Jihadists underscore the West's alleged clinging to life with a verse from the Quran (2:96): "Indeed, you will find them [the evildoers] of all people the most attached to life, even more than those who associated other gods with Allah. Every one of them wishes to live for one thousand years. This long life, however, will not spare them the punishment."

Jihad and martyrdom are hence presented as the very antithesis of everything that the West stands for. In early 2002 Abu Ayman al-Hilali, who interprets many of bin Laden's ideas on Salafi-Jihadist Web sites, gave the following suggestion of how the enemy could be eliminated: "First we have to acknowledge a basic fact, proved by experience and reality, already acknowledged by the enemy, which is that the vital contradiction to the Zionist and American enemy is the doctrine of Jihad and Martyrdom (Istishhad)."[39]

Salafi-Jihadist preachers who venerate martyrdom help inspire thousands of Muslim youth to develop a cultlike relationship to self-sacrifice. On April 23, 2004, Abu Hamza al-Masri told a crowd of 200 Muslims gathered at London's Finsbury Park mosque to embrace death and the "culture of martyrdom."[40] In an address to Muslims at a tennis center community hall near London on April 22, 2004, Omar Bakri Muhammad, the leader of the Salafi-Jihadist Al-Muhajiroun group,[41] urged Europeans to accept a truce offered by bin Laden lest Muslims "be obliged to become [bin Laden's] sword" in a new battle, while adding that "it is foolish to fight people who want death—that is what they are looking for." At the same speech, he also told the listeners what awaits the martyrs in paradise, namely "sweet kisses and the pleasures of bathing with scores of women."[42]

Much of the literature that describes the characteristics of paradise flourished in the aftermath of the 1991 Gulf War, yet most original references regarding the benefits of the martyr in paradise can be found in hadiths that were collected following the prophet Muhammad's death.[43] The martyr is usually said to have six privileges granted by God:[44]

- He is forgiven his sins on the shedding of the first drop of his blood.
- He has a place in paradise.
- He is redeemed from the torments of the grave and the fear of hell.
- A crown of glory is placed on his head of which one ruby is worth more than the world and all that is in it.
- He will marry seventy-two of the huris with black eyes.
- His intercession will be accepted for seventy of his kinsmen.

Many narrations about Muhammad's sayings regarding the merits of martyrdom are found in the hadiths collected by Muhammad Ismail al-Bukhari, whose collection of the prophet's sayings is acknowledged as one of the most authentic hadiths. The hadiths collected by Bukhari contain sayings attributed to the prophet related to the place of the martyr in paradise (vol. 1, book 2, no. 35); the martyr's reward (vol. 9, book 83, no. 29); and the pleasure Allah reaps from the martyrs (vol. 4, book 54, no. 57).

Most Westerners, and some Muslims, believe that martyrdom operations are tantamount to suicide. Traditionally, Islam sanctions suicide (*intihar*), which is regarded as a sin.[45] Salafi-Jihadists, therefore, must draw a sharp distinction between martyrdom and suicide, and always use the terms martyrdom operations (*amaliyyat istishhadiyya*) or sacrifice operation (*amaliyyat fidaiyaa*) rather than the term suicide operation (*amaliyyat intihariyya*) when describing this modus operandi. They also "solve" the problem of Islam's sanctioning of ordinary suicide by placing the emphasis on the intent of the perpetrator, arguing that the ordinary suicide kills himself for personal reasons, such as distress or depression, whereas the martyr kills himself for the sake of God and the *umma*. Because most conservative Sunni Islamic preachers would agree with this distinction, Salafi-Jihadists and many conservative Muslims have a common understanding that the tactic in itself may be legitimate.[46]

Theoretical Antecedents of Salafi Jihad

The doctrine of Salafi Jihad can be traced back to Imam Ahmed bin Hanbal (780–855), a Muslim scholar and theologian who founded the Hanbali *fiqh*, the most conservative of Islam's four schools of jurisprudence with the most stringent guidelines regarding social and personal conduct. Yet, the individual who had the deepest impact on Salafism was the thirteenth-century theologian Taqi al-din ibn Taymiyyah, a professor of Hanbali law whose family had to flee Syria as a result of repeated invasions by the Mongols. Taymiyyah was a strong opponent of the distinction between religion and politics in Islam, and thus formulated the importance of *tawhid* adopted by Salafi-Jihadists centuries later. Among the many legacies he left for future Salafi-Jihadists, his justification of jihad against both external and internal opponents of Islam ranks especially high.

Taymiyyah also applied the concept of *jahiliyya* to modern times. *Jahiliyya* is the term that refers to the state of ignorance, disorder, and paganism that existed prior to the arrival of Islam. He argued that Muslims who strayed from the path of Islam and who do not abide by God's laws were *jahilis*.[47] Specifically, he declared the king of the Mongols to be *jahili* because of his refusal to implement Sharia law.

The previously mentioned Wahhab (1703–92), an Arab theologian born in the Najd region of modern-day Saudi Arabia, was the next major influence on Salafi-Jihadists. Wahhab was drawn to the works of Taymiyyah and preached a puritanical version of Islam that would abide closely by the traditional sources of Islam—the Quran and the hadith. His most relevant work for radical Islamists was a small book titled *The Ten Voiders of Islam*, in which he described ten things that would automatically lead to the expulsion of Muslims from their religion. One of these is supporting nonbelievers against Muslims, which is apostasy—a point that has frequently been cited by Al Qaeda to justify its opposition to Muslim regimes in the Middle East, including the leaders of Saudi Arabia for allowing the stationing of American troops beginning in 1990.[48]

In the late nineteenth and early twentieth centuries, at a time in which Islam was in decline, Salafism reemerged most strongly in India and Egypt, and for good reason—these two countries with large Muslim populations were among the first to feel the impact of modern Western culture and power. Understandably, the intellectual discussion during that time revolved around how to reconcile Islam with modernity and the advent of Western ideas and institutions.[49]

In Egypt, this debate paved the way for the establishment of the Muslim Brotherhood in 1928 by Hassan al-Banna, as was already discussed. The Muslim Brotherhood's goal was the revival of Islam by creating an Islamic system that would be incompatible with the West and its institutions, as reflected in its credo: "God is our objective; the Quran is our constitution; the Prophet is our leader; Struggle is our way; and Death for the sake of God is the highest of our aspirations."[50]

A similar development took place in India, where the Islamist reaction was centered around the *dar ul-ulum* (realm of learning), an institution of Islamic learning second in stature only to Egypt's al-Azhar. Established 1867 in Deoband, in the Indian Uttar Pradesh province, *dar ul-ulum* became the "wellspring of South Asian Islamic orthodoxy," whose alumni and followers, known as Deobandis until today, propagate Salafi tenets of Islam.[51] One of the products of Indian Wahhabism was Abu al-Ala Maududi, a journalist bent on purifying Muslim society of Western influence and corrupt Muslim traditions alike. Maududi, who regarded all nationalism as anathema to religion, called for an Islamization from above, which would be achieved through the creation of a state guided by Sharia. In 1941 he founded Jamaat i-Islami, a Salafi party that eventually became the dominant religious party in Pakistan, where Maududi moved in 1947. Maududi regarded the Jamaat i-Islami as the vanguard for the future jihad.

Maududi picked up Taymiyyah's *jahiliyya* theory and went a step further. While Taymiyyah limited his charge of *jahiliyya* mostly to the Mongols, Maududi suggested that most Muslim rulers had veered off the original doctrines of Islam and were thus apostates. By crafting their own, man-made laws, Maududi charged that these Muslims had usurped the authority reserved for God alone through hubris. He accused all governments in Muslim countries that refused to abide by Sharia as apostates and called upon the true believers to wage jihad against them.

Few thinkers were as crucial for the development of Salafi Jihad as the Egyptian Sayyed Qutb, who combined Maududi's beliefs of modern *jahiliyya*, Taymiyyah's propagation of the need to wage jihad against apostates, and the notion of *tawhid* as unity of worship. Qutb influenced many Afghan Arabs, including Ayman al-Zawahiri. His book *Milestones*, which was published in 1964, became a manifesto of sorts for Salafi-Jihadists. Qutb's arguments were in line with traditional Salafism, but went further than any of the other theologians in calling upon true Muslims to engage in violent jihad as a method to create the genuine Muslim state. He criticized Muslim scholars for whom jihad had symbolized merely the defense of Islam. Rather than a defensive and temporary undertaking, Qutb called for jihad to be waged aggressively and permanently. Qutb also called upon Muslims to fight those "nominally" Muslim regimes who in reality were an obstacle only to those who truly worshiped God. This posed a problem of *fitna*, however, Muslim internecine fighting, which required Qutb to justify the use of violence against Muslims. To bypass the problem of *fitna*, Qutb argued that righteous Muslims were fighting infidels, not other Muslims.[52]

Qutb wrote that what stood in the way of mere *dawa*, the peaceful spread of Islam, were illegitimate and oppressive regimes like those in Egypt under Nasser. These regimes prevented their Muslim citizens from freely choosing Islam and were thus heretical. Qutb referred to the Nasserite regime—and almost all other governments, for that matter—as *jahili* regimes, tantamount to a morally corrupt entity akin to the barbarism that reigned prior to the arrival of Islam. *Dawa* by itself, he argued, could not bring about God's rule on earth because the *jahili* regimes would not give up their power. Hence, to remove this obstacle, a Muslim vanguard movement was needed that would engage in jihad by the sword (*jihad bis sayf*).[53]

Qutb also inherited from Taymiyyah a deep resentment toward Jews, which he passed on to modern-day Salafi-Jihadists as well. Qutb wrote that anybody who led the Islamic community astray could only be a Jewish agent. To him, the Jews were the epitome of all that is un-Islamic, and he portrayed them as the archenemy of Islam who longed for that religion's destruction.[54]

Qutb's influence on Salafi-Jihadist groups such as Al Qaeda is particularly striking in the writings of Ayman al-Zawahiri. In his book *Knights under the Prophet's Banner*, Al Qaeda's deputy leader credits Qutb with being the catalyst of the Islamic revolution. Qutb's "call for loyalty to God's oneness and to acknowledge God's sole authority and sovereignty was the spark that ignited the Islamic revolution against the enemies of Islam at home and abroad," Zawahiri writes. The Al Qaeda deputy leader greatly admires Qutb as "an example of sincerity and adherence to justice. He spoke justice in the face of the tyrant [Gamal abd-el-Nasser] and paid his life as a price for this. The value of his words increased when he refused to ask for pardon from [Nasser]."[55]

Among the most influential disciples of Qutb was Muhammad abd al-Salam Faraj (1954–82), who led the Cairo branch of the Egyptian Islamic Jihad and authored one of the most important books for the jihad movement, *The Neglected Duty*. Like Taymiyyah, Faraj viewed jihad as central in Islam. Jihad was the "neglected duty" and should be placed alongside the other pillars of the faith.

Faraj echoed Qutb's belief that the strategy of the nonviolent spread of Islam (*dawa*) was useless because mass communication was controlled by the state, which in turn was run by apostates who deserved death. He concluded that rather than waiting for the defeat of imperialism—the "far enemy"—Muslims should focus on overthrowing their own governments first, which he, too, termed apostate. Faraj made local rulers responsible for the existence of imperialism in Muslim lands, but thought that fighting the imperialists directly was a waste of time. Instead, he argued, "we must concentrate on our own Islamic situation: we have to establish the rule of God's Religion in our own country first, and to make the Word of God supreme. . . . There is no doubt that the first battlefield for jihad is the extermination of these infidel leaders and to replace them by a complete Islamic Order. From here we should start."[56]

Contemporary Salafi-Jihadist Preachers and Strategists

Al Qaeda and Salafi-Jihadist groups today rely on a vast network of preachers and strategists to propagate jihad, as understood in the Salafi-Jihadist interpretation. Following the death of Dr. Abdullah Azzam, who introduced Salafi-Jihadist doctrine to the Afghan mujahideen and their Arab supporters and inspired Osama bin Laden in creating Al Qaeda, a younger generation of ideologues came of age. Their takeover of global jihadist propaganda occurred in two stages.

In the first stage, during the first half of the 1990s, the younger ideologues appeared alongside the Taliban, as well as in the Balkans. The most dominant figure at this first stage was Dr. Ayman al-Zawahiri of the Egyptian Islamic Jihad, who not only consolidated Azzam's doctrine but also contributed his experiences from Egypt to his attempt to form the only true Salafi-Jihadist state in modern Afghanistan.

The second stage took place during the second half of the 1990s, when another generation of ideologues emerged out of the global jihadist terrorism perpetrated by Al Qaeda.[57] That group included Sheikh Abu Muhammad al-Maqdisi, a Palestinian-Jordanian who combined doctrines of Salafi Jihad with the most stringent principles of Wahhabism. Maqdisi helped form the group Tawhid wal Jihad, which operated in Jordan and Iraq. He also mentored several important Salafi-Jihadist ideologues, including Abu Anas al-Shami and Abu Qatada al-Falestini, but his most famous disciple was Abu Musab al-Zarqawi, with whom Maqdisi spent time in prison.[58]

The aftermath of the 9/11 attacks saw the emergence of a new group of interpreters of bin Laden and Al Qaeda. By 2002 many of these interpreters, who included intellectuals such as Abu Ayman al-Hilali, Abu Saad al-Ameli, Lewis Atiyyat Allah, and Abu Ubayd al-Qurashi, had their own Web sites. Other intellectuals from Saudi Arabia, Yemen, Egypt, and other countries also published on jihadist Web sites such as the Center for Islamic Study and Research as well as in on-line magazines. The postings of these individuals generated a multiplier effect of additional waves of interpretations of Al Qaeda and global jihad. Although these interpreters were not the main Salafi-Jihadist strategists of global jihad, they served as a backbone to them.[59]

By mid-2003 the center of gravity of Salafi-Jihadist indoctrination shifted to Saudi Arabia, which became the movement's new epicenter. The radicalization of a group of younger Saudi Islamists, which challenged the older generations of Saudi Wahhabism, gave way to increasingly vocal condemnations of the United States, Western culture, and even the Saudi ruling family.[60] The most striking figure in this process was Sheikh Youssef al-Ayeri, a Saudi scholar and commander of Al Qaeda in Saudi Arabia who was killed in June 2003. Ayeri, a veteran of the Afghan jihad against the Soviets who was among the leading architects of the notion of global jihad in Iraq, wrote an estimated forty books and many more articles in the three years before his death. In his writings, all of which were unsigned and published on the Internet, he described the future strategy of the Salafi Jihad, which in large part hinged on the jihadists' success in Iraq. In one of his books, *The Crusader War against Iraq*, for instance, he wrote that the Iraq war is not important because "a brother Arab country is attacked by the United States" but because Iraq is the first link in a chain of attacks that are bound to follow. Therefore, he continued, "if the Mujahidin do not resist in Iraq, they are going to fail in the future aggressions."[61] Ayeri also stressed the importance of jihadist volunteers from outside of Iraq, who are a powerful source that will guarantee the success of the jihadist resistance. As the reality of the war in Iraq suggests, Ayeri's recommendation has been implemented. He warned that the main threat to Muslims today was the spread of secular democracy, which he cited as the main reason why Muslims needed to resist the Americans in Iraq.[62]

After 2005, and especially in the aftermath of the July 7 London bombings, some cracks appeared in the ideology of the Salafi Jihad. Several ideologues of the older generation increasingly criticized younger generations of Salafi-Jihadists for abandoning the true jihad as envisioned by Abdullah Azzam and for promoting indiscriminate violence. Abu Basir al-Tartusi, for example, a Syrian jihadi scholar residing in London and one of the key Salafi-Jihadist thinkers, published a fatwa on his Web site in which he protested the London bombings as a "disgraceful and shameful act, with no manhood, bravery, or morality."[63] Another highly publicized internal dispute was one involving Maqdisi and his former protégé, Abu Musab al-Zarqawi. In 2005 Maqdisi criticized Zarqawi, saying that the latter's "indiscriminate attacks might distort the true Jihad."[64]

At the core of these disputes lies a tension within the Salafi-Jihadist movement alluded to earlier—namely, that between hard-line Salafi purists and extremist jihadists. While the former are intent on providing ideological justifications for their actions, the latter are pragmatists who are primarily concerned with action rather than words. In recent years, the Salafi-Jihadist movement appears to have seen a relative rise of the strategists who focus on technical and tactical issues of the jihad, while displaying less concern with the ideological component. One example is Muhammad Khalil al-Hakaima, whose writings focus on tactical and operational issues related to intelligence and warfare. On his Web site, al-Hakaima provides the readers with a number of recommendations about what tactics to use in the jihad. In a document issued in September 2006, he called for the establishment of effective counterintelligence capabilities in order to prevent the enemy from penetrating the jihad.[65]

Another key strategist is Abu Bakr Naji. In his book, the *Management of Savagery*, Naji explains how Al Qaeda plans to defeat the United States and its allies in the Middle East. He states Al Qaeda's need to establish sanctuaries in security vacuums and create more resonant propaganda. Naji offers a particularly exploitative plan to strengthen the jihadist movement and establish the caliphate. He advocates a strategy of deliberate destabilization of weak states, followed by the entry of jihadists into the chaotic theater. As the jihadists enter, they present themselves as the only force able to enforce security, all the while establishing a state based on Sharia law.[66]

Perhaps the most important strategist of global jihad after 9/11 is Mustafa Setmariam Nasar, better known as Abu Musab al-Suri. Born in Aleppo in 1958, Suri's political socialization occurred while he was a member of the Syrian Muslim Brotherhood. Following President Hafez Assad's violent suppression of the Brotherhood in the town of Hama in 1982, Suri went first to Spain and in 1987 to Afghanistan, where he met Abdullah Azzam and participated in the war against the Soviet army. In 1992 Suri joined Al Qaeda, and he would spend much of the second half of the 1990s in London, running an institution called Conflicts of the Islamic World. While in the United Kingdom, he also served as the editor of an Arabic-language newsletter, *Al-Ansar*. Throughout these years, he maintained ties to bin Laden and other senior figures in Al Qaeda. During Suri's stay in London, he also helped found the Algerian Armed Islamic Group (GIA).

In 1998 he moved back to Afghanistan and pledged allegiance to Taliban leader Mullah Omar. Although he rejoined Al Qaeda, he considered himself an independent operator. The U.S. State Department believed that, while in Afghanistan, Suri was running two training camps, in Kabul and Jalalabad, where he allegedly trained the mujahideen in toxic materials and chemical substances. He made his views on unconventional weapons clear after the September 11 attacks, which he praised, adding that it would have been far more useful had the planes been loaded with weapons of mass destruction.[67] He would later be linked to Abu Musab al-Zarqawi and to the train attacks in Madrid on March 11, 2004, although he denied charges of personal involvement.[68]

After the U.S. invasion of Afghanistan in 2001, Suri went into hiding and did not surface until 2004, when he posted a massive, 1,600-page book on the Internet titled *The Call of the International Islamic Resistance*—a treatise that outlines future strategies for the global jihad movement, placing terrorist attacks and decentralized urban warfare at the forefront of methods that will guarantee success to the global jihad movement.[69]

Suri, who was captured in Quetta in October 2005, saw his role as that of educating the "third generation" of Muslim fighters, that is, more-dispersed mujahideen who did not receive systematic training in Afghan camps. Among his recommendations to the new generation of mujahideen was his call on Muslims to wage a decentralized global jihad against the United States and other infidel countries. Links to the organization's leadership cadre should be kept to a minimum in order to evade enemy security advances. The old, traditional model of centralized, hierarchical, regional, and secretive forms of jihadist organizations, he believed, has not proved its value because their pyramidal structure made it highly vulnerable to external attack. In August 2005, after the London bombings, he encouraged sleeper cells around the globe to launch a general front as part of a "global conflict" against the entire West and its allies.[70] In this decentralized war, Suri believed that propaganda and jihadist indoctrination was of key importance. He recalled the failure of the jihadist experience in Syria, blaming the defeat of the Muslim Brotherhood on a lack of strategy and planning, a lack of ideological grounding, a dearth of jihadist theory, and weaknesses in the foundations of propaganda.

Suri recommended that future forms of jihadist warfare should adopt the form of the "jihad of individual terrorism" that would be practiced by autonomous cells of jihadists combined with the participation of jihadists in "open fronts." The leadership's role in this "jihad of individual terrorism" should be limited to "general guidance." Leadership should be exercised on the level of small cells. The common bond in this decentralized movement, Al-Suri believes, should be the "common aim, a common doctrinal program and a comprehensive (self-) educational program." The most important component of this decentralized jihad, according to Al-Suri, is the moral motivation and willingness to engage in the struggle, rather than the ability to handle weapons. Without adequate mental preparation, armed struggle is useless.[71]

Suri, whose writings are prominently featured on Web sites close to Al Qaeda, such as the Global Islamic Media Front (GIMF), has become possibly the prime theoretician of Al Qaeda after 9/11. He acts in a systematic and organized manner and exhibits the patience of the first generation of Al Qaeda that is often lacking in younger jihadists.

Suri's writings not only lay bare the current focus of many jihadists on tactical elements of the jihad but also provide a window into the ongoing debates within the Salafi-Jihadist movement's doctrinal purists and pragmatists. In his 1,600-page book, Suri strongly criticizes Salafis, arguing that they have endangered the jihadist project due to their doctrinal stubbornness, which has invited internal feuds. Although Suri acknowledges that most Salafi-Jihadists have adopted Salafi elements, he nevertheless expresses his displeasure with the arrogant exclusiveness of the Salafi purists. Suri believes that the jihadist movement should be inclusive and enable as many Muslims as possible to join it. Instead, Suri rants, the arrogance of the Salafis kept the bulk of Muslims away from the jihadist movement.[72]

Nevertheless, individuals with strong Salafi credentials and beliefs continue to remain in the forefront of the Salafi Jihad. One of them is Kuwaiti cleric Hamid al-Ali, one of the most influential Salafi-Jihadists today, who sanctioned suicide bombings—and specifically the flying of aircraft into targets—in early 2001.[73] After studying at the Islamic University of Medina, Ali returned to Kuwait, where he declared the Kuwaiti government to be apostate. Although he is banned from teaching, he nevertheless influences hundreds of thousands of Muslims through his popular Web site and other forums that publish his work. In 2005, after a series of arrests in Kuwait, Ali was accused of actively recruiting young Kuwaitis for the jihad in Iraq. He is also accused by the U.S. Department of the Treasury of providing funds for training camps in Kuwait and posting training material and technical assistance on explosives on his Web site.

Another central Salafi-Jihadist figure acting in the intersection of insurgency and theology is Hasan Muhammad al-Qaed, better known by his nom de guerre, Abu Yahya al-Libi. Libi was one of the first volunteers who fought in Afghanistan and was captured in 2002 by Pakistani and U.S. forces. He escaped from U.S. detention at Afghanistan's Bagram Airbase in July 2005. In the aftermath of his regained freedom, he has frequently contributed to journals and Web sites associated with Al Qaeda and the global jihad movement and has crystallized as one of the key ideological hard-liners of the movement active on the Internet. Libi is a highly active participant in the internal discussion among Salafi-Jihadists over the question of *takfir*. He has strongly criticized the "enemies within," namely the Muslim Brotherhood (and especially Hamas), the Shia, and the Saudi clergy. He condemns Hamas for following the democratic rulebook when it participated in—and won—the Palestinian elections. Libi also criticizes those Salafis who refuse to accept Al Qaeda's Salafi-Jihadist message, often repeating that jihad is not a matter of choice but an individual duty and obligation for all Muslims. He calls openly for a "total jihad" in which the only way to win involves the sacrifice of "rivers of blood of martyrs, high mountains of remains of torn organs, and souls carried by zealotry for religion, searching for martyrdom, and running towards the broad gardens of paradise."[74] Since his escape from Baghram, Libi has quickly climbed up the leadership ladder and, in early 2008, is assumed to be part of Al Qaeda's innermost circle. His claim to fame is his unique ability to present himself not only as a military strategist but also as a scholar. In that role, he often lashes out at the Saudi clergy, whom he criticizes of apostasy for, among other infractions, allowing the Shia to participate in the *hajj* to Mecca.

What Explains the Rise of Al Qaeda and Salafi Jihad?

The rise of Salafi-Jihadist ideology and Al Qaeda's transition into a global terrorist actor are the primary drivers of the globalization of martyrdom. Yet, what accounts for the rise of Al Qaeda and its guiding ideology in the first place? This section identifies six central factors that help explain the spread of Al Qaeda and its guiding ideology, the Salafi Jihad. They are the rise of Islamism; the crisis of Islam; globalization; the mediated diffusion through Salafi-Jihadist and Wahhabi leaders and institutions; the perceived Western domination of Islam; and the role of the Afghan jihad as an opportunity for the formation of Al Qaeda (figure 3.1).

Islamism

The origins of Islamism—the entry of Islam into the political sphere—date to the 1920s in Egypt, although its most significant theoretical evolution did not occur until the late 1960s. Until the 1960s, Islam was practiced in two general forms:. popular Islam, which emphasized a personal form of devotion to God mediated at best through spiritual guides; and a more scholarly Islam, which was favored by Islamic intellectuals who read and interpreted sacred texts of the *ulema* —officially acknowledged scholars of the Quran. Most Muslims were situated somewhere in between these two poles.[75]

Toward the end of that decade, three ideologues in Pakistan, Egypt, and Iran—Abu al-Ala Maududi, Sayyed Qutb, and Ruhollah Khomeini—helped turn the burgeoning Islamic movement into a powerful political force. Its goal was to reshape states in accordance with the conservative formulations of Islamic law, known as Sharia. Islamists believe that the Quran, with its universal principles, provides a complete system and contains all the answers to life's pressing questions. As a result of its broad message, its promise to reestablish social justice, its criticism of the authoritarian and corrupt regimes in the Middle East, and its ability to provide services for the poor and needy, the movement historically appealed to a broad array of social groups.

Two groups were particularly susceptible to the Islamist message in the post–World War II period. The first group consisted of a generation of sometimes educated and often unemployed youth whose numbers grew continually due to a spectacular population growth in the Middle East between the mid-1950s and 1970. Yet, as urbanization and literacy advanced, the housing needs and employment demands of this group were not met, causing this generation to become

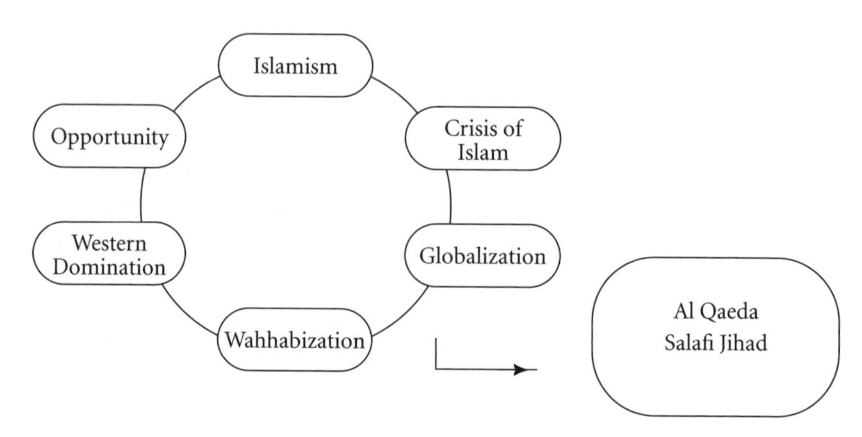

Fig. 3.1. The Rise of Al Qaeda and Salafi Jihad

increasingly disgruntled. The second group consisted of the traditional, devout middle class, many of whom were the offspring of merchant families associated with the bazaars. In the postwar era, this traditional bourgeoisie was without political power and was economically disadvantaged due to the corruption and nepotism of the ruling military and political establishment. According to Gilles Kepel, the divergence of these two groups' interests lies at the heart of contemporary Islamism, as both groups are committed to the notion of an Islamic state ruled by Islamic law—the Sharia—but have differing views of the state. While young urban youths provided that state with "social-revolutionary content," the devout middle class "saw it as a vehicle for wresting power for themselves from the incumbent elites, without fundamentally disturbing the existing social hierarchies."[76] A third group, the Islamist intelligentsia, mobilized these two groups and reconciled their diverging interests with an "ideology that offered a vague social agenda but a sharp focus on morality."[77]

That ideological appeal further heightened after the 1973 Arab-Israeli War—a war that sealed the fate of Arab nationalism and opened the way for a new religious ideology to fill the vacuum. In the aftermath of the 1973 war, the Islamist movement became even more popular in countries such as Egypt, Malaysia, and Pakistan. It was only in February 1979, however—when a revolution in Iran deposed the shah—that Islamism became a global force to be reckoned with. The revolution was made possible due to the charismatic Ruhollah Khomeini, who had managed to unify the diverging interests of different classes—masses of youngsters who had moved to the larger cities, the devout bourgeoisie, the Shiite clergy, and even the secular middle class—while focusing them on the only common denominator uniting them, namely their hatred of the shah and his regime. Within a few months after the ouster of the shah, Khomeini neutralized his erstwhile secular allies and made the Islamic revolution perfect.

During the 1980s the focus of the Islamist movement shifted to Afghanistan. In December 1979, the same year that the Pahlavi dynasty crumbled in Iran, the invasion of Afghanistan by the Soviet army further galvanized the Islamic movement, providing an opportunity to defend a Muslim country from an attack by "godless" Russian soldiers. Like no other event in the 1980s, the "jihad" to oust the Red Army unified both moderate and radical members of the Islamic *umma*. That unity was symbolized by the flocking of Muslims from numerous Arab and Islamic countries to Afghanistan to support their brethren in a struggle against the atheist superpower, financed largely by Saudi Arabia and supported by Pakistani and U.S. intelligence agencies.

In the first decade after the Islamic revolution, a string of successes gave a solid boost to the Islamic movement. They included the start of the Intifada against Israel and the related emergence of Hamas as a rival to the Palestine Liberation Organization (PLO), the victory of the Islamic Salvation Front (FIS) in elections in Algeria, and a successful Islamist coup in Sudan orchestrated by Hassan al-Turabi. The rout of the Soviet Union from Afghanistan in 1989 by the Afghan mujahideen crowned the 1980s as the most successful decade of the Islamist movement. The soon-to-be-followed implosion of the Soviet Union would raise additional hopes that Islam could spread to the newly independent, Muslim-majority states of Central Asia and the Caucasus and, with Bosnia, reach Europe proper.

The Crisis of Islam

The second factor that has contributed to the rise of Salafi-Jihadist ideology and the emergence of Al Qaeda is the crisis that has beset Islam especially since the late 1970s. The crisis has manifested itself in the deterritorialization of Islam, a decline of social authority, and an economic paralysis in Islamic countries, especially in the Arab world. These developments have been accompanied by a religious revivalism that culminated in the Islamic revolution of Iran in 1979.

According to Olivier Roy, the Muslim world contends with a process by which Islam is trying to live up to its "de facto political marginalisation."[78] Several processes are responsible for this marginalization, including the privatization of religion, the formation of closed religious communities, the construction of "pseudo-ethnic or cultural minorities," the identification by many Muslims with Western forms of religious practices, and the attraction to violent interpretations of Islam.[79] A key challenge to Islam is what Roy calls the growing "deterritorialization" of the religion.

Largely a product of globalization and the decreasing relevance of territorial borders, the deterritorialization of Islam denotes a trend whereby perhaps as many as a third of all Muslims today live as minorities. This creates a host of problems revolving around the question of how these Muslims identify themselves and their religion in a globalized world. Simply put, "deterritorialization leads to a quest for definition."[80] The search for a new meaning has resulted in the definition of a new universal Islam that rejects local, cultural forms of Islam.[81] This "re-Islamization," which adopts the form of Salafism,[82] attempts to rebuild a new, global Muslim community of believers (*umma*) on a purely religious, as opposed to cultural and local, basis.[83] By transforming Muslims into a larger, transnational group—Salafism provides Muslims with a new identity.

The crisis of Islam does not affect merely those Muslims living as minorities in the West, but also many Muslims in the Arab and Muslim world. Because of the process of globalization, many Muslims living in Muslim countries share the sense of belonging to a minority with their coreligionists in the West. More conservative Muslims may even feel as if they are a minority in their own countries if they believe that the regime does not truly represent them. As a consequence of these processes, there is a weakening connection between the *umma* and a territorial entity. Instead, the Muslim community has to be conceptualized increasingly in "abstract or imaginary terms."[84]

Another manifestation of the crisis of Islam is the crisis of its social authority. Religious teaching institutions are in poor shape and in need of reform, as is the *ulama*, the body of Islamic scholars. Large religious schools (*madrassas*) are challenged by the emergence of smaller, private ones, as well as by clerics who now speak on radio and television rather than in the madrassas.[85] Another indication of the crisis of social authority is the growing use of brutal punishments called for in religious law, the Sharia, in countries like Afghanistan, Iran, Sudan, and Nigeria. Roy points out that these countries have meted out these punishments out of fear and weakness. Traditional Muslim societies are endangered, Roy suggests, and these regimes know it.[86]

How does this crisis of Islam affect Muslims, especially in places where they live as minorities? Farhad Khosrokhavar, who conducted extensive interviews of several Salafi-Jihadists in prisons, writes that Muslims living in the West—especially second- or third-generation immigrants—often feel dislocated and mentally confused. Their parents' or grandparents' generation had high hopes to integrate, become successful, and maintain part of their Muslim identity, but the interviewees do not cherish these hopes any longer. Instead, they feel as if the West excludes and represses them—an exclusion made all the worse because the West has attempted to seduce them with its initial promise of integration, and continues to seduce them with the temptations that liberalism has to offer. In a similar vein, Holmes hypothesizes in a thoughtful essay on the 9/11 suicide hijackers that one possible explanation for the motivations of the 9/11 attackers may be that "the ripest recruits for [suicide missions] . . . would be half-way men, stuck in transit between the Middle East and the West, whose frustration is mingled with a feeling of being *tainted* by a society that seduces them. The hijackers' felt need to erase such a stain on their souls could conceivably have become so obsessive that it eclipsed all thought of future consequences."[87]

Many Muslims in the West appear torn between their parents' and grandparents' traditional values and traditions—nuclear family structures, patriarchal authority, and sexual chastity—and the realities of the West, which include sexual promiscuity, the deregulation between men and women, homosexuality, family instability, and the loss of traditional family structures. The interviewees view life in the West as being dictated by consumerism and "a mediocrity that do not seem to offer any future," rendering life meaningless. Coupled with deep feelings of repression by the West, this emptiness helps fuel Islamic radicalism. It is this struggle with an existential question that leads these young Muslims to adopt a militant faith. "Struggle," Khosrokhavar writes, "is the best way to purify their faith and to protect the believer from the temptations of a corrupting modernity that serves the purposes of a perfidious West."[88] The repression and emptiness sensed by these young Muslims produces intense feelings of humiliation, which is experienced in several forms. According to Khosrokhavar,

> First, there is the humiliation they experience in everyday life because they feel that they have been economically marginalized and made to feel socially inferior, as is the case with the excluded Maghrebin youth in France, or young West Indians and Pakistanis in Great Britain. Second, thanks to the media, they experience the humiliation of the Muslim world in Bosnia, Afghanistan, Iraq or Palestine. Mechanisms of identification then lead to the internalization of that feeling. Finally, there is sometimes a feeling that their immersion in the Western world has defiled them. For immigrants or their sons, the fact that they left their country of origin, either as children or at some later date, makes them feel that they have unfairly been spared the sufferings of their coreligionists in Muslim societies.[89]

Humiliation is one of the most underestimated forces in international and human relations, argues Tom Friedman, adding that when people or nations are humiliated, they may engage in extreme violence. Feelings of humiliation are easily sensed in a globalized world, he writes, when "you get your humiliation dished up to you fiber-optically."[90]

Globalization

Globalization has changed the world in fundamental ways.[91] Global interconnectedness among societies, organizations, and individuals has proceeded at a remarkable speed and breadth and has resulted in increased travel, productivity, new technological innovations such as the Internet, and, at least for some segments of the global population, a rise in standard of living. At the same time, globalization has had some unintended consequences, four of which had a direct bearing for the emergence and strength of Al Qaeda and Salafi Jihad.

The first unintended consequence is the clash between globalization and Islam. The impact of globalization on Muslims living in the West is particularly profound—and hence challenging—because many Muslims are used to traditional social and family structures, as well as values that appear to be threatened by globalization. According to Reuven Paz, the "inability of a large section of the Muslim public to cope with the technological, cultural, or economic aspects of Western modernization" lies at the root of the development of the doctrine of global jihad. This is the reason why a substantial part of Muslims seek salvation in the idea of a return to the past, the glorious past of Islam.[92] Many Muslims in Arab or Muslim countries, for example, are used to communalized forms of life, yet globalization and life in the West highlight what Khosrokhavar labels an "exaggerated individualism."[93] As a result, many young Muslims consider the West to be impersonal, insular, and lonely, a place where they sense a loss of dignity.[94]

Muslims in general are particularly affected by globalization because Islam teaches that it is the ultimate religion, which prevails above all others. Yet, Islam has been in decline for centuries. Globalization has contributed to this cognitive dissonance felt by many Muslims because, according to Friedman, it has made "the backwardness of the Arab-Muslim region, compared to others, impossible to ignore."[95]

The second unintended consequence of globalization is the use by terrorist organizations, including Al Qaeda, of technological innovations for its own purposes. Terrorists have often used inventions originally designed for peaceful purposes to help them carry out acts of wanton violence. Alfred Nobel's invention of dynamite in 1866, for example, was supposed to revolutionize the construction business. It ultimately revolutionized terrorism, too, when many anarchist groups, including some in the United States, began using dynamite to terrorize their political opponents. Today, Al Qaida has exploited the Internet for communication among its members, to gather information, to plan and execute attacks, to recruit potential terrorists, and to indoctrinate future terrorists.

A third way in which globalization has helped produce Al Qaeda relates to the organizational structure of terrorist groups. Some of the changes introduced by globalization have enabled the formation of a new generation of terrorist organization—terrorist networks—which pose the most challenging threat to Western countries and their allies around the globe. Al Qaeda, a transnational terror network, is a shadowy and opaque organization with no precise leadership structure and no apparent physical headquarters. This places new challenges to countering terrorism; because networks are not static and lack a formal hierarchy, they cannot be eliminated through decapitation. Nodes forming the network can be removed without affecting the integrity of the network.[96]

Al Qaeda–type terrorist networks are an outgrowth of globalization because networks are dependent on the modern technologies that are characteristic of globalization. The products of globalization include cellular and satellite phones, fax machines, laptop computers, news networks such as CNN, and e-mail. Transnational networks would not exist if it were not for the ease of travel in modern times. Networks also use modern means of communication that enable its members to exchange messages across continents quickly and inexpensively.

Fourth, globalization has been a platform for the immediate transnational diffusion of grievances. While human tragedies in a local area have always elicited empathy among humans in another area, globalization has enabled the immediate and global diffusion of human tragedies, with the result that local conflicts, tragedies, and grievances can now be seen, watched, or heard by an unprecedented number of people in nearly all countries of the world. This has led some people who are far removed from the area of crisis or conflict to produce vicarious grievances—grievances that result from a suffering that an individual has not personally experienced. As one young man in Luton, England, said shortly after the July 7, 2005, London bombings, "It's not just the BBC and ITV any more. We have al-Jazeera, we have the internet. If something happens to innocent people in Iraq, the Muslims of Luton will know about it and feel that grief."[97]

Globalization has also increased grievances in some areas because, as Friedman points out, the modern tools and innovations of globalization, such as broader and cheaper access to information about various parts of the world, have "deepened these grievances by making it easier for individuals from one culture to compare their circumstances with those of people from other cultures."[98] Cases reviewed in chapters 5 to 7 show that a large number of suicide bombers have produced vicarious grievances based on footage from regions they had never visited, in order to undo a humiliation they have never personally experienced. Evidence in chapter 5 shows that the Internet has, more than any other medium, been used to indoctrinate many young Muslims (and a growing number of converts).

The spread of Salafi Jihad through the Internet or satellite television is a form of direct or "nonrelational" transfusion that does not require a broker. Salafi Jihad, however, has also been diffused by means of what Sidney Tarrow has called "mediated diffusion," aided by brokers that "help to bridge cultural and geographic divides and diffuse new forms of collective action across borders."[99] This mediated diffusion has played a key role in the global spread of Wahhabi preachers and institutions, including mosques and religious schools.

Wahhabization: The Spread of Salafi-Jihadist Actors and Institutions

According to Tarrow, collective action "requires activists to marshal resources, become aware of and seize opportunities, frame their demands in ways that enable them to join with others, and identify common targets."[100]

The spread of Salafi and Salafi-Jihadist doctrine, and the rise of Al Qaeda cannot be explained without the physical diffusion of individuals, institutions, and financial assets around the globe. Beginning in the mid-1970s, Saudi Arabia embarked on a massive spending spree to spread its fundamentalist form of Wahhabism—a puritan form of Islam virtually synonymous with Salafism—to as many countries as possible. Taking advantage of the void left by the failure of Arab nationalism (which culminated in the Arab defeats in the 1967 and 1973 wars against Israel) as well as the rising prices of oil after 1973, it build a vast network of associations, mosques, and *ulema* that would adhere to and further spread the Wahhabi creed of Islam to all corners of the world.

The Saudi Wahhabization program was driven in no small part by the rivalry with the detested Shia regime in Iran, with whom the desert kingdom competed for the leadership of the Muslim world. The Iranian revolution had seriously threatened the status of Saudi Arabia as the dominant religious, political, and moral center of the Islamic world. As Iran was attempting to become the spokesman for Muslims and the "oppressed" throughout the world, the Saudi kingdom went to great lengths to suggest that the Islamic revolution in Iran was really the outcome of and catalyst for Shia Islam and Persian nationalism.

Over the next three decades, the kingdom would muster some $70 billion in overseas aid, more than two-thirds of which was destined for "Islamic activities," such as the building of mosques, religious learning institutions, or Wahhabi religious centers. The campaign resulted in an estimated construction of 1,500 mosques, 210 Islamic centers, 202 colleges, and almost 2,000 schools in non-Islamic countries by 2003.[101] At the same time, Saudi Arabia attracted immigrant labor forces, which began to arrive in large numbers to Saudi Arabia and other Gulf states in the mid-1970s. As these immigrants—both recent college graduates and professors—enriched themselves, they also absorbed Wahhabi tenets of Islam.

Led by Wahhabist clerics, charities closely linked to the royal family, such as the Muslim World League, the International Islamic Relief Organization, or the al-Haramain Foundation, provided money, relief services, and Wahhabist literature that preached mistrust of infidels, and extolled the practice of *takfir* and the pursuit of jihad as the key to the eventual domination of true Islam, thus paving the way for Al Qaeda and like-minded terrorist groups that came in its wake. While money was also used to fund commendable projects such as orphanages and medicine for refugees, many charities provided funding for terrorist groups, some doing so knowingly. Al Qaeda alone is said to have collected between $300 and $500 million, mostly from Saudi charities.[102]

At least $150 million poured into Bosnia in 1994 alone, much of it to charities that abetted terrorist activity; a CIA investigation later found that about a third of Islamic charities active in the Balkans facilitated the activity of groups such as Hamas and Hizballah. The 1996 report compiled by the CIA found that of more than fifty Islamic charities engaged in international aid, a third were linked to terrorist groups. These charities—some of which were present in as many as thirty, perhaps even ninety countries—at times acted as fronts, providing terrorist groups with safe houses, false identities, and travel documents. They were overseen by religious leaders and members of the Saudi royal family.[103]

Naturally, the spread of Salafist institutions and schools was accompanied by the spread of Wahhabi and Salafist scholars. In the mid-1990s, many young Salafi scholars repressed by the Saudi kingdom, including such figures as Saad al-Faqih and Abu Basir al-Tartusi, left Saudi Arabia for London. There, they met with other radical Algerian and Palestinian scholars such as Abu Qatada al-Falestini to further develop the Salafi-Jihadist doctrine.[104] These clerics would subsequently help radicalize young Muslims in the West by playing on their sense of victimhood, exclusion, and solitude, calling on them to join jihad in distant countries, and sometimes at their host societies.

The importance of the physical diffusion of individuals, institutions, and assets lies in the geographic spread of Salafi and Salafi-Jihadist ideas. Over time, these nonviolent NGOs and movements have created an atmosphere of radicalism by carrying out Islam's political, social, and educational work, while acting as a "greenhouse" for the emergence of violent groups "and the preservation of worldviews of hostility toward the West or Western culture."[105] They would often preach in private, unregulated mosques, which would become hotbeds of Salafi Jihad.

Western Domination

The narrative of Al Qaeda and its guiding Salafi-Jihadist ideology revolves in large measure around the perception that Islam is under attack by a global conspiracy of Crusaders, Zionists, and apostates. The contempt for what Salafi-Jihadists view as a Western domination of Islam is not the only grievance that lies at the root of the surge of Salafi Jihad and Al Qaeda, but it is the most central grievance.

Al Qaeda's list of examples of Western aggressions is long. It contains real and perceived, past and present factors, such as Western occupation of Muslim lands by Britain, France, the Soviet Union, the United States, and Israel; the existence of despotic, "apostate" regimes such as Egypt, Jordan, and Saudi Arabia that Salafi-Jihadists regard as puppets of the West, with which they collaborate in the subjugation of ordinary Muslims; the West's exploitation of Muslim riches; and the belief that the West, and especially the United States, is on a quest to dominate the Middle East militarily, politically, economically, and culturally.

According to Salafi-Jihadists, by far the most severe aggression against Islam is the physical presence of foreign troops in Muslim countries. In August 1990 King Fahd invited the U.S. Army to Saudi Arabia to defend the country from a possible attack by Saddam Hussein, while rejecting a counteroffer by Osama bin Laden to have an international army of Muslim fighters protect the kingdom instead. By doing so, the Saudi royal family committed a sin of unimaginable proportions in the eyes of Salafi-Jihadists. Bin Laden and his fellow jihadists found unbearable the notion that infidel troops accompanied by Christian and Jewish clergy now defiled Islam's two holiest places—Mecca and Medina.

Beginning in March 2003, the U.S. presence in Iraq provided further proof to Salafi-Jihadists that the United States was on a mission to rein in and dominate Islam. Much as Afghanistan had served as a haven and training ground for jihadists during the 1980s and 1990s, Iraq would subsequently attract thousands of Arab and Muslim mujahideen who would stream to Iraq to fight the occupiers and their collaborators and realize their dream of establishing a caliphate from the heart of the Arab world.[106] According to Paz, an Israeli authority on radical Islamist ideology, Iraq presented Salafi-Jihadist ideologues and terrorist operatives affiliated with or inspired by Al Qaeda with a golden opportunity "to consolidate, direct, and reinforce the insurgency and to reinvigorate militant and radical Islam around the Muslim world by elaborating a new set of ideas about the meaning and purpose of Jihad."[107] Iraq, however, also inspired Salafi-Jihadists outside the traditional Muslim world. As a study by Nesser showed, the war in Iraq serves as a "significant motivational factor for the militant radical milieus in Western Europe." Nesser showed this influence in the case of the Madrid bombers as well as in the actions of Mohammed Bouyeri, the murderer of Dutch filmmaker Theo van Gogh.[108]

According to Al Qaeda's guiding ideology, the perceived infractions against Muslims constitute a clear attack on Islam. Attacks on Islam, in turn, require a defensive jihad waged against the aggressor—a jihad in which every Muslim must participate in one way or another. Violence is an integral part of this jihad because of the belief that the United States—the devil incarnate—and its cronies understand no other language.

U.S. policies play an important role in fomenting anger and mistrust among many individuals who are subsequently attracted to Salafi-Jihadist ideology. Blaming U.S. policies alone for the emergence of jihadist terrorism, however, ignores the intrinsic goals of Al Qaeda and its guiding ideology, which adopts an aggressive form of expansionist Islam that attempts to establish a caliphate in as many countries as possible. While a more openly pro-Arab or pro-Muslim policy on the part of the United States may help appease some elements within the larger jihadist movement, the United States will always remain an infidel in the eyes of the movement's hard core. Short of a complete surrender and obsequiousness to Al Qaeda and its maximal demands, the United States will find itself in an ongoing war against an enemy inspired by a religious ideology.

Opportunity: The Afghan Breeding Ground of Salafi Jihad

It is difficult to imagine the creation of Al Qaeda and the formulation of Salafi-Jihadist ideology without the unique opportunity that presented itself in the aftermath of the Soviet invasion of Afghanistan in December 1979. Afghanistan presented a unique gathering opportunity for thousands of Muslims willing to fight against an occupying superpower. Thousands of foreign fighters joined the Afghan mujahideen in the nine-year long attempt to rout the Soviet army from Afghanistan. Later, after many of the fighters would return to their home countries or would continue on to fight in third countries, the deep friendships and bonds that had been forged among some of these fighters would enable the formation of transnational terrorist cells.

Afghanistan also helped internationalize the jihad through the friendships and personal ties bin Laden was able to forge during the war, which helped him create a virtual rolodex of global leaders of the Islamic movement. These ties would later help bin Laden to establish bonds with similar-minded organizations, thus contributing to the global diffusion of Al Qaeda's ideology, while providing itself and other groups with the synergistic benefits of cooperation between terrorist groups. The result was the establishment of a transnational terrorist network whose geographic spread had been unprecedented in scope.

The Afghanistan experience also helped build up self-confidence and an aura of invincibility among the mujahideen. After all, a handful of poor and poorly fed warriors had just defeated one of the world's two superpowers. Seizing upon the momentum of the humiliating defeat of the Red Army, Azzam began propagating his idea of a global Islamic jihad, while bin Laden suspected that, henceforth, future battles would be a cakewalk. "Having borne arms against the Russians in Afghanistan," the Al Qaeda leader told an interviewer, "we think our battle with America will be easy by comparison. . . . We are now more determined to carry on until we see the face of God."[109]

Similarly, the experience of the Afghan war gave rise to the idea of creating a global Islamic *umma*. The obstacle in the way of establishing this universal nation of believers was identified, first, in the local regimes. These, however, were perceived as merely pawns in the game of larger Western powers, led by the United States. In this way, the United States became the main obstacle in the way of establishing a global Muslim community of believers.

Afghanistan also afforded Al Qaeda the opportunity of a physical safe haven—thanks to the generous support of Mullah Omar and the Taliban regime, which provided Al Qaeda with virtual freedom of action. The carte blanche given to Osama bin Laden, coupled with the necessary space provided, helped Al Qaeda train the members of the future global Islamic insurgency without disturbance. Beginning in 1996, after spending some five years in Sudan, Osama bin Laden helped transform Afghanistan into the key training ground for Islamic militants. In the next five years, between 10,000 and 20,000 fighters would undergo training in camps in Afghanistan supported by Osama bin Laden.[110]

CHAPTER FOUR

From Al Qaeda to Global Jihad

Prelude to the Global Jihad Movement
The Affiliates Phenomenon

From the very outset, Al Qaeda's goal was not to become the leader of the Islamic movement per se, as much as to serve as a vanguard that would spark international waves of jihad. The hope was for this awakening to result in a globally active jihadist movement.

From its early days, Al Qaeda regarded the establishment of links with other Islamist groups that adhered to a more or less similar outlook on the world as a benefit rather than a burden or threat. It regarded cooperation, support, and coordination with other groups as creating a multiplier effect that would strengthen the forces of "true" Muslims against those of the infidels and apostates.

At any one time, Al Qaeda's formal membership probably did not exceed several hundreds of fighters.[1] Its reach, however, extended to thousands of jihadists who were members of groups who benefited from Al Qaeda's organizational support, training, and financing. These groups are known as Al Qaeda affiliates.

The level of cooperation between Al Qaeda and a particular affiliate varied from case to case as well as over time. In some instances, Al Qaeda's links to other groups buttressed jihadist groups in places where a mujahideen presence had already been established. Al Qaeda's financial and material aid also supported the establishment of jihadi groups and movements in places where no such presence existed, or where that presence was weak. Al Qaeda also offered funding and fighters to Afghanistan in return for protection by a nation-state and the advantage of a safe haven. In some cases, bin Laden and his associates also provided aid to freelancers such as Khalid Sheikh Muhammad, the organizer of the 9/11 attacks, some of whom formally joined Al Qaeda by swearing allegiance to bin Laden. In June 2001 Al Qaeda even formally merged with one group, the Egyptian Islamic Jihad, after which it officially renamed itself Qaedat al-Jihad (Base of Jihad).[2]

From an operational point of view, Al Qaeda's years in the Sudan proved crucial for the expansion of links with similar-minded groups. In these years, from 1992 to 1996, Al Qaeda persistently attempted to form an international insurgent organization to attack American, Israeli, and other pro-Western, Christian, and Jewish targets. During the Sudan years, Al Qaeda was involved in international terrorist or insurgent activities in various ways, including funding, operational support, guidance, and sometimes complete direction of attacks. It was in these years that Al Qaeda turned into a terrorist organization of global reach. These groups and individuals with various ties to Al Qaeda were present in such countries as Algeria, Bosnia, Eritrea, Ethiopia, Jordan, Philippines, Somalia, Uganda, and Yemen. Radical Islamists were also supported in Burma, Chechnya, Egypt, Lebanon, Libya, Kashmir, Pakistan, Saudi Arabia, and Tajikistan, among other places.[3] It was also in the Sudan when Al Qaeda formalized its links with terrorist groups allied to it by creating the Islamic Army Shura, a coordinating body for the consortium of these groups.[4]

Most of the groups that received support from Al Qaeda during the Sudan years were focused on liberating lands that had once been under Muslim control, such as Kashmir or the Philippines, or were fighting in places like Bosnia or Chechnya, where they believed Muslims to be under attack. Bosnia in particular offered an opportunity for the jihadists to make inroads into Europe proper. The country had declared its independence from Yugoslavia in 1992, a move that was followed by attacks from Serb militias. The three-year-long war that followed killed an estimated 150,000 and displaced an estimated 2 million people as a result of the Serb policy of "ethnic cleansing." According to Kepel, a total of about 4,000 jihadists from Peshawar, mostly Saudis, had fought in Bosnia. Their arrival followed the 1992 seizure of Kabul by the mujahideen. The most important leader of the Bosnian mujahideen was a veteran of the Afghan war, Abu Abdel Aziz, better known as Barbarossa. He commanded the Kateebat al-Mujahideen (Mujahideen Battalion) regiment that was created in August 1993, and which was responsible for horrific acts of violence against its enemies. When they were not fighting the Serbs, the foreign mujahideen attempted to impose a Taliban-style form of Islam on the local population, particularly in the Zenica region, their stronghold. The result was further estrangement from the local Muslim population.[5]

During Al Qaeda's Sudan period, many mujahideen joined the battle against the "near enemy," that is, Arab or Muslim regimes they deemed to have abandoned the true religion, such as Egypt and Algeria. Some of these local movements had begun their jihad rather spontaneously, oftentimes under the influence of Afghan Arabs who had returned to these countries after the defeat of the Soviets, such as the Algerian Armed Islamic Group (GIA) or the Abu Sayyaf in the Philippines. Al Qaeda saw its role as coordinating these local movements by providing funds, training, and at times weapons.[6]

Attacking the Far Enemy: Al Qaeda's Strategic Shift

Sudan was also crucial in another respect. It was in this African country where the internal debate took place about where next to take the jihad, and especially about whether to focus the struggle against the near enemy (*al-Adou al-Qareeb*)—local Arab regimes that were regarded as apostates—or the far enemy (*al-Adou al-Baeed*), which consisted of the United States and its Western allies. Eventually, those who advocated a strategy of hitting the far enemy, such as Al Qaeda official Mamdouh Mahmud Salim (aka Abu Hajer al Iraqi), the zealous head of Al Qaeda's fatwa committee, prevailed. The decision, however, came at a price, because many of the less radical elements, who opposed taking the fight to the far enemy, left the group. When Al Qaeda returned to Afghanistan in May 1996, it returned as a smaller, yet more radical organization.[7]

The strategic shift in the mid-1990s from attacking the near enemy to attacking the far enemy would become a watershed for Al Qaeda and helps explain the subsequent diffusion of SMs into dozens of countries. The jihadists' shift of focus was not only strategic but also tactical and was linked to several significant events. By far the most important was the jihadists' military victory over the Soviet Union in Afghanistan, which encouraged the victors to seize the momentum of the jihad's success and export it to new battlefields. That export occurred both in the realm of ideology, with the spread of Salafi-Jihadist texts, and through the dispersal of the Arab Afghans to a host of other countries beginning in the late 1980s. A second event that influenced the decision to target the United States was the presence of U.S. forces in Saudi Arabia in the wake of Iraq's invasion of Kuwait. Jihadists viewed the presence of infidels in the midst of the *dar al-Islam* as a desecration of Islam's holiest places, which were located nearby. They also dreaded an encirclement by the United States, which in their eyes already occupied the Persian Gulf and was in the process of establishing a foothold in Somalia. U.S. government claims to the contrary notwithstanding, many Muslims believed that the United States and its allies were conducting a war not against Iraq but against Muslims. A third reason—and a possible explanation for why Salafi-Jihadists began targeting the West at that particular time—also lay in the jihadists' defeat in the battle against the near enemy. After having suffered heavy losses in places like Egypt and Algeria, Al Qaeda had to focus elsewhere. As Gerges explains, "jihadis in Egypt, Algeria, and elsewhere had to choose between surrender and a new mission that would keep their sinking ship afloat. They lost the battle against the near enemy and had few options at their disposal."[8]

A second group of reasons for the shift in strategy by bin Laden was tactical. Bin Laden believed that extending attacks against Americans and Israelis would boost Arab and Islamic self-confidence. There was also a second tactical rationale. The Al Qaeda leader believed that attacks against local regimes were counterproductive, reducing the military effectiveness of Al Qaeda's potential allies, such as the EIJ.[9] At first, he disagreed on this issue with Zawahiri, who believed that the fight against the far enemy depended on the victory of the jihad against the near enemy. In Zawahiri's words, Jerusalem could not be liberated until the battle for Egypt and Algeria was won and until Egypt itself was liberated.[10] Bin Laden may have also decided to shift the focus to the United States and its Western allies in order to overcome some internal disputes among Al Qaeda members and sympathizers. In an October 1996 interview in *Nida al-Islam*, a radical Islamic magazine, he advised, "it is crucial to overlook many of the issues of bickering to unite our ranks so we can repel the greater kufr."[11]

Apart from strategic and tactical reasons, a number of personalities had strongly influenced the shift toward Al Qaeda's new internationalist outlook. Key among these individuals was Abu Hajer al-Iraqi, who assumed the leadership of Al Qaeda's fatwa committee during the Sudan years, although he never officially became a member of Al Qaeda. A former soldier in Saddam Hussein's army of Kurdish origin, Abu Hajer had fought together with bin Laden in Afghanistan. Acting as bin Laden's imam, his religious authority surpassed that of other bin Laden associates because Abu Hajer had memorized the Quran. He regularly addressed bin Laden and other members of Al Qaeda about the legitimacy of killing innocent civilians. A frequently mentioned figure in his lectures was Taymiyyah, the medieval theologian who regarded the Mongols as infidels despite their eventual conversion to Islam. He preached that those who had aided the Mongols in the Middle Ages were infidels, too. Likewise, all contemporary enemies of Islam, be they civilian or military, were part of a conspiracy against Muslims. Anyone who aided the Americans and their infidel and apostate allies was fair game. If innocent Muslims were erroneously targeted in the process, then they would go to paradise. By legitimating the killing of innocents, Abu Hajer helped turn Al Qaeda into the international terrorist network that it is known today.

Another individual who adopted the strategy of targeting the far enemy was

Zawahiri, who gradually reversed his early focus on targeting the near enemy, especially Egypt, toward a more global approach. By the mid-1990s, Zawahiri's writings reflected his new stance, which favored targeting the United States and its allies over the targeting of Egypt and other local enemies. In his book *Knights under the Prophet's Banner*, Zawahiri elaborated on the reasons why Al Qaeda decided to "go global":

> The Islamic movement and its jihad vanguards, and actually the entire Islamic nation, must involve the major criminals—the United States, Russia, and Israel—in the battle and do not let them run the battle between the jihad movement and our governments in safety. They must pay the price, and pay dearly for that matter. The masters in Washington and Tel Aviv are using the regimes to protect their interests and to fight the battle against the Muslims on their behalf. If the shrapnel from the battle reach their homes and bodies, they will trade accusations with their agents about who is responsible for this. In that case, they will face one of two bitter choices: Either personally wage the battle against the Muslims, which means that the battle will turn into clear-cut jihad against infidels, or they reconsider their plans after acknowledging the failure of the brute and violent confrontation against Muslims. Therefore, we must move the battle to the enemy's grounds to burn the hands of those who ignite fire in our countries.[12]

Zawahiri believed that the United States and other Western countries would forcefully resist Al Qaeda's attempt to establish a global caliphate. Because a war between Muslims and the Zionist-Crusader alliance was inevitable, he reasoned that Al Qaeda might as well start attacking the West now:

> The struggle for the establishment of the Muslim state cannot be launched as a regional struggle. It is clear from the above that the Jewish-Crusade alliance, led by the United States, will not allow any Muslim force to reach power in any of the Islamic countries. It will mobilize all its power to hit it and remove it from power. Toward that end, it will open a battlefront against it that includes the entire world. It will impose sanctions on whoever helps it, if it does not declare war against them altogether. Therefore, to adjust to this new reality we must prepare ourselves for a battle that is not confined to a single region, one that includes the apostate domestic enemy and the Jewish-Crusade external enemy.[13]

Upon Al Qaeda's return to Afghanistan, the group solidified its transition into a global terrorist organization. A dramatic step occurred on August 8, 1996, when bin Laden declared war against the United States—a step that "marked the emergence of the true global Salafi jihad."[14] In his declaration of war against America, bin Laden explained his decision to wage war against the far enemy: "the situation cannot be rectified . . . unless the root of the problem is tackled. Hence it is essential to hit the main enemy who divided the ummah into small and little countries and pushed it, for the last few decades, into a state of confusion. . . . People of Islam," he urged, "should join forces and support each other to get rid of the main 'Kufr' who is controlling the countries of the Islamic world, even to bear the lesser damage to get rid of the major one, that is the great Kufr."[15]

Another radicalization of Al Qaeda took place around 1997. In 1996, and again early in 1997, bin Laden stressed the importance of driving the United States out of Muslim territories, but he had not yet included U.S. civilians among his preferred targets.[16] That changed on February 23, 1998, when the Al Qaeda leader issued another statement—a declaration by a previously unknown group, World Islamic Front against the Crusaders and the Jews. The 1998 statement, which was drafted by Zawahiri, was a testimony to the Al Qaeda leaders' attempts to broaden their group's platform by including in this fatwa a number of radical Islamist groups other than Al Qaeda. For the most part, however, the other groups listed were rather obscure. Bin Laden had signed in his own name, still keeping the name Al Qaeda secret. Nevertheless, the 1998 declaration became the "manifesto of the full-fledged global Salafi jihad," as Sageman put it. Bin Laden had now openly declared war on the far enemy and announced that the United States would henceforth be hit wherever possible, including on its own homeland:

> The ruling to kill the Americans and their allies—civilians and military—is an individual duty for every Muslim who can do it in any country in which it is possible to do it. . . . We—with Allah's help—call on every Muslim who believes in Allah and wishes to be rewarded to comply with Allah's order to kill the Americans and plunder their money wherever and whenever they find it. We also call on Muslim ulema, leaders, youths, and soldiers to launch the raid on Satan's U.S. troops and the devil's supporters allying with them, and to displace those who are behind them so that they may learn a lesson.[17]

Bin Laden reiterated his inclusion of U.S. civilians among targets in an ABC interview in 1998: "We do not differentiate between those dressed in military uniforms and civilians. They are all targets."[18]

By the time Al Qaeda had issued the 1998 fatwa, foreign fighters had returned to Afghanistan in large numbers to train at the dozen or so training camps that were financed or equipped, in part or in full, by Al Qaeda. Few of these foreigners were connected to Al Qaeda. Most were either freelancers who simply wanted to contribute to jihad in any way possible or members of existing groups, such as Harkat-ul-Mujahideen (HUM), the Islamic Movement of Uzbekistan (IMU), or the Taliban. Others were involved with local groups in their native countries, such as the GIA.[19]

When Al Qaeda linked up with individuals or groups for a joint terrorist project, it tended to be approached more by the other party than vice versa. The militant groups that sent members to be trained in the camps, or who sought bin Laden's financial assistance, had various reasons to seek Al Qaeda's support, which were sometimes purely local. Fighters from Uzbekistan and Tajikistan, for example, had an agenda of installing an Islamic government in Uzbekistan, ultimately aiming at uniting Central Asia and Xinjiang Province into a Muslim region to be called Turkestan.[20]

The connection to each group differed from case to case, as did the relationship. Bin Laden penetrated Algerian networks, for instance, by offering training camps, which helped him raise his profile. When the volunteers returned to Algeria or to Europe and joined such outfits as the GIA or GSPC, they were as much bin Laden's operatives as they were those of other groups. Over time, as a result of combat, surrender, and internecine fighting, more senior operatives were killed, and the proportion of operatives linked more closely to bin Laden in any group increased, as did his influence. According to Jason Burke, these relationships were reinforced by the granting of substantial funds by bin Laden to older and more established activists, particularly the individuals who recruited new volunteers and arranged their travel and training. These men developed dual loyalties to bin Laden and to their own domestic groups, be they the GIA, the GSPC, or EIJ.

From Al Qaeda to the Global Jihad Movement
The Fall and Rise of Al Qaeda, 2001–2003

The attacks of September 11, 2001, which killed nearly 3,000 individuals, were a strategic success for Al Qaeda, but the group was unable to rest on its laurels for long, given the swiftness and magnitude of the American response that followed under the framework of the "global war on terrorism" declared by the United States. Its first stage was Operation Enduring Freedom, which consisted of an attack on Afghanistan by a U.S.-led alliance that aimed to destroy Al Qaeda and the Taliban regime, which had provided a safe haven to bin Laden and his cohorts during the previous five years. From Al Qaeda's standpoint, the situation immediately following 9/11 looked bleak. In the first year and a half, Al Qaeda had lost up to 75 percent of its original members and had lost its infrastructure of training camps to other groups.[21] The loss of its operational bases severely disrupted the group's command and control capabilities. Cells affiliated with Al Qaeda were rounded up in Europe, Africa, and Asia, and successes were made in disrupting terrorist financing and in foiling a number of terrorist plots.[22] As a result of these initial successes, a number of intelligence analysts and officials of the Bush administration believed that the United States was winning the war against Al Qaeda.[23]

Others were more cautious and warned of the dispersal of jihadists into a global movement. One of the first analysts who described the ongoing threat posed by Salafi-Jihadist groups in the aftermath of the U.S. invasion of Afghanistan was Israeli terrorism analyst Reuven Paz. One month after the 9/11 attacks, Paz circulated a paper in which he suggested that the new centers of gravity of jihadist groups would migrate to the Muslim communities living in the West, and to other countries in the periphery of the Muslim world, such as the Philippines. Pockets of jihadists in these countries, he argued, would begin cooperating closely with one another and form a special bond he termed the new "brotherhood of global jihad"—a network that would replace the base that had previously roamed in Afghanistan.[24] The term global jihad, Paz wrote, "marks and reflects the solidarity of a variety of movements, groups, and sometimes ad hoc groupings or cells" that act under an ideological umbrella of a radical interpretation of Islam. The interpretations themselves, he wrote, stem from developments in the Arab world since the 1960s, ignorance of principal elements of orthodox Islam due to secularization, and difficulties coping with Western modernization and its values.[25]

Paz believed that what helped make jihad a concept accepted on a global level was the adoption by more and more Muslims of the view that jihad is a religious duty designed to fend off a perceived global conspiracy against Islam. It also resulted from a growing acceptance by Muslims of the notion of the "non-territorial Islamic state"—itself an outcome of a more intense global interaction of different Muslim communities that helps strengthen the perception that Muslims are under threat. "The globalization of the reaction to this threat," Paz concluded, "has led to the doctrine of a global Jihad."[26]

Paz's analysis proved prescient. Most likely even before Operation Enduring Freedom, Al Qaeda, which could hardly have been surprised by the U.S. reaction to the attacks on the U.S. homeland, began to plan the dispersal of its fighters to the Afghan countryside, Pakistan, Central Asia, and their various home countries. In Pakistan, many Al Qaeda figures remained in the mountainous region near the Afghan border; others absconded to the larger cities like Karachi and Rawalpindi, where some key Al Qaeda figures, such as KSM and Ramzi Binalshibh, would be arrested in subsequent years. Some Al Qaeda leaders fled to Iran, aided most likely by the Revolutionary Guards.[27]

According to Michael Scheuer, who headed the CIA's bin Laden unit, Al Qaeda used its ties to Pashtun tribes and to Afghan heroin smuggling networks for its dispersal. It was also assisted by members of Pakistan's bureaucracy and Islamists in Pakistan's army and security services, Islamic NGOs, and insurgent and terrorist groups in Kashmir such as Jaish-e-Muhammad (JEM), Lashkar-e-Taiba (LET), and Hizb-ul-Mujahideen (HM).[28]

In forming the global jihad movement over the next years, jihadists benefited from and exploited the links they had made while undergoing training in Afghanistan or subsequent jihads that were fought in places like Bosnia and Chechnya. These common experiences and bonds enabled the exchange of ideas, knowledge, and experience. Thanks to shared funding, training, and logistics, as well as the benefits of globalization—notably a greater ease of travel and access to modern technologies and communication systems such as the Internet—jihadists would now be able to form a dedicated and empowered brotherhood that was truly global in nature and aspiration.

As Al Qaeda members and insurgents dispersed in late 2001, bin Laden transferred funds to jihadists with workable plans to attack U.S. and other Western targets of interest. One jihadist, Mohammed al-Tubaiti, reportedly received $5,000 from a bin Laden lieutenant. With the money, he planned to dispatch a cell to organize a suicide boat attack against U.S. and British warships in the Straits of Gibraltar. The attack was to occur in May 2002, but it never took place.[29] According to Burke, the SM on the synagogue in Djerba described in chapter 2 had also originated during the last days of fighting in Afghanistan in the fall of 2001. The bomber, Nizar Nawar, apparently received money and was sent off to perpetrate an attack while the Taliban collapsed. Several SMs that took place in Saudi Arabia between 2002 and 2004 were similarly perpetrated by jihadists who were directed by "Saudi Afghans."[30]

Saif al-Adel, one of the top lieutenants of Al Qaeda, confirmed the group's post-9/11 strategy to scatter and broaden the front of attacks against infidels and apostates. "Our plan was to spread in the territory and open new and several battlefronts with the Americans to disperse their forces and deny them the chance to focus on one region," he told Jordanian journalist Fuad Husayn. The dispersal was "very important for the project to survive . . .," he continued. "The young men who spread all over the world would open new battlefields with the Americans, polytheists, and hypocrites."[31]

In November 2002, while Al Qaeda continued to suffer the loss of key leaders, the group reportedly convened a strategic summit in northern Iran, at which the *shura majlis* decided that it could no longer act as a hierarchy. According to Spanish counterterrorism judge Baltasar Garzon, the summit was held without bin Laden present, but with many of the top leaders attending. The discussion was led by Abu Musab al-Suri, whose great impact on the global jihad was discussed earlier. Al-Suri suggested that Al Qaida was no longer capable of surviving as a hierarchical organization and would need to transform into a network, with operations spread out over the entire globe, carried on in large part by individuals rather than organizations.[32]

In retrospect, Al Qaeda's decision in late 2001 to disperse its members and fighters and to decentralize its operations—formalized in the meeting of the *shura majlis* in Iran in late 2002—guaranteed the group's survival in the face of massive military pursuit by the United States and its allies. Al Qaeda's diffusion, of course, had not been planned hastily. It was the logical consequence of a deliberate strategy to breed a network of affiliated fighters, cells, and organizations long before September 11, 2001. Since its years in the Sudan, the group had been *primus inter pares* in a network of affiliated and like-minded groups eager to wage jihad in places where Muslims were deemed to be threatened, oppressed, or besieged. September 11, as is sometimes argued, did not transform Al Qaeda from an organization into a network—Al Qaeda had been the leader of a network at least since 1992. The real shift that Al Qaeda was forced to undergo after September 11 was a relative and temporary shift in its center of gravity from the group's core leadership to the group's affiliates. Whereas prior to 9/11 it was relatively free to plan operations and lead an international terrorist network, its ability to do so after the September attacks was eroded to some degree. As its ability to conduct operations diminished (although never to the extent that it vanished altogether), the relative importance of its ability to send strategic messages—and hence serve as an *inspirational leader* of a *global* network—became even more important.

As a result of these transformations, and given Al Qaeda's loss of a safe haven and operational command post, the aftermath of 9/11 witnessed the relative increase in attacks planned and executed by Al Qaeda affiliates and associates, when compared to the period before 9/11. Even after 9/11, many attacks by Al Qaeda affiliates were planned with financial, operational, or material support of the remaining leadership of Al Qaeda, now often referred to as Al Qaeda

Central or Al Qaeda Core. The extent of this support was and remains different from case to case.

One factor that worked in Al Qaeda's favor is that the aftermath of 9/11 did not alter the fact that individuals who had trained in camps in Afghanistan were present in a multitude of countries in the world. In many cases, Al Qaeda–affiliated fighters had been present in these regions—including Africa (Somalia, Kenya), Southeast Asia, Chechnya, Kashmir, Central Asia, Western Europe, the Middle East, and North America—before 9/11. Training camps would soon re-emerge first in Central Asia, then spread to Asia, Southeast Asia, the Far East, and Africa.[33]

Now that the center of gravity of Al Qaeda shifted increasingly to its affiliates, Al Qaeda suddenly appeared not only as highly robust but also as a truly global network of terrorists and insurgents—one whose members were able to strike in such distant places as Aceh, Chechnya, Indonesia, Iraq, Kashmir, Kenya, Morocco, Saudi Arabia, and Yemen. In sum, Al Qaeda's forced reliance on local groups, brought about by the pressures exerted on the group after September 11, helped render the group more resilient.

The Global Jihad Movement after 2003

During the course of 2003, U.S. officials began acknowledging that Al Qaeda had survived the onslaught of the United States and was a reinvigorated entity, with bases of operations established in places like Kenya, Sudan, Pakistan, and Chechnya.[34] By 2004 the optimism reflected in the statements of American officials shortly after 9/11 vanished almost entirely. Reports that Al Qaeda had suffered a deathblow as a result of Operation Enduring Freedom and the war in Iraq, which began in March 2003, were reversed. More important, perhaps, was the admission—based in part on evidence gathered after the arrest of Mohammed Naeem Noor Khan, an Al Qaeda computer engineer—that Al Qaeda's senior command structure may not have taken as strong a hit as had long been assumed.[35] Officials now believed that Al Qaeda had retained some of its previous command and communications structure.[36]

Experts credited this resiliency to Al Qaeda's ability to continue to recruit, mobilize, and animate actual and potential fighters, supporters, and sympathizers.[37] Jessica Stern, for example, attributed Al Qaeda's survivability to its "protean nature,"[38] which involved the group's adoption of tactics of "leaderless resistance," used prominently by right-wing American extremists in order to evade law enforcement agencies. Popularized by Louis Beam of the Aryan Nations,

Beam warned that hierarchical organizations endangered the survival of insurgencies. Instead, he suggested, individuals and groups should operate independently of one another, and avoid reporting to a central headquarters or single leader for directions.[39] Bruce Hoffman likened Al Qaeda to the archetypal "shark in the water, having to constantly move forward, albeit changing direction slightly, in order to survive."[40]

Some analysts even believed—prematurely, as it turned out later—that Al Qaeda ceased to be an organization altogether and transitioned entirely into a movement.[41] Many of the analysts who predicted the death of Al Qaeda as an organization based their assessment on the investigation of the March 11, 2004, Madrid train bombings. Because the investigation of the Madrid bombings had failed to produce clear evidence of involvement by Al Qaeda's core leadership, some researchers believed that Al Qaeda had been completely replaced by "homegrown terrorism" consisting of self-radicalized Muslims and converts not dependent on the training and direction of a terrorist organization.

In February 2006 Director of National Intelligence John Negroponte testified before the Senate Select Committee on Intelligence and described the contemporary threat to the United States as the global jihad movement, which, the intelligence community believed, consisted of three different types of groups and individuals.[42] The first constituent part of the global jihad movement is Al Qaeda, "a battered but resourceful organization." Second, the movement consists of other Sunni jihadist groups, some that are affiliated, and some that are not. All of them, however, are allied with or inspired by Al Qaeda's global anti-Western agenda. Negroponte added that these groups posed less of a danger to the U.S. homeland than Al Qaeda, but they posed a growing threat to U.S allies and U.S. interests abroad. Further, these Sunni jihadist groups persisted in their attempts "to expand their reach and capabilities to conduct multiple and/or mass casualty attacks outside their traditional areas of operation."[43] Third, the global jihad movement consisted of networks and cells that are the "self-generating progeny of al-Qaida."[44] Negroponte went on to describe the origin, nature, and threat posed by these networks and cells:

> Emerging new networks and cells . . . reflect aggressive jihadist efforts to exploit feelings of frustration and powerlessness in some Muslim communities, and to fuel the perception that the US is anti-Islamic. . . . This has led to the emergence of a decentralized and diffused movement, with minimal centralized guidance or control and numerous individuals and cells—like those who conducted the May 2003 bombing in Morocco, the March 2004 bombings in Spain, and the July 2005

bombings in the UK. Members of these groups have drawn inspiration from al-Qaida but appear to operate on their own. Such unaffiliated individuals, groups and cells represent a different threat than that of a defined organization. They are harder to spot and represent a serious intelligence challenge.[45]

Negroponte's testimony strongly suggested that Al Qaeda's demise had been prematurely predicted. In early 2007, he reiterated that the entity was far from dead, and instead posed "the gravest terrorist threat to the United States."[46] Indeed, between September 11, 2001, and early 2007, Al Qaeda had been able to inflict massive damage by initiating or inspiring terrorist attacks in Egypt, Turkey, Morocco, Madrid, Iraq, the United Kingdom, Jordan, Saudi Arabia, Pakistan, India, and Indonesia. After 9/11, jihadists also regrouped in the Horn of Africa and made inroads in Afghanistan and Iraq.

No less important, between 2005 and 2007 the group managed to convince at least forty organizations to adopt Al Qaeda's focus on the far enemy and thus become an integral part of the global jihad movement.[47] Well-known examples include the merger of the Egyptian Islamic Jihad and the GSPC with Al Qaeda, but other, lesser-known groups have adopted Al Qaeda's worldview, too, such as Al Qaeda in Bilad al-Sham (Syria), Al Qaeda Organization in Lebanon, and Qaedat al-Jihad in Yemen.

Reports about the resilience, and even a "return" of Al Qaeda, appeared even more frequently in the course of 2006 and 2007.[48] The picture drawn by the reports was one of a growing reconfiguration of Al Qaeda on the Afghan-Pakistani border, where Al Qaeda had been able to establish a new safe haven. European intelligence agencies, for instance, reported about increased movements among jihadist recruits to the tribal area of North Waziristan, a remote area where Pakistani soldiers were unable or unwilling to exercise their authority. The poorly controlled terrain enabled Al Qaeda to establish training centers where some ten to twenty recruits per camp were taught skills similar to those that previous jihadists had acquired in training camps in Afghanistan. Although these new training camps, which recruit and train Westerners, including most likely U.S. citizens, did not reach the size and level of sophistication of the Al Qaeda camps of the 1990s, recruits nevertheless received valuable lessons in the construction of IEDs and suicide bomb vests, communication techniques, and, most importantly, jihadist indoctrination.[49]

According to several U.S. officials, Al Qaeda's renewed ability to regroup and establish training camps was a result of an agreement reached between Pakistani President Musharraf and tribal leaders in the area. Musharraf promised the leaders to withdraw troops from the area in exchange for the leaders' ending their support for cross-border attacks into Afghanistan by the Taliban and Al Qaeda.[50] The agreement, which collapsed during the summer of 2007, was widely regarded as detrimental to the ability to confront the militants with force. Other factors, however, have also contributed to Al Qaeda's ability to create a new safe haven in Pakistan. For one, the Iraq war has diverted crucial assets away from Afghanistan to Iraq, including Special Forces and CIA operatives, leaving the Afghan government in a weakened position to stabilize the country. A second major factor in Al Qaeda's ability to regroup along the Afghan-Pakistani border was the mobilization of Pakistani forces along the Pakistani-Indian border following an attack by Al Qaeda–affiliated Kashmiri separatist groups on the Indian parliament. After India had mobilized its forces along the border in response to the attack, Pakistan shifted hundreds of thousands of soldiers from the western border eastwards.[51]

In July 2007 a threat assessment by the National Counterterrorism Center titled "Al-Qaida Better Positioned to Strike the West" lent additional credence to claims of a reconstituted Al Qaeda. While the report acknowledged that Al Qaeda was still considerably weaker than before September 11, the authors of the report stated that the group was stronger than it had been in years.

Increasingly, leading U.S. officials suggested that Al Qaeda had coordinated closely—indeed, established a virtual merger—with the Taliban and established a haven along the Afghani-Pakistani border—a 1,400-mile-long mountainous stretch.[52] Another indication of Al Qaeda's renewed strength is its ability to upgrade its propaganda operations, with As-Sahab, its main production arm, distributing highly polished videos, sometimes within days of an attack.

At the time of this writing, most of Al Qaeda's leaders are presumably based in Pakistan, but also travel to places such as Afghanistan, and occasionally to Iraq, Turkey, Iran, the Caucasus, and North Africa. Much of the leadership of Al Qaeda has changed, when compared to the leadership that existed in September 2001. With the killing or capturing of many senior operatives in the months and years following the U.S.-led invasion of Afghanistan, lower ranking personnel have quickly taken their place and assumed leadership responsibilities, according to the testimony of CIA director Michael Hayden.[53] The new leadership continues to be dominated by Egyptians, most of whom are associates of Zawahiri, as well as a growing contingent of Libyans, including Abu Yahya al-Libi and—until his death in January 2008—Abu Laith al-Libi, a veteran of the Afghan-Soviet War who led Al Qaeda's retreat from Kabul after the U.S. invasion. More recently, he was believed to have organized the SM on the Bagram Airbase in

Iraq, which coincided with a visit by Vice President Cheney. Another key Libyan operative, Atiyah Abd al-Rahman, is believed to act as a liaison between Al Qaeda's central leadership and Al Qaeda in Iraq.[54]

Al Qaeda's Adaptive Strategy

In early 2006 Al Qaeda's top operational priorities, according to the U.S. National Counterterrorism Center, were attacks on the U.S. homeland and U.S. interests overseas, as well as on U.S. allies, in that order.[55] The strategy to achieve these aims, however, was subject to a number of adaptations. For one, the preferred targets after 9/11, and especially after March 2003, tended to be "softer" civilian targets that were not necessarily symbols of Western, especially American, economic and military power, as most targets up until that time had been. After 9/11, and especially after 2003, attacks against purely civilian targets such as dance clubs, restaurants, shopping malls, wedding ceremonies, and even funerals increased relative to attacks against more symbolic installations such as embassies, military bases, or financial centers. SMs planned and executed by jihadist groups in places like Bali, Riyadh, Morocco, and Iraq left no doubt that civilians now had become fair game.

A second element of the new strategy was the deliberate attempt by Al Qaeda and the global jihad movement to erode popular support for the United States by targeting mostly Western countries in what, per Al Qaeda's calculation, would result in a chasm between the United States and its traditional allies. Several books published in 2003 and early 2004 appealed to jihadist cells to adopt just such a strategy. One of these books, *Iraqi Jihad: Hopes and Risks*, was published on an Islamist Web site by The Information Institute in Support of the Iraqi People—The Center of Services for the Mujahideen. On eight pages of the book, the author made a case that Spanish troops present in Iraq should be attacked because Spain was the "weakest link" of support for the United States. Attacking Spanish forces, the author(s) argued, would be a useful starting point in a domino effect by which Al Qaeda would gradually erode Western support for the United States, thus isolating Washington. On December 8, 2003, the Global Islamic Media Front (GIMF) published a more explicit threat, hinting at the possibility of attacks against Spain outside of Iraq. Indeed, on March 11, 2004, three days before Spanish elections, Madrid was shaken by bombings on four commuter trains that killed 191 people.[56]

The strategy to drive a wedge between the United States and its allies is part of a growing political sophistication in the strategy of Al Qaeda. The SMs in Istanbul of 2003, which coincided with a Bush-Blair summit in London, and the Madrid attack's timing, which coincided with the Spanish elections, suggest that Al Qaeda is increasingly exploiting the political calendar in the West for its own purposes, thus becoming a more pragmatic actor. Al Qaeda's growing political activity was also apparent in April 2004, when bin Laden offered a truce to European countries, albeit not to the United States—an offer clearly designed to cause disagreements between the United States and its allies in the West.[57]

Norwegian terrorism analysts Lia and Hegghammer showed that Al Qaeda's growing political sophistication was reflected in the publication of a new genre of "jihadi strategic studies"—writings that draw on Western secular-rationalist sources; identify and analyze weaknesses of both parties; consider political, economic, and cultural factors in the conflict; and recommend realistic strategies. The writers of these tracts, which include such strategists as Youssef al-Ayeri and Abu Musab al-Suri, often refrain from long religious justifications of the need to fight the West based on the Quran and the Sunna and instead focus on practical strategies and tactics of how to wage that struggle. Lia and Hegghammer added that these strategic thinkers adopted an academic approach, constructing arguments in a rational and organized fashion, while extensively drawing from Western media and academic sources.[58]

Third, in 2005 Al Qaeda sought to significantly expand the audience to which it appealed, aiming, on the one hand, to widen the circle of individuals drawn to Al Qaeda and, on the other, to create rifts within infidel countries. In an essay published in February 2005 titled "The Freeing of Humanity and Homelands under the Banner of the Quran," Zawahiri, for the first time, attempted to appeal to a non-Muslim audience, thus trying to increase anti-Americanism among such groups as the antiglobalization movement and environmentalists or nuclear disarmament activists, that is, within the camp of the infidels proper. In a statement issued on July 27, 2006, Zawahiri called upon "all oppressed and wronged people in the world, the victims of Western oppressive civilization led by America: Stand by Muslims in the face of this injustice which humanity has never witnessed before."[59] In the same statement, Zawahiri even made overtures to Shias by praising Hizballah, a Shia organization, and invoking the names of Ali and Hussein, two of the most central figures in Shia Islam. In another videotape distributed on the fifth anniversary of the 9/11 attacks, Zawahiri further distanced himself from the bloody campaign that Al Qaeda's vice-regent in Iraq, Abu Musab al-Zarqawi, had waged until his death in June 2006. In the interview, Zawahiri suggested that Al Qaeda's central leadership had never initiated the infighting among Sunnis and Shia that had emerged in Iraq, adding that Al

Qaeda was too busy fighting the infidels. Repeating Al Qaeda's perennial efforts to unify the *umma*, he stressed that Muslims were "one nation, waging one war on multiple fronts."[60]

An interview broadcast on May 5, 2007, was a further sign that Al Qaeda attempts to widen its appeal among segments even of the American population, thus attempting to erode domestic support for the Bush administration while creating a rift among Americans. Zawahiri portrayed Al Qaeda as a group fighting on behalf of the oppressed of the world, including the oppressed in North America. He stated that Al Qaeda was not waging jihad "to lift oppression from Muslims only; we are waging jihad to lift oppression from all mankind . . .," but he still called upon the underdogs of the world to convert to Islam, "the religion of freedom and rejection of tyranny."[61] In the videotape, Zawahiri for the first time invoked Malcolm X, calling him a fellow Islamic struggler and martyr, while referring to Condoleezza Rice and Colin Powell as "house slaves." Zawahiri asked rhetorically why African Americans were joining the U.S. Army when they should instead turn against their own government, which continues to oppress them. Bin Laden hit on the same theme in a September 7, 2007, statement, when he invoked, seemingly for the first time, the African American icon, before calling upon Americans to accept Islam.

The fourth adaptation of its strategy, and one that mushroomed after 9/11, was the jihad movement's growing presence on and exploitation of the Internet. For Al Qaeda, this medium was the perfect tool for what has been traditionally its most important priority, namely to spread the spirit of jihad in as many countries and to as many people as possible.

Al Qaeda, the Global Jihad Movement, and the Internet

On April 28, 2003, a forum of 225 Islamist clerics, scholars, and businessmen established a new body of supporters of global jihad against the United States and the "Crusader West." They opened a Web site at the URL www.maac.ws in both Arabic and English. The secretary-general of this virtual body was Safar al-Hawali, a man regarded as a key mentor of Osama bin Laden.[62]

October 2005 saw the inaugural broadcast of *Sawt al-Khilafa* (Voice of the Caliphate), a television program announced as the new weekly Al Qaeda news broadcast to appear on the Internet. A masked newsreader presented the week's news from a Salafi-Jihadist standpoint, sitting next to a machine gun and a copy of the Quran.[63]

In September 2006 a group of Salafi-Jihadists launched a new Web site called

Electronic Jihad (www.al-jinan.org). Its stated purpose was to help organize an electronic jihad against Web sites that insult Islam. Their move was sparked by comments from an address by Pope Benedict XVI, which the jihadist Web site developers had found offensive. By June 2007 the Web site operators claimed to have launched successful attacks against more than fourteen Web sites that were deemed "un-Islamic" and "pro-Zionist."[64]

These examples tell an alarming tale of the role the Internet plays in the indoctrination and incitement of Salafi-Jihadist terrorism. The number of Web sites featuring radical Islamist and Salafi-Jihadist content have risen constantly after a spike in numbers in 2000 and numbered at least 5,000 in late 2007.[65]

No other medium of communication has been more important in abetting the rise of Salafi Jihad than the Internet, which serves not only as an instrument to wage terrorist operations but also as an important arena in which Salafi-Jihadist doctrine is formulated, attacks are planned, and new jihadist recruits are won. The Internet serves as a perfect tool to wage the war against its enemies in the media—a place where, by Ayman al-Zawahiri's own admission, at least half of the overall battle against the Crusader-Zionist foe takes place.[66] So far, Al Qaeda seems to have the upper hand in the cyberbattle. In September 2006, at the fifth anniversary of the 9/11 attacks, Paz declared, "global jihad has clearly won the battle over the internet. As a means of indoctrination, Al-Qaeda and its affiliates dominate this medium, while the West and the Muslim world have so far failed to devise . . . a serious 'counter-Jihadi' response." While the Western media community was "swimming in the sea of Jihadi web sites," the jihadists' response was "swift, technologically advanced, highly adaptive to changing situations, and consumed by the Western media as a serious source of information."[67]

Instrumental Use of the Internet to Conduct Terrorist Operations

INFORMATION GATHERING AND SHARING

Terrorists are widely known to engage in "data mining" on the Internet in order to gather information—and at times ideas—that will maximize the chances of success in the execution of terrorist operations. Such information may include data on how to produce weapons, maps and other detailed descriptions of critical infrastructure, details of access routes, troop deployment, and similar pieces of information. Terrorists use search engines, chat rooms, discussion groups, or social networking services like Friendster and MySpace to find information, maintain contact with each other, or build communities based on similar interests.[68] Web forums serve a similar purpose. Jihadist forums often include separate sections titled "jihadi cells" or "electronic jihad." Jihadi cell sections contain exchanges by forum participants related to information on military technology, requests for supplying and funding, or inquiries on how to join a cell in a distant country where jihad is waged. The electronic jihad section of Web forums contains updated instructions and warnings of penetrations of Web sites, as well as suggestions for terrorist attacks.[69]

One on-line magazine, *Technical Mujahed*, published by the Al Fajr Information Center, for example, is designed to disseminate technical information to jihadists about covert communications, secret transfer of information, the design of Web sites, and more operational tactics such as firing weapons. According to the editor of *Technical Mujahed*, the magazine aims at providing jihadists with a sense of security, vigilance, and confidence, given that many jihadists are allegedly hesitant to engage in electronic jihad for fear of being monitored.[70]

According to a recent report by the Norwegian Defence Research Establishment, the Internet's use as a global library containing training manuals and handbooks is the main function of the Internet for jihadist groups.[71] One such library is Abu Muhammad al-Maqdisi's *Tawhed* Web site, which serves as a repository of more than 3,000 books and articles written by jihadist authors. The articles have been downloaded tens of thousands of times, and many more copies have been downloaded to CD-ROMs.[72]

INSTIGATION AND INDOCTRINATION

As a tool of indoctrination, information spread through the Internet provides aspiring martyrs with the theological justification—and, indeed, the imperative—to join the jihad and act in the defense of Islam. In doing so, the global jihad targets its indoctrination particularly at the youth, a segment that is better-versed in the technology of cyberspace than any other group. In an article published in the Internet magazine *Sawt al-Jihad* on April 27, 2005, for instance, Sheikh Youssef al-Ayeri told mujahid youths not to ask their parents for permission to join jihad. At the same time, he calls upon parents not to prevent their sons from fulfilling their religious duty.[73]

As examples from the case studies in chapters 5 to 7 show, Salafi-Jihadist scholars and strategists appeal to Muslim youth to display a sense of duty, responsibility, honor, and manhood in the face of what they portray as the humiliation of the entire Muslim nation by a conspiracy of Christians and Jews. The Internet is used widely to disseminate movies and film segments in which the suffering of Chechen, Iraqi, and Palestinian Muslims is highlighted. Suicide bombers are being filmed as they drive their booby-trapped cars toward their targets, featuring a smile on their face and a thumbs-up to the camera. Oftentimes, songs venerating *istishhad*, or martyrdom, are heard in the background, while a voice calls upon the viewer to follow the example of other martyrs and join the struggle against the infidels. Humiliation and the suffering of women and children are particularly prominent themes and are often accompanied by gory pictures of slain babies and mutilated women.

As a technique that lowers the moral threshold of potential jihadists, the creators of these Web sites and the jihadists featured in the movies use mechanisms of moral disengagement such as dehumanization. Conspiracy theories—rampant in jihadist videos as they are in popular discourse in Arab and Muslim countries in general—serve a similar purpose, namely to lower the moral inhibitions that keep individuals from inflicting violence upon others. As one political scientist observed, conspiracy theories are easily conveyed on the Internet because this medium transmits irrationality more easily than rationality: "irrationality is more emotionally loaded, it requires less knowledge, it explains more to more people, it goes down easier."[74]

Instigation is one of the most important instrumental uses of the Internet for Al Qaeda and the global jihad movement and keeps this opaque formation tied to a common ideology. Its importance is second to none for the Al Qaeda core leadership because bin Laden has consistently repeated Al Qaeda's first priority to be the instigation to jihad of as many Muslims in as many regions as possible. Although Al Qaeda may not fund or manage the Web sites or their contents, Salafi-Jihadist articles and their messages of indoctrination are nevertheless a "valuable and ubiquitous force-multiplier for its program of propagation and incitement," as Scheuer notes.[75]

The instigation is not necessarily conducted by jihadist groups themselves, but increasingly by young, technically adept Muslims (and a growing number of converts) who are attracted by Salafi-Jihadist ideology. Perhaps the most famous young Internet propagandist was a twenty-two-year-old U.K. citizen of Moroccan origin, Younes Tsouli. Using an Internet alias, Irhabi007—*irhabi* being the Arabic word for terrorist—he set up a number of sites that hosted massive video files spitting out pro-jihadist propaganda. Irhabi007's specialty was hacking into ordinary Web sites such as the Arkansas Highway and Transportation Department, and then using those sites as hosts for large computer files—including videos of beheadings and suicide bombers. In addition to distributing videos of attacks, he also interpreted communiqués by Al Qaeda and disseminated a number of tutorials about how to hack Web sites while protecting one's anonymity on line. Toward the latter stages of his short career, Irhabi007 also seemed to have attempted to participate in actual terrorist attacks, according to information found on his laptop. Irhabi007 became such a legend among Internet jihadists that many subsequent users adopted variations of his name.[76]

For Western counterterrorism officials, a worrying trend is Al Qaeda's and the global jihad movement's increasing technical sophistication, coupled with its efforts to communicate to Western audiences. Al Qaeda's deputy leader, Zawahiri, appeared in highly sophisticated video productions at least a dozen times between 2006 and 2007. Increasingly, his messages were aimed at a Western and American audience, as evidenced by the translation of videos into English, Kurdish, French, German, and other languages. Al Qaeda's efforts to appeal to audiences in the West were underscored by the presence of Adam Gadahn, an American Al Qaeda member known as Azzam al-Amriki (Azzam the American). A convert to Islam, Gadahn appeared as early as 2001 in a videotape that commemorated Al Qaeda's successful suicide boat attack against the USS *Cole*. The propaganda film created in the aftermath of the USS *Cole* attack was Al Qaeda's first serious attempt to maximize the propaganda utility of successful attacks. The USS *Cole* propaganda movie was the first film for which Al Qaeda used As-Sahab (Clouds), its production company. As-Sahab would later also produce a propaganda movie of the 9/11 attacks.[77] After 2005 the number of its productions increased significantly. In 2005 it released sixteen videos, while in 2006 it produced more than sixty.[78] In the course of 2007, the production company disseminated more than ninety videos.[79]

As-Sahab is one of a large number of jihadist on-line media groups that have sprung up since about 2000. Some of them are tied to one entity only—such as Al Qaeda in the case of As-Sahab. Other jihadist on-line media groups, such as the GIMF and Al-Fajr, operate more independently, distributing material on behalf of a larger range of jihadist groups to Web forums. The media groups not only disseminate material but also verify that the material is authentic. Sometimes, they also interpret the distributed material, making them important agenda setters in the cyber-jihad.[80]

On-line discussion forums, rather than the media groups or official Web sites of jihadist organizations, appear to be the key nodes of what can be described as the on-line jihad. On the Web forums, active or aspiring jihadists discuss all matters of jihad, including issues related to ideology, or more technical issues related to forming a jihadist cell. These forums are usually password-protected, and they frequently change their URL address.

PLANNING

A third instrumental purpose of the Internet is its use for planning of operations. Data mining can be used for developing initial attack plans. The anonymity of the Internet makes it relatively easy for terrorist operatives to conceal their identities. Terrorists have also developed ways to encrypt messages. One tactic, known as "dead-drop," enables the passing on of messages without actually sending them. Dead-drop involves, first, the creation of an e-mail account, such as Hotmail. The sender of the message writes an ordinary e-mail message, but instead of sending it to the intended receiver, simply saves it as a draft. The sender then transmits the e-mail account name and password to the receiver during chatter on a message board. The recipient can simply access the e-mail account and read the message, which was never actually sent.

TRAINING

The Internet also provides a whole range of instructions for how jihadists and potential jihadists can wreak havoc on infidels and apostates thanks to openly available on-line manuals and encyclopedias that provide information on a range of activities needed to stage successful attacks. In the Al Qaeda on-line periodical *Muaskar al-Battar* (The Al-Battar Training Camp), for example, two senior Al Qaeda operatives described how to preexamine targets for attacks, remain vigilant during the planning phase, organize small, compartmentalized cells, mislead the enemy, and conduct surprise attacks.[81]

Technical aspects of training found on Web sites run the gamut from instructions on artillery and range-finding, the production of poison and chemical and biological weapons, suicide explosive belts, antiarmor shells, to the assembly of rockets. In mid-2005, for example, several Islamist Web sites featured a twenty-six-minute-long video containing detailed guides on how potential suicide bombers can produce suicide belts that are difficult to detect.[82]

In early 2003 a media organization known as Global Islamic Media—a precursor to the GIMF—issued a series of nineteen training lessons called *The Series of Preparation to Jihad.* The series was extremely popular on line and was also found on a computer belonging to a member of the cell responsible for the Madrid attacks.[83]

The Internet also performs the function of a virtual classroom for jihadi training, mainly in subforums found on jihadist discussion forums dedicated to training and preparations. According to a recent study, however, most of these training forums seem to be directed by amateurs, not experienced jihadists.

Moreover, new technologies are not shared on the Internet on a wide scale, probably because jihadists are aware that they may be tracked by investigators. The study concluded that personal, face-to-face encounters among terrorist operatives are still important when the newest technologies, such as IED technologies from the war in Iraq, are shared.[84]

RECRUITMENT

The Internet is also used for the recruitment of jihadists, including suicide bombers. Gabriel Weimann observed, for instance, that "Iraqi insurgents and their sympathizers are monitoring users of their sites, then contacting those who seem the most sympathetic to killing American soldiers, Iraqi military and others."[85] In other cases, small cells have formed among strangers who met on the Internet, or where personal connections made in real life have been nurtured in cyberspace.[86]

It appears that jihadist groups themselves rarely engage in the training of recruits on the Internet. An exception to that is Al Qaeda in the Arabian Peninsula (AQAP), which used the Internet in 2004 after a clampdown on its activities by Saudi security services. AQAP launched the previously mentioned on-line magazine *Muaskar Al-Battar*, which facilitated training and preparation of its fighters and attempted to instigate current and potential jihadists to use this knowledge to create additional camps and cells.

FUNDRAISING

The Internet has also become a popular fundraising tool for terrorist organizations. Given its global use, the Internet provides a sheer unlimited pool of potential recruits and financiers. Organizations openly raise funds on their Web sites, sometimes even using the popular on-line payment service PayPal.[87]

Terrorist organizations not only use the Internet for fundraising among its supporters but increasingly conduct identity theft of ordinary Web users, including the stealing of credit card information, to help them finance terrorist attacks. A resident of New Jersey, for instance, who was urged in an e-mail message to verify her eBay account information, unknowingly reached Tariq al-Daour, a young man in the United Kingdom who was involved in planning terrorist attacks in the United States, Europe, and the Middle East. Along with two accomplices (one of whom was Irhabi007), he used the stolen information to make purchases in hundreds of on-line stores totaling more than $3.5 million. They purchased items that would assist in the planning and execution of attacks. The woman's data first made its way to the black market for stolen identities and then ended up in Daour's hands. Along with Irhabi007 and another man, Daour also admitted in court to having incited Web surfers to murder innocent people. The investigation in the United Kingdom that led to the arrest of Daour and his two accomplices was the first successful prosecution for inciting murder on the Internet. It also revealed significant links between Islamist terrorist groups and cybercrimes.[88]

The Significance of the Internet for Jihadists

The Internet is not merely used by Salafi-Jihadist operatives as a tool to stage terrorist attacks but also fulfills several important needs for the rank and file. The Internet helps bestow upon those who want to feel part of a larger Muslim *umma* a sense of solidarity and identity, empowerment and pride, and a virtual utopia.

The Internet helps generate a forum where individuals who feel humiliated and jilted can regain a sense of community, solidarity, brotherhood, and a new identity. As Thomas Friedman writes, globalization has been kind to Al Qaeda "in that it has helped to solidify a revival of Muslim identity and solidarity, with Muslims in one country much better able to see and sympathize with the struggles of their brethren in another country—thanks to the Internet and satellite television."[89]

The Internet also bestows a feeling of empowerment and pride on many young and alienated Muslims because, thanks to the Internet and what Friedman calls "the flattening of the world," in which the playing field is leveled, small actors can appear larger than life. Regular posts on the Internet by terrorist groups or jihadist sympathizers can create a false image of a large volume of activity and, if picked up by Western media, can significantly raise the level of fear and anxiety among members of the target audience.

The Internet is also empowering to Salafi-Jihadists because it helps them celebrate such "victories" as the attacks of 9/11, thus humiliating their enemies while undoing their own humiliation, which they claim to have endured through centuries of perceived anti-Muslim policies and Western subjugation. On the fifth anniversary of the attacks of September 11, 2001, for instance, As-Sahab published a seventy-eight-minute propaganda clip called *Attack on Manhattan*. The pseudodocumentary tells the story of 9/11 from the perpetrators' perspective, and even included testimonies by two of the 9/11 suicide hijackers.[90]

In a more direct sense, the Internet also helps empower Salafi-Jihadists in that the restrictions that they tend to face in Islamic countries do not apply on the

Internet—a virtual space where anyone with access to a computer and an Internet connection can let their voices be heard.

The Internet also empowers Arab and Muslim women in particular. These women are oftentimes unable to participate in ordinary political life in their home countries due to restrictions and the strength and persistence of traditional, patriarchal, forms of social conduct. One researcher has pointed out that in the course of 2006, the number of Web sites devoted to female mujahideen (*mujahidat*) has sharply increased.[91]

For Salafi-Jihadists and other Muslims seriously striving to realize the global unity of Muslim believers in the form of an *umma*, the Internet presents itself as a virtual realization of such an imagined community. Sageman astutely points out that given the Internet's virtual nature, which has no earthly counterpart, the community becomes idealized as a just, egalitarian *umma*, "unified in an Islam purged of national peculiarities, and devoid of corruption, exploitation, and persecution. The appeal of this approximation of paradise can become irresistible, especially to alienated young Muslims and potential converts suffering from isolation or from ordinary discrimination."[92] The flip side of this virtual community, Sageman adds, is that the mass nature of this medium "encourages sound bites and other reductionist answers to difficult questions. Drawn to their logical conclusion, theses views encourage extreme, abstract, but simplistic solutions, without regard to the reality and complexity of life."[93]

CHAPTER FIVE

Suicide Missions from Afghanistan to Uzbekistan

In the aftermath of 9/11, the instigation of jihad continues to be the centerpiece of Al Qaeda's strategy. The evolution of the global jihad movement, with Al Qaeda at its helm, underscores the movement's success in spreading its message and inciting local individuals and cells to adopt violence for the sake of Allah. Much of this violence has taken the form of suicide attacks. This chapter provides an overview of SMs conducted by cells and networks affiliated with the global jihad movement. Many of the attacks described in this chapter have not been planned and perpetrated by Al Qaeda proper but by affiliates with varying degrees of ties to Al Qaeda. Also included are homegrown cells—some of which appear to have limited or perhaps no operational ties to Al Qaeda—that are clearly inspired by its message. Although the discussion is extensive, it is not exhaustive. Its main intention is to underscore the Salafi-Jihadist nature of many suicide attacks of the past decade.

Afghanistan

Suicide attacks were first introduced in Afghanistan with the killing of Ahmed Shah Massoud, the commander of the Northern Alliance, by a pair of suicide bombers on September 9, 2001. SMs had not been used in Afghanistan in the preceding decades, including during the Afghan-Soviet War. The tactic made its next appearance only in 2003, when two suicide attacks were conducted, followed by three SMs in 2004. The number of SMs then increased dramatically. In 2005, 17 suicide bombers detonated themselves in Afghanistan, followed by 123 successful suicide attacks in 2006 and 160 suicide attacks in 2007.[1]

By late 2007 the main perpetrators of SMs in Afghanistan were from the Taliban, although attacks have also been carried out to a lesser extent by Al Qaeda and by Gulbuddin Hekmetyar's Hezb-e Islami. Attacks are targeted primarily at the International Security Assistance Force (ISAF), which was deployed in the aftermath of Operation Enduring Freedom. SMs in Afghanistan also target the Afghan military and police forces, as well as softer targets such as government and community leaders, government workers, and politicians. Civilians, however, are the most affected segment. Although civilian casualties are low when compared to those in Iraq, innocent bystanders constitute the majority of casualties of SMs in Afghanistan.

The relatively few suicide bombings in 2005 targeted mainly military forces. The next year saw a dramatic increase in SMs as well as a number of highly dramatic attacks, including an attempt to assassinate U.S. ambassador Ronald Neumann and a successful suicide assassination of Canadian diplomat Glyn Berry in Kandahar.

High-profile SMs continued in 2006. In August SMs in Kandahar and Helmand provinces killed nearly 40 people.[2] In September 2006 SMs targeted an American military vehicle, killing sixteen; a provincial governor and close friend of President Hamid Karzai; a NATO patrol, killing four Canadians; and a security checkpoint near the governor's office in Lashkar Gah in southern Helmand.[3] In some cases, SM cells have used mosques to plan their operations and to store weapons and explosives.[4] In 2007 there was a steep rise in the lethality rate of Afghan suicide bombings. In June 2007, a bomb ripped through a bus carrying police instructors in Kabul, killing thirty-five people. On November 6, 2007, a bomb exploded in the town of Baghlan, killing nearly 80 lawmakers. The most lethal suicide bombing in Afghanistan to date occurred at a dog-fighting arena near Kandahar on February 17, 2008, which killed close to 100 people.

As in Iraq, SMs in Afghanistan are a tactic used in a broader insurgency waged against foreign forces and the local regime, which is perceived as a tool of the West. The goal of SMs appears to be to depose the present Afghan regime led by President Karzai. Suicide attacks are believed to be a useful strategy that can help undermine the regime's efforts to achieve its goals of stabilizing the country, while sapping the motivation of member countries of the ISAF to remain in Afghanistan through persistent targeting of the force's member states. As a result of the lack of stability created by ongoing attacks, the Taliban attempts to portray itself as the only group in the country that can provide security.

In its insurgency, the Taliban has benefited from alliances with several veteran mujahideen, including Hekmatyar and Maulana Jalaluddin Haqqani, the leaders, respectively, of Hezb-e Islami and Hezb-e Islami Khalis. This coalition is all the more dangerous as it has a number of seasoned fighters in its ranks—members of the Taliban who were not captured or killed during the U.S.-led invasion of Afghanistan in October 2001 and its aftermath.

Given long-standing historical Afghan opposition to foreign influence and occupation, the emergence of resistance to foreign forces in Afghanistan is hardly surprising. As Taliban spokesman Abdul-Hai Mutamen has pointedly explained, "the people of Afghanistan . . . never accept foreign dominance. . . . We want NATO and other foreign troops to leave Afghanistan as soon as possible."[5]

A study of the 158 suicide attacks carried out between 2001 and February 2007 by Williams and Young appears to support the notion that SMs in Afghanistan are targeted at the occupation forces.[6] Only eight attacks appear to be aimed primarily at civilians. Of these eight attacks, the Taliban apologized for two for causing casualties among civilians and denied involvement in a third case. In four of these eight cases, the civilians may have been "collateral damage," as the primary targets seem to have been military convoys or governmental representatives.

As in other cases, the Taliban uses SMs not only as a strategic weapon but also for its tactical benefits. Asked why the Taliban adopted SMs, the group's spokesman Mohammad Hanif told a Western journalist that "this is an effective way of destroying our enemy. It is a tactic that has been used by mujahideen all over the world."[7] In February 2007 Al-Jazeera reported that then–Taliban leader Mullah Dadullah presented the Taliban's "new weapon" that would confront NATO's "lethal weapons," namely the weapon of suicide operations.[8]

The Taliban has also recognized and applied the value of SMs to instill fear. In the previously cited report, Mullah Dadullah claimed that he recruited 500 additional suicide bombers for the coming spring. A day after a suicide attack near Bagram Airbase was staged while U.S. vice president Cheney was present about a mile away, Taliban commander Mullah Hayatullah Khan said that the Taliban sent 1,000 suicide bombers to northern Afghanistan, repeating earlier warnings that the group had prepared 2,000 bombers to help bring about a particularly bloody year for the coalition forces.[9] In early June 2007 a Pakistani journalist was invited to attend a Taliban graduation ceremony of suicide bombers who were said to have been trained to carry out attacks against Western countries, including the United States, Canada, and the United Kingdom. It was chaired by Mansur Dadullah, brother of Mullah Dadullah, who had been killed the previous month. In the tape, he threatened to unleash a wave of SMs against the West, asking why the Taliban should wait for the West to come to Afghanistan, when Afghans could take the war to the enemy.[10]

Suicide belts and vests are increasingly the preferred weapon of suicide attackers in Afghanistan, although car bombs are also used, and both yielded—at least until late 2007—a low killing rate in Afghanistan.[11] A field study confirms the relatively low technical aptitude of Afghan suicide bombers. In most cases, the bombers approached foreign convoys on foot or in cars, but were unable to inflict casualties on their targets. In several cases, the suicide vest exploded prematurely.[12] A follow-up study by Williams published in July 2007 provided additional details. It stated that in 44 percent of all SMs conducted in the preceding two years—a number equal to about ninety bombers—the only death caused by the bombing was that of the attacker himself. Ten additional bombers managed to kill only one person in addition to the bomber in the same time period. Williams explains that this low kill ratio could be due to a strong tribal code, Pashtunwali, that emphasizes acts of valor and revenge. As a result of this code, suicide bombers are more likely to attempt to strike at more fortified, military targets rather than maximize civilian deaths.[13]

Williams also found "considerable evidence" for the existence of an additional reason for the poor success rate of Afghan suicide bombers—a reason having to do with the nature and background of the suicide bombers in Afghanistan. Based on his field research, he concluded that it is highly likely that some suicide bombers in Afghanistan have been duped, are mentally deranged, or were merely acting due to financial payments promised to their families, which can reach up to $23,000. Thus, Afghan police told him about an individual who threw his vest at a patrol, expecting it to detonate by itself. Others were caught with sedatives or hallucinogens, which they were asked to take in order to calm their fears. A particularly telling story offered by Williams is that of an inept attacker who tried to push his booby-trapped car against the intended targets when it ran out of gas.[14]

Although attempts by Afghan officials to present suicide bombers as mentally deranged or duped by organizations should be approached with suspicion, similar findings were made in a study conducted by the United Nations Assistance Mission to Afghanistan (UNAMA). One failed suicide bomber interviewed by UNAMA analysts claims to have been deceived and coerced into the operation. He was allegedly given "tablets" that intoxicated him and had been warned that he would be beheaded were he to fail to comply with the request.[15]

Perhaps most disturbingly, UNAMA has concluded that at least some suicide bombers in Afghanistan are children, many of whom come from Pakistan. A fair number have been recruited in schools and madrassas situated on the Afghan-Pakistani border. The report cites a case in July 2007 in which a fourteen-year-old boy who studied in a madrassah in South Waziristan encountered two men who came to his school. They showed him and his classmates videos of "martyrs," taught him how to drive, and even let them ride on motorcycles. The men tried to persuade the boy to cross the border and kill an Afghan governor. After the boy walked for eight hours across the border, he found the handler, who threatened to kill the boy if he backed out. Various additional stories of the recruitment of children for suicide bombings in Afghanistan have been reported by other sources.[16]

Information about the composition of suicide bombers in Afghanistan has proved particularly difficult to establish. Afghans consistently claim that foreigners are responsible for what they believe to be an utterly un-Afghan tactic, and they oftentimes cite Pakistanis, Arabs, and Central Asians as likely suicide bombers. In terms of their origin, there are persistent reports of foreigners infiltrating Afghanistan in order to detonate themselves. In early February 2006 Afghan police arrested a citizen of Mali who apparently planned to assassinate a governor of a northern province. A Bangladeshi was reportedly arrested in connection with SMs a day later.[17] Rita Katz of the SITE Institute noted that in videos of SMs from Afghanistan the Taliban claim responsibility, but suicide bombers are heard speaking Arabic.[18] In October 2006 a report appeared in the daily *Al-Hayat* that a growing number of Saudis are joining the insurgency in Afghanistan,[19] while *Der Spiegel* reported in March 2008 that German authorities believe that a Turk from Bavaria, Cüneyt Ciftci, detonated himself on March 3, 2008, in Khost, thus entering German history books as the first suicide bomber from Germany.[20]

The most plausible foreign connection to suicide attacks in Afghanistan, however, is the one to Pakistan. In February 2006 the *New York Times* reported that transcripts of interrogations of arrested suspects believed to be involved in the series of SMs that rocked Afghanistan in the winter of 2005–6 revealed that the attacks were orchestrated from Pakistan by members of the ousted Taliban government. The suspects said that the bombers are recruited in the Pakistani city of Karachi and were then moved to safe houses on the Pakistani side of the Afghan-Pakistani border, before being transferred into Afghanistan. In November 2006 Afghan and NATO security forces said that frequently the trail of the organization, financing, and recruiting of suicide bombers in Afghanistan can be traced back to Pakistan. An Afghan intelligence official quoted in the same article said that suicide bombers in Afghanistan come from two different strands—those linked to extremist groups that have long been aided by Pakistani intelligence; and those allied with Afghan groups like the Taliban or Hezb-e Islami.[21] According to an October 2006 report in the *Sunday Times*, captured Taliban fighters and failed suicide bombers told Afghan security services that they had been trained by the Pakistani Inter-Services Intelligence.[22]

Interviews conducted by UNAMA officials with local intelligence, military, and police officials corroborated the suspicion that logistics for suicide operations were provided partly in Pakistan, whose Federally Administered Tribal Areas (FATA) and Northwest Frontier Province (NWFP) have undergone a "Talibanization" that attracts a growing number of militants, including those related to Al Qaeda. The militarization of the region, the long-established ties between Pakistani intelligence and the Taliban, and Pashtun identities that transcend the Afghan-Pakistani borders abet recruitment of operatives based in Pakistan who move to Afghanistan.

Despite the undeniable support structure that exists in Pakistan, the UNAMA report's authors did not absolve Afghans of responsibility for SMs in their own country. Bomb factories, for example, were discovered in Kabul and Kandahar, leading the authors to stress that their report "attests to the Afghan involvement in the supply of suicide attacks in the country."[23]

Salafi-Jihadist ideology is a clear influence on the Taliban, which has increasingly adopted Al Qaeda's global jihadist ideology justifying suicide attacks. The Taliban, which conducts the majority of suicide attacks, is part of the Hanafi Deobandi school and, as such, is not entirely congruent with Salafi-Jihadists. Yet, both the Taliban and Salafi-Jihadists share a common literalist understanding of sacred texts, and both believe that jihad should be waged to spread their forms of Islam. Traditionally, the Taliban focused its jihad internally, expressing a disinterest in foreign affairs. The Taliban's excesses in 2001, particularly the destruction of Buddhist statues in Bamiyan and the persecution of foreigners on Afghan soil, may have indicated the growing influence of Salafi-Jihadists on the Taliban.[24] Early bonds between the Taliban and Al Qaeda existed based on their shared traits (including a hatred of Shias), and these bonds grew after the mid-2000s.

A month earlier, at a time when the Al Qaeda–Taliban coalition was in full swing, Al Qaeda nominated Mustafa Ahmed Muhammad Uthman Abu al-Yazid as the general leader of Al Qaeda's activities in Afghanistan. Yazid had previously sworn allegiance to Taliban leader Mullah Omar, and Al Qaeda's move was an important gesture designed to show the Taliban the importance Al Qaeda places in a successful insurgency in Afghanistan.[25]

According to Waliullah Rahmani, a freelance journalist in Afghanistan, Al Qaeda and the Taliban published several books in which they call upon Muslims to join them and other Salafi-Jihadist groups such as Hekmatyar's Hezb-e Islami. In one series of these books titled *Zad al-Salam* (The Muslim Provision), they justify their tactics. The fourth series of *Zad al-Salam*, a 158-page-long tract, focuses on SMs. In it, the authors suggest that the legitimacy for the use of martyrdom operations is anchored in the Buruj chapter of the Quran, which stresses jihad, bravery, and the toleration of difficulties. Al Qaeda and the Taliban stress a particular part of the chapter in which Allah is said to prefer those Muslims who fight against threats to their religion. The authors also quote sayings of the Prophet Muhammad in which he promises paradise to those fighters martyred during the struggle against the infidels.[26]

Videotapes featuring the wills of suicide bombers are a relative rarity in Afghanistan, unlike Iraq and some other countries. The few that are known contain Salafi-Jihadist messages. One video that was released features the will of a suicide bomber who introduces himself as Amanullah Ghazi from the province of Khost. Ghazi decries the "infidels" who have "defiled" Afghanistan, where they are "misleading" Muslims from the righteous path. He then invokes *fard ayn*, the notion that each Muslim must join the jihad if Islam is under attack, saying, "it is the duty of every Muslim to sacrifice oneself in the path of God." Ghazi also urges other Muslims to follow his lead, adding that the Quran offers the martyr paradise: "Inshallah, I will meet you in paradise."[27]

Another video features an unidentified suicide bomber who attacked Canadian soldiers in October 2005 and shows footage of Osama bin Laden calling for the expulsion of "infidels" from Islamic lands through jihad.[28]

To motivate Afghans to fight the jihad, organizations use tactics similar to those used in Iraq. In particular, they attempt to appeal to young Afghans' sense of honor and manhood. According to a report published by the Jamestown Foundation, videotapes are played in madrassas for Afghan students in which Western women are shown wearing bikinis while going to discotheques. In addition, these seminary students are taught that Afghan girls employed by Western NGOs are sexually exploited by the male employees.[29] As in Iraq, this direct challenge to Afghans to protect their women's honor is likely to have a strong influence on their willingness to punish the alleged culprits with suicide attacks.

The Afghan insurgency seems to have copied much of the sophisticated media campaign used by Salafi-Jihadists in the war in Iraq. Prior to the U.S.-led invasion of 2001, the Taliban made little, if any, effort to wage a systematic media campaign designed to support the psychological battle against its enemies. Today, in contrast, the Taliban is relatively successful in waging a propaganda campaign, which includes the dissemination of news, incitement, and instruction for the insurgent and terrorist battle.

Algeria

On April 11, 2007, Algeria witnessed its first suicide attacks in a decade, when two suicide bombings killed 24 people and injured more than 220. Al Qaeda in the Islamic Maghreb (AQIM) claimed responsibility for the attack in an Internet statement in which the group provided details of the attacks and posted images of the bombers. One suicide bomber drove an explosives-laden vehicle through the gate of the prime minister's office, killing 12 and wounding 135. A second SM occurred at the police station in Bab Ezzouar, an eastern suburb of Algiers, killing 12 people and injuring 87. A man who called Al-Jazeera's Rabat bureau identified himself as a spokesman for Al Qaeda and said that the group also attempted to bomb the Interpol office in Algiers: "we won't rest until every inch of Islamic land is liberated from foreign forces."[30]

AQIM also took responsibility for additional attacks in the course of 2007, including a suicide attack in July, when a bomber blew up a truck inside a military encampment, killing ten soldiers; and on September 6, 2007, in a failed attempt to hit President Abdelaziz Bouteflika at Batna that killed twenty-two civilians. Two days later, AQIM suicide operatives drove a truck filled with explosives into a Coast Guard base in the eastern city of Dellys. Twenty-eight members of the guard were killed and several buildings destroyed in that attack.

On December 11, 2007, AQIM struck with a deadly pair of attacks. The first bomb targeted the Algerian constitutional court in the Ben Aknoun neighborhood of the capital. Ten minutes later, another bomb detonated at the offices of the United Nations. The bombs killed at least thirty-seven people, including a dozen UN employees. In its claim of responsibility, AQIM stated that the attacks were carried out to "defend the wounded Islamic nation [in] defiance to the Crusaders and its agents, the slaves of America and the sons of France."[31] The attackers were soon identified as Larbi Charef, aka Abdul Rahman Abu Abdul Nasser al-Assemi, and Rabah Bechla, aka Ibrahim abu Otmane. Charef, who detonated himself near the court, was thirty years old and had a history of trouble. He was raised in poverty in Oued Ouchayeh, a notoriously poor and rough neighborhood of Algiers. In 2004 police arrested him and accused him of providing logistical support to the GSPC. He spent nearly two years in prison, where he underwent a profound change, according to relatives. Bechla, the UN bomber, was a sixty-four-year-old man who had lost two sons to the Islamist cause. Suffering from cancer, Bechla was moribund when he approached the UN offices, having reportedly only days or weeks to live. Authorities described him as one of the oldest terrorists in the history of the nation.[32]

The roots of SMs in Algeria are inseparable from the country's recent history of savage violence, especially between 1992 and 1997. Salafi-Jihadists have been the main perpetrators of the violence in those years, beginning with an attack carried out on November 28, 1991, on a military outpost in Guemmar by a group headed by a veteran of the Afghanistan war, Aissa Massudi (aka Tayyeb al-Afghani).

Fighting and gruesome violence in Algeria were triggered when in January 1992 the Algerian government thwarted the all-but-certain victory of the Islamic Salvation Front (FIS), which was poised to win the elections for the National Assembly. The subsequent fighting between Islamist militants and the Algerian army claimed a total of about 100,000 lives. One particular violent faction was the Armed Islamic Group (GIA), an amalgamation of several Salafist groups whose ranks were filled mostly by poor, urban youth joined by Algerian alumni of Afghanistan. Many of its urban poor members were among the 40,000 Islamists who had been arrested and sent to detention camps in the Sahara, before being released in the summer of 1992.

In late 1992 the GIA's emir, or leader, Abdelhaq Layada, decried the fall of the caliphate in 1924 and called upon Muslims to proclaim that the struggle in Algeria was—similar to Afghanistan—a jihad in defense of Islam that required every Muslim's participation. Following Layada's arrest, the next GIA leader, Mourad Si Ahmed (aka Jafar al-Afghani) further escalated the violence and also forged connections with the global jihad. Two of these connections were to Abu Qatada al-Falestini and Abu Musab al-Suri, who edited *Al-Ansar*, a weekly bulletin, in London. Henceforth, they would publish the GIA's propaganda material in the bulletin.[33]

Under its next emir, Sharif Gouzmi (aka Abu Abdallah Ahmed), the GIA was strengthened when two other Islamist movements joined the group. Gouzmi's successor, Jamal Zitouni, took the war abroad. Under his leadership, the GIA hijacked a French Airbus in December 1994 and flew it to Marseille, where the hijackers were killed by French special forces. The GIA also began killing Algerian dissidents in France.

Internally, the GIA under Zitouni established the principle of *takfir*. In a publication titled *The Way of God: Elucidation of Salafist Principles and the Obligations of Jihad Fighters*, the GIA leader called upon Muslims to accept the GIA's Salafi Jihad or else face death. The *takfiri* line and the suspension of *Al-Ansar* on May 31, 1996, did not bode well for the GIA's future. Under its next emir, Antar

Zouabri, violence reached unprecedented heights. Taking *takfir* to a new limit, the GIA under Zouabri killed anyone who dared defy his authority. Undeterred even by the criticism of other Salafi-Jihadists abroad, he applied the principle of *takfir* to the majority of Algerians, arguing that they had "forsaken religion and renounced the battle against its enemies."[34] One of his few supporters was Abu Hamza al-Masri, who then headed the Finsbury Park mosque in London. Even he, however, distanced himself from the GIA when the latter officially declared virtually every Algerian an infidel in a statement in September 1997—the GIA's final communiqué. Under his rule, the war saw its sad climax, when indescribable massacres were conducted in the Ramadan months of 1997.

As a result of the GIA's indiscriminate killing of civilians, Hassan Hattab, a former regional commander of the GIA, founded the Salafist Group for the Call and Combat (GSPC) in 1998. Unlike the GIA, the GSPC claimed that it would limit its attacks to military and political institutions. Its stated goal was to overthrow the Algerian government and establish an Islamic state in its stead. In the late 1990s, the GSPC carried out a number of attacks aimed at government and military targets in the more rural areas of Algeria. The GSPC was also able to take over much of the GIA's external networks across Europe and North Africa and eventually eclipsed the GIA as Algeria's most dangerous outfit. In recent years, cells that had links with the GSPC hatched several terrorist plots across Europe, including in Germany, Italy, Spain, France, Belgium, the Netherlands, and Britain. Among the plots were planned attacks against the U.S. embassies in Paris and Rome, attacks on the Christmas market in Strasbourg, and the G-8 summit in Genoa.

On September 11, 2006, the fifth anniversary of the 9/11 attacks, Zawahiri announced the formal integration of the GSPC with Al Qaeda. The merger may not have come as a complete surprise, given the GSPC's earlier expressions indicating an ideological overlap with Al Qaeda. Even before Zawahiri's announcement, the GSPC had clarified that it was not focused solely on attacks against France but was a global jihadist group. Its fighters began spreading to Europe as early as 2001, and already in 2003 the GSPC had announced its full support of the 9/11 attacks. In May 2006 it even threatened to attack U.S. military bases in Mali and Nigeria, warning that planning for these operations was already under way.[35] In late January 2007 the GSPC renamed itself Al Qaeda in the Islamic Maghreb (AQIM), thus pledging allegiance to Al Qaeda and formalizing its transition from a local to a global jihadist organization.

From the point of view of Al Qaeda, the merger with the GSPC was significant for a number of reasons. For one, the merger created the impression that Al

Qaeda continues to appeal to Muslim groups and is thus successful in its efforts to "awaken" Muslims to join the battle against the far enemy—the United States and its allies. Although this successful inspiration is a key goal in and of itself, Al Qaeda also hopes for the process of awakening to create additional stress and fear among the West—or, in the words of Zawahiri, become "a bone in the throat of the American and French Crusaders."[36] The merger implied increased opportunities for Al Qaeda to rely on an enlarged pool of European jihadists in order to execute terrorist attacks, especially in the West. Al Qaeda is also able to exploit the working relationships the Algerian group has with criminal enterprises in Europe.

A few months after the merger, AQIM proved that it internalized its new identity as a global jihadist outfit. Communiqués released by the group in 2007 reflect the Salafi-Jihadist arguments proffered by Al Qaeda. The group's leader, Abdelmalik Droudkel (aka Abu Musab Abdul Wadud), began labeling France as a participant in the "Christian crusade" to dominate the Muslim world and deprive Muslims of their religious values.[37] In May 2007 he followed up with a logical step, issuing a statement calling upon Muslims to make a commitment to martyr themselves in the cause of Islam.[38]

In addition to the GSPC's suicide bombings in Algeria, Algerian jihadists have also been involved in SMs abroad. Apart from the GIA's hijacking of a French airliner in 1994, which it threatened to fly into the Eiffel Tower, more recent reports from Iraq persistently suggest that at least a portion of foreign jihadists there are Algerians, some of whom have become suicide bombers. Intelligence officials in Europe told the *Washington Post* in May 2007 that more than 100 Algerians are imprisoned in Europe after being detained on their way to Iraq or after returning from there.[39] Moreover, interrogations and wiretapping of terrorism suspects, as well as recovered documents, suggest that the GSPC/AQIM has associates in a number of European countries, including France, Germany, Italy, Turkey, and Greece—the last-named country a preferred entry point for terrorists to Europe due to its lax immigration controls.[40] A West Point study on the foreign fighters in Iraq based on captured documents disclosed that Algerians were the fifth-most-common group of foreigners entering Iraq with the purpose of waging jihad. Out of 595 foreign fighters for whom information on their nationality was available, 43 (7.2%) were Algerians. Of these 43, 22 listed their hometowns: 36.4 percent of Algerian jihadists in Iraq hailed from El Oued, while 22.7 percent were from the capital of Algiers. Constantine and Baraki each accounted for an additional 9 percent. Compared to other nationalities listed in the study, however, relatively few Algerians seemed to have intended to become suicide bombers. Only 5 out of the 36 Algerians (13.9%) who indicated their "work" listed "suicide bomber" as their intended mission.[41]

At least some Algerians can be expected to return to the country after gaining valuable experience in Iraq. Non-Algerians, however, are also streaming to Algeria to fill the ranks of the GSPC. According to a former leader of the Libyan Islamic Fighting Group (LIFG), Libyan Iraq war volunteers are joining AQIM in growing numbers.[42] After having been warned by the Libyan government against returning to Libya, many of these Iraq veterans are now heading to Algeria—a disconcerting development given the high proportion of Libyans among Iraqi foreign fighters as well as in Al Qaeda's leadership circles.

In the aftermath of the wave of suicide bombings in Algeria in 2007, which continued into 2008 with a suicide attack on January 29 in the town of Thenia, a fiery debate ensued about the legitimacy of suicide attacks. Following the attack in Thenia on January 29, 2008, which killed four and wounded an additional twenty-three people, five Muslim scholars from Algeria, Saudi Arabia, and Syria strongly condemned AQIM's use of "martyrdom operations" as "only increasing the Muslims' difficulties" and "having no religious basis." Although these scholars were quickly denounced by AQIM as "Bush's scholars" and "mouthpieces of the tyrants," AQIM nevertheless felt the need to justify its apparent intent to limit civilian casualties through focused targeting of police barracks.[43] AQIM's quick rebuttal indicates its sensitivity to ongoing accusations on the part of Muslims questioning the motives of the jihadist use of suicide attacks.

Chechnya

The first suicide bombing in Chechnya took place on June 7, 2000, when a Chechen man and a Chechen woman detonated a bomb-laden truck at a checkpoint on the compound of the elite Omsk OMON unit at Alkhan-Yurt in Chechnya. The suicide attackers received support from other rebels who hid in a nearby forest, and fired at the Russian forces after the explosion. Only four days later, a former Russian soldier who converted to Islam carried out another SM at a checkpoint in Khankala, killing two senior OMON sergeants.[44] Chechen rebels staged five more SMs on Russian positions on July 2 and 3, in which at least thirty-three soldiers were killed, eighty-four wounded, and six more were missing.[45]

From the very outset, the Chechen conflict had elements of a global struggle. Rather than attempting to keep the focus on its Russian enemy, the Chechen rebels noted on their official Web site (www.qoqaz.net) after their first SM that the operation was meant as a message to all Muslims. The operation, according to the rebels, "was a cry that said no to the crimes against the Muslim Ummah, but will the people of the Ummah heed to this call and rush to support their brothers and sisters who are in need? Will the hearts of the believers come alive with this example of pure faith and courageous sacrifice?"[46]

In the following years, several SMs were carried out by Chechen groups, most of them by the so-called Black Widows, an exclusively female group of suicide attackers that adheres to radical Islamist principles.

On December 27, 2002, three Chechen bombers driving a truck and a car devastated a government center in the Chechen capital of Grozny that housed a pro-Russian regional government. On May 14, 2003, a woman suicide bomber, who apparently intended to assassinate the pro-Russian leader of Chechnya, Ahmad Kadyrov, killed at least fifteen people during a religious festival in Ilishkan. The attack came only two days after a truck bombing aimed at a compound housing Chechen officials in Znamenskoye had killed at least fifty-nine people. Shamil Basayev, an Islamic warlord killed in early July 2006, claimed responsibility for both attacks.[47] Roughly three weeks later, another woman bomber detonated herself near a bus carrying military workers from the town of Mozdok to a Russian air base, killing at least eighteen people, including many women.

On July 5, 2003, two women detonated themselves at the entrances of the Tushino Aerodrome, a north Moscow airfield, during a rock festival attended by 30,000 fans. The blasts killed at least sixteen people and wounded perhaps four times as many. The bombs were equipped with ball bearings and metal fragments to maximize the effects of the blasts.

In 2004 suicide bombers detonated themselves in the Moscow subway in February and outside a subway entrance in August.

Altogether, some 40 Chechen suicide bombers have staged approximately 26 SMs in Chechnya and Russia between June 2000 and December 2005. If the two hostage situations of the Moscow theater and the seizure of a middle school in Beslan are included in the count—attacks that are not traditional SMs but where the attackers professed an expectation to die in the course of the attack—the total number of Chechen suicide attackers is 112, including 48 women and 64 men, who have claimed the lives of 939 people and wounded 2,913.[48]

Chechnya is a valuable case study in demonstrating how an originally localized conflict has adopted the global characteristics of Salafi Jihad. After the Soviet-Afghan War and the collapse of the Soviet Union that followed, Central Asian countries and the Caucasus were a favored destination for hundreds of recently unemployed Afghan Arabs, who wanted to re-create their victory against the Soviet Union. In the early 1990s, small groups of Afghan Arab fighters arrived in Chechnya, influenced by the conflicts in Abkhazia and Nagorno-Karabach. These foreign jihadists linked up with Shamil Bassayev, a young warlord, who spearheaded the jihad in Chechnya, along with the foreign jihadists' commander, Omar ibn al-Khattab. In the subsequent decade and a half, this small group would have a tremendous effect in shaping the conflict and the struggle against Russia that would far surpass their relatively small numbers.[49]

Along with their manpower, these fighters brought with them experience, money, and the Salafi-Jihadist ideology, which at the time was relatively unknown in the Sufi-dominated region.[50] Despite the predominance of the Sufi tradition of Islam in Chechnya and the relative indifference to Salafism, Salafi-Jihadist ideology was able to gain a foothold in Chechnya when the need for money to face the militarily superior Russian enemy became evident. That money was provided mostly by Saudis, with the understanding that they would be allowed to build mosques and schools in Chechnya that would promote Wahhabism.[51] The arrival of the Afghan Arabs was accompanied by the distribution of Salafist (known locally mostly as Wahhabist) literature, including the wide circulation of a book called *One God*, which rejected local cultural influences of Islam.[52] Foreign funds helped establish Wahhabist schools and mosques where students and preachers were urged not only to repel the Russians from Chechnya but to join the jihad against all infidels in the name of God.[53]

The Afghan Arabs and subsequent jihadists they attracted from a variety of places—some of the 9/11 hijackers, for example, had wanted to fight in Chechnya until they were ordered to participate in the planes operation of 9/11—were relatively scattered until 1995. In that year, the foreign fighters organized under Khattab, a Jordanian jihadist who had fought in Afghanistan and Tajikistan. Khattab had reportedly trained in Al Qaeda–affiliated training camps in Afghanistan and shared personnel and resources with the Al Qaeda leader. Once in Chechnya, Khattab, who was widely known as Barbarossa, became operations chief under Shamil Basayev, the overall commander, who had close personal ties with bin Laden.[54]

Following the end of the first Russian-Chechen War in 1996, foreign jihadis were able to expand their influence. The Chechen government, expecting the confrontation with Russia to resume at a future time, asked Khattab to establish a center in which both local and foreign fighters would be trained in such tactics as mine laying and ambushing, while receiving a Wahhabist indoctrination. Some 2,500 fighters were trained in these camps between the first and second war, according to estimates by Russian authorities.[55]

After 1997 a growing number of Chechen commanders adopted Wahhabism as their creed and slowly helped turn the Chechen struggle from one dominated mostly by ethnonationalist motivations to one in which nationalist motivations are joined by religious motives. This confluence of local and global characteristics is visible in the current, second installment of the Chechen-Russian War, which began in 1999.

Egypt

Beginning in 2004, a number of devastating SMs took place in Egypt, the birthplace of the Islamist movement. On October 7, 2004, three suicide bombers targeted two popular Sinai resorts, killing 34 people, including 13 Israeli vacationers, and injuring some 170 others. One suicide bomber detonated a car bomb at the Taba Hilton, which led to most of the fatalities. A second suicide bomber detonated himself at a bungalow campground at Ras a-Sultan near Nuweiba, while a third attacker died close by when his car bomb detonated prematurely before reaching its target.[56]

On April 7, 2005, a suicide bomber detonated himself at Cairo's main bazaar as he fled the authorities, killing two French tourists and a U.S. citizen. Nine months later on the southern tip of the Sinai Peninsula, on July 23, 2005, three powerful explosions hit the popular Red Sea resort of Sharm el-Sheikh, killing at least 64 people and wounding more than 150 in the deadliest terrorist attack in Egyptian history. Two suicide attackers detonated bomb-laden cars near the city's Old Market bazaar and the Ghazala Gardens Hotel on the city's beach front. A third suicide bomber detonated a suitcase filled with explosives near a taxi stand. Although several groups linked to Al Qaeda took responsibility for the attacks, and despite reports of heightened Al Qaeda activity on the Sinai Peninsula,[57] Egyptian authorities initially insisted that the bombers were Egyptians of Bedouin origin from Al-Arish, who had no apparent links to international organizations.[58] In March 2006, however, as the investigation into the bombings proceeded, Egyptian authorities reported links between the local Bedouin cell responsible for the bombing and Al-Tawhid wal-Jihad, a group with links to international Islamists. The authorities also suggested that the cell responsible for the Sharm el-Sheikh attacks were responsible for the 2004 bombings in Taba as well.[59]

The next major SM in Egypt again targeted the resort town of Taba on the Gulf of Aqaba. The attack, which occurred on April 24, 2006, killed at least twenty-three people and injured more than eighty and bore all the hallmarks of an attack organized by, or at least inspired, by Al Qaeda. Two days later, two bombers targeted Egyptian police and a U.S.-led multinational peacekeeping force, but killed only themselves in the process.

In 2006 Egypt sentenced three men to death in connection with the 2004 bombings in Taba, announcing that they belonged to Tawhid wal-Jihad, which, the prosecution charged, consisted of Bedouins from the Sinai who entertained Islamist views. Ten additional defendants were sentenced to shorter prison terms. All defendants pleaded not guilty, and several told the court that they were forced to make confessions under duress.[60]

It remains unknown whether the SMs in Egypt that began in 2004 have been planned and executed by local Egyptian Islamists, perhaps of Bedouin origin, nationalists, international jihadists like Al Qaeda, or perhaps a combination of local elements holding a grudge against the Egyptian regime and being guided by the steering hand of Al Qaeda. That Al Qaeda regards the Mubarak regime as apostate is undisputed. An attack on Egypt would certainly conform to attacks of traditional Salafi-Jihadist groups on the near enemy, as called for by radical Islamist preachers, such as Faraj and Zawahiri.[61]

Islamism has a long history in Egypt, beginning with the formation of the Muslim Brotherhood there and providing a long line of Islamist and jihadist ideologues from Banna to Qutb and Faraj. After their suppression by President Gamal abd-el Nasser during the height of Arab nationalism in the 1960s, his successor, Anwar Sadat, allowed the Muslim Brothers to return from their exile in Saudi Arabia in the mid-1970s. Like other regimes would do in subsequent years and decades, Sadat struck an implicit deal with the Egyptian Islamists: in exchange for their political support (including against more radical factions within the Brotherhood), he would allow the Islamists a significant degree of cultural and ideological autonomy. The agreement evaporated only a few years later, when Sadat went to Israel as part of his efforts to reach a peace agreement with the Jewish state.

After the assassination of Sadat in 1981, Egypt's militant Islamists split into two movements. The first, the EIJ, was led by Abboud al-Zomor and Ayman al-Zawahiri. A second faction, the Islamic Group (Gamaa al-Islamiyya, GI), was led by the "Blind Sheikh," Omar Abd el-Rahman. The two movements had the common goal of deposing the Egyptian government, but the groups differed in their ideology, goals, and strategy. The Blind Sheikh, who would later gain notoriety for his role in the first World Trade Center bombing of 1993, had a more inclusive vision of Islam, arguing that all of humanity was able to embrace Islam. This contrasted sharply with Zawahiri's approach, which held that those who did not agree with the radical tenets of the EIJ were infidels. Zawahiri believed that violence was the only way to crush the regime and establish an Islamist state, while the Islamic Group advocated a combined strategy of jihad and the *dawa*, the nonviolent call to Islam. Beginning in 1987, both groups were responsible for numerous attacks, with the GI focusing on attacking Christian Copts in the Upper Nile region. By 1992 the GI had entirely adopted a strategy of violence at the same time as it was able to vastly expand its presence in the Nile Valley. At that point, it encountered a fierce response by the government of Mubarak. The EIJ exploited the government's focus on GI for a surreptitious buildup of its power in Middle Egypt.

It cannot be ruled out that Bedouin elements, particularly those in the northern part of the Sinai, who are impoverished and whose relationships with the regime in Cairo have been particularly poor, have decided to adopt violence to express their resentment against the regime. Traditional resentments against the regime are harbored not only due to economic destitution—more than 90 percent of the local Bedouin population depends on low-paying, seasonal work—but also because of Cairo's interference in local and tribal affairs, a gross infraction in a region where tribal identity far outweighs national patriotism. Disillusionment and hostility toward the national government have led many young Bedouins to adopt Islam as their main identity.[62] If Bedouin tribes from the north are responsible for the bombings, as the Mubarak regime claims, it is likely that they were influenced by the message of Al Qaeda, and possibly received financial or operational support from abroad.[63]

Indonesia

On October 12, 2002, two suicide bombers affiliated with Jemaah Islamiyah (JI), a radical Islamist network that aims to create a regional Islamic superstate in Southeast Asia, bombed two nightclubs—Paddy's Pub and the Sari Club—on the tourist island of Bali, killing 202 people, including 88 Australian tourists. The attacks were conducted by a radical minority faction of the JI that split from the moderate majority of the group in the course of a leadership crisis between 1999 and 2000. The radical faction was led by Riduan Isamuddin, better known as Hambali, Al Qaeda's senior operative in Southeast Asia who also unsuccessfully planned a series of attacks (including suicide bombings) in Singapore. Hambali appointed an individual named Mukhlas to direct the 2002 Bali bombings and relied on the help of an additional dozen others. Plans for the 2002 Bali attacks began earlier that year in Thailand.[64] The attacks were funded by 9/11 organizer

Khalid Sheikh Muhammad (KSM), who transferred funds to Hambali. The planning of the Bali attacks lasted for about eight months and was facilitated by means of a local infrastructure of operatives from Afghanistan who had previously acquired operational experience. In deciding to employ the tactic of suicide operations, the planners were heavily influenced by Al Qaeda, who had long preferred SMs to maximize both casualties and the element of fear.[65]

Following the October 2002 bombings, one JI defendant said that the attacks were a result of imperialist, pro-Israeli, and anti-Muslim policy. Bin Laden, meanwhile, blamed "Australian imperialism" for the attack in a videotape he sent to the Al-Jazeera satellite TV station. Australian intervention in East Timor, bin Laden asserted, was a usurpation of Muslim land. Schweitzer believes that blaming U.S. policies was the result of indoctrination and training JI members received in bin Laden-sponsored training camps in Afghanistan.[66]

According to transcripts of police interviews made available in 2003, Imam Samudra, a prime suspect, told police that the attack meant to punish Australia for its close relationship with the United States and its involvement in East Timor's transition to independence from Indonesia in 1999. Samudra listed a number of other reasons for the attacks, including revenge for "the barbarity of the US army of the cross and its allies England, Australia, and so on." On a Web site that Samudra set up after the attack, he reportedly cited additional reasons, writing: "For all you Christian infidels, if you say that this killing was barbaric and cruel, and happened to innocent civilians from your countries, then you should know that you do crueler things than that."[67] In 2007, after three members of the 2002 Bali attack cell lost their final appeal against a death penalty, they issued a two-page statement through their lawyer. In it, they wrote that once executed, they would meet their lovers, their prophets, and their "beautiful angels." After their death, they continued, "the drops of our blood, God willing, will become a ray of light for the faithful Muslim people and a burning hell or fire for the infidels and hypocrites."[68]

On August 5, 2003, the JI offshoot staged another suicide operation at the JW Marriott Hotel in Jakarta, using a sports utility vehicle to maximize the effects of the blast.[69] The attack was financed by the same funds that KSM had transferred to Hambali for the previous year's attacks in Bali. The attacks at the JW Marriott were carried out by remnants of the radical faction around Hambali, who was in hiding during 2003. Muhammad Noordin Top and Azhari Husin, who had both been part of the cell that perpetrated the 2002 Bali bombings, planned and executed the attack. They were also responsible for another suicide attack conducted on September 9, 2004, in which two suicide bombers detonated themselves in a white delivery truck near the Australian embassy in Jakarta, killing 9 people and injuring 180.[70]

On October 1, 2005, three suicide bombers struck Bali a second time, killing twenty people and wounding some ninety. Many of the casualties were dining in the three restaurants that were targeted, one on a busy street and two located at a beach front five miles away. Indonesian security services blamed Husin and Top with masterminding this operation as well.[71] Husin detonated himself some five weeks after the bombings, when counterterrorist units closed in on his safe house in Java.

A thirty-four-page report titled "The Bali Project" that was found on Husin's computer shed some additional light on the October 2005 bombings. Investigators said they found no evidence of any link to Al Qaeda in the 2005 bombings, but there was compelling evidence that some members of Jemaah Islamiyah were involved in the planning and execution. The document described the targets of the operation as "foreign tourists from America and its allies," although, in effect, "all white people" would be considered the enemy. The bombers surveyed potential targets in Bali, including several fast-food chains, theaters, tattoo parlors, and nightclubs, but they eventually decided that restaurants were the most appropriate targets because they were frequented by foreigners and security was low. They chose two restaurants in Jimbaran and a restaurant at Kuta Square. The restaurants in Jimbaran added the additional incentive of being frequented by foreign businessmen whose death, the plotters believed, would have a "greater impact."[72]

Jordan

On November 9, 2005, at around 8:30 pm local time, three men and one woman walked into the Grand Hyatt, the Radisson SAS, and the Days Inn hotels in the Jordanian capital of Amman.[73] A few minutes later, the three men detonated the suicide belts that they carried on their bodies. The woman, thirty-five-year-old Sajidah Mubarak al-Rishawi, failed to follow suit after apparently leaving a crucial component of the device in the taxi that took her and one of the male bombers to the Radisson SAS.[74]

Four days after what came to be known as the Amman bombings, and to Jordanians as their own 9/11, the three bombers were identified as Ali Hussein, who detonated himself at the Radisson SAS; twenty-three-year-old Safa Mohammad, who attacked the Days Inn Hotel; and twenty-three-year-old Rawad Jassem, who blew himself up at the Grand Hyatt.[75] All of them, including Sajidah al-Rishawi, were Iraqis.

Nearly half of the fifty-seven people killed in the three attacks died at the Radisson SAS, where the bombers targeted a wedding of a middle-class couple. Twenty-five relatives of the couple were killed in the attack, in addition to a hotel employee and a member of a performing group. At the Days Inn, three Chinese citizens died. They were part of a thirty-five-member Chinese military delegation that was visiting the country.[76] All three affected hotels were popular with foreign visitors.

A subsequent indictment issued by Jordan's state security public prosecution mentioned a total of eight conspirators. Two of them were Jordanians, one of whom was the leader of Al Qaeda in Iraq (AQI), Abu Musab al-Zarqawi, and five were Iraqis. According to the indictment, the accused were members of AQI, a group that had tried to attack Jordan on numerous occasions, sometimes successfully.[77]

Prior to the Amman attacks, Al Qaeda had offered frequent warnings to the Hashemite Kingdom of Jordan because of its pro-American and pro-Israel stance. Islamists hold Jordan in contempt for signing a peace treaty with the despised Israeli neighbor in 1994. Since Al Qaeda's attacks on the U.S. homeland in September 2001, Jordan has provided logistical support to the United States in its war in Iraq, which included serving as the staging ground for many of the private contractors collaborating with U.S. forces in Iraq. Most important, perhaps, many of Iraq's military and security forces are trained on Jordanian territory and schooled by an American staff.[78] Many Islamists have been sentenced to death in absentia and scores of militants have been arrested in Jordan. In April 2004 Abu Musab al-Zarqawi claimed responsibility for a number of bombing attempts in Jordan and reiterated his interest in attacking the country. In December 2004 Osama bin Laden attacked the kingdom verbally in an audiotape released to Al-Jazeera, saying that ruling Arab families, including among them the "pagan-infidel" regime in Jordan, "defer to America and play their role in its treacheries. [The late Jordanian] King Hussein continued in the treacherous course set by his grandfather, Abdallah, son of Sharif Hussein, and his father too, against Palestine. And his [i.e., Hussein's] son, Abdallah II, follows this same course."[79]

Abu Musab al-Zarqawi, who helped organize the Amman bombings, was a Jordanian native with a long history of enmity toward his home country. He was involved in the assassination of U.S. diplomat Lawrence Foley in Amman in

October 2002, according to the indictment of the captured assassin. In neighboring Iraq, in August 2003 Zarqawi's group staged the suicide bombing of the Jordanian Embassy in Baghdad, which killed at least fourteen people. His most elaborate plot was to target Jordanians and Americans in Amman with attacks using chemical weapons against the Jordanian General Intelligence Department (GID), the Office of the Prime Minister, and the U.S. Embassy in Amman. The plot, for which Zarqawi recruited a cell leader called Azmi al-Jayousi, was foiled in 2004.[80]

The Amman attacks were in large part a political message sent by Zarqawi to the Hashemite regime.[81] Following the attacks, Al Qaeda in Iraq issued a statement:

> A squadron of the lions of the finest and noblest of battalions, the Battalion of the al-Bara bin Malik . . . undertook a new raid on some of the dens implanted in the land of the Muslims in Amman. After studying the targets and keeping them under surveillance, the choice of site for the operations to be carried out was made on some hotels which the Jordanian tyrant has made into the back garden for the enemies of the Faith—the Jews and the Crusaders, a filthy resort for the traitorous apostates of the [Islamic] Nation, a safe refuge for the infidel intelligence services who are directing from there their conspiracy against the Muslims, and springs of fornication and debauchery [designed] as a war against God and his Prophet.[82]

In a second communiqué released on the day after the Amman bombings and posted on several Islamist forums, the group justified its choice of targets. The posting claimed that the three hotels were targeted because they "have become favored centers of activity for intelligence apparatuses—especially the [intelligence apparatuses] of America, Israel, and several Western European countries —from which they wage their secret campaign, as part of what is called the 'war on terror,' in collaboration with the intelligence [services] of Egypt, the Palestinian Authority, Saudi Arabia, and the Jordanian traitor."[83] The communiqué stated further that,

> from these hotels, the Crusaders also operate the bases that they have established on Jordanian soil in order to train cohorts of apostates for the army of the infidel government in Baghdad. Consequently, they have turned into meeting places for officers of the so-called "NATO Alliance" which supervises these bases in order to turn the Muslim land of Jordan into a safe rear base for the armies of the Crusaders and deserters of the faith, [a base from which they] set forth to Iraq in order to kill Muslims, shed their blood, and violate the honor of their women, while the Jor-

danian scoundrel and others shed crocodile tears over them. Thanks to the wall of security around these hotels, they have become safe breeding grounds for the filth of Jewish and Western tourists, who spread their licentiousness and lechery at the expense of the blood and suffering of the Muslims in this land.[84]

A third communiqué posted on various forums on November 11, 2005, provided additional details about the attacks and further justified the bombings and the reason why suicide attacks were chosen as the modus operandi. It listed the noms de guerre of the four dispatched bombers and explained that "all the squad members . . . vowed to one another that they would die, and chose the most expedient way to satisfy Allah and receive what no eye has ever seen and no ear has ever heard [i.e., Paradise]. . . . Explosives belts were chosen in order to hit the targets with accuracy and cause the maximal number of deaths." Finally, AQI gave a warning to Israel: "The Jews should know that the separation fence they erected to the east of the Jordan River in the time of the British Empire is now within the range of the lions of monotheism . . . and it will not be long before they feel the wrath of the jihad fighters, who will not be deterred by the false rumors of the traitors and the lies of the perverts, and this will be the beginning of the salvation."[85]

On November 18, in the face of persistent condemnations of the attack by the Jordanian public, Zarqawi himself deemed it necessary to explain the reasons behind the bombings in an audiotape. He listed the following reasons for attacking the Hashemite Kingdom of Jordan:

1. The heresy of the Jordanian government, which declared war on God and his true followers
2. The regime's ties to Israel
3. The corruption—including "obscenity" (i.e., moral corruption)—that has spread in Jordan
4. Israel's influence in Jordan, and Jordan's encouragement thereof (citing as evidence the joint Israeli-Jordanian Qualifying Industrial Zones in Irbid)
5. The existence of secret American prisons in Jordan "directly supervised by the Jordanian intelligence apparatuses," and the torture and humiliation that the jihad fighters endure there
6. Jordan's active collaboration with the United States in its war in Iraq

Zarqawi also warned that his group would continue its attacks unless the Hashemite regime met a number of conditions, including ending the presence of U.S. and British forces stationed in Jordan; closing the U.S. and Israeli embassies in Amman; ending the training of the Shia police force in Iraq and the Iraqi army; closing the secret prisons for jihad fighters; and removing the Jordanian diplomatic representation in Iraq.[86]

The November 2005 bombings in Amman were hardly the first time that Salafi-Jihadists had planned to attack the Hashemite Kingdom with self-described martyrs. In 2004 Fahd Nouman Suweilem al-Faqihi, a Saudi national, attempted to blow himself up on the Saudi-Jordanian border.[87] In July 2005 a cell of five Iraqis, a Libyan, and a Saudi acting on behalf of AQI were involved in a plot to conduct SMs against Jordan's Queen Aliya International Airport, as well as hotels in the Dead Sea and the Red Sea resort of Aqaba. Four of them were arrested in February 2006. According to the charge sheet, some of the suspects rented apartments in Zarqa and Jabal Hussein, and they said they chose the hotels because they were frequented by Americans and Israelis. Authorities had also seized roughly seven pounds of PE-4A heavy explosives, which one of the suspects had concealed in a children's game in a rented Amman apartment.[88]

Mainstream Salafism has existed in Jordan at least since the 1960s. Many jihadists from Jordan, like those from other Arab countries, however, were radicalized during the 1980s, when a few hundred of them joined the mujahideen in Afghanistan in their war to oust the Soviet Army from their lands. Abdullah Azzam, who helped organize the arrival of Jordanians in Afghanistan, was himself a Jordanian of Palestinian origin. The Jordanians who went to Afghanistan to participate in the jihad against the "godless Soviets" were poorly educated. Eager to rid itself of problematic elements within its territory, the Jordanian regime encouraged the Jordanian contingent of the Afghan Arabs to leave for Afghanistan. One of them was a young man by the name of Ahmad Fadhil Nazzal al-Khalaileh, better known as Abu Musab al-Zarqawi.

When these Jihadists returned to Jordan from Afghanistan in the early 1990s, they came in the wake of 250,000 Palestinians who had arrived from Kuwait, which had expelled them for their support of Saddam Hussein during Iraq's invasion of Kuwait. Most settled in Zarqa, a poor town east of Amman that in subsequent years became a breeding ground for Salafists, as well as in Salt (and fewer in Irbid). Originally a place ravaged by problems of alcoholism and drug abuse, Salt witnessed a religious resurgence after the 1990s and subsequently produced many Jordanian suicide bombers and insurgents in Iraq.[89]

The returning "Afghans" were disillusioned at the sight of these Palestinians, and wondered whether this was why they had been fighting a holy war.[90] They also faced a generally high rate of unemployment in Jordan and were disappointed by the result of the 1991 Gulf War and the normalization of ties between Jordan and Israel. Because many faced problems integrating into Jordanian society, some went to Europe and became part of the European Muslim diaspora. Others went underground to organize themselves for the struggle against the "apostate" Hashemite regime.

The immigrants from Kuwait also included Salafi-Jihadist preachers such as Issam Muhammad Taher al-Barqawi, better known as Abu Muhammad al-Maqdisi, a key Salafi-Jihadist figure who would later become the religious mentor of Zarqawi. Once Maqdisi settled in Jordan in 1992, he traveled around the country to preach. Together with his protégé Zarqawi, he formed a group called Al-Tawhid (Unity of God) in 1993, which later became Bayat al-Imam. The group's aim was to mobilize the Jordanian returnees from Afghanistan.[91]

After forming Bayat al-Imam and as a response to it, Maqdisi and Zarqawi were arrested and transferred to a number of prisons, eventually ending up at Suwaqa prison south of Amman. Maqdisi became the emir of the imprisoned jihadists and published a number of books while behind bars. Zarqawi, meanwhile, deepened his religious education and increased the number of his followers. Many would die years later under his command in Fallujah and other places in Iraq.[92]

In 1997, when Zarqawi and Maqdisi were transferred to a prison in Salt, they established an informal recruitment network, using mostly petty criminals who went in and out of prison. Zarqawi and Maqdisi were eventually moved to another prison and released in 1999 as part of a general amnesty declared by the newly crowned King Abdullah.[93] Zarqawi left Jordan, first to Pakistan and later to Afghanistan. After his departure, and especially after 2004, Maqdisi began to criticize Zarqawi, warning him not to use violence as an end in itself.[94]

The attacks in Jordan are consistent with the ideology of Al Qaeda, including that of its Iraq branch, and with Salafi Jihad in general. In statements attributed to Zarqawi and Al Qaeda in Iraq, there are a number of recurrent themes. First and foremost is the notion that Islam is under attack by a Crusader-Zionist coalition that enjoys support from Jordan and other "apostate regimes." Real Muslims, the "defenders of the faith," must act in defense of Islam and help reverse the ongoing humiliation of its men, the pillaging of its cities, and the raping of its women. Indeed, communiqués issued by AQI are replete with calls to uphold the honor of Muslim men and women. The overthrow of Jordan and other apostate regimes is at the top of the Salafi-Jihadists' agenda because the ongoing control of Muslims by Western countries and Western institutions, such as the UN, the World Bank, and NATO, is perceived to be possible only thanks to the collaboration of these "treacherous" regimes that have sold out to the United States and Israel.

Morocco

On May 16, 2003, fourteen suicide bombers attacked a Spanish-owned restaurant, a hotel, a Jewish cemetery, a Jewish community center, and an Italian restaurant in the Moroccan city of Casablanca. Twelve of the attackers completed their mission, killing thirty-three innocent civilians in the process and injuring more than three times as many. According to reports, the perpetrators were loosely linked to the Moroccan Islamic Combatant Group (GICM). The cell responsible for the attacks had formed around a nucleus of Moroccan veterans of terrorist training camps in Afghanistan who regarded bin Laden as an inspirational leader.[95] The suicide bombers all came from Sidi Moumen, a squalid shantytown (*bidonville*) outside central Casablanca.[96]

The men regularly prayed in local mosques, where clerics preached jihad against infidels and advocated the severing of ties to the Moroccan establishment.[97] Their target selection, as well as subsequent investigations, has revealed that hatred directed against the Moroccan regime and an intense enmity toward Jews partly motivated the bombers. Religious fanaticism, combined with an expectation to reap rewards after death, helped convince the fourteen individuals to perpetrate suicide attacks. The bombers told interrogators that in the process of radicalization, they displayed a growing religious piety, in part as a result of the indoctrination by radical clerics such as Mohammed Fizazi, Omar Haddouchi, and Zakaria el Miloudi. They also met privately at the home of one of the suicide attackers, where they regularly discussed martyrdom and watched videotapes about jihad and self-sacrifice for God.[98]

In 2007 several smaller SMs took place in Morocco. On March 11, 2007, a suicide bomber blew himself up in an Internet café in Casablanca, injuring four people. The owner of the café said that the man was surfing radical Islamic Web sites.[99] Less than a month later, on April 10, three men sought in connection with the Internet café suicide bomber detonated explosive devices in the course of a police raid on their hideout in the Casablanca's El Fida district. The attacks killed a police officer and wounded twenty-one bystanders. A fourth man belonging to the group, Mohamed Mentala, was killed before being able to set off the IED he was carrying on his body.

Four days later, suicide bombers targeted the U.S. Consulate and an American cultural center in Casablanca when two brothers wearing explosive belts, Mohamed and Omar Maha, detonated themselves in coordinated SMs. Unable to breach the security barriers at the sites, the brothers managed to injure one bystander only slightly. The attacks were the first terrorist attacks on U.S. targets in Morocco.

Moroccan officials at first believed the bombers from March and April to be amateurs but later found out that they had stumbled across a sophisticated cell that planned to strike hotels, cruise ships, and other tourist targets.[100] At least three operatives within the network had trained in Al Qaeda camps in Afghanistan. The first, Saad al-Houssaini, known as "The Chemist," was arrested on March 6, 2007. The son of a professor, Houssaini studied chemistry in college and won a scholarship to attend graduate school in Valencia, Spain. While in Spain, he was radicalized under the influence of a Tunisian man who urged him to support Islamic fighters in Afghanistan. He left Valencia in 1996 and traveled to Afghanistan, where he remained until 2001. Besides being an expert bomb maker, Houssaini spent several years building a terrorist network that helped recruit Algerian fighters to Iraq. Eighteen Moroccans he helped recruit left for Iraq in early 2007. Thirty-eight years old at the time of his arrest, he helped found the GICM, an Al Qaeda affiliate, while training in Afghanistan. He later became the operational commander of the GICM. The second man, Abdelazize Benzine, is believed to be the right-hand man of Houssaini, while the third, Abdelaziz Habbouch, is believed to have played a leading role in the 2003 attacks, in addition to helping recruit Moroccans to Iraq.[101]

The nature of the connection of the Moroccan cell to Al Qaeda remains unknown. What is certain, however, is that Morocco constitutes an apostate country in the eyes of Salafi-Jihadists, as indicated by Osama bin Laden himself in a taped message released in 2003. Morocco sentenced Abdelkarim Mejjati, a former medical student from Morocco who died in a gun battle in Saudi Arabia in April 2005, to a jail term of twenty years in absentia for his involvement in the Casablanca attacks. A multilingual jihadist and skilled bomb maker of privileged upbringing, Mejjati was also believed to have helped organize the network that blew up three residential compounds for foreign workers in Riyadh on May 12, 2003. The *Washington Post* reported in 2005 that Moroccan investigators at first believed that the operation was conceived and planned locally. When they apprehended a suspect who divulged Mejjati's name to interrogators, however, they concluded that those responsible for the attacks were taking cues from Al Qaeda's top leadership.[102]

Apart from the successful SMs described previously, a number of suicide attack plots have been foiled by Moroccan authorities. In December 2002 three Saudi men were put on trial in Morocco for forming an Al Qaeda cell and planning to conduct SMs on NATO ships in the Straits of Gibraltar. Several months after the 2003 attacks, Moroccan security services foiled a plot involving thirteen-year-old twin sisters, Imane and Sanae Laghriss, who planned to blow themselves up first at a liquor store and then at the Moroccan parliament, using gas cylinders.[103] In the summer of 2006, another plan was thwarted when fifty-nine individuals were arrested on suspicion of planning to carry out SMs.[104]

Apart from their involvement in SMs at home, Moroccans have also become increasingly active in terrorist plots and attacks abroad, and many have joined the insurgency in Iraq or established recruiting networks in Europe with that aim. Moroccans were also among the Arab Afghans who went to Afghanistan during the 1980s and 1990s, and Moroccan nationals were prominently featured in the March 11, 2004, Madrid train attacks. Weeks after the Madrid bombings, seven individuals suspected in involvement in the bombing blew themselves up in the Madrid suburb of Leganes when Spanish security forces stormed their apartment. Five of those were Moroccan nationals.[105]

Three years later, in March 2007, Spanish security services broke up a cell that had trained more than thirty jihadists slated to be sent to Iraq to become suicide bombers. According to the Spanish National Police, the recruiter, a Moroccan named Mbark El Jafaari, urged the would-be bombers to avoid growing long beards and to dress in jeans and other Western clothes in order to arouse less suspicion.[106]

Moroccans appear to be among the most dedicated volunteers for suicide attacks in Iraq today. According to a recent study based on captured documents, a whopping 91.7 percent of Moroccans who have entered Iraq between August 2006 and August 2007, and who have indicated their mission preference, suggested that they hoped to become suicide bombers. Only 8.3 percent volunteered to become "ordinary" fighters.[107]

A recent study examining the evolution of jihadist terrorism in Morocco has concluded that three major factors have influenced the emergence of jihadist terrorism in Morocco: the influence of global jihad, the growing Islamization of the country, and deteriorating socioeconomic conditions.

In terms of the growing Islamization, the authors highlight the strong influence of the Saudi Wahhabi brand of Sunni Islam. The Moroccan monarchy entertained strong ties with Saudi Arabia since the mid-1970s for both financial and political reasons. Domestically, the expansion of Wahhabism in Morocco was endorsed by the monarchy as a counterforce to both domestic leftist and

Islamist organizations who challenged the legitimacy of the regime, as well as internationally to counteract the potential effects of the Iranian revolution on Morocco. Meanwhile, the steady stream of income from Saudi Arabia that accompanied the growing Wahhabi presence helped the regime finance its war in Western Sahara.[108]

Apart from the rise of Islamism and Salafism in Morocco, socioeconomic causes too appear to weigh heavily in the emergence of jihadists in Morocco. Morocco probably has the largest income gap among all the North African countries. The rates of unemployment and illiteracy are staggering and among the worst in the Arab world. Radical Islamist and Salafist ideas have nurtured especially in the impoverished suburbs of the larger cities, where radical Wahhabi preachers—many of whom were educated in Saudi Arabia—are dominating the mosques. Field research has suggested that "the influence of socioeconomic factors has contributed to the radicalization and recruitment of disadvantaged individuals who are particularly receptive to the inspiration provided by global jihad and jihadi Salafism."[109]

Pakistan

Suicide attacks, a rarity in Pakistan until 2002, are now a common tactic against the Shia community, foreigners, Pakistani government and military targets, and political figures. They increased drastically after 2007. Between 1995 and 2007, more than sixty suicide attacks took place in Pakistan, with fifty-six of these attacks occurring in 2007 alone.[110] The first occurred on November 19, 1995, when a suicide bomber rammed a bomb-laden truck into the Egyptian Embassy in the Pakistani capital of Islamabad, killing fifteen people and wounding at least fifty-nine more. The attack was carried out by the Egyptian Islamic Group and was targeted at Egypt rather than Pakistan.[111] The most lethal suicide attack in Pakistan was the first attempt to kill former Prime Minister Benazir Bhutto in October 2007 upon her return to Pakistan. Although Bhutto survived that attack on her life, the bombing killed 143 bystanders and wounded about 500.[112] Bhutto was assassinated in a second attack two months later, which combined gunfire targeted at the chairwoman of the Pakistan People's Party (PPP) with a suicide bombing.

Many SMs in Pakistan, especially between 2002 and 2006, had a strong anti-Shiite character. Tensions between Sunnis and Shiites in Pakistan flared during the 1980s in Pakistan, when Zia ul-Haq attempted to impose Sunni Hanafi Islam on a national scale, which led to revolts of the country's Shia population. A pro-

Iranian Shia party was established in Pakistan in 1980, prompting Iran's rival Saudi Arabia to subsidize organizations prepared to fight the Shia, as well as Deobandi madrassas in general. A number of virulently anti-Shia Deobandi organizations were established beginning in the mid-1980s, starting with Sipah-e-Sahaba in 1985. In 1993 and 1994, Harkat al-Ansar (renamed to Harkat-ul-Mujahideen in 1998) and Lashkar-e-Jhangvi were formed. Aided by Afghan Arab veterans of the Afghan-Soviet War supported by Pakistan, these anti-Shia groups also engaged in violent jihad against India in Kashmir, where many of the SMs took place before the tactic picked up in Pakistan proper.[113]

High-profile SMs against Shias, who account for roughly 15 percent of Pakistan's 140 million citizens, began on July 4, 2003, when three suicide bombers detonated themselves during Friday prayers at the Hazara Mosque in the south-western city of Quetta in an attack that killed forty-seven Shia Muslims and injured more than sixty. Lashkar-e-Jhangvi, a radical anti-Shia terrorist outfit linked to Sipah-e-Sahaba, was held responsible for this and many other attacks against Shia that were to follow. Other SMs on Shia mosques took place in February 2004, when sixty Shia died after two suicide bombers attacked a religious procession in Quetta; in May 2004 in Karachi, in an attack that killed fifteen and wounded ten times as many; as well as in October 2004, when thirty Shia were killed during Friday prayers in Sialkot. The attacks on the Shia spurred a number of Shia counterattacks on Sunnis, thus raising the specter of ethnic strife.[114] Similar attacks targeting the Shia community and its leaders occurred throughout 2005 and 2006.

The first Pakistani suicide bomber was a middle-class woman who, on November 6, 2000, entered the advertising section of Pakistan's most widely circulated newspaper, asking to place a small ad. She detonated shortly after placing a call on her mobile phone in which she was heard saying, "I am in the right place."[115]

Between 2000 and mid-2003, most SMs attributed to Pakistanis or to groups supported by Pakistan occurred in Kashmir or targeted foreigners in Pakistan. SMs were first employed by radical Islamist groups in Kashmir and India beginning in April 2000. On December 25, 2000, a twenty-four-year-old Muslim from Birmingham who had joined the Salafi-Jihadist Jaish-e-Muhammad (JEM), rammed a booby-trapped car into the Indian army's headquarters in Srinagar, killing nine people.[116] Almost a year later, on December 13, 2001, a spectacular SM targeted the Indian parliament, killing seven people. India blamed Lashkar-e-Taiba (Army of the Pure, LET), a group that had declared war on India and aims to drive the world's largest democracy from the predominantly Muslim region of Kashmir—a border area that India claims for itself.[117]

Over the next years, a number of radical Islamist groups would employ SMs against foreigners, Shia groups, and Pakistani government targets. On May 8, 2002, eleven French citizens were killed along with three Pakistanis, when a suicide bomber detonated himself in a car parked next to the Sheraton Hotel in the port city of Karachi, which is frequented by foreign businessmen. Some five weeks later, a suicide car bomb detonated outside the U.S. consulate in Karachi, killing eleven and injuring more than twenty. In March 2006 a U.S. foreign service officer, David Foy, and three others were killed in an SM. Additional attacks against American and other foreign targets were prevented by Pakistani security services.

Pakistani groups, perhaps aided by foreign jihadists, also made several attempts on the lives of key political figures. On December 25, 2003, two suicide attackers driving pickup trucks carrying some fifty pounds of explosives attempted to ram President Musharraf's motorcade on a main road in Rawalpindi. Musharraf narrowly escaped injury, but the attack killed seventeen people. The assassination attempt was the second on the Pakistani president in eleven days, and the third attempt on his life using SMs.[118] On July 30, 2004, Pakistan's designated prime minister, Shaukat Aziz, narrowly escaped an assassination attempt in a suicide bombing that killed nine people, including Aziz's driver.[119] On April 28, 2007, a suicide bomber who struck a political rally in Peshawar narrowly missed killing Pakistan's interior minister, Aftab Khan Sherpao, and his son, but killed twenty-eight bystanders. Sherpao, who was running for parliament, was again targeted by a suicide bomber on December 21, 2007. He again escaped the attempt to kill him, but the suicide bomber, who detonated himself in a mosque, killed forty-eight people attending prayer and wounded twice as many.

The assassination of former prime minister Benazir Bhutto in December 2007 was the sad climax of the stepped-up suicide bombing campaign waged by members of the Taliban, Al Qaeda, and other groups in Pakistan over the course of that year. The Pakistani government, as well as the U.S. Central Intelligence Agency, quickly blamed Al Qaeda–linked groups for the attacks, focusing on Baitullah Mehsud as the chief suspect, but in reality Bhutto did not suffer from a lack of other enemies with the desire and capability to kill her. She herself suggested on several occasions that individuals linked to the government had an interest in killing her. Unfortunately, the Bhutto assassination may never be solved.

Bhutto's assassination was preceded by a period of growing violence in Pakistan's tribal belt. Beginning in 2005, militants along the Afghan-Pakistani border began sending out suicide bombers to blow themselves up near American and NATO forces in Afghanistan. In the summer of 2006, SMs and the use of improvised explosive devices (IEDs) against government security forces also surged in Waziristan, in Pakistan's tribal belt. In the course of 2006, a growing number of SMs were carried out against targets in Pakistan proper, opening a new front that some observers believed was proof of a growing "Talibanization" of the conflict between the Pakistani government and militants. Most of these radical Islamists are members of the Taliban and Al Qaeda, who are working closely together, coordinate attack plans and pool their skills. They draw their membership from Arabs and Salafi-Jihadists from Western countries, but also from a larger number of Uzbeks, Tartars, and Tajiks and a growing contingent of Pakistanis.[120]

Al Qaeda, the Taliban, and allied movements roam predominantly in the remote, semiautonomous tribal areas of Waziristan, along the Afghan-Pakistani frontier, but they are also present in major cities such as Karachi, Quetta, and Peshawar. The concentration of militant Salafi-Jihadists in this border region (and increasingly in some major cities) underscores the fact that nation-state borders matter little in this region. Both sides of the Afghan-Pakistani border are dominated by ethnic Pashtuns, whose solidarity among each other supersedes their identification with the states whose territory they legally inhabit. For that reason, it is also difficult to differentiate between who are Afghans and who are Pakistanis, including when it comes to identifying many of the suicide bombers. Hundreds of thousands of Afghans who were displaced during the 1980s and early 1990s grew up in Pakistani refugee camps or lived and studied in the madrassas, making it extremely difficult to tell these two peoples apart. Taliban fighters in Afghanistan cross the border to Pakistan with relative ease. According to one British officer in Helmand, "round here the distinction [between Afghans and Pakistanis] is meaningless. Nation states don't really exist in the way we imagine them to."[121]

In September 2006 the Pakistani government, whose army had suffered set-backs in the tribal regions, signed a deal with tribal militants in Northern Waziristan. Although the government lauded the truce deal as a peace pact with tribal elders, the deal was reportedly cut directly with militant leaders, while tribal elders "did the militants' bidding."[122] The deal stated that the local tribal forces were to police the area and expel foreign fighters, while preventing additional foreign jihadists from entering the area. In return, the Pakistani military agreed to return to its bases. The militants, however, had no intention of honoring the agreements, and it thus had the opposite effect, allowing the Taliban, Al Qaeda, and allied Salafi-Jihadist movements to regroup in the area and institute strict versions of Islam in many of the areas now under its full control.

In July 2007, following a government crackdown on Lal Masjid, the Red Mosque, in which scores of Islamist radicals were killed, the Taliban renounced the truce, and an unprecedented number of SMs followed. On July 17 and ten days later, on July 27, suicide bombers killed a combined total of least thirty-two people in the Pakistani capital. In the months following the attack on the Red Mosque, pro-Taliban and foreign Salafi-Jihadist fighters waged a violent campaign against the Pakistani regime, killing 250 members of the security forces in less than three months. The Pakistani government, meanwhile, found itself in a dilemma. It was unable to defeat the jihadist threat militarily, but leaving them alone would enable them to plot additional attacks against Pakistan. Meanwhile, the Taliban–Al Qaeda alliance cleverly exploited the disarray of the Pakistani military and the paralysis of the Musharraf regime to spread its influence—and increase its attacks—on both Afghanistan and Pakistan, where it now waged open war not only at the regimes and their Western allies but also at locals who dared denounce the Salafi-Jihadists and their violent tactics.

A constellation of the Taliban, Al Qaeda, and other, lesser-known movements allied to them are believed to be the main perpetrators of SMs there. The bombers are often trained in ancient mud-walled fortresses, and their graduates travel both to Afghanistan and to Pakistan to detonate themselves or otherwise join the fighting. These various groups, Jason Burke believes, are not part of a single movement but rather "a new state without formal borders . . . a chaotic confederation of warlords' fiefdoms." Worse, Burke adds, is that it is now evident that Al Qaeda has been able to "rebuild a version of the terrorist infrastructure that existed in Afghanistan in the late Nineties."[123] *Newsweek* magazine put it even more bluntly by suggesting that Pakistan was more dangerous in 2007 than any other country in the world and had "everything Osama bin Laden could ask for: political instability, a trusted network of radical Islamists, an abundance of angry young anti-Western recruits, secluded training areas, access to state-of-the-art electronic technology, regular air service to the West and security services that don't always do what they're supposed to do."[124]

Similar to Afghanistan during the late 1980s and 1990s, a growing number of Westerners make their way to the region, too, where they often link up with one of the many Salafi-Jihadist organizations that have also nested in the area[125]—another phenomenon eerily familiar from the 1980s and 1990s, when it was

Afghanistan that offered a perfect ground not only for Al Qaeda but for a plethora of like-minded organizations to establish training camps.

Accompanying the rising influence of Al Qaeda is a notable growth in the appeal of Salafi Jihad, which, according to Burke, "has spread among the Pashtun tribes in both Afghanistan and Pakistan, providing a new language and justification for age-old resentments against central authority, buttressed by new ideas about 'the global attack on Islam by the West' and a powerful call to 'jihad.' "[126] One result of the growing appeal of the Salafi Jihad among locals is that Al Qaeda and a growing number of elusive associate groups are increasingly made up of homegrown militants bent on replacing Musharraf's government with a regime adhering to Salafi-Jihadist principles.[127]

One of these lesser-known militant movements is Tehreek Nifaz-e-Shariat Muhammadi, a Salafi-Jihadist group linked to Al Qaeda, and closely supporting it and the Taliban.[128] That group was likely behind an attack that killed forty-four military cadets in November 2006 in Dargai—the most costly SM against the Pakistani military up to that point. For the first time, ordinary Pakistanis were now subjected to what appeared to be an indiscriminate escalation of violence, with SMs being a preferred tactic.

Another group sending suicide bombers to Pakistan is led by Qari Zafar, who stems from the southern Punjab and is linked to the radically anti-Shia group Sipah-e-Sahaba and to Jaish-e-Muhammad.[129]

The SMs, whose number increased further in the course of 2006 and 2007, seemed devoid of a clear strategy. Some of them attacked government and military targets, in a clear attempt to hit the Pakistani symbols of power. Ever since President Pervez Musharraf made an alliance with the United States following the 9/11 attacks, Islamic militants of Salafi-Jihadist persuasion marked him as a potential target who deserved to die for his alleged treason to Muslims.

Other SMs in Pakistan's tribal areas, however, seemed to originate in sectarian, ethnic, and tribal differences, both between Sunnis and Shia, but also between competing tribes, and between Salafi-Jihadists such as the Taliban and Al Qaeda on the one hand and less extreme Muslims on the other hand.

Many of the SMs seem to be motivated by revenge for government attacks. Baitullah Mehsud, a former Taliban fighter based in South Waziristan who is believed to have sent several suicide bombers to Afghanistan and Pakistan, said that he began targeting Pakistan after the Pakistani military conducted helicopter strikes at a presumed hideout of his followers. Several attacks that followed were then attributed to him, including the assassination of Bhutto.[130] Mehsud, who is said to have close ties to Al Qaeda, now leads a coalition of local Taliban cells formed in December 2007 known as Tehrik-e-Taliban. The group is dedicated to the establishment of a Sharia-based regime in Afghanistan and Pakistan, while fighting the Musharraf regime and foreign forces in Afghanistan. According to several sources, he commands between 5,000 and 20,000 fighters (mostly from his Mehsud clan) and has hundreds of suicide bombers at his disposal.[131]

Revenge is a key element of the Pashtun tribal code known as Pashtunwali. According to Mushtaq Minhas, chief news correspondent at Pakistan's Aaj television network, "whenever a village or houses are bombed in tribal areas, it creates more suicide bombers. It's not just because they have been lured by a cleric with a promise of heaven, but it's also because of the Pashtun *badal* tradition."[132]

In 2006 and 2007 SMs against the Pakistani military and the security services have witnessed a substantial increase. On November 8, 2006, a suicide bomber detonated explosives in the midst of 130 Pakistani army recruits on a military training ground in Dargai, in northwestern Pakistan, killing 44 army recruits and wounding 20 more. It was the most deadly SM against the Pakistani military up to that point. The attack took place a week after an air strike on an Al Qaeda–linked madrassa in Afghanistan's Bajaur district that killed about 83 people. An unidentified caller told a journalist that "Pakistani Taliban" were behind the attack and were avenging the air strike in Bajaur.[133] In mid-July, a week after the Pakistani government raided the Red Mosque, SMs killed 24 Pakistani troops in North Waziristan and 14 recruits at the police headquarters in Dera Ismail Khan on the same weekend, and injuring a combined total of 70. In September 2007, a suicide bomber attacked a bus carrying workers associated with the Inter-Services Intelligence, Pakistan's notorious spy agency, killing 22 people. A week later, a bomber wearing a uniform breached commandos headquarters, one of the most secure army installations, killing 17 soldiers who were having dinner.

The attack on the Inter-Services Intelligence was a testament to the paradox of violence in Pakistan. During the 1980s and 1990s, it recruited, financed, armed, and trained many of the radical Islamists that now turned against their erstwhile supporters. Even more worrisome for the Pakistani regime, a growing number of Pakistanis appeared to focus their anger—and their attacks—on Pakistan, after having previously gone to Afghanistan to attack U.S. and NATO forces there. A growing number of Pakistani tribesmen from border regions and members of banned extremist Sunni groups were joining Al Qaeda's Pakistan contingent, according to the *Daily Times*.[134]

Radical Islamists and Salafi-Jihadists of Pakistani origin have also played prominent roles in SMs in the West. In the United Kingdom, three of the four London bombers—Mohammed Siddique Khan, Shehzad Tanweer, and Hasib Mir

Hussein—were of Pakistani origin. British citizens of Pakistani origin also dominated the composition of more than twenty would-be-bombers involved in the August 2006 plot to detonate airliners en route from Western Europe to the United States. Many of the suspects in that plot had close family ties to Pakistanis residing in Pakistan, suggesting an apparently close ideological and organizational affinity between British suspects of Pakistani origins and elements in Pakistan proper.[135]

Saudi Arabia

Saudi Arabia has long been a prime target for Al Qaeda and its affiliates, especially since the early 1990s, when the ruling family welcomed American troops on its soil. Saudi Arabia first became a target of suicide attackers in 2003. In May, three cells of members of a terrorist network supported by Al Qaeda in the Arabian Peninsula (AQAP), each consisting of between nine and twelve members, staged simultaneous attacks on three residential complexes in the capital Riyadh. The attacks combined traditional SMs with rifle attacks against the compound, which housed mostly foreigners consulting Saudi businesses and the military. The attackers first gunned down guards at the complex, thus clearing the path for the entry of bomb-laden cars driven by suicide operatives. Twenty-nine people, including eight Americans, were killed in these attacks.[136]

Additional SMs were staged first on November 8 of the same years at the Al-Muhi residential complex in Riyadh, which housed foreign workers. The attacks killed 17 people and injured 122. The operation was similar to the May 2003 attack in that rifle firing units cleared the way for explosives-laden cars.

Another attack occurred on April 21, 2004, at the headquarters of the Saudi special forces, which again took the form of a suicide car bombing, killing 4 people and injuring 150. An unknown group, the Battalions of the Two Holy Sites on the Arabian Peninsula, posted an announcement on an Islamic Web site claiming that it was "following the path of Bin Laden and Al Qaeda."[137] The attack was a turning point because, unlike in previous attacks, most casualties were Saudi civilian employees, leading many Saudis to condemn these attacks.[138]

In Khobar, on May 29, 2004, a cell consisting of four men attacked three Western oil company offices. Although it planned to detonate a suicide car bomb, the plan did not materialize and turned into a siege situation, in the course of which the attackers killed sixteen hostages, all non-Muslims. Seven months later to the day, terrorists detonated an explosives-laden car near the Ministry of the Interior through remote control, while two suicide bombers detonated a booby-trapped car that they tried to ram into a recruitment center of the Saudi Emergency Forces, which had recently begun to focus its work on counterterrorism.[139]

Following frequent calls by Osama bin Laden and Zawahiri,[140] Salafi-Jihadists have also targeted the oil industry in an additional effort to undermine the Saudi royal family's grip on Saudi Arabia and hit Western oil interests. A first SM against an oil-processing plant was foiled in February 2006 when Saudi security opened fire at two cars approaching the Abqaiq plant in the eastern Dammam Province, causing the vehicles to detonate. Shortly after the attempted attack, Al Qaeda assumed responsibility for the failed operation and promised to launch additional strikes on oil facilities to force "infidels" out of Saudi Arabia and prevent further "theft" of Muslim wealth by "Crusaders and Jews."[141] In 2007 Saudi authorities foiled another apparent SM against oil installations, as well as public figures and military bases in an arrest wave during which more than 170 suspects were taken into custody. According to a Saudi government spokesman, some of the individuals arrested trained as pilots in a neighboring country and hoped to use planes for SMs.[142]

AQAP was established by Saudi Islamists who went to Afghanistan in 1999 to join Osama bin Laden's training camps. Upon their return to Saudi Arabia, bin Laden and Saudi returnees established a sophisticated recruitment infrastructure with the support of local representatives such as Youssef al-Ayeri. In 2002 they were joined by additional Saudis returning from Afghanistan in the wake of the U.S.-led invasion of Afghanistan. Directed by bin Laden to engage in terrorist activities in Saudi Arabia beginning in 2002, Ayeri helped establish AQAP by building rural and urban training centers.[143]

Ayeri and another commander, Abdul Aziz al-Muqrin, were primarily responsible for importing the concept of self-sacrifice into the peninsula. Schweitzer concludes that "the adoption of suicide attacks as the leading mode of operation for terrorist activity in Saudi Arabia and the accompanying rhetoric appearing in claims of responsibility attests to the internalization of al-Qaeda's principles and ideology by its affiliates."[144] These principles were also reflected in a video statement released by AQAP's production arm, which featured Sheikh Sultan bin Bajad al-Oteibi (aka Abu Abdul Rahman al-Athari), who was reportedly killed in the attacks of December 29, 2004. Al-Oteibi laid out the reasons for Al Qaeda's sustained attacks on Saudi Arabia, saying, "at this time, traitors have come to rule us, servants of America . . . they betrayed noble Jerusalem and gave it to the Jews, and opened up the country of the Two Holy Mosques to the soldiers of the Jews and Christians. Muslims, these rulers have allied the Jews and Christians, and helped them against the Muslims." Al-Oteibi also suggested that the battle of the mujahideen extends far beyond Saudi Arabia: "As to our targets, and our path in battle: these pertain to the Jews and Christians. We will target their interests everywhere. We advise all Muslims and all wise infidels who are guarding these interests or who are working in them, to leave them and not even to come close to them. The Mujahideen might attack them at any moment."[145]

Following the first SM by AQAP, the Saudi regime clamped down on the group, severely weakening Al Qaeda's Saudi branch. Although the group would never completely recover, it managed to partially reorganize itself through a sophisticated public relations campaign waged mainly on the Internet.[146]

A socioeconomic study of members of AQAP in 2006 found that, at the height of the campaign in 2003, Saudi militants were overwhelmingly Saudi nationals, mostly in their late twenties, who came from different parts of the kingdom. Poor areas were not overrepresented, as most members belonged to the middle and lower middle class. Many seemed to have been unemployed or in unstable professions, and unlike other members of the global jihad, there were few engineers and doctors among the jihadists. The only common thread identified by Hegghammer, who authored the study, was that most jihadists had a previous experience with jihad in Afghanistan, Bosnia, or Chechnya. Those who went to Afghanistan were motivated by political, religious, or personal reasons. Many had wanted to participate in jihad somewhere, especially in Chechnya. Personal reasons included the loss of life of a friend or relative. Religious conviction also featured heavily. According to Hegghammer, "many seem to have gone out of a desire to meet the individual obligation of jihad and to achieve martyrdom, without paying much attention to the political content of their jihad activities."[147]

In terms of how the jihadists were recruited to join the jihad, the study states that there are indications that some may have radicalized themselves over the Internet, while others have become radicalized relatively quickly after watching images from Chechnya in 1999. Most importantly, however, the study points to the significance of social networks, as many jihadists prepared for their jihad together with friends or relatives. In terms of recruitment to AQAP proper, the recruitment was mostly a "top-down" process coordinated by senior commanders who systematically targeted returnees from Afghanistan. These returnees, in turn, were also motivated by a mix of political, personal, and religious factors that included "a genuine belief in, and desire for, martyrdom."[148]

Apart from staging suicide attacks in Saudi Arabia, scores of Saudis have also flocked to Iraq to conduct "martyrdom operations." Saudi suicide bombers in Iraq are discussed in chapter 7.

Turkey

On November 15, 2003, two cars exploded at the Beth Israel and Neve Shalom synagogues in Istanbul. Five days later, on November 20, two trucks detonated nearly simultaneously at the British Consulate and the local branch of HSBC Bank. The four bombings that shook Istanbul killed 58 people and wounded 750 others. The plot originated in a meeting in 2000 of four men on the outdoor terrace of Hassan Company, a textile factory in the center of the city on the Bosporus. The four men included Yusuf Polat, a Turk who sold socks and toys at an open bazaar, and Habib Aktas, a Turk from Mardin, an ancient city where Arabic is the dominant language. Aktas became the leader of the small group.

In the first week of September 2001, several Turkish jihadists, including Aktas, met Osama bin Laden in Kandahar, where they expressed their interest in staging a spectacular attack in Turkey for the sake of jihad. Although they declined to pledge allegiance to bin Laden, the Al Qaeda leader was willing to support the operation, and he instructed an Al Qaeda operative to deliver seed money to the Turkish guests after the meeting.[149]

The cell suggested staging an attack on a meeting of TUSIAD, the Turkish Industrialists and Businessmen's Association, which the group believed to include many "Jewish bosses." According to subsequent testimony by a member of the cell, the conspirators planned to hijack the two dozen assembled businessmen and collect a ransom. Should something go wrong, they would kill the hostages as well as themselves. It was Al Qaeda's notorious operations chief, Muhammad Atef (aka Abu Hafs al-Masri), who suggested using truck bombs instead, arguing that losing a group of fifteen men in one operation would be too much.[150] Bin Laden, on the other hand, recommended that to punish Ankara for its secular, "anti-Islamic" policies and its ties to the United States and Israel, the Turkish cell should unleash attacks on the Eastern Turkish U.S. Airbase at Incirlik and on Israeli boats that docked at Turkey's southern port of Mersin.[151]

Aktas, a Turkish citizen of Arab origin, became the crucial connecting link between Al Qaeda's core leadership and the local cell—a cell that was already in place at the time that Aktas met with bin Laden in September 2001. Aktas also provided the know-how for the bomb production.[152] During Aktas's visits to the burgeoning terrorist cells in Istanbul, much of his influence stemmed from his ongoing experience on the various jihadist battlefields, including Chechnya and Bosnia, and his known connections with the Al Qaeda leadership. He benefited greatly from the prestige of being in touch with the commanders, as well as his personal religious charisma as a jihadist practitioner. Confession reports show that local operatives viewed him as an almost holy figure.[153] Aktas hosted study groups, in which participants received lessons on the merits of jihad and learned to memorize the Quran. He also played videotapes to his audience that showed alleged crimes committed by Israel and the United States.[154]

By mid-2002 a slightly modified plot was under way. The cell, known in Turkish as El Kaide Turka, or Turkish Al Qaeda, revised its list of targets when it found that the U.S. Airbase at Incirlik and the U.S. Consulate and Embassy were too well guarded. The cell decided to strike at softer British targets instead. When the group learned that the port at Mersin was too closely monitored, it also changed its plan with regard to the attacks on Jewish interests, deciding instead to attack less heavily guarded synagogues in Istanbul.[155] Aktas rented an industrial workshop on the European side of Istanbul. Using a recipe that he learned in an Afghan training camp, he prepared an explosives cocktail based on hydrogen peroxide. Another veteran of Afghan training camps, Gurcan Bac, helped Aktas in the process, drawing on information also obtained from chats on the Internet. Once assembled, two tons of explosives were placed on each of four pickup trucks that were registered to relatives of the conspirators.

The cell leaders approached the suicide bombers privately. The four suicide bombers were all from the same town in eastern Turkey and had poor backgrounds that contrasted starkly with the image of the experienced terrorists. They had to be taught how to drive the trucks that were used in the suicide bombings. Two of them, Mesut Cabuk and Gokhan Elaltuntas, had traveled together to Pakistan. Feridun Ugurlu, the third bomber, had also been in Pakistan in 1996. Ugurlu reportedly used to spend hours underlining passages in radical Salafi-Jihadist books. The fourth bomber was Ilyas Kuncak, a forty-seven-year-old pious spice merchant. According to a friend of Kuncak, the fourth bomber used to be a communist once, "fighting against what he became."[156]

Another central figure in the plot was Louai Sakka, a Syrian Al Qaeda operative. Sakka provided a safe house to Aktas and other members of the Turkish cell in Aleppo, Syria, where several of the Istanbul cell members fled after the attack. Five months later, the group moved on to Iraq, where Sakka, now known as Louai al-Turki, participated in insurgent operations in Fallujah as a senior lieutenant of Abu Musab al-Zarqawi. He helped organize the insurgent attack on

Abu Ghraib, where two other organizers of the Istanbul bombings were detained.[157] While Aktas died in Fallujah, Sakka was arrested in the southeastern Turkish town of Diyarbakir on August 6, 2005. Two days earlier, his apartment had blown up when he was assembling a bomb intended for an attack using an explosives-laden yacht, which he wanted to steer into a ship filled with Israelis.

Turkey has long been a favored target of Islamist radicals and Salafi-Jihadists. Local militant Islamic groups such as the Great Eastern Islamic Raiders' Front (IBDA/C) and the Turkish Hizballah, as well as global jihadists such as Al Qaeda hold Turkey in contempt for a variety of reasons. Following World War I, Atatürk transformed Turkey into a secular state and abolished first the sultanate and then the caliphate in 1924. More recently, Turkey's orientation toward the West, such as its efforts to be included in the European Union; its status as the only Muslim state that is a member of NATO; its strong political, economic, and military ties to the United States and Israel; and its support of U.S. military engagements in Afghanistan and Iraq have provided Al Qaeda with a variety of incentives to launch attacks on the most democratic of Muslim majority states.

Transcripts of the interrogations of individuals involved in the plot provided additional insights into the motivations of the Istanbul cell. According to these transcripts, the cell aimed to "take action against American and Israeli targets and to break their dominance over Islamic countries," according to one suspect. Another suspect expressed the belief that the Islamic *umma* was oppressed.[158]

On February 16, 2007, a Turkish court handed down life sentences for seven conspirators—Louai Sakka, Haroun Ilhan, Fevzi Yitiz, Yusuf Polat, Baki Yigit, Osman Eken, and Adnan Ersoz. Thirty-one of the seventy-four people who were put on trial received lesser sentences, and twenty-six were acquitted.[159]

Turkey has in recent years become an increasingly important venue for Salafi-Jihadists. On May 3, 2004, for example, Turkish authorities announced that they had foiled a plot by members of Ansar al-Islam to bomb a NATO summit in Istanbul that was to take place a month later. The event was to be attended by several world leaders, including British prime minister Tony Blair and President George W. Bush. The police arrested a total of sixteen men and confiscated guns, explosives, guides for bomb making, as well as 4,000 compact discs containing training instructions by bin Laden. In December 2006 Turkish police arrested ten suspected Al Qaeda operatives after monitoring the cell for more than a year. The captives were preparing to conduct bombing attacks. The arrested men included an attorney who admitted being Al Qaeda's leader in Turkey. On May 30, 2007, eleven additional alleged members of Turkish Al Qaeda were arrested.[160]

Uzbekistan

In April 2004 the Islamic Jihad Group (IJG), an organization responsible for a number of violent attacks in Uzbekistan, carried out a series of SMs around Tashkent and Bukhara, in which forty-seven people were killed. The attacks targeted both political and civilian sites, including local government offices and a crowded market. An offshoot of the Islamic Movement of Turkestan (formerly the Islamic Movement of Uzbekistan, IMU), the IJG is on the U.S. State Department's list of Specially Designated Global Terrorist Groups. A statement in which the IJG claimed responsibility for simultaneous bombing attacks against the U.S. and Israeli embassies and the Uzbek prosecutor general reveals the Salafi-Jihadist nature of IJG:

> A group of young Muslims executed martyrdom operations that put fear in the apostate government and its infidel allies, the Americans and Jews. The mujahidin belonging to Islamic Jihad Group attacked both the American and Israeli embassies as well as the court building where the trials of a large number of the brothers from the Group had begun. These martyrdom operations that the group is executing will not stop, God willing. It is for the purpose of repelling the injustice of the apostate government and supporting the jihad of our Muslim brothers in Iraq, Palestine, Afghanistan, the Hijaz, and in other Muslim countries ruled by infidels and apostates."[161]

The bombers in Uzbekistan included several women, one of whom was nineteen-year-old Dilnoza Holmuradova, who detonated an IED strapped to her body at the Choru Market in Tashkent. Holmuradova did not fit the profile of the poor and uneducated suicide bomber. She came from a middle-class family and was a computer programmer. She was enrolled at the police academy and spoke five languages. At some point in 2002, she began adopting a strict form of Islam, after which she stopped wearing modern clothes and refused to watch television or listen to music. Together with her sister, they left home in January 2004, never to return.[162]

CHAPTER SIX

The United Kingdom and the 7/7 Bombings

On the morning of July 7, 2005, four explosions rocked London's transportation system. At around 8:50 am, three nearly simultaneous explosions hit the London Underground system in a Circle Line tunnel between Liverpool Street and Aldgate stations; in the Circle Line just outside Edgware Road; and in a Piccadilly Line tunnel, between King's Cross and Russell Square. Less than an hour later, at 9:47 am, a bomb carried in a backpack exploded on the upper deck of a No. 30 bus in Tavistock Square. The bombs vaporized the four suicide attackers and killed an additional 52 people, while injuring some 700 more. The four bombers were identified as Mohammed Siddique Khan, Shehzad Tanweer, Germaine Lindsay, and Hasib Mir Hussein.

The quadruple bombings in London on July 7, 2005, were the first major suicide attacks by Salafi-Jihadists against a European country on its own turf. Examining the London bombings more closely is important because Al Qaeda and the global jihad movement have stated repeatedly that Europe is a main battlefield in their struggle against its enemies. This chapter closely examines the 7/7 attacks, as they came to be known, from three perspectives: that of the bombers, that of the group, and that of the Salafi-Jihadist context in Britain.[1]

Who Are the London Bombers?

To many Britons, the most shocking fact about the four suicide bombers was that they were all British citizens. The official account of the bombings ordered by the House of Commons described the personal backgrounds of the bombers as "largely unexceptional," with the partial exception of Lindsay.[2] Tanweer, Khan, and Hussein were all second-generation British citizens whose parents were of Pakistani origin, whereas Lindsay was of Jamaican descent.

Thirty-year-old Mohammed Siddique Khan, who detonated his explosive device in the Circle Line outside Edgware Road, was the oldest member of the London suicide cell. He was from the Leeds area, married with a pregnant wife, and the father of an eighteen-month-old daughter. Investigators of the London attacks regard him as the senior and dominant figure and the overall ringleader of the cell who was responsible for identifying, cultivating, and supporting the other members. Khan is also the person likely to have liaised with Al Qaeda contacts outside Britain, including in Pakistan.

In Britain, Khan was employed as a "learning mentor" at a local primary school until December 2004, where many of his students perceived him as a "father figure."[3] According to the House of Commons report, he "developed a vocation for helping disadvantaged young people," and he worked part time in youth and community counseling while completing his degree.[4]

In the mid-1990s, Khan was part of a group of fifteen to twenty second-generation Britons of Pakistani origin known as the Mullah Boys. The group was known for kidnapping young Pakistani drug addicts and, with the consent of their families, keeping them locked up in an apartment where they were forcibly cleansed of their drug habits. The Mullah Boys turned more religious after 9/11.[5]

It is unclear precisely when Khan developed more extreme views, although his brother Gultasab contends that the transition was gradual rather than sudden. He told a reporter that his brother left the traditional, community-run mosque on Hardy Street when he found that it had nothing to offer him. According to Gultasab, "the people who ran the mosque had no idea how to connect with the second generation. . . . They spoke and wrote in Urdu, and the only time they interacted with the younger Muslims was when they taught them to recite the Koran by rote—in Arabic." Gultasab added that his brother was attracted to the Wahhabi approach, which was different. "They delivered sermons and printed publications in English. Siddique's Urdu was poor, so the only things on Islam he could read were Wahhabi-approved publications."[6]

Gultasab added that "Sid," as the 7/7 ringleader was known, had a run-in with his family when he insisted on marrying his future wife, Hasina Patel, whom he met while studying at Leeds Metropolitan University in 1997. She was a Deobandi Muslim of Indian origin whose background was directly opposed to Khan's family's Barelvi Islam.[7] Wahhabists and Salafi-Jihadists are likely to have appealed to Khan in part because their version of Islam was, in a way, more inclusive and was dismissive of the traditional Islam of his parents, which dictated certain terms regarding whom Khan was able to marry. Khan's eventual wedding to Patel destroyed his ties to his father.

By 2001 Khan was clearly very serious about Islam. He prayed regularly at work and attended mosque on Fridays, but he was not remembered as being aggressive when he spoke to colleagues about religion. He had spoken out against the 9/11 attacks in school. Some of his friends, however, remembered that there had been "a subtle change in his character" about a year after he began studying, when he became less talkative, more introverted, and slightly more intolerant about dissenting views. Still, teachers and the children's parents held him in high regard because he had "a real empathy with difficult children," helped calm down a number of distressed youngsters, and even managed to bring a few excluded students back into school.[8]

Shehzad Tanweer, the twenty-two-year-old bomber responsible for the blast between Liverpool Street and Aldgate Station, was from Leeds. His father Mumtaz, who is considered a pillar of the Pakistani community in Beeston, the working-class suburb of Leeds where Shehzad grew up, immigrated to Britain in 1961 from the eastern Pakistani city of Faisalabad. In the quarter century during which he had lived in the United Kingdom, he slowly built a business for himself that eventually included a slaughterhouse and a fish-and-chips shop. Mumtaz and his family, including Shehzad, lived in a large house, and Shehzad led a seemingly ordinary live. He wore brand-name clothes, worked out at a gym, took classes in martial arts, and played for a local cricket team, where he excelled. He studied sports science at Leeds Metropolitan University and occasionally helped out at his father's shop. Tanweer grew up in a pious, although not radically religious environment, praying five times a day and attending mosques regularly.[9] Although his dream had been to become a professional cricketer, at around age eighteen he apparently underwent a political and religious transformation in the course of which he began to feel distant from all things British. Around the time of the 9/11 attacks, he became more religious and began socializing with people who were convinced that Islam was besieged. According to one friend, "Shehzad definitely opened his eyes because of September 11. That's when many young people got back into Islam around here."[10]

Beginning around mid-2002, religion became a major focus of his life, and he increasingly lost interest in his studies. Nevertheless, nobody seemed to have observed that he became more and more extreme.[11] Together with Khan and Hussein, he began frequenting a local Islamic bookstore, the Iqra Islamic Learning Center. In December 2004 he went to Lahore, accompanied by Khan, where they stayed for two months and may have received terrorist training at a madrassa run by Lashkar-e-Taiba (LET), according to Pakistani intelligence officers.[12] He did not have paid employment at that point and was financially supported by his father, who wanted him to work in his business.

Germaine Lindsay, nineteen, who detonated himself in the Piccadilly Line tunnel between King's Cross and Russell Square, was the only one of the four bombers who had no Pakistani origins. Born in Jamaica, Lindsay came to the United Kingdom as a five-month-old baby, together with his mother. He did not have an easy childhood. His natural father had remained in Jamaica, and his stepfather had treated him harshly. His relationship with his second stepfather was better, but he left the family in 2000.

Lindsay was described as a bright child, and he did well both in school and in sports, and showed some artistic and musical talent. He spent his childhood in the outskirts of Leeds, and adopted Islam "zealously" about four years before the London bombings.[13] After his conversion, he began referring to himself as Jamal. His name change was part of a larger personal transformation he underwent after adopting Islam, according to some acquaintances. He turned away from some of his old friends, quit smoking, and stopped listening to music and playing soccer, while attempting to convert others to Islam. He began wearing the traditional white thobe, learned Arabic quickly, and attended mosque frequently—first the Omar Mosque, and later the Leeds Grand Mosque where, according to other worshipers, "he was an enthusiast of Arabic recitation of the Koran and prayed loudly and fervently."[14]

After his conversion, Lindsay socialized with known troublemakers and was disciplined for distributing leaflets in support of Al Qaeda. He apparently suffered a crisis when his mother moved to the United States in 2002, leaving Lindsay alone in his family home. After his mother's departure, he performed occasional odd jobs.

In October 2002 he married Samantha Lewthwaite, another Muslim convert, who bore him a child in April 2004. Lindsay worked as a carpet fitter at that point, although at the time of the London bombings he was unemployed.[15] After November 2004 Lindsay apparently underwent another personal transformation. Although he had previously avoided contact with other women, he began flirting with women openly and soon had a girlfriend. He shaved his beard, began wearing western clothes, and associated with petty criminals. After his wife realized that he had cheated on her, Lindsay left the house.

The fourth bomber, Hasib Mir Hussein, eighteen, of Leeds, who detonated himself on the No. 30 bus in Tavistock Square, was a tall and shy youth described by his classmates as "docile, until provoked," at which point he had a tendency to become violent.[16] Hussein attended college, where he enrolled in an advanced business program, but his academic achievements were poor, as was his attendance record.[17] He is also said to have smoked marijuana with friends.[18] He turned very religious around 2003, and his extremism intensified when he returned from a visit with his parents to Saudi Arabia, where he went on the *hajj*, the pilgrimage to Mecca. He became more openly supportive of Al Qaeda after the *hajj*, and stated frankly that, in his opinion, the 9/11 bombers were martyrs.[19] Around 2004 Hussein began to wear Western clothes again, and shortly before the attack he shaved off his beard, possibly to attract less attention to himself.[20]

The four bombers led a rather similar social life, which revolved around mosques, youth clubs, gyms, and an Islamic bookshop in Beeston. Tanweer and Khan had known each other from childhood, but over the years had lost touch with each other. As adults, they reconnected at a fitness gym and grew increasingly close to each other. After Hussein befriended Tanweer and Khan, the three formed a clique and spent much time in a local youth club and an Islamic bookshop. In the second half of 2004, Khan and Lindsay became close associates.

Motives and Justifications of the Bombers

Justifications for the Bombings

The bombers were from Beeston and the neighboring district of Holbeck on the outskirts of Leeds. Beeston, a densely populated working-class neighborhood in Leeds, is also one of the more culturally diverse districts of the city. Beeston has a relatively high rate of unemployment, 7.8 percent (vis-à-vis 3.3 percent in Leeds at large). About a third of the population receives the British equivalent of welfare.[21] Khan, Hussein, and Tanweer, however, were not poor by the standards of the area. It is widely known that Tanweer, who was especially well-off by local standards, received a red Mercedes from his father as a present.

Thus, the main motive of the London bombers did not result from unemployment or poverty. A far more likely factor influencing their radicalization is a severe crisis of identity typical of many second- and third-generation immigrants in Europe today. Muslims in the United Kingdom, their parents, and/or grandparents overwhelmingly hail from Pakistan, Bangladesh, and India.

Children and grandchildren of the original immigrants from the Indian subcontinent often report that they do not quite know where they belong. The expectation that they should adapt to Western life-styles clashes head on with their parents' or grandparents' more traditional upbringing, creating intergenerational tensions. Some have tried to adopt a British identity, but in many working-class neighborhoods, this attempt has often been synonymous with sexual promiscuity, drinking of alcohol, and drug usage. Many second- and third-generation immigrants have sought proficiency in martial arts and boxing in these neighborhoods and frequently divide into gangs. One young Muslim from Beeston said that unlike their parents, youths today are not passive; they will fight for their rights. In the context of Beeston, youngsters told a reporter, Islam saved them from Britain.[22]

In the absence of a clear identity, these young Muslims appear to be searching for an alternative identity, which a growing number of them seem to find in Islam. According to a poll published in July 2006, for example, four out of five Muslims in the United Kingdom identified themselves first as Muslims, while only 7 percent saw themselves as British citizens first—a much higher percentage than their coreligionists in the United States, France, Germany, or Spain.[23]

A more interesting and perhaps revealing angle is an examination of how the suicide bombers justified their actions, and how the larger community of Salafi-Jihadists views the world around them and their own place in it. At least two of the bombers, Khan and Tanweer, recorded their wills on tapes, which were published along with footage featuring Al Qaeda's deputy leader, Ayman al-Zawahiri. Their words, along with statements by other Salafi-Jihadists residing in the United Kingdom, paint a picture of the mental universe of the bombers.

The London bombers regard themselves first and foremost as Muslims, and they claim to act in the name of, and in the interest of, their religion. In the words of Tanweer, in an audiotape released on the first anniversary of the London bombings, "We are 100 percent committed to the cause of Islam."[24] However, a closer look at the statements of the bombers reveals that their beliefs are more closely aligned to Salafi-Jihadist ideology than to Islam per se. In their video statements, Khan and Tanweer reflect nearly all central tenets of the Salafi Jihad. First and foremost, they perceive Islam to be under attack from the West, and they believe that it is their duty to defend their religion against this onslaught for the sake of protecting the Muslim community, but also in order to avenge the perceived cruelties committed by the West. According to Khan, "Your democratically elected governments continuously perpetuate atrocities against my people all over the world. And your support of them makes you directly responsible, just as I am directly responsible for protecting and avenging my Muslim brothers and sisters. Until we feel security, you will be our targets."[25]

The list of alleged atrocities against Muslims is rather long. Tanweer, for example, accuses non-Muslim U.K. citizens of being

> those who have voted in your government, who in turn have, and still continue to this day, continue to oppress our mothers, children, brothers and sisters, from the east to the west, in Palestine, Afghanistan, Iraq, and Chechnya. Your government has openly supported the genocide of over 150,000 innocent Muslims in Falluja . . . You have offered financial and military support to the U.S. and Israel, in the massacre of our children in Palestine. You are directly responsible for the problems in Palestine, Afghanistan, and Iraq to this day. You have openly declared war on Islam, and are the forerunners in the crusade against the Muslims.[26]

The bombers clearly want the West, in this case U.K. citizens, to have a taste of its own medicine. Khan, for instance, warns that "until you stop the bombing, gassing, imprisonment and torture of my people we will not stop this fight. We are at war and I am a soldier. Now you too will taste the reality of this situation."[27]

In a videotape message released on the first anniversary of the London attacks on Al-Jazeera, Tanweer similarly justified his actions in part with the ongoing British military involvement in Afghanistan and Iraq, as well as British support of the United States and Israel. He also warned that similar attacks would follow: "What you have witnessed now is only the beginning of a string of attacks that will continue and become stronger until you pull your forces out of Afghanistan and Iraq and until you stop your financial and military support to America and Israel."[28]

Whether British involvement in Iraq is a cause, a motivation, or an excuse for the London bombings is difficult to establish. Certainly, however, Britain's close alliance with the United States in the "global war on terror" has heightened its risk of suffering terrorist attacks, at least in the short term. Two key reports published in 2005 confirmed that the war in Iraq has contributed to a radicalization of British Muslims. In April 2005 a report by the British Joint Intelligence Committee stated that "Iraq is likely to be an important motivating factor for some time to come in the radicalization of British Muslims and for those extremists who view attacks against the UK as legitimate." The report further warned that the Iraq war had "reinforced the determination of terrorists who were already committed to attacking the West and motivated others who were not." The report, titled "International Terrorism: Impact of Iraq" further stated that "Iraq has re-energised and refocused a wide range of networks in the UK."[29] In July 2005 the influential Royal Institute of International Affairs (commonly known as Chatham House) came to a similar conclusion in its own report, stating that Britain's participation in the war in Iraq and its supporting stance of U.S. foreign policy had increased the risk of falling victim to a terrorist attack.[30]

Hatred for the West's perceived atrocities is coupled with a complete rejection of all that is Western, made possible by the Salafi-Jihadists' tendency to view the West as a conspiratorial super-entity that is decadent and threatens to defile Muslims. The consequence is the framing of the struggle of Islam against the West as a cosmic war between good and evil, whereby the evil of the West encompasses every aspect, from the government to the economy to the military to the press. Khan, for example, says that "I'm sure by now the media's painted a suitable picture of me, this predictable propaganda machine will naturally try to put a spin on things to suit the government and to scare the masses into conforming to their power and wealth-obsessed agendas."[31]

Khan's statements also reflect his internalization of another central tenet of Salafi Jihad, namely *tawhid*, the strict and absolute unity of God, which dictates the entire life of the "true" Muslim. "Our religion is Islam," he says, "obedience to the one true God, Allah, and following the footsteps of the final prophet and messenger Muhammad, may peace be upon him. This is how our ethical stances are dictated." Adherence to the notion of *tawhid* requires that Muslims reject all man-made laws, because only God's laws are relevant. This, too, is reflected in Khan's statement, when he declares that "Our so called scholars today are content with their Toyotas and semi-detached houses. They seem to think their responsibilities lie in pleasing the kufar [i.e., the heretic] instead of Allah so they tell us ludicrous things like you must obey the law of the land. . . . How on earth did we conquer land in the past if we were to obey by this law? By Allah, these fellows will be brought to account."[32]

As a Salafi-Jihadist, Khan also accepts the centrality of jihad within Islam and asserts that if Muslims are deserting the holy jihad, "Allah will cover you with humiliation, and it will not be removed until you turn back to your religion."[33] Naturally, like all Salafi-Jihadists, he defines jihad not as a peaceful internal struggle against one's evil inclinations but as "fighting in Allah's cause" and an individual duty for every Muslim. "Jihad is an obligation on every single one of us, men and women," whereas "turning your backs on jihad . . . is a major sin."[34] Like all Salafi-Jihadists, Khan then elevates the status of jihad to that of the five core pillars of Islam. He also calls for the restoration of the caliphate, a declared goal of Al Qaeda, warning that "You're not safe, nor in the East or the West and you'll never have peace until Allah's Sharia reigns supreme over these lands."[35]

Salafi Jihad extols martyrdom as the most honorable way to fight jihad, and Khan's and Tanweer's statements are filled with calls upon their Muslim brethren to emulate them and seek martyrdom, lest they go to hell. Khan, for example, urges his coreligionists, "Muslims all over the world, I strongly advise you to sacrifice this life for the hereafter. Save yourselves from the fire and torment,"[36] while Tanweer repeats the Salafi-Jihadist mantra, "We love death the way you love life."[37] It is easy to dismiss statements such as these as mere propaganda. However, a close watching of the footage of the London bombers, who were caught on CCTV on the day of the attacks, appears to strengthen Tanweer's insistence that indeed the suicide bombers were looking forward to their deaths. When the four bombers arrived at King's Cross station at around 8:30 am on July 7, 2005, a camera captured them hugging each other. According to the authors of the House of Commons report into the bombings, they appeared "happy, even euphoric."[38]

Mechanisms of Moral Disengagement

Apart from the statements and wills left behind by two of the London bombers, which reveal, beyond a shred of doubt, an intense adherence to the central tenets of Salafi Jihad, it is worthwhile to examine the factors that appear to have helped the bombers to disengage morally from the act of dying and killing. The concept of moral disengagement was coined by psychologist Albert Bandura. According to Bandura, ordinary individuals who interact with each other in their daily lives abide by certain codes of behaviors, or moral standards. These moral standards are what he calls "self-sanctions," because they help prevent the individual from behaving in a way that may offend other people. There are, however, several ways in which individuals can gradually remove these self-sanctions. Bandura calls the processes by which these self-sanctions may be discarded "mechanisms of moral disengagement."[39]

A number of these psychological mechanisms are evident in the case of the London bombers, as well as the statements of other British Salafi-Jihadists who have shaped the London bombers' mental universe. One mechanism includes the psychological division between "ingroups" and "outgroups," that is, between true Muslims and heretics. This mechanism is often combined with the dehumanization of the outgroup, another prominent means of moral disengagement. Taped by a British reporter working undercover, for instance, Omar Bakri Muhammad, the leader of what was then called the Al-Muhajiroun, a Salafi-Jihadist group, said after the London bombings that "The toe of the Muslim brothers is better than all the kuffar on the earth."[40] A member of the Savior Sect—an offshoot of Al-Muhajiroun—who identified himself as Zachariah said that "they're kuffar. They're not people who are innocent. The people who are innocent are the people who are with us or those who are living under the Islamic state."[41] Use of the term *kuffar*, or "dirty kuffar," is a widely used term in Salafi-Jihadist popular culture, such as jihadist rap videos.

The London bombers are known to have immersed themselves in footage showing the killing of Muslims at the hands of Israelis and Americans.[42] Such viewing is likely to have enhanced another process of moral disengagement known as advantageous comparison, in which one's own actions are seen as relatively moderate when compared to the actions of the outgroup, which are perceived as far more vicious. This process of advantageous comparison seems to have taken root not only among the London bombers but also among members of the larger community condoning the activities of the bombers, or at least voicing understanding for their deeds. Thus, one youngster in Beeston who sympathized with the London bombers asked a reporter, "Why should we care about the London bombings when thousands of innocent Muslims are being killed in Iraq?"[43]

Conspiracy theories, which are widespread not only among Salafi-Jihadists but also among less radical Muslims, serve a similar purpose in that they further intensify anger and thus radicalize potential jihadists. An undercover *Sunday Times* reporter spent six weeks in Beeston and reported that conspiracy theories pervaded the local Muslim community. Several people he met were convinced that the four London bombers were not involved in the attack. Some family members too were in denial. Hasib Mir Hussein's father Mahmoud, for instance, refused to believe that his son was capable of blowing himself up, saying that "no-one has shown me any evidence that he did it."[44]

Additional Motives

A few additional elements must be added to the complex mix of motivations that may have led the London attacks to perpetrate a suicide attack. The first is the promise of benefits in paradise, which was mentioned by both bombers who left behind wills. Tanweer, for example, recites a passage from the Quran, from *Surat Al-Touba*: "Oh you who believe, what is the matter with you, that when you are asked to march forth in His cause, you cling heavily to the earth. Are you pleased with the life of this world rather than the Hereafter? But little is the enjoyment of this world as compared to the Hereafter."[45] Khan was even clearer, and in his statement to the video camera, he invoked the promised benefits of paradise several times, saying: "By preparing ourselves for this work [i.e., jihad and martyrdom], we are guaranteeing ourselves paradise and gaining the good pleasure of Allah . . . and by turning our backs on this work, we are guaranteeing ourselves humiliation and anger of Allah."[46] He concluded his statement by saying that "With this I leave you to make up your own minds and I ask you to make *dawa* to Allah almighty to accept the work from me and my brothers and enter us into gardens of paradise."[47]

Second, the obvious element of vengeance that was a clear motive of the London bombers was supplanted by the belief that becoming a martyr confirms and strengthens one's honor and manliness. This element is, again, evident from statements by both Khan and Tanweer. Khan, for example, castigates "so called scholars" of Islam who "fear the British government more than they fear Allah." He calls upon his brethren to prevent these "fake" Muslims from giving lectures and issuing fatwas and suggests that these so-called scholars "need to stay at home . . . and leave the job to the real men, the true inheritors of the Prophet's." Eventually, he calls upon them: "Come back to your religion and bring back your honor."[48] This appeal to one's honor appears to be a widespread technique by which Salafi-Jihadist groups attempt to shame impressionable Muslims and converts into perpetrating acts of terrorism in the name of the defense of Islam. The statement of Omar Brooks (aka Abu Izzedine), a convert to Islam and member of the group Al-Ghurabaa, a successor organization to the Salafi-Jihadist Al-Mujahiroun,[49] is particularly telling. At a meeting of the group on July 3, 2005, Brooks claimed that he did not want die "like an old woman. . . . I want to be blown into pieces with my hands in one place and my feet in another."[50]

Radicalization on the Group Level

Like all suicide attacks organized or inspired by Al Qaeda and the global jihad movement, the SMs in London were a result not only of the personal motivations of the bombers but also of the strategic and tactical interests of the group. Apart from their intrinsic value as an attack against an infidel state, the attacks in London were also staged to send several strategic signals to various British audiences. The attacks sent a message to the government that its support of the United States was duly punished. The attacks were also designed to alienate the British public from its government, by suggesting that its own government had brought this suffering on its people. The attackers intended to convince the British public that it has the ability to prevent further suffering by protesting those actions that allegedly have led to the attack, namely support for the United States and Israel. The goal, of course, was the attempt to alienate the British public from its representatives, and thus to undermine British unity and sow divisions among its ranks. From a tactical perspective, suicide attacks have been used first and foremost because they are a cheap, effective, highly lethal, and extremely shocking mode of attack that can leave a particularly severe psychological impact on the target audience.[51]

The Pakistan Connection and Links to Al Qaeda

Two groups initially claimed responsibility for the attacks: the hitherto unknown Secret Group of Al-Qaeda of Jihad Organization in Europe and then the Abu Hafs al-Masri Brigades. Experts deemed the claim of the former more credible.[52] In a video statement released by Al Qaeda after the bombings, Ayman al-Zawahiri took credit for the operation, saying that "London's blessed raid is one of the raids which Jamaat Qaidat al-Jihad was honored to launch. . . . In the Wills of the hero brothers, the knights of monotheism—may God have mercy on them, make paradise their final abode and accept their good deeds."[53]

Investigators quickly learned that Khan and Tanweer visited Pakistan from November 19, 2004, to February 8, 2005. The writers of the official government report on the bombings thought it "likely that they had some contact with Al Qaida figures" and that Khan had recorded his farewell video during that visit. Khan was also believed to have had "some relevant training" on the Pakistani side of the Pakistani-Afghan border during a brief visit in the summer of 2003.[54] They concluded, however, that as of May 2006 there was "no firm evidence to corroborate this claim [Al Qaeda's involvement] or the nature of Al Qaida support, if there was any. But, the target and mode of attack of the 7 July bombings are typical of Al Qaida and those inspired by its ideologies."[55]

About a year after the bombings, however, the ongoing investigation suggested closer links between Al Qaeda and the bombings than was initially assumed. Already in September 2005 a video that featured Khan had lent strong support to the claim that, at a minimum, the London bombers were inspired by Al Qaeda's ideology to a great extent. In his statements, Khan declared his gratitude to Allah for having been raised "amongst those whom I love like the prophets, the messengers, the martyrs and today's heroes like our beloved Sheikh Osama Bin Laden, Dr Ayman al-Zawahiri and Abu Musab al-Zarqawi, and all the other brothers and sisters that are fighting in Allah's . . . cause."[56] Peter Bergen noted that one of the key pieces of evidence overlooked in the British government report was that Khan's statements, which had been interspersed with statements by Al Qaeda's alleged no. 2, Ayman al-Zawahiri, were made on a videotape that bore the distinctive logo of As-Sahab, Al Qaeda's television production arm. Bergen also argued that Khan's appearance on the videotape strongly suggested that he met with members of Al Qaeda's media team, which is based on the Afghan-Pakistani border.[57] This led Bergen to conclude that "the more you delve into the London bombings, the more they look like a classic al-Qaeda plot."[58]

In early July 2006 the BBC reported that Pakistani intelligence suggested that Khan and Tanweer met with Zawahiri in Pakistan's tribal areas in January 2005. In the three months that led up to the bombing, the bombers were in contact with one or several individuals in Pakistan and may have obtained advice from them.[59] The alleged Pakistani intelligence report and Bergen's assertion were further corroborated when, on the first anniversary of the London attacks, the second videotape appeared. That tape featured Shehzad Tanweer alongside segments showing Ayman al-Zawahiri and Adam Gadahn, the American member of Al Qaeda. Although the three were not shown together on the video, the tape made evident that Al Qaeda had invested heavily in its sophisticated production.

Other aspects of the attacks seemed to suggest at least some professional involvement by a terrorist organization in the bombings. For instance, the attacks were financed by methods that would arouse little suspicion and, as the official account into the attacks concluded, "the group showed good security awareness and planning discipline."[60] Tanweer's statements have helped advance some of Al Qaeda's tactical goals, namely to instill fear among a large audience, while attempting to rally Muslims to jihad by presenting Al Qaeda as the vanguard of a global Islamic insurrection that aims to liberate all Muslims from the perceived yoke of the Crusader-Zionist alliance. On the tape, Tanweer warned:

> What you have witnessed now is only the beginning of a series of attacks, which, *inshallah*, will intensify and continue, until you pull all your troops out of Afghanistan and Iraq, until you stop all financial and military support to the U.S. and Israel, and until you release all Muslim prisoners from Belmarsh, and your other concentration camps. And know that if you fail to comply with this, then know that this war will never stop, and that we are ready to give our lives, one hundred times over, for the cause of Islam. You will never experience peace, until our children in Palestine, our mothers and sisters in Kashmir, and our brothers in Afghanistan and Iraq feel peace.[61]

In October 2006 unnamed "senior military intelligence officers" were quoted in the *Wall Street Journal* as having dismissed the previously held notion that the London bombers had acquired know-how on the production of the explosive material solely from the Internet. Instead, they now believe that the bombers received "crucial weapons training" in Pakistan.[62] A significant individual in this regard is Abd al-Hadi al-Iraqi, a former major in Saddam Hussein's army, who was detained by American forces in 2006 when he attempted to cross from Iran to Iraq. Now a prisoner in Guantánamo Bay, Abd al-Hadi al-Iraqi identified Britain as a key battleground in the struggle of Al Qaeda against the West. Between 2002 and 2004, he led efforts to attack American forces in Afghanistan, employing units based in Pakistan. According to senior counterterrorism sources quoted by the *Times* of London, Abd al-Hadi had sought out British recruits, believing that their possession of British passports and natural command of English would make them ideal contenders for attacks in Britain. The Al Qaeda commander reportedly met Siddique Khan and Tanweer at a training camp in Pakistan in late 2004 and "retasked" them to become suicide bombers. Abd al-Hadi al-Iraqi was also linked to Rashid Rauf—one of the key figures in the August 2006 plot to hijack ten airliners taking off from Heathrow Airport and explode them over American cities.[63]

Whether Al Qaeda is responsible for the London attacks (which is likely) or not, it is in its interest to claim direct or indirect responsibility for the London bombings. Successful attacks such as the London bombings generate pride among those young Muslims who accept Al Qaeda's narrative that Islam is under siege and hence required to defend itself. By using SMs, the most shocking and awe-inspiring tactic available in its arsenal, Al Qaeda is able to present itself as fearless, determined, and omnipotent. These characteristics help Al Qaeda fortify its role as the vanguard of a resurrected and self-confident Islamist movement that strikes back at its attackers with the only means left at its disposal—its willingness to sacrifice its own members' bodies in an act that, they argue, pleases God and helps redeem Muslims at large. Al Qaeda firmly counts on the attraction that this act of heroism bestows upon the Muslim who has no other means to restore his honor other than by creating a balance of terror. This explains why bin Laden, Zawahiri, and other members of Al Qaeda keep repeating the perceived grievances and sufferings of Muslims and the need to avenge these injustices through the total devotion to jihad, manifested in its ultimate form, through martyrdom operations.

Target Selection

In the mind-set of Salafi-Jihadists, Britain is part and parcel of the Crusader-Zionist entity that has subjugated Islam. In the case of Britain, the perceived sins it committed against Muslims reach even farther back into history than the sins committed by Americans and Zionists, and they include Britain's alleged responsibility for the demise of the Mughal Empire in India in the early eighteenth century. Perhaps most importantly, Salafi-Jihadists blame Britain for colonizing large swaths of the Middle East after World War I, including Egypt, Iraq, and Palestine; for exploiting their natural riches; and for cheating the Arabs of their chance to create a single Arab homeland.

Such accusations, some of which contain elements of truth, while others seem grossly exaggerated, are constantly referred to in the statements of bin Laden, Zawahiri, and other key members of Al Qaeda. In 2000 bin Laden accused the British of being responsible for destroying the caliphate system in 1924 and for creating the problems in Kashmir and Palestine, as a result of which many Muslims died. He blamed Britain for establishing an arms embargo on the Muslims of Bosnia, which led to the alleged killing of 2 million Muslims. Britain is also blamed for "starving the Iraqi children" when it embargoed Iraq under Saddam Hussein and for its continuous bombings and killings of innocent children in Iraq as the primary ally of the United States in the war in Iraq.

The London bombings were likely carried out as part of a string of campaigns announced by Ayman al-Zawahiri in September 2002. At the time, Al Qaeda's deputy leader warned that countries that would assist the United States in a future attack in Iraq would suffer the consequences. "The Mujahed youth had already sent messages to Germany and France," he warned then. "However, if these doses are not enough, we are prepared with the help of Allah to inject further doses."[64] As Michael Scheuer put it after the London bombings, "As always for Al Qaeda, a threat made yields an attack executed."[65]

On September 1, 2005, in his first statements after the London bombings, which also featured, for the first time in Al Qaeda's history, English subtitles, Zawahiri again stated that Islam is under attack by the West. He said that the attacks in London were designed as vengeance for Western occupation and aimed at carrying the battle onto the enemy's turf. He called the attacks a "slap in the face to the conceited crusader British arrogance," which made Britain "drink from the same cup from which it had long made the Muslims drink. This blessed raid, like its glorious predecessors in New York, Washington, and Madrid, brought the battle to the enemy's soil." Zawahiri also blamed Britain not only for ignoring Al Qaeda's previous offer of a truce but for rejecting Al Qaeda's offer with contempt, thus laying the blame for the London attacks on the British government:

> Didn't the Lion of Islam, the mujaheed Sheikh Osama bin Laden, may Allah protect him, offer you a truce, so you would leave the lands of Islam? But you were obstinate and your arrogance has led you to crime, and your Foreign Secretary Jack

> Straw said that these proposals should be treated "with the contempt which they deserve." So taste the consequence of your governments' arrogance. Blair brought calamities upon his people in the heart of their capital, and he will bring more, Allah willing, because he continues to exploit his people's heedlessness, and stubbornly insists on treating them like uncomprehending idiots. He keeps reiterating to them that what happened in London has nothing to do with the crimes he perpetrated in Palestine, Afghanistan, and Iraq.[66]

Zawahiri also justified the targeting of all Britons, including specifically civilians, arguing that whoever elects and pays taxes to his government cannot be absolved from responsibility for that government's actions. Indeed, Zawahiri argues that even those who did not elect the government but abide by the country's man-made laws are accomplices of the government and must be punished.

> We say to them that these civilians are the ones who pay taxes to Bush and Blair, so they can equip their armies and give aid to Israel, and they are the ones who serve in their armies and security services. They are the ones who elected them, and even those who did not vote for them consider them legitimate rulers who have the right to give them orders and must be obeyed, and who also have the right to order strikes against us, killing our sons and daughters, and to wage war in their name, and to kill Muslims on their behalf. Moreover, they consider disobeying their orders a crime punishable by law.[67]

Finally, Zawahiri warns of future attacks should the West not cease its attacks against innocent Muslims. He warns that anybody who participates in any kind of aggression against Islam, be it in Iraq, Afghanistan, or Palestine, will be repaid in kind.[68]

Given Al Qaeda's portrayal of Muslims' struggle against the Crusader-Zionist alliance as a cosmic war of epic proportions—a war of good against evil—it cannot be ruled out that the London bombers, who at the very least were profoundly inspired by Al Qaeda's Salafi-Jihadist ideology, chose the particular targets in London also for their symbolic significance. Thus, it may not be a coincidence that it was King's Cross station which served as the epicenter of the attacks on London's transportation system. In a video released in July 2006 by As-Sahab, the narrator said, "The knights of London continued to train and plan for the operation, and the targets were identified with precision, so much so that even the names of the targeted stations held symbolic meaning and spiritual significance for the Crusader West. And after completing their training and preparation, the knights departed for the field of operation."[69]

Recruitment and Indoctrination

Zawahiri's words leave little doubt that, for Al Qaeda, taking responsibility through a video statement is a great opportunity to recruit additional jihadists by portraying *shuhada* such as Tanweer as modern-day Robin Hoods who are redeeming the Muslim nation through their selfless acts of devotion to God and the entire Muslim *umma*. Thus, Zawahiri says:

> What made Shehzad join the camps of Qaeda Al-Jihad was the oppression carried out by the British in Iraq, Afghanistan, and Palestine. He would often talk about Palestine, about the British support of the Jews, and about their clear injustice against the Muslims. . . . That is why Shehzad joined the camps of Qaeda Al-Jihad, where he spent some time, along with Muhammad Al-Siddiq [i.e., Khan]. Both of them were striving for martyrdom, and were hoping to carry out a martyrdom operation. Both of them were very resolute in this. If the brothers discussed some other issue, they would not pay any attention, because their goal, for which they came to the camps of Qaeda Al-Jihad, was to carry out a martyrdom operation. They were bonded by a great love, for the sake of Allah. Together, they formed a great team, even though each excelled at different things. The love of martyrdom for the sake of Allah was not motivated by poverty, unemployment, and emptiness, as some mercenary media outlets try to portray to us. It was motivated by the love of Allah and His messenger. A person who is about to carry out this act has complete conviction that this act of his is one of the best acts in the eyes of Allah. Whoever looks at the life of the martyr Shehzad can see this with absolute clarity. Shehzad Tanweer, Allah's mercy upon him, was well read, loved sports, and kept physically fit, and that is why he studied physical education at university. He had a passion for boxing. Even though his family was well off, his clothes and look did not disclose this. Allah's mercy upon him, he used to pray all night long, and loved reading the Koran. While his brothers spent their time reading the *Hadith*, he would spend his time reading the Koran. He would contemplate what he read in the Koran, and often he would stop at a specific verse and say to his brothers: "Look, this is exactly what is happening today."[70]

Al Qaeda's "strategic indoctrination" through such statements increases the possible pool of young Muslims who are attracted to Al Qaeda's ideology and motivates some to seek ways in which they can link up to the jihad. Friendship, and at times kinship ties, play an important role in the radicalization process of the group and its efforts to link up to global jihad.

In his seminal book, *Understanding Terror Networks*, Marc Sageman discusses the importance of friendship and kinship bonds for the radicalization of today's jihadists at length. Sageman collected biographical details of nearly 200 members of what he terms the "global Salafi jihad" for his book and found that unlike in hierarchically structured terrorist organizations, where recruitment tends to occur from the top down, the global jihad movement is characterized by bottom-up recruitment. Friendship among individuals in this case is formed prior to the joining of the movement. Once that friendship is forged, rhetorical extremism escalates, and the condemnation of the West readies the small circle of friends to join the jihad. Sageman believes that, in this process, a strong desire for adventure combines with religious and political motives. "Formal affiliation with the jihad . . . seems to have been a group phenomenon. Friends decided to join the jihad as a group rather than as isolated individuals."[71] Hence, rather than being recruited by Al Qaeda, many of the young men in Sageman's sample are volunteering to join the organization themselves, in the absence of traditional recruiters. An encounter with some link to jihad is necessary to join the movement; otherwise, the small group will remain isolated. Persons with whom the small group has weak ties, and who are sometimes highly visible and have prestige, can be of crucial importance. Sometimes, the encounter with the link to the jihad happens by pure chance.[72]

According to Sageman's sample of members of the global jihad movement, preexisting friendship bonds "played an important role in the formal affiliation of 68 percent of mujahideen on whom there was adequate information.[73] Sageman summarizes the process of joining the jihad in three steps: social affiliation with the jihad, accomplished through friendship and kinship ties; a progressive intensification of beliefs and faith, leading to acceptance of the global Salafi jihad ideology; and the formal acceptance into the jihad through the encounter of a link to jihad.

Although it is not clear whether the friendship of the London bombers preceded their connection with Al Qaeda or followed it, the bonds among the London bombers seem to have generated an internal dynamic of intense self-radicalization in a way that supports some of Sageman's findings. From the report, it appears that Khan, the probable ringleader of the clique, used places such as gyms, youth clubs, and an Islamic bookshop to identify suitable candidates for future terrorist attacks. Subsequent indoctrination of the group likely occurred on the small group level and took place in less public spaces, such as private apartments, in order to avoid detection.[74]

In the months before the bombings, Khan, Tanweer, and Hussein spent a large amount of time together, and some of their activities included camping, canoeing, white-water rafting, paintballing, and similar outdoor activities that help create strong personal bonds among a group of individuals. The activities were oftentimes arranged by Khan and other young Muslims who frequented the youth center and bookshop. Some of these trips likely served as opportunities to identify candidates for indoctrination and perhaps for operational training and planning.[75]

Hence, the most frightening aspect of the London attacks was the relative lack of outward signs that the clique was highly radicalized. Apart from Lindsay, none of the London bombers came from problematic backgrounds that would seem to render them particularly vulnerable to radicalization. The speed with which the clique radicalized is additional cause for concern. Although the precise date at which the plans of the attacks were originally concocted remains unknown, the period of radicalization seems to have occurred in the year prior to the attack.

Londonistan: Salafi Jihad in the United Kingdom

Since the nineteenth century, Britain has served as a refuge and center for dissidents from the Middle East, and in the second half of the 1990s London became a central hub for militants from all over the world. These included militants who had fought in Afghanistan and who benefited from Great Britain's lax immigration policies. One of the tightest connections existed between the British capital and Algiers, thanks to the publication in London of *Al-Ansar*, a bimonthly newsletter run by Abu Musab al-Suri and Abu Qatada al-Falestini that helped wage the GIA's propaganda war.

The connection between the United Kingdom and Al Qaeda dates back to the 1980s. During the Afghan war against the Soviet Union, between 300 and 600 British Muslims are believed to have trained in Afghan camps,[76] and many of them are likely to have returned to the United Kingdom after the Soviet army's retreat from Afghanistan. Osama bin Laden first established a foothold in London around the mid-1990s. Shortly before, the Saudi government clamped down on a number of Saudi dissidents whose criticism of Riyadh was deemed a threat to the Saudi regime. When a number of these Saudis moved to London to continue their verbal attacks against the ruling family of Saudi Arabia, bin Laden did not want to be left out and opened an office in the North London suburb of Dollis Hill. The office bore the name Advice and Reform Committee and was led by Khalid Fawaz, who became bin Laden's first local lieutenant. Years later, Fawaz was arrested in connection with the bombings of the U.S. embassies in Kenya and

Tanzania.[77] Other members of Al Qaeda also lived in the United Kingdom during the 1990s; for example, Abu Anas al-Libi, an Al Qaeda computer expert who was also implicated in the embassy bombings, resided in Manchester.

Al Qaeda's Salafi-Jihadist ideology has been propagated in the United Kingdom through a number of radical clerics, who have openly called upon their listeners to adopt the doctrine of jihad. Among these radical preachers are men like Abdullah al-Faisal, a Jamaican-born cleric who called upon his followers to kill infidels using guns and chemical weapons. He is said to have had a strong influence on Jermaine Lindsay, the Jamaican-born member of the London bombing cell.

Another radical cleric is Omar Mahmoud Uthman abu Omar, better known as Abu Qatada al-Falestini, who has been described in court documents as the spiritual leader of Al Qaeda in Europe, and whose sermons have inspired, among others, lead September 11 hijacker Muhammad Atta.

Among the most venomous Islamic preachers residing in London was Omar Bakri Muhammad, founder of the radical Salafi-Jihadist group Al-Muhajiroun which, in late October 2004, split into two groups, the Savior Sect and Al-Ghurabaa. Bakri's admiration for bin Laden dates back at least to 1999, the year that Bakri published an open letter to bin Laden on his group's Web site, offering his service to the Al Qaeda leader. A year earlier, bin Laden had sent a fax to Bakri in which he guided the preacher on how to conduct a jihad against the United States.[78] Since 2003, the Syrian-born preacher has regularly urged young British Muslims to volunteer to fight the jihad in Iraq. His lectures in Islamic law were reportedly attended by two young Britons who in April 2003 went to Israel to conduct a suicide attack at Tel Aviv's Mike's Place pub.[79] In December 2004 Omar Bakri Muhammad warned in a sermon in central London attended by more than 500 people that if the West failed to change its policies in the Middle East, Muslims would give them "a 9/11, day after day after day."[80]

The most prominent among the London-based Salafi-Jihadist clerics is Abu Hamza al-Masri, an Egyptian veteran of the Afghan-Soviet War who preached at London's notorious Finsbury Park mosque, which was frequented by London bombers Khan, Tanweer, and Lindsay. Known for his incitement to violence, Masri regularly called for violence against infidels. He urged his listeners to get an infidel and "crush his head in your arms, so you can wring his throat. Forget wasting a bullet, cut him in half!"[81] Among the individuals he helped radicalize during his tenure as the mosque's imam are Zacarias Moussaoui, who was convicted of conspiring to kill Americans as part of the September 11 attacks, as well as convicted "shoe bomber" Richard Reid, who attempted to ignite an explosive device hidden in his shoe during an American Airlines flight from Paris to Miami on December 22, 2001.[82] Saajid Badat, another would-be shoe bomber who was supposed to detonate an explosive device on board an airliner flying from Amsterdam to the United States but who changed his mind and was subsequently arrested, also worshiped at the Finsbury Park mosque.[83] Under Masri's tenure, the North London Central Mosque, as the Finsbury Park mosque is officially called, also stocked an arsenal of deadly weapons. In 2003 a raid on the mosque discovered a cache of equipment for chemical warfare, chemical warfare protection suits, three pistols, a stun gun, CS spray, gas masks, handcuffs, and hunting knives.[84]

Radical Muslim clerics have substantially contributed to an Islamist atmosphere that produced a growing number of terrorists and insurgents with links to the United Kingdom. In no small part, they have helped turn "Londonistan" into a destination and crossroads for potential terrorists who used the city as a base from which to conduct fundraising and recruitment of terrorists.[85] These include Omar Saeed Sheikh, a British citizen educated at the London School of Economics who was arrested in 2002 in connection with the murder of *Wall Street Journal* reporter Daniel Pearl.

London was also the target of several high-profile terrorist plots. In January 2003 Scotland Yard arrested twelve men and charged them with making traces of ricin in North London, apparently planned for use in an attack on the Heathrow express train. All but one of them, however, were released due to lack of evidence.

In this atmosphere, it is not surprising that several British individuals were linked to suicide attacks long before the 7/7 bombings. Some of the individuals involved in the planning and execution of the U.S. embassy bombings in Kenya and Tanzania in August 1998, as well as the bombings in Casablanca in 2003, had links to the United Kingdom. A plot to conduct an SM against the U.S. Embassy in Paris was carried out by a group with ties to Al Qaeda, two members of which lived in Britain.[86]

In 2006 British authorities disclosed that the first Al Qaeda plot to use a large bomb to attack a target in Britain was disrupted in November 2000 in Birmingham.[87] In addition, Khalid Sheikh Muhammad, the mastermind of the 9/11 attacks, had planned to attack at least three British targets, including Heathrow Airport; Canary Wharf Tower, Britain's tallest skyscraper; and the British Embassy in Cambodia. Of these attacks, KSM told U.S. interrogators that the Heathrow plot was the most advanced of the three plans. It involved plans that had been devised over the course of several months, including a plot to hijack several London-bound aircraft and crash them into crowded terminals and fuel depots.

Four Saudi suicide hijackers had been recruited for the plot in 2002. They were apparently seen in a video together with Osama bin Laden published several days before the fifth anniversary of 9/11.[88]

The July 2005 bombings in London were not the first attacks on British targets. On November 20, 2003, a dual suicide truck bombing targeted the HSBC Bank and the British Consulate in Istanbul, killing 30 people and wounding 400 others. Most of the victims were Turks, but the attacks also killed several Britons, including among them Roger Short, the consul general of Britain in Turkey. British citizens were also among the victims of the attacks of September 11.

Two young British Muslims made history as the first British citizens to conduct an SM in 2003. On April 30 of that year, twenty-one-year-old Asif Muhammad Hanif and twenty-seven-year-old Omar Khan Sharif approached Mike's Place pub in Tel Aviv, a popular bar on the beach front adjacent to the U.S. Embassy. After being denied entry into the pub, Hanif blew himself up at the entrance to Mike's Place, killing three civilians and wounding fifty. Sharif, a married resident of Derby, however, failed to detonate his device, fled the scene, and later drowned in the Mediterranean. His body washed ashore on the Tel Aviv beach front two weeks later. Hanif and his family were from the suburb of Hounslow in West London, where they lived in a modest row house in a mostly Asian neighborhood. Hanif's brother, Taz Hanif, said that his brother, whom he described as "a big teddy bear," had traveled to Syria to study Arabic. He studied business at college, worked part-time at Heathrow Airport, and grew increasingly religious.[89] Sharif's background was somewhat different. His family was relatively affluent and came from the English Midlands town of Derby. According to neighbors, he came from a Westernized family, was educated in a private school, and enjoyed playing football and skateboarding.[90] After spending a few years in university in London, Sharif became more religious, and his wife dressed in a burka.[91] In 2006 two British journalists discovered that in the summer of 2001 Mohammed Siddique Khan had worked with the two Mike's Place bombers to recruit youngsters for training in Afghanistan.[92]

British jihadists also went to Iraq, where a British brigade of an estimated 150 jihadists is believed to have joined the insurgency against coalition forces in Iraq.[93] According to a Whitehall document, Al Qaeda had plans to recruit many more of the estimated 1.8 million Muslims to its cause. A joint Home Office and Foreign Office dossier titled "Young Muslims and Extremism" prepared for Prime Minister Tony Blair in 2004 said that Britain may be harboring thousands of Al Qaeda sympathizers and that Al Qaeda was secretly recruiting affluent, middle-class Muslims in British universities and colleges to carry out terrorist attacks in the kingdom.[94] By 2006 the search for British recruits for suicide operations had reportedly also reached foreign countries. In April 2006 an Iranian-based group, the Committee for the Commemoration of Martyrs of the Global Islamic Campaign, said it was targeting potential recruits in Britain because they faced fewer restrictions in entering Israel.[95]

Even a year after the July 7 bombings, the terrorist threat in the United Kingdom, and that emanating from British Muslims in other countries, remained high. On August 12, 2006, John Reid, Britain's highest-ranking law enforcement official, disclosed that some twenty-four terrorist conspiracies were still under surveillance in the United Kingdom. He added that, since the 7/7 attacks, British security services had foiled what he described as four other major conspiracies.[96] Three months later, the director of MI5, Dame Eliza Manningham-Buller, revealed in a speech that British police were contending with "some 200 groupings or networks, totaling over 1,600 identified individuals . . . who are actively engaged in plotting, or facilitating, terrorist acts here and overseas." She added that the MI5 is aware of some thirty terrorist plots, many of which have links to Al Qaeda in Pakistan.[97] In November 2007 the new head of MI5 provided a figure of 2,000 Al Qaeda–linked individuals operating in the United Kingdom, 400 more than during the previous year.[98] Worse perhaps, an inquiry exposed in February 2008 that some of these individuals—including several members of the 7/21 bombers—were trained in British terrorism training camps in national parks in the Lake District of northern England, the New Forest in the south, and southern counties of Berkshire, Kent, and East Sussex. If this news was not bad enough, the London Metropolitan police force found out in 2008 that four individuals had infiltrated it as "al-Qaeda spies."[99]

A mere two weeks after the July 7, 2005, bombings there was another attempt by five suicide attackers to stage a strikingly similar series of attacks on the London transportation system. Officials had initially believed the 7/21 bombing attempts to be a copycat act of terrorism. In January 2007, however, when the trial against the 7/21 bombers was in full swing, the prosecution suggested that the plot had been concocted long in advance. The plotters—Muktar Ibrahim, Manfo Asiedu, Hussein Osman, Yassin Omar, Ramzi Mohammed, and Adel Yahya, all of whom were originally from Africa—were between twenty-four and thirty-three years old. They had prepared six bombs using a mix of liquid hydrogen peroxide, chapatti flour, acetone, and acid and placed the bombs in plastic containers filled with screws. The bombs failed to detonate, however, after the defendants miscalculated the amount of hydrogen peroxide needed. Except for Adel Yahya, the prosecutors charged that all the defendants were supposed to die as suicide bombers. Ramzi Mohammed had left behind a suicide note. Manfo Asiedo had apparently lost his nerves and dropped the bomb, as a result of which the British media initially reported stories about four suicide bombers. Muktar Ibrahim had been trained for jihad in the Sudan in 2003 and traveled to Pakistan the following year. Yassin Omar's one-bedroom apartment in New Southgate served as the cell's bomb factory.[100] As of July 2007 four of the defendants were sentenced to life in prison.

Probably the most elaborate terrorist plot foiled to date was that of a conspiracy to detonate a number of airliners in midair, in a plan strikingly similar to the 1994–95 Bojinka plot concocted by Ramzi Youssef and Khalid Sheikh Muhammad.[101] On August 10, 2006, more than twenty people, most of them British citizens of Pakistani extraction but also including at least two converts, were arrested in London, High Wycombe in Buckinghamshire, and Birmingham. They were suspected of playing a role in an SM plot that, had it been successfully executed, could have rivaled the 9/11 attacks in fatalities and destruction. The plot reportedly involved the attempted detonation of between ten and a dozen American and British aircraft flying from the United Kingdom to various destinations in the United States and Canada. The would-be hijackers allegedly intended to use sophisticated and highly effective liquid explosives, to be carried in the conspirators' hand luggage, possibly disguised in soda bottles. Several days after the arrests, investigators found several martyrdom videos on laptop computers they seized, which had apparently been made by some of the suspects.[102]

The Heathrow plot, for which eight men were eventually put on trial, was probably planned to commemorate the fifth anniversary of 9/11, and an involvement at the highest levels of Al Qaeda is likely.[103] British authorities reported evidence of links between the August 2006 plotters and individuals directly related with Al Qaeda, and unnamed officials told the *Sunday Times* that one man arrested was Al Qaeda's commander in the United Kingdom. Reports suggesting that the plotters received training on the Afghan-Pakistani border matched other reports of new training camps that had been established in the same tribal areas.[104]

The arrested plotters of August 2006 had profiles similar to those of the 7/7 bombers. Three plotters were converts to Islam, including Don Stewart-Whyte, the son of a British Conservative Party official. Most of the arrested individuals were married and some had children. Like the 7/7 bombers, most of them were from the middle class, held jobs, and liked sports. Two of the arrested were women. The arrested plotters included a biomedical student and a record company executive.

Three months after the arrests in the Heathrow plot, Dhiren Barot, a thirty-four-year-old British Muslim from Kingsbury in northwest London, was sentenced to life in prison for planning several terrorist attacks, including suicide operations, in Washington, New York, New Jersey, and London. Barot came to London with his parents as a small child from India. After converting to Islam from Hinduism at the age of twenty, he quit his employment with Air Malta and subsequently traveled to Pakistan to obtain terrorist training with Al Qaida. Once back in the United Kingdom, he began to plot terrorist attacks against the United States and the United Kingdom. Barot traveled to the United States on two separate occasions to case potential targets. Pakistani authorities provided information that led to Barot's arrest, and his plans were subsequently discovered on a laptop computer seized during a raid on a house in Gujrat, Pakistan, in July 2004. The document listed several possible targets for attacks, including several London train stations and the Savoy Hotel, as well as several different types of weapons to be used for these attacks, such as a planned dirty bomb containing radioactive material. The prosecutor of the case also said that Barot plotted to detonate a bomb under the Thames River, with the aim of flooding the London Underground network and drowning hundreds of commuters. He also plotted to strike at a number of targets in the United States, including the headquarters of the International Monetary Fund (IMF) and the World Bank in Washington, D.C., the New York Stock Exchange building and Citigroup headquarters in New York, and the Prudential building in Newark, New Jersey.

Barot's plans for attacks in the United States were first hatched prior to September 9/11, then shelved, but adopted for plans against the U.K. targets. In the seized document, Barot had written that his primary purpose was to "inflict mass damage and chaos."[105] After monitoring Barot for several weeks, security services arrested him in August 2004. Barot's case is clear testimony to the fact that radical Islamists were contemplating ways to hit the United Kingdom already as late as the 1990s.

In November 2006 another terrorism case dominated British news. It was the trial of seven young British Muslims, aged nineteen to thirty-four, who were arrested on March 30, 2004, after one of Britain's largest antiterrorist undercover investigations, known as Operation Crevice. They were charged with involvement in a criminal conspiracy to make explosives to commit murder, although all of them denied these allegations. Among the targets they discussed were the Ministry of Sound nightclub, the Bluewater shopping mall, a train, a pub, a British airliner, and a list of synagogues. Six of the seven cell members had family roots in Pakistan, and some allegedly had connections, albeit vague, to Al Qaeda.

According to prosecutors, the ringleader of the group was twenty-four-year-old Omar Khyam, a talented cricket player who was influenced in his teens by Al-Muhajiroun. Khyam, the grandson of a British army colonel and the son of a wealthy businessman, enjoyed a comfortable middle-class upbringing. He became interested in religion and took a turn toward Salafi Jihad around the age of fifteen. One day, however, he decided to run away from high school and go to Pakistan, where he was taught guerrilla warfare in training camps. Another member of the cell, thirty-one-year-old Salahuddin Amin, was independently indoctrinated in London, apparently influenced both by videos showing the slaughter of Muslims in Chechnya and Bosnia and by lectures of Finsbury Park mosque imam Abu Hamza al-Masri.

Following another stint in Pakistan, cell members were monitored storing large amounts of fertilizer at Access Storage, a self-storage warehouse near Heathrow. Meanwhile, some of the accused were overheard on surveillance tapes talking about plans to blow up a number of targets, including a nightclub. Shortly after, the police arrested the suspects. During the raids, officers found CD-ROMs with detailed plans of Britain's electricity and gas system, a list of British synagogues, and parts of an electronic explosives handbook.[106] On April 30, 2007, five of the seven cell members were found guilty of planning to use 1,300 pounds of ammonium nitrate fertilizer to produce bombs for attacks in Britain in revenge for its support of the United States after 9/11.

Based on testimony by the prosecution's star witness, Mohammed Babar, a Pakistan-born American Al Qaeda operative arrested in the United States in early April 2004, investigators found that two men from Luton—identified only as Q. and Abu Munthir—played key roles in recruiting the cell around Omar Khyam. Both Q. and Abu Munthir reported directly to Al Qaeda.[107] Furthermore, as was disclosed in late April 2007, Omar Khyam had met with Mohammed Siddique Khan at least four times in England while he was under surveillance by MI5, and at least once also with Shehzad Tanweer. The link between Khyam and the London bombers, however, was never followed up.[108] Babar was shown a picture of Siddique Khan after the 7/7 attacks and said he recognized his face from the Malakand training camp in Pakistan.

The most recent attack that took place in the United Kingdom involved a group of medical doctors and also involved a suicide operation. Early in the morning on June 29, 2007, police in London found two cars rigged to explode with gasoline, gas canisters, and nails. The two Mercedes cars were parked around the corner from each other in London's Haymarket. Investigators later learned that two men—Bilal Abdullah and Khalil Ahmed, had attempted to blow up the cars with the intention of killing visitors to a nearby nightclub, Tiger Tiger. Bilal Abdullah was later identified as a twenty-seven-year-old, British-born Iraqi who worked as a junior doctor under supervision in a diabetes ward at Royal Alexandra Hospital near Glasgow. Colleagues described him as radical in his views.

After their failed attempt, the pair drove 400 miles from London to Glasgow, where they conducted an apparent suicide operation by ramming their Jeep Cherokee into a hall at Glasgow Airport. In the course of the attack, Khalil Ahmed, also a medical doctor, apparently doused himself with gasoline, suffering severe burns during the attack, to which he succumbed several weeks later. Several doctors were arrested in connection with the attacks, but only two in addition to Abdullah have been formally charged. Several of the detainees met in Cambridge in 2005. Unlike many of the previous terrorist plots in the United Kingdom, at least half of the suspects of the "Doctors' Plot" were of Arab origin, as opposed to South Asian or African.

In mid-December 2007 British investigators and U.S. intelligence officers indicated that the plotters had connections to Al Qaeda in Iraq. Phone numbers found on their cell phones contained the numbers of members of AQI. Although the officials did not suggest that the plot was directed by AQI, the attack was the result of the closest collaboration detected thus far between the Iraqi group and plotters outside the Middle East.[109]

Conclusion

The bombings in London were the first successful Islamist terrorist attacks in the United Kingdom and were all the more shocking to Britons because, for the first time, it was British citizens who perpetrated SMs on British soil. As with other suicide attackers, the motivations of the suicide bombers remain unclear, although several elements seem to have come together to produce a deadly confluence of factors. The bombers likely suffered from an acute crisis of identity that appears to befall many children or grandchildren of immigrants to Europe who appear to be stuck in between two worlds. Neither able to identify with their parents' or grandparents' home country, nor fully accepted in the United Kingdom, where nationalism is strong, xenophobia rampant, and opportunities for professional advancement scarce, the bombers were searching for a new source capable of providing a sense of community, belonging, identity, and purpose. They found it in a virtual community of Muslim believers, and they chose to adopt Salafi-Jihadist ideology apparently because it offered them a simplistic worldview and provided solace and a sense of belonging in a new globalized *umma*. That ideology was also attractive because it explained in very simple terms the origins of the bombers' predicament and laid out a concrete plan of action by which these problems could be fixed.

They adopted this ideology together, as a group, while undergoing a process of intensive radicalization led by a highly charismatic leader, Mohammed Siddique Khan. These bonds provided emotional support to all members of the group and encouraged the adoption of Salafi Jihad. Their bonds were strengthened by the secret pact that they held, which they had to conceal until their death. Sageman is perhaps correct in saying that "it may be more accurate to blame global Salafi terrorist activity on in-group love than out-group hate."[110]

The adoption of Salafi-Jihadist ideology also opened the gates for a gradual readying for the act of killing and dying, aided by various mechanisms of moral disengagement offered by the ideology. Perceiving Britain and the United States as the absolute evil on earth, and their citizens as *kuffars*, the bombers dehumanized their enemies, which made it easier to mistreat them. They were also convinced that what would await them after their act of martyrdom would be the pleasures of paradise. Whether this posthumous benefit acted as a motivator in itself, as an added benefit, or as a mechanism to overcome the fear of death is impossible to know. What is highly probable, however, is that the bombers really believed that they would attain these benefits.

Apart from a new meaning of life, the expectation of posthumous benefits, and the desire for revenge for the perceived attacks against their fellow Muslim brothers and sisters, the bombers also appear to be driven by a desire to fulfill the role of men, as they see it. Both Khan and Tanweer stressed the heroism of their deeds and labeled those who are "appeasing" the West and fail to join the battle on the side of true Islam as people who are acting in an unmanly fashion.

The statements by Khan and Tanweer, and findings by the Home Office and the Royal Institute of International Affairs, strongly suggest that the wars in Iraq and elsewhere have served as a motivator. Once the bombers have accepted that they are acting on behalf of, and for the sake of, a globalized community of Muslims, then the attacks against their brethren in Iraq, Chechnya, and Palestine became highly personalized. Attacks against their fellow Muslims were likely perceived as attacks against their most immediate family, and certainly as attacks against Islam, their adopted community, adding to an overwhelming sense of humiliation and frustration.

Incidents in Britain proper can also stir up additional anger. In June 2007 a botched raid by 250 officers in the Forest Gate section of London stirred up resentment among some Muslims. During the raid, officers shot and wounded a Muslim suspect, destroyed his house, and arrested him and his brother. The police said that they suspected the men of involvement in the production of chemical weapons, but the men were later released, with the police acknowledging that they had made a mistake.

Blaming British policies alone for the attacks, however, would miss the important point that the United Kingdom had been a preferred target of Salafi-Jihadists long before Tony Blair and George W. Bush had created a strong alliance, and years before the British marched into Iraq. As the director-general of MI5, Eliza Manningham-Buller, correctly pointed out, "Let there be no doubt about this: the international terrorist threat to this country is not new. It began before Iraq, before Afghanistan, and before 9/11."[111]

The London bombings also highlighted the inherent danger emanating from policies that are highly tolerant of indoctrination by preachers of hate.[112] It is in large part due to Britain's relative tolerant policies vis-à-vis these minorities that radical networks were allowed to flourish in Britain for years, leaving Islamist imams a free rein to spread their radical propaganda.

CHAPTER SEVEN

The Rise of Suicide Attacks in Iraq

On March 22, 2003, less than a week after the beginning of the U.S.-led invasion of Iraq, four civilians, including Paul Moran, a thirty-nine-year-old Australian cameraman on assignment for the Australian Broadcasting Corporation, were killed in a suicide car bombing on the outskirts of the northern Iraqi village of Khurmal. The attack heralded what was to become the most dramatic and lethal campaign of SMs conducted since the Japanese kamikaze attacks during World War II. Over the next four years, at least 627 additional suicide attacks would take place in Iraq—nearly as many SMs as occurred in the preceding quarter century in all other countries combined.[1]

In 2003 twenty-five suicide attacks were conducted in Iraq, including many high-profile SMs that targeted mostly U.S. and allied forces. On April 4, 2003, for example, two women detonated themselves near U.S. forces in western Iraq. The Al-Jazeera satellite station aired a video in which one of the two attackers, identified as Nour Qaddour al-Shanbari, swore to "defend Iraq . . . and take revenge from the enemies of the (Islamic) nation, Americans, imperialists, Zionists," and Arabs who have collaborated with the intruders.[2]

One of the most notorious suicide bombings was directed at the United Nations. On August 19, 2003, a suicide bomber drove an explosives-laden cement mixer into the three-story converted hotel that served as the United Nations Headquarters in Baghdad, killing seventeen people, including Sergio Vieira de Mello, the UN secretary-general's special representative in Iraq. Other major SMs in 2003 included the August 7 attack at the Jordanian embassy and the August 27 attack directed at the International Committee of the Red Cross.

In 2004 the number of SMs tripled to seventy-five, and the attacks were no longer confined mostly to international forces and institutions perceived as occupiers. Increasingly, SMs now also targeted Iraqi "collaborators" and members of Iraq's Shia community. On March 2 a suicide bombing timed to coincide with the Shia holiday of Ashura killed some 180 Iraqis, nearly all of them Shia worshipers, in Karbala. On May 17, two suicide bombers killed the president of the Iraqi governing council, Izzedine Salim, and six others. On July 28, some 70 people, mostly Iraqis, were killed in an SM aimed at new police recruits in Baquba, north of Baghdad. The spate of suicide bombings was a major contributor to the U.S. offensive in Fallujah in November of that year.

In 2005 the number of suicide attacks skyrocketed to 339. On January 19, during the run-up to Iraq's legislative elections, at least five suicide bombers blew themselves up in various districts of Baghdad, including at the Australian Embassy and the Baghdad International Airport, killing some 26 people, mostly Iraqis.[3] A suicide car bomb at an Iraqi clinic on February 28, 2005, where a crowd of Iraqi police and army recruits were gathered, killed at least 122 people and was one of the most deadly suicide operations in Iraq since the beginning of the war.[4]

Attacks on Shia gatherings, already a favored target of the mostly Sunni suicide bombers, continued unabatedly in 2005 as well as 2006. On September 14, 2005, for instance, at least 112 Shias were killed in a suicide car bombing in the Shia-dominated Khadimiya district of Baghdad.

The most serious escalation of violence in 2005 came in the aftermath of the formation of a new Iraqi government, which was sworn in on May 3. Partly in order to stem the flow of foreign fighters, who constituted the bulk of suicide bombers, the U.S. military embarked on an offensive in western Iraq's Al Anbar province in May 2005. In the spring of 2005 American commanders declared that suicide bombings had become the operational priority of American commanders.[5]

The escalation came at a time when the insurgency appeared to be shifting its focus increasingly toward a political and sectarian polarization of Iraq in the apparent hope of igniting a civil war. The overall increase in sophistication and size of improvised explosive devices (IEDs) used for suicide and nonsuicide attacks during the spring and summer of 2005 heightened the number of fatalities that resulted from the bombings.[6]

Even prior to 2005, the decision taken by Salafi-Jihadist elements of the insurgency to ignite ethnic tensions led to stepped-up attacks targeting the Shia, Sufi, and Kurdish communities. Kurdish Iraqis had been subjected to SMs already before 2005, primarily by the Ansar al-Sunna Group, an offshoot of Ansar al-Islam, a group based in northern Iraq that entertains strong ties to Al Qaeda. June 2, 2005, saw the first major SM against the Sufi community—a mystical branch of Islam—when a suicide bomb attacked a Sufi congregation in the northern Iraqi village of Balad, killing eight worshipers and injuring twelve. More attacks on Sufis were to follow in subsequent months.[7] The attack on the

Sufis was a testament to the radicalization of the Islamist element of the insurgency, which increasingly adopted a radical Salafi-Jihadist form.

In 2006 the total number of SMs in Iraq dropped to 179, but included many particularly lethal bombings. One week in late September 2006 saw the highest number of SMs of any given week since the insurgency began.[8] The Shia continued to be the single most targeted community in Iraq.[9]

Suicide attacks continued in 2007, with at least 111 attacks recorded by early April.[10] Attacks were conducted against a wide range of targets, from newspapers to the Iraqi parliament, and from cultural sites such as the Sarafiya bridge to soccer fans celebrating the victory of the Iraqi soccer team. February 3, 2007, saw the most devastating suicide attack to date. The attack was targeted at a Shia market in Baghdad. Around dusk, a bomb-laden truck exploded at the crowded market, killing 135. Attacks against Shias increasingly led to revenge attacks against Sunnis. In late March 2007, after the explosion of truck bombs in the northern city of Tal Afar that killed more than 80 Shias, Shia gunmen, apparently including police officers, took revenge on Sunnis by shooting perhaps as many as 70 of them.[11]

Who Are the Suicide Bombers in Iraq?

Since the beginning of hostilities, the majority of insurgents in Iraq have been Iraqis, with foreign fighters constituting only a small part of the insurgency.[12] Between 2003 and 2007, however, foreign jihadists have continuously been responsible for the majority of SMs. In May 2007, for instance, General David Petraeus said that "80 to 90 percent of the suicide bombers come from outside Iraq,"[13] and in the preceding years various officials suggested that foreigners constituted around 90 percent of suicide bombers.[14]

In March 2005 Reuven Paz published statistical information on 33 members of the Salafi-Jihadist insurgency who died in Iraq while carrying out SMs: 23 (70 percent) were from Saudi Arabia, 5 (15 percent) from Syria, 2 from Kuwait, and 1 each from Libya, Iraq, and Morocco.[15] A study conducted in late 2005 with a sample of 429 fighters in Iraq by and large confirmed Paz's findings. It also suggested that the composition of suicide bombers largely reflected the overall composition of foreign fighters in the insurgency, including those who did not perpetrate SMs. Based on that study, 53 percent of the fighters were Saudis, 13 percent Syrians, 8 percent Iraqis, 6 percent Jordanians, and 4 percent each Kuwaitis and Libyans, with the rest distributed among other countries. The average age of 85 of the 429 fighters about whom information was available was twenty-seven, and at least 22 of the 429 were married. Only a few of them (5 percent) had combat experience in other regions, indicating that the recruits to the Iraqi jihad were part of a new generation of foreign fighters. Information on the educational status of the 429 fighters was available in only 31 cases. Of these, 17 had apparently quit their education in order to join the jihad in Iraq.[16]

Even though foreign jihadists play a disproportionately active role in SMs, some Iraqis too have manifested a willingness to die in order to kill. One of the first Iraqi suicide bombers was Namir Awaad, who struck near a U.S. army base in Rashidiya on December 9, 2003.[17] On January 30, 2005, a mentally challenged Iraqi boy blew himself up at a polling station.[18] On June 20, Al Qaeda in Iraq (AQI) issued a statement announcing the creation of a separate SM brigade composed entirely of Iraqi volunteers. The new Iraqi suicide brigade was called Abu Dujana al-Ansari Brigades and was said to be subordinated to AQI's suicide operations squad, the Al-Baraa bin Malek Brigades.[19] The actual number of Iraqi suicide bombers appears to have risen since the formation of the al-Ansari Brigades, although it remains unclear whether the proportion of Iraqi suicide bombers compared to foreign suicide attackers has risen as well.[20] A more recent study featuring information on 101 identified suicide bombers in Iraq, for instance, confirmed that Iraqi suicide bombers are a minority. Of the 101 bombers listed, only 7 were Iraqis. Of the remaining 94, 44 were Saudis, 7 Kuwaitis, 7 Europeans, 6 Syrians, 3 Libyans, and 2 each were from Jordan and Egypt.[21]

There are several possible reasons for the relatively high number of Saudis among the foreign fighters, including suicide attackers. Saudi volunteers are heavily influenced by the kingdom's Wahhabi stream of Islam, which is a close cousin of Salafism. The two movements share a strong anti-Shia sentiment, which could explain why many Saudis are eager to help Salafi-Jihadist insurgents stir up ethnic unrest in Iraq by targeting the Shia. A second reason for the large number of Saudis (as well as Kuwaitis) among foreign fighters has to do with their relative wealth. As one Iraqi who smuggled Arabs from Syria to Iraq for years has said, "our brothers in Iraq are asking for Saudis. The Saudis go with enough money to support themselves and their Iraqi brothers. A week ago, we sent a Saudi to the jihad. He went with 100,000 Saudi riyals [roughly $27,000]. There was celebration amongst his brothers there."[22]

Finally, Saudi jihadists were instigated by more than two dozen Saudi religious rulers to wage a jihad in Iraq to end the occupation of a Muslim country. The fatwa was issued just as the Saudi regime had clamped down on the activities of Al Qaeda in the Arabian Peninsula.

According to Paz's study, the social origin of the Saudis killed in Iraq suggests that they come from respected and well-known tribes or families and have never participated in terrorist attacks prior to joining the jihad in Iraq. Many came from wealthy or upper-middle-class families. Further, many of the Saudis killed were twenty-five to thirty years old and married, some highly educated, and several among them professionals, including two businessmen. In ten cases, two brothers volunteered to fight in Iraq and were killed, while in three cases, two brothers carried out an SM (both joint and separately).[23]

Paz's study suggests that recruitment of jihadists streaming to Iraq, including those who end up as suicide attackers, in many cases occurs through bonds of friendship and kinship ties, reflecting the type of recruitment other researchers have identified for members of the global jihad at large.[24] This thesis is corroborated by a study based on figures posted on the Al Saha Web forum, which found that the majority of recruits who came from the same areas either entered Iraq together or were recruited through relatives. The recurrence in the list of the names of major tribes, the study argued, supported this interpretation. The study also concluded that by far the largest component of foreign jihadists in Iraq were from neighboring Arab countries.[25]

During the summer of 2005, General John Abizaid, former commander of the United States Central Command, reported on an influx of suicide bombers from North Africa, specifically from Algeria, Tunisia, and Morocco.[26] Officials at the European Command confirmed that one in four foreign fighters captured in Iraq was African and added that forensic investigations disclosed that up to 20 percent of suicide car bombers in Iraq were of Algerian origin.[27]

An additional group of foreign fighters comes from Europe and consists mostly of Muslims living in European countries such as France, Germany, and the United Kingdom. One of the most notorious suicide attacks by a foreigner took place on November 9, 2005, when Muriel Degauque—a Belgian woman who converted to Islam—carried out an SM in Baghdad.[28] She was the second woman suicide bomber dispatched by Al Qaeda to Iraq. A month earlier, the group had dispatched a woman to Tel Afar, where, dressed as a man, she killed five men and wounded another thirty.[29]

In September 2007 U.S. forces seized a trove of documents and computers at a tent camp in the desert near Sinjar, close to the Syrian border. The raid targeted a cell that was thought to be responsible for smuggling the vast majority of foreign fighters into Iraq. Among the information that was confiscated were biographical sketches of more than 606 foreign fighters that also listed places of origin. Of the 606 individuals recorded, 389 designated their "work" in Iraq, which over half of them, 56.3 percent (217) specified as "suicide bombers," while a minority, 41.9 percent (166) designated themselves as "fighters." Of those who intended to become suicide bombers, the single largest group were Saudis (76), followed by Libyans (52), Moroccans (22), Syrians (21), Yemenis (18), Tunisians (10), and Algerians (5). Interestingly, however, Saudis were not the most eager to become suicide bombers. Out of all nationalities included in these records, Moroccans were most willing to sacrifice themselves, with 91.7 percent of all Moroccans who indicated their "work" preferring to become suicide bombers, followed by Libyans (85.2%), Syrians (65.6%), Saudis (50.3%), Yemenis (46.1%), and Tunisians (41.7%). According to the West Point study, the "Sinjar Records support the conclusion that the plurality of suicide bombers entering Iraq between August 2006 and August 2007 were Saudi. However, they challenge the notion that, once in Iraq, Saudi foreign fighters are more likely than their comrades from other locations to become suicide bombers."[30]

Biographies of Suicide Bombers in Iraq

Obtaining insights into the individual motivations of suicide bombers is always a challenging task, and this is particularly true for perpetrators of suicide attacks in Iraq. Because researchers are unable to interview most suicide bombers, they are often compelled to rely on published biographies. Save for a few suicide bombers whose biographies stand out, such as that of Muriel Degauque, however, researchers are often limited to biographies provided by radical Islamist Web sites. These Web sites obviously portray the "martyrs" in a heroic light and the information they contain can therefore hardly serve as a reliable reflection of the bombers' real personalities. It is nevertheless worthwhile to briefly examine the biographies of several suicide bombers that have been published.[31] While these biographies shed little light on the mental universe of the "martyrs," they may be able to provide us with some additional clues to the puzzle of why these individuals have chosen to become human bombs.

One published biography is that of Ahmad Said al-Ghamidi, a twenty-year-old who wanted to be a doctor. He was enrolled at the University of Khartoum in Sudan, for which he paid the tuition himself. He hardly made it to school, however, deciding instead to travel to Iraq, where he killed twenty-four people, including nineteen American soldiers in a suicide operation.[32]

Faisal al-Mutairi, another suicide bomber, had apparently wanted to fight in Afghanistan but was arrested in Iran. He was a boxing coach who also distributed messages and propaganda material on the Internet and in mosques for the sake of jihad.[33]

Abu Osama al-Maghribi blew himself up at the UN headquarters in Baghdad. According to a fellow mujahideen, Abu Osama was a twenty-six-year-old Moroccan who owned a restaurant together with his father, earning no less than $3,000 every month. Six years before he joined the jihad, he got married and bought a piece of land. Nevertheless, his biographers note, "he was unable to resist the urge to join jihad."[34]

Abu Abdul Malik al-Najdi was one of three suicide bombers who participated in an attack on two hotels in Baghdad. In his will, which he read before a camera,[35] he said: "I tell you that there is no good in this life, while the Muslims are humiliated and the sacred places were dishonored. . . . to my family . . . I also tell you that I found my happiness that can't be described."[36]

Beginning in 2005, Al Qaeda in Iraq began posting a series of written biographies on the Internet featuring mujahideen who died in Iraq. The series, which is called the "Biographies of the Prominent Martyrs of al-Qaeda in Iraq," is written by a man calling himself Abu Ismail al-Muhajir and includes the biographies of several suicide bombers.

One biography describes Saif al-Ummah, a Saudi who participated in jihad operations in Afghanistan, Chechnya, and Iraq. According to the narrator, al-Ummah was impressed with the tactic of suicide operations and wanted to become a suicide bomber himself. He is quoted saying that "the sound of the suicide operations deafens the ears and no force can escape from their shrapnel. The whole world hears about them." He also believed that he had committed sins in his life for which "only martyrdom for Allah can purify me. I ask that you do not refuse me and that you give me speed in seeking to meet my Lord." Al-Ummah drove a pickup truck loaded with C4 explosives into the al-Iskandariyya police station south of Baghdad on an unspecified date.[37]

Abu Umayr al-Suri was a suicide bomber originally from the Syrian city of Aleppo and was responsible for hitting the headquarters of the Polish forces in Karbala. His biographer writes about him that he was from a well-off family that owned a textile factory. When he was a young child, his father died, and he was raised by his mother. He studied engineering, but left his studies early to join jihad.[38]

The story of Abu Osman al-Yamani, known as the "Paradise Lover," was published in April 2006. Al-Yamani, according to the biography, was chosen to participate in a suicide operation targeting the new American barracks in Husaiba. Prior to his bombing, he is described as having consoled his fellow mujahideen by saying that he was "going on a picnic, and not to death." From the biography, it appears that the future suicide bomber had a criminal background.[39]

Abu Maaz al-Janoubi, aka Saad bin Saleh, was married with eight children and perpetrated an SM on behalf of Al Qaeda in Iraq in Al-Qaim. Two days before the attack, he contacted his wife to tell her goodbye. His wife told him that he "should not let any of the beautiful girls [of heaven] enter his house before her." According to the narrator, "this was encouraging for him. The heroic operation resulted in killing thirty-one American snipers and destroying the building they were in."[40]

Another video featured prominently on jihadist Web sites was released on February 11, 2006. The video features Abu Mouwayia al-Shimali, who refers to himself as "Fatimah's Fiancé," in reference to a woman called Fatimah who allegedly had been mistreated at Abu Ghraib prison. Fatimah is said to have written a letter during her time at Abu Ghraib, and the alleged contents of the letter are scrolled vertically down during the video. Al-Shimali is first seen sitting against a wall, with a Quran propped atop a gun at his right. He asks for marriage to Fatimah upon becoming a martyr. Next, footage is seen including explosive material in the rear and front seat of his car. Al-Shimali is smiling and appears overjoyed for minutes, while sitting in his car and giving a thumbs up to the cameraman. He then rides toward a combined checkpoint of American soldiers and Iraqi National Guards at an unidentified location, and the viewer can then see a big explosion that allegedly led to the death of twenty Americans.[41]

These biographies are short and provide only tiny fragments of the lives of the suicide bombers to which they are devoted. Nevertheless, what little information can be gleaned from these biographies supports some of what is known about the personal motivation of suicide bombers to date.

First, suicide bombers are mostly in their twenties, and they are not necessarily poor. At least three of the bombers described here abandoned either well-paying jobs or promising career tracks. Suicide bombers are not exclusively single, as once believed. Many suicide bombers are married, and some have children (one of the bombers described was the father of eight).

Second, suicide attackers keep referring to the humiliation of Islam and to their need to preserve the honor of Islam. Notions of manhood appear to be very prominent, as is particularly evident in the example of Fatimah's Fiancé.

Third, several of the suicide bombers appear intensely happy, even elated. They seem to anticipate their pending martyrdom with much excitement. There is no reason to doubt al-Yamani's conviction that he indeed felt as if he was going on a "picnic" rather than to his death. The case of Saif al-Ummah shows that he drew much satisfaction from the very use of the weapon of suicide bombing. He praises the tactic of suicide attacks and is obviously happy to have found a way to inflict heavy damage on his enemies.

Fourth, some of the biographies suggest that martyrdom is viewed as a mechanism of self-purification. For some, martyrdom may be a device with which past sins can be erased—as perhaps for al-Yamani, who had a criminal background before he became a suicide bomber, or for Saif al-Ummah, who admitted that he wanted to be purified for his sins. Indeed, radical Islamist martyrs generally believe that dying for the sake of Allah washes away all their sins at once.[42]

Fifth, these biographies strongly suggest that martyrs indeed believe that their actions will guarantee them a place in paradise, as the biographies of Paradise Lover al-Yamani as well as of Fatimah's Fiancé suggest. At least for some of them, the promise of marriage to the virgins of paradise appears to be an added incentive to seek martyrdom. The statement of al-Janoubi's wife, who mentions the "beautiful girls [of heaven]," suggests that, if nothing else, the belief in the "black-eyed houris" is relatively widespread among some of the communities that produce suicide bombers. Biographical sketches of members of Zarqawi's organization posted on Islamist Web sites also suggest that the promise of heavenly rewards plays at least some role in the motivation of some young Muslims to come and die in Iraq. One announcement on a radical Web site stated that Abu Anas Tuhami, who is believed to have carried out an SM on Iraq's election day on January 30, 2005, was to have been married a month after his martyrdom. "Instead, he chose to be with the virgins of paradise. He used to talk frequently about the virgins of paradise and their beauty and he wished to drink a sip from the sustenance of paradise while a virgin beauty wiped his mouth," the statement read.[43]

Finally, the biographies confirm that one of the most obvious motivations for suicide bombers appears to be revenge. This is particularly striking in the biography of Saif al-Ummah, who expressed his elation at having found the perfect weapon to exact vengeance. It is also a motif in the video of Fatimah's Fiancé, whose main reason for seeking death and martyrdom appears to rest with the desire to avenge the alleged mistreatment of Fatimah.

Several reports available from press accounts support these findings, while providing clues to additional motives. In June 2005, for example, *Time* published an interview with a twenty-year-old suicide bomber in training who used the pseudonym "Marwan abu Ubeida."[44] Abu Ubeida, a member of AQI, provided a rare glimpse into the motivations of suicide bombers in Iraq. Unlike most suicide bombers in Iraq, he was a native Iraqi. The day on which he was approved for a suicide operation, he said, was the happiest day of his life. Even though he was happy to see Saddam fall from power, after the dictator was deposed, he turned against the United States. Deeply influenced by Abu Anas al-Shami, the Zarqawi organization's spiritual guide, he adopted the jihadist worldview, which commands him to abstain from music, alcohol, and other "Western influences." Asked what motivates him to volunteer for a suicide attack, the Fallujah native said that he volunteers, first, to fight for Islam; second, to become a martyr and win acceptance into heaven; and, third, to defend his country. Waiting to be assigned his mission, he says, is the most difficult period.[45]

Suicide attackers seem to be motivated by the desire to defend Iraq, and by extension the larger Muslim world, from what is perceived as a U.S.-led attack on Islam. This defense simultaneously punishes the arrogant aggressor—the United States—and its main collaborators, especially Iraqi policemen and members of the National Council, Shia "apostates," and other coalition members. As one Lebanese teacher said, "I decided on jihad because I wanted to stop the occupation, not out of the love of blood." His anger, he said, was fed by almost daily scenes on television of Iraqi women and children dying, "not to mention Palestinians suffering the same fate."[46]

Organizations deliberately feed these feelings of humiliation and helplessness with statements that appeal to the honor and manliness of potential recruits. "They are slaughtering your children and shaming your women,"[47] said Abu Musab al-Zarqawi in a thirty-four-minute-long video released in April 2006, clearly implying that a true Muslim must defend women and children from the claws of the infidels by joining jihad.

Like their brethren in Palestine, volunteers for martyrdom in Iraq are also told that the martyr's death is a relatively painless matter. In the words of one Iraqi fighter, "even if your body was totally torn out, all that you will feel is a slight itch."[48]

The suicide bomber's willingness to die seems to be the product of a combination of motivations that includes anger at the United States and, by extension, the West; a belief in the need to defend a religion that is perceived to be under attack; the desire to defend one's honor and dignity in light of the humiliating defeat in this battle; and reaping the benefits of martyrdom. It is important to note that this willingness to die is not limited to the suicide bomber but is also present in many "ordinary" fighters, especially those belonging to the Islamist groups. During major battles such as the one in Fallujah during November 2004, as well as during a major offensive by U.S. Marines in western Iraq in May 2005, insurgents did not seem intimidated by the prospect of their own death and were reported to have fought until the very end. One Marine, Gunnery Sergeant Chuck Hurley, who participated in the May 2005 battles against insurgent strongholds in western Iraq, told a reporter that the insurgents "were willing to stay in place and die with no hope. All they wanted was to take us with them."[49]

Not all martyrs, however, appear to act entirely of their own volition, as there are persistent reports of suicide bombers, including a growing number of children among them, who may have been subjected to various degrees of psychological pressure or even duped into perpetrating an attack in which they die. In the province of Dayala on November 9, 2007, for instance, a ten-year-old suicide bomber—perhaps the youngest bomber ever recorded—detonated himself along with six tribal elders who had formed an alliance against AQI.[50]

Reports of bombers who have been duped appeared more frequently in the course of 2006 and 2007. In March 2007 the *New York Times* reported that insurgents detonated a bomb in a car with two children inside after using the children as decoys in order to pass through a checkpoint. According to an unidentified U.S. military official, the blast killed the children and three other civilians.[51] In 2004 a Saudi national, Ahmed al-Shayea, was allegedly tricked into becoming a suicide bomber against his will. After arriving in Iraq to join the jihad, his "emir" told him that his first assignment was to take a fuel tanker to a Baghdad neighborhood. Two Al Qaeda operatives drove with him, but then jumped out 1,000 yards before they arrived at the destination. His tanker exploded, but Shayea miraculously survived the attack, although it left him disfigured. Today he spends his time warning would-be-jihadists from joining Al Qaeda.[52]

The Groups behind the Suicide Attacks
Evolution and Nature of the Sunni Insurgency

The suicide attack campaign in Iraq is part of a larger insurgency that formed in the aftermath of the U.S.-led invasion in March 2003 and intensified in the summer months of that year. Rather than a hierarchically structured formation, the insurgency has crystallized as a constellation of perhaps 100 different groups. They include, among other elements, members of Saddam Hussein's former Baath Party and other Saddam loyalists such as security guards; Iraqi Islamists, rebellious tribespeople, aggrieved Iraqis, and criminals (many released by Saddam Hussein shortly before the U.S.-led invasion); and foreign jihadists from Arab and Muslim countries and also from Europe. The insurgency consists of a web of constantly shifting connections built on networks of trust (*ahl al-thiqa*).

As Major James West of the First Marine Expeditionary Force in Anbar Province observed about the insurgents, "Sometimes they work with each other, sometimes not. . . . You don't know where the next alliance is going to be."[53]

Although there are a number of militant Shia groups active in Iraq, the insurgency is largely Sunni-based. Insurgent groups have employed diverse tactics, of which explosive devices detonated in a suicide attack (usually taking the form of suicide vests or an explosives-laden vehicle) are only one. Others include direct fire attacks with small arms and rocket-propelled grenades (RPGs), indirect fire attacks with rockets and mortars, remotely triggered improvised explosive devices (IEDs), and vehicle-borne IEDs, among other tactics.[54]

The extent of Saddam Hussein's role in the emergence of the insurgency is under debate.[55] Most likely, the cells composing the insurgency developed over time, fed by increasing resentment and built, as suggested in a report by the International Crisis Group, on "pre-existing party, professional, tribal, familial or geographic—including neighborhood—networks."[56] Former members of the Baathist regime were ideally suited to lead the emerging insurgency, because they were experienced and knew the whereabouts of weapons stockpiles.

The constituent parts of this "composite insurgency"[57] are naturally guided by a variety of motivations whose boundaries may be blurred. Major motivational streams include a desire to end foreign occupation, to undermine the U.S.-supported Iraqi government, and to establish an Islamic caliphate in Iraq. The Baathist component appears particularly bent on regaining the power and privileges it has lost in the wake of the collapse of the Baathist regime. There is little doubt that the Baathists' sense of entitlement is accompanied by a growing fear of being politically, economically, and militarily dominated by Kurdish groups in the north and by the Shia majority of Iraq, especially in the south of the country. To achieve the intermediate goal of ousting the U.S. forces, the Baathists appeared willing to collaborate with Islamist organizations. As one senior Baath Party official who was asked how he felt about Al Qaeda said, the Baathists will "support anyone who carries arms against the Americans."[58]

The domestic Islamist component of the insurgency has welcomed the fall of Saddam Hussein and regards the insurgency as an opportunity to turn Iraq into a state ruled on the basis of Sharia. Iraqi Islamists have witnessed a resurgence of religion in their country since the early 1990s, which has provided added momentum to this movement. Religion offered comfort to many who were persecuted under Saddam Hussein or were affected by sanctions imposed on Iraq by the West, and it is a significant source of support for insurgents. The high resonance of religion is reflected in the widespread usage of religious terms of references among insurgents and insurgent groups. Not surprisingly, about 50 percent of all Sunni insurgent groups bear names that have an Islamic connotation.[59]

Groups Conducting Suicide Missions

Salafi-Jihadist groups are the most visible and aggressive elements of the insurgency, and responsible for the bulk of SMs. Of these, AQI, led until June 2006 by the charismatic Jordanian Abu Musab al-Zarqawi, is responsible for most SMs and other brutal forms of violence, such as beheadings. Following Zarqawi's death, the group is currently led by Abu Ayyub al-Masri, an Egyptian who has been an active terrorist since 1982, when he joined the Egyptian Islamic Jihad under Zawahiri.

The formation of AQI is intricately linked to Zarqawi, who arrived in the Kurdish regions of Iraq around May 2002. At the time, the region was controlled by a group known as Ansar al-Islam, an Al Qaeda affiliate with which Zarqawi quickly joined forces. Convinced that a future American attack on Iraq was inevitable, Zarqawi began preparing for the future battle in the "land of the two rivers" by establishing local support networks in Baghdad and the Sunni triangle of Iraq.[60]

On October 17, 2004, Zarqawi officially pledged allegiance to Osama bin Laden in a message on an Islamist Web site. Two days later, he announced that the organization he led, Al-Tawhid wal-Jihad (Unity and Jihad), was now operating under the name Al Qaeda in Iraq.[61] AQI claims to consist of more than a dozen brigades, including two suicide brigades. The group released communiqués on a daily basis and had two official Web sites, which were shut down in December 2005.[62]

Osama bin Laden responded to Zarqawi's swearing of allegiance in an audiotape, in which he praised Zarqawi's efforts and called him the "prince of Al Qaeda in Iraq." His greatest wish, bin Laden said in the audiotape was "for [Zarqawi] to keep the resistance alive and growing, to increase the number of local insurgents and give the Iraqis more decision-making powers."[63]

While Zarqawi successfully courted Osama bin Laden, the most formidable alliance of the insurgency was being established, namely that between Salafi-Jihadist groups, on the one hand, and ideological Baathists and homegrown Iraqi guerrilla groups, on the other.[64] Tribal elements, which were previously allied with Al Qaeda in Iraq, were increasingly sidelined in the process.

The strategy of Al Qaeda in Iraq was posted by the Global Islamic Media Front, the Al Qaeda mouthpiece, in a new analysis on August 29, 2005. The document asserted that the West was convinced that a jihadist victory in Iraq would be followed by a continued expansion of jihad to other parts of the Middle East and would eventually result in a true global jihad movement. The West, according to the document, is thus committed to victory in Iraq, and it was incumbent upon the mujahideen to defeat the occupation forces. The following strategy was deemed most appropriate for the jihadists to achieve that objective:[65]

- Isolating US forces in Iraq, which is achieved in two ways: first, by attacking translators working for Americans and the Iraqi administration; and, second, by targeting the new Iraqi policemen, who became "shields" for the Americans
- Targeting Arab and foreign diplomats in Iraq, who are representatives of infidel regimes
- Attacking the "heretical" Alqami[66] Shii groups, especially as represented through the Badr Brigades, which the author claimed are assisted by Iran, Syria, and other foreign elements

On January 15, 2006, Abu Maysara al-Iraqi, a spokesman for AQI, suddenly announced the birth of the Mujahideen Shura Council (MSC), an alliance of six Salafi-Jihadist groups, including AQI, which was established to lead the "fight to face the infidels and their followers the converters."[67] Five days later, the council announced its new emir: Abdullah Rashid al-Baghdadi. The MSC was ostensibly created to integrate all the various Sunni insurgent groups under one common movement.

On October 15, 2006, the MSC announced that the member groups of the council established the Islamic State of Iraq (ISI). They blamed what they termed the de facto existence of a Kurdish and Shia state in Iraq for the need to create a Sunni Islamic state. Its goal was to unite the Sunni jihadist fighters "so that Allah's word will reign supreme."[68] The new leader of the ISI was Abu Omar al-Baghdadi, to whom Abu Hamza al-Muhajir, the successor of Abu Musab al-Zarqawi as AQI's leader, pledged allegiance. Over the course of 2007, the ISI would embark on a campaign to position itself as the sole, legitimate political and administrative body of Sunni Arabs. That effort resulted in military campaigns against some of its former allies, including the 1920 Revolution Brigades and the Islamic Army, which refused to join the ISI.[69]

The establishment of the ISI threatened to split the insurgency. In mid-March 2007, following the killing of the leader of the 1920 Brigades by AQI, the 1920 Brigades announced that it had divided into two groups—a split that resulted in part from internal debates over the group's relationship with AQI. The ISI has become increasingly aggressive in its stance vis-à-vis Sunni groups who refuse to join it, to such extent that it created much resentment against the group. The Islamic Army of Iraq, for example, accused Al Qaeda of killing many of its members and posted these accusations on its Web site. It especially criticized AQI's practice of *takfir* and called upon Osama bin Laden "to purify his faith and honor."[70]

AQI appears to have weakened after the proclamation of the ISI. The internecine fighting that ensued between AQI and other Sunni groups that resisted joining the ISI appears to have grown in intensity, while the emergence of the Anbar Salvation Council (ASC)—a coalition of Sunni tribes that formed as a result of AQI's encroachment on tribal interests—deprived the group of crucial tribal support. As a result of that weakening, the center of gravity of AQI toward the end of 2007 appears to have shifted largely to northern Iraq, especially the city of Mosul.[71]

Apart from AQI, another organization relying heavily on the use of SMs is the Ansar al-Sunna Group (ASG). On February 1, 2004, this hitherto unknown group claimed responsibility for a double SM in Irbil in the Kurdish-dominated north. ASG, which also adheres to a rigid Salafi-Jihadist ideology and presents itself as a pan-Islamist movement, officially declared its existence on the Internet in September 2003. It was established out of a coalescence of Kurdish Ansar al-Islam operatives, Iraqi Sunnis, and foreign members of Al Qaeda.[72] Iraqis are believed to be the dominant group within ASG, which targets Americans and their collaborators, including secular Kurds.[73] The group claims to have some sixteen brigades, including a suicide attack brigade known as the Martyrs Brigade of Ansar al-Sunna. It publishes daily communiqués and had a Web site that was shut down in November 2005.[74]

Strategic and Tactical Factors

The groups discussed thus far are not the only entities involved in terrorist violence. Dozens of other groups have claimed responsibility for terrorist attacks, including suicide operations. In the course of 2005, however, probably due to intense competition, many of the smaller groupings have disappeared and merged with the larger, more prominent groups such as AQI, ASG, and the Victorious Army Group. These larger umbrella movements began to serve as front organizations providing money, general direction, and expertise to other, smaller groupings, and at times taking responsibility for their attacks.[75]

As in other countries, groups employing SMs in Iraq do so for a number of strategic and tactical reasons. From a strategic standpoint, groups using SMs in Iraq believe that it is the best means to achieve their goals, which include their attempt to undermine the success of the Iraqi state by delegitimizing it in the eyes of Iraqis. As the burgeoning Iraqi state plunges into chaos, AQI and other groups employing SMs can better present themselves as the only force able to bring stability to the country.

Another strategic goal of groups employing SMs in Iraq is the stirring of ethnic tensions. Attacks against the Shia and Sufis are justified ideologically as attacks against apostates. These attacks, however, also have an additional purpose: by dividing the country along ethnic lines, Salafi-Jihadist groups are able to present themselves as leaders of one side of the divide, namely of the new "underdogs" in Iraq—the recently disempowered Sunni minority. No other tactic is better at igniting ethnic hatred and conflict than persistent SMs, which are often timed to coincide with prayers or sectarian holidays.

A recent study by Mohammed Hafez argues convincingly that what unites all groups employing SMs in Iraq is their pursuit of a strategy aimed at the collapse of the Iraqi political system. Those groups seeking a reintegration of the Iraqi system, on the other hand, tend not to use suicide operations.[76] Groups seeking the eventual reintegration of Iraq are composed of displaced Iraqi officers, soldiers, and security personnel who lost their jobs and other privileges as a result of the war and the "de-Baathification" measures that followed. This category includes such groups as the Islamic Army in Iraq, the Islamic and National Resistance Movement (1920 Revolution Brigades), the Mujahideen Army in Iraq, and the Islamic Front for Iraqi Resistance (Salah al-Din al-Ayubi Brigades). According to Hafez, these groups aim at expelling the coalition forces from Iraq "in order to improve their bargaining power vis-à-vis the Shia-Kurd dominated state."[77] They employ both Sunni Islam and Arab nationalism as a source of their legitimacy, and the ideological commitment of the Baathists among them tends to be weak. Groups pursuing a system reintegration strategy, Hafez adds, tend to limit their attacks against coalition forces and rarely use SMs.

The category of groups pursuing a "system collapse" strategy, on the other hand, is composed mainly of Salafi-Jihadists and ideologically committed Baathists. Most SMs are conducted by groups pursuing this strategy, with the Salafi-Jihadist component of this category carrying out far more SMs than the Baathist component.[78]

Like groups elsewhere that use SMs, groups in Iraq are also keenly aware of their tactical benefits. First, suicide operations draw an enormous amount of attention to the group's cause, in part because of a fascination with suicide bombers on the part of the media. To compound the media effect of its SMs, AQI and other groups regularly videotape their SMs and their perpetrators. These videotapes serve the purpose of not only sending a signal to the target audience but also increasing recruitment.

Second, SMs always create extreme fear in the larger population, and this is also the case in Iraq. "No other weapon is so efficient in terrorizing and intimidating the population," one U.S. officer serving in Iraq said.[79] In Iraq, SMs often occur simultaneously or sequentially, within a short time lag of each other, to increase the shock effect, and to confuse and kill additional security and medical personnel, thus rendering consequence management efforts more difficult. On October 25, 2005, for example, three suicide car bombings occurred within minutes, targeting the Palestine and Sheraton hotels, which are frequented by foreigners and house the Ministry of Agriculture.[80]

Beginning in January 2007, SMs in Iraq were employed using chlorine gas. Chlorine gas was among the first chemical weapons to be used as a weapon in modern warfare. In World War I, both the German and the British armies employed chlorine, releasing the gas from large cylinders in a favorable wind. The use of chlorine in terrorist attacks, however, is relatively rare. In 1997 a serial bomber detonated several chemical bombs containing chlorine across Sydney's eastern suburbs that injured some three dozen people. In Japan, on the third anniversary of the sarin gas attacks on the Tokyo subway system, a chlorine-like gas was found in three beer cans in the Kasumigaseki subway stations. Other than that, reports of the use of chlorine in terrorist attacks are sparse, and prior to Iraq, there had not been an SM that employed the use of chlorine gas. Apart from the desire to maximize damage to the target audience, groups combining chemical material with suicide attacks clearly attempt to heighten the sense of fear among the target population.[81]

Third, SMs are sometimes intended to provoke a heavy-handed response by the targeted entity. The attacking party hopes that such a response might heighten sympathies and support for the group's cause.[82] Terrorist organizations described U.S.-led offensives in Anbar Province alternatively as acts of despair, barbarism, or cowardice on the part of infidels. The struggle of the mujahideen, on the other hand, has been portrayed in countless recruiting videos and DVDs as heroic.

Finally, suicide operations are adopted due to their tactical benefits, including their great accuracy, high lethality, and cost efficiency. A senior U.S. military intelligence officer confirmed these tactical advantages of SMs in the Iraqi case, saying that "suicide bombings are the biggest killers in Iraq but they are the most difficult attacks to prevent."[83] SMs can be even more effective when the explosive device is placed in a car. Most suicide bombings in Iraq generally take the form of car bombs, which can take less than an hour to assemble and, unlike suicide belts, do not need to be custom-fit to the bomber.[84] SMs offer perhaps the best means to penetrate a heavily fortified target. In Iraq, this tactic is often used in combination with conventional shooting attacks, whereby initial suicide bombers may detonate themselves to create an opening in a fortified barrier, through which subsequent attackers can then penetrate the facility and carry out additional bombings—a tactic frequently used by the LTTE in Sri Lanka. In the attack against the Palestine Hotel, for instance, one vehicle first blew a hole in a concrete wall, thereby opening the way for an explosives-laden cement truck to penetrate the compound and maximize damage and fatalities.

Recruitment and Training

When joining the jihad, some volunteers for martyrdom are recruited by clerics or activists in their native countries, where many are influenced by imams who issued fatwas calling upon Muslims to fight the alien occupiers in Iraq. In Europe, some universities and radical mosques have become recruiting grounds for young Muslims willing to fight—and often die—for a larger cause.[85]

Some volunteers for the jihad in Iraq are assisted by veterans of other wars, including those in Afghanistan, Chechnya, and Bosnia. Most, however, appear to have voluntarily linked up to a terrorist network themselves, often through some of the thousands of jihadist Web sites and chat rooms. The Internet, which plays a key role as a recruitment tool, offers freely available on-line guides on how to join the jihad in Iraq.[86]

Once the volunteer decides to join the jihad, the most likely route by which he will arrive in Iraq is through neighboring Syria, although Iran is playing an increasingly prominent role in sending insurgents and even car bombs into Iraq.[87] In a speech on August 1, 2005, U.S. ambassador to Iraq Zalmay Khalilzad said that "terrorists are moving into Iraq through Syria. Leaders of hardcore Baathist insurgents reside there. Terrorists and insurgents are trained in Syria and funding goes through that country. Syrian government media are broadcasting anti-Iraq propaganda."[88] Indeed, jihadist volunteers themselves have been frank about the underground network that smuggles fighters through Syria. In the summer of 2005, American frustration with Syria escalated into a prolonged firefight along the Iraqi-Syrian border between U.S. Army Rangers and Syrian troops, in the course of which several Syrians were killed.[89] In the spring of 2007, the State Department still believed that up to 90 percent of all suicide bombers in Iraq entered the country via Syria.[90]

Hard-line religious indoctrination is an integral part of the preparation for jihad. In the words of a Lebanese teacher who volunteered to become a suicide bomber, "I had to agree with the idea of jihad, with the ideology behind it, before I was ready to act. It wasn't enough just to say I want to go be a martyr; I had to know why."[91] Apart from spiritual and religious indoctrination, the foreign jihadist volunteers also receive a crash course in the military aspects of the insurgency at secret training camps in the Syrian desert, near the Iraqi border. This course includes training in using Kalashnikov rifles, using remote detonators, and firing rocket-propelled grenades.[92]

The second stage of the journey leads the insurgent from Syria to a safe house in Iraq, usually in Baghdad, although some take the northern route, heading to Tal Afar and onward to Mosul in the north.[93] One volunteer said that crossing into Iraq was simply a matter of money. He paid an Iraqi smuggler $500 to be included in a group that was then guided across the border toward Iraq. To get from the Syrian-Iraqi border to Baghdad, the jihadists use Sunni Arab mosques sympathetic to the insurgency along nearly every town from Damascus to Baghdad, a path informally known as Iraq's Ho Chi Minh Trail.[94] According to an American officer who studied suicide bombings, this network of mosques exists in towns along the Euphrates such as Qaim, Haditha, Ramadi, and Fallujah, onward to central Iraq. At each stage, the handlers are organized in cells in order to protect the network's secrecy.[95]

Once they arrive in Baghdad, the officer said, the volunteers are put in safe houses and receive their missions rather quickly. The Lebanese teacher provides additional detail. When he arrived in Baghdad, he was placed in a room with sealed windows, where more than a dozen other Arabs from Libya, Egypt, Kuwait, and Saudi Arabia waited for instructions. The Iraqi in charge then told him that there were three ways in which the occupiers could be attacked: a roadside bomb and shooting at patrols were the first two options. "The third and best jihad was to drive a car into the enemy."[96]

According to "Marwan abu Ubeida," a would-be bomber interviewed by *Time*, after the suicide bomber's dispatchers disclose the details of the mission to the *shahid*, he is expected to spend his few remaining days in a secluded safe house, where he is to immerse himself in prayer, while abstaining from television, music, and cigarettes. He will not have much of a say with regard to the actual operation. The bomber, in fact, may not even be told the exact location of his attack until minutes before the operation.[97]

The services of handlers of suicide bombers vary, and at times the same handler is responsible for providing everything from a safe house to information on the target and explosives, in addition to acting as guardian and father figure for the would-be bombers. Some handlers do not have a sturdy group affiliation and instead provide their services to a number of insurgent and terrorist groups, who pick these handlers based on their reputation. Sometimes, groups approaching the handlers have a specific target in mind. At other times, they ask the handler for advice on the best time and location for an attack. One such handler, Abu Qaqa al-Tamimi, said that in the days before the operation, he will also help the would-be bomber to familiarize himself with his surroundings, showing him alternative routes and side streets leading to his destination. At times, he will drive the bomber to his target himself and may even videotape the attack for the sponsoring group.[98]

Incitement and Radicalization

Recruits for jihad in Iraq appear to fit the model of "bottom-up" radicalization much more than the traditional "top-down" recruitment pattern. The story of "Abu Ibrahim" is a case in point. The twenty-four-year-old citizen of Zarqa, Jordan, and five of his friends gradually radicalized themselves by watching videos depicting the tortures and killings of Muslims on the Internet. A local imam with an intense hatred for Shias helped them find a link to Iraq. The six friends left Zarqa in the fall of 2006, and two of the friends died as suicide bombers.[99]

Much of the recruitment of jihadists, including future suicide attackers, takes place on the Internet, where groups such as AQI and ASG regularly distribute videos that often feature one or several suicide attackers reading their wills. In nearly all cases, the videos of suicide attackers are accompanied by statements of the groups' leaders, urging more young Muslims to follow the footsteps of the bombers. A narrator usually praises the heroic deeds of the bomber, while songs extolling jihad and martyrdom are heard in the background.[100]

In attempting to recruit additional jihadists, terrorist organizers use a variety of rhetorical and psychological devices to incite and radicalize potential suicide bombers.

CONSPIRACY THEORIES

Al Qaeda in Iraq and other Salafi-Jihadist groups make extensive use of conspiracy theories, which are rampant in the Arab and Muslim world in general.

These conspiracy theories include claims that the United States is involved in a campaign aimed to subjugate Islam. Salafi-Jihadists regularly accuse Jews (or "Zionists") of pulling strings behind the scenes. One conspiracy theory suggests that infidel armies have used mysterious poisons. In one videotape, Zarqawi charges, "It has been proven to us beyond a shadow of a doubt that the Crusaders are using toxic gases in their battles against the mujahideen, even if the masters of the Black [i.e., White] House and their followers deny it."[101] Another video that celebrates three suicide bombers who targeted the Al-Hamra and the Ad al-Zohoor hotels in Baghdad is combined with footage of the imprisoned Blind Sheikh, Omar Abdul Rahman. The narrator suggests that Abdul Rahman receives poor treatment in his American prison—"The sheikh always complains of a bad odor that fills his room. He is convinced that it will cause a slow death for him."[102]

APPEALS TO MANLINESS, HONOR, AND GLORY IN THE FACE OF HUMILIATION

AQI and other groups frequently charge U.S. troops and other infidels, including the Shia, with the mistreatment of Muslims, including accusations of sexual violence against Muslim women. One of the main purposes of such claims is to personalize the sense of humiliation felt by ordinary Muslims and consequently to shame them into action. In one tape, for example, Zarqawi asks, "Have you not heard that many of your chaste and pure sisters from among the Sunnis of Tel Afar had their honor desecrated, their chastity slaughtered, and their wombs filled with the sperm of the Crusaders and of their brothers, the hate-filled Rafidites [i.e., the Shia]. Where is your religion? Moreover, where is your sense of honor, your zeal, your manliness?"[103] The terrorist recruiters expect potential jihadists to react to such allegations "honorably" by adopting vengeful jihad for the sake of God. A video issued on July 21, 2005, by AQI called upon young men "to follow . . . in jihad and give their lives for the sake of Allah's religion." In the tape, a suicide bomber is seen embraced by a group of other men after reading his will. Rifles are seen in the background of the video, while songs praising martyrdom are heard.[104]

In the fall of 2005, Al Qaeda in Iraq released a one-hour video providing details of a massive operation in Baghdad, in which the group sought to motivate Muslims to join jihad and seek martyrdom in the name of God. The film features footage from the preparations of the attack and statements from the four bombers, in addition to a number of still shots of imprisoned women, Iraqi men hurt by U.S. soldiers, and a mutilated corpse of an Iraqi. A voice asks, "how can your conviction be weakened and your determination be diminished, when you see the enemy taking possession of your houses and violating your honors?" When one of the bombers is asked what he wishes to say to the U.S. Army, he answers: "Queues of martyrs await them, with the help of Allah." The suicide bombers all repeat the same message, saying "you must continue this path. It is the path of glory," and then they read their wills, in which they urge Muslims to act to protect Islam. The narrator concludes by saying, "Sons of Islam, men of belief, Allah almighty has opened an opportunity for jihad in Iraq. Recall those who followed the path of jihad and martyrdom: the path of glory, and not of humiliation; of pride, and not of subjection; of paradise, and not of hell. . . Where are those striving to defend their religion? Where are the lovers of virgins in paradise? Where are the seekers of the Garden of Eden?"[105]

Another video mentions the black-eyed virgins who are supposed to await the martyr in heaven. In the opening shots of the movie, scenes are shown of people from Palestine, Afghanistan, Chechnya, and Indonesia who have allegedly been tortured. A voiceover of bin Laden states, "Don't you see what's happening? Are you not angry about your religion?"[106]

EXAMPLES TO BE EMULATED

AQI and other Salafi-Jihadist groups are keen on finding individuals whose willingness to sacrifice themselves is likely to be accepted by others with awe and a desire to emulate these martyrs. Here, too, the group attempts to shame potential recruits into action. In a video issued in August 2005, AQI released footage of the "oldest suicide bomber," Abu Sayed al-Iraqi. The video shows an old man reading his will before the execution of a suicide operation, which is seen next. The old man says that "old men, children, and women will follow the young men from the Muslim nation in the fight against the infidels."[107] The footage of the old man may well have served to shame younger potential jihadists into action—if an octogenarian can become a martyr, why shouldn't young Muslims be able to? In another video released February 7, 2006, Zarqawi is heard saying about suicide attackers that they "left their families, their money, everything just for the sake of Allah," clearly insinuating that these individuals are examples that should be emulated by others.

A SENSE OF ADVENTURE AND EXCITEMENT

Finally, in their videos, jihadist groups often seem to appeal to the thirst for adventure, excitement, and purpose that characterizes many men and women in their young adulthood. Following an attack on a U.S. base in Mosul on December 21, 2004, for example, the Ansar al-Sunna Group posted a video on line that featured footage of the planning of the attack, complete with pictures of the floor plan apparently used, with the word "restaurant" clearly written on it. The narrator says, "Let the Americans, their allies and their apostate collaborators know that, thanks to Allah, the Ummah has woken up from its sleep, and has prepared itself to confront the enemy. . . . For Allah, may He be praised, Has prepared men who are keen to die just as the infidels are keen to live."[108] The video indirectly suggests to young men that joining the jihad will make them a part of a group that fights for a cause, has a sense of purpose, and provides a sense of belonging.

The Salafi-Jihadist Environment

Most suicide attacks in Iraq are perpetrated by groups that adhere to a strict Salafi-Jihadist interpretation of Islam. These include, among others, Ansar al-Islam, Ansar al-Sunna Group, the Victorious Sect, Jaish-e-Muhammad, Ahl al-Sunna wal-Jamaah Army, and the Conquest Army.

The quintessential Salafi-Jihadist group active in Iraq is AQI, which is dominating a larger Salafi-Jihadist umbrella organization, the Islamic State of Iraq. The goals of AQI, which are paradigmatic for those of other Salafi-Jihadist organizations, were summarized in an on-line magazine in March 2005 by a commander of the group, Abu Maysara. The group's goals include the renewal of pure monotheism; waging jihad for the sake of Allah; coming to the aid of the Muslims wherever they are; reclaiming Muslim dignity; and finally, reestablishing "the Rightly-Guided Caliphate in accordance with the Prophet's example, because 'whoever dies without having sworn allegiance to a Muslim ruler dies as an unbeliever.' "[109]

While the war in Iraq has done much to intensify Salafi-Jihadist ideology in Iraq, Salafi-Jihadist networks in Iraq had existed prior to the 2003 invasion of the country. In the course of the 1990s, these networks came into being partially in response to the military and economic crisis brought on by the first Gulf War. In the aftermath of 9/11 and Operation Enduring Freedom, when Al Qaeda lost Afghanistan as a safe haven, additional Salafi-Jihadists entered Iraq, where they were joined by members of Salafi-Jihadist networks from places like Jordan, Kuwait, Lebanon, North Africa, Saudi Arabia, Syria, Yemen, and Europe.[110]

In the course of the insurgency, the rhetoric especially of groups that perpetrate SMs, but even of some of those that do not, gradually adopted elements of Salafism. According to a 2006 report by the International Crisis Group (ICG), the insurgency has "converged around more unified practices and discourse, and predominantly Sunni Arab identity. . . . For now, virtually all adhere publicly to a blend of Salafism and patriotism."[111] While many Web sites depicted the insurgency as patriotic and nationalistic, for example, "the rhetoric from the groups most visibly active on the ground was of an increasingly religious and, more precisely, salafist bent."[112] More insurgent groups, for example, began referring to their struggle as one against Crusaders, and an increasing number began making an explicit link between the war in Iraq and a broader struggle on behalf of Muslims.[113]

This convergence around Salafi-Jihadist themes came in spite of the internecine fighting that plagued the insurgency in the first half of 2005. Rather than leading to a permanent fragmentation of the insurgency, the infighting helped create a more unified discourse centered around Salafist themes. Thus, for instance, insurgent groups turned to Salafist *ulema* in increasing numbers for moral and juridical justification for jihad and for specific forms of violence.

The strengthening of the Salafi Jihad has also become evident in the growing support that an increasing number of Islamist clerics have voiced for tactics favored by Salafi-Jihadists, such as SMs and beheadings. Paz points out that prior to the war in Iraq, for example, Islamic clerics debated the legitimacy of SMs. In the course of the Iraq war, however, many Islamist clerics condoned suicide operations. To the extent that there has been a debate over what constitutes legitimate tactics, it was largely over other issues, such as the legality of beheadings, kidnapping, and the killing of Muslims, or the question of whether terrorist acts can be perpetrated outside of Iraq.[114]

Salafi rhetoric has been able to dominate the discourse probably because Salafi-Jihadist groups use the Internet's resources more effectively. On-line researchers at the International Crisis Group reported that the groups most closely affiliated with transnational, Salafi-Jihadist networks were the first to implement a "genuine internet-based communication strategy." To that end, Salafi-Jihadist groups established links between Salafi Iraqi preachers (especially from Fallujah) and like-minded Salafi *ulema* abroad. These contacts are likely to have facilitated subsequent contacts among jihadist groups.[115]

Salafi-Jihadist groups in Iraq are not merely interested in ending the occupation and are unlikely to abandon their activities if and when the occupation eventually ends. As Zarqawi has made clear before his death, his group was "not fighting to chase the occupier out or preserve national unity or keep borders delineated by the infidel intact. We are fighting because it is a religious duty, just as it is a duty to take Shariah law to the government and create an Islamic state."[116] Everyone who stands in the way of the establishment of the future caliphate is a heretic—a *kufr*—and must be fought. Hence, Salafi-Jihadists target not only the occupiers but all those who resist the attempt to create an Islamist super-state ruled in accordance with the strictest Salafi-Jihadist tenets. To quote Zarqawi again,

> We do not fight for a fistful of dust or illusory boundaries drawn by "Sykes-Pikot." We are not fighting so that a Western evil would replace an Arab evil. Ours is a higher and more sublime fight. We are fighting so that Allah's word becomes supreme and religion is all for Allah. Anyone who opposes this goal or stands in the way of this aim is our enemy and will be a target for our swords, regardless of their name or lineage.[117]

Since 2003, Iraq has assumed an increasingly central place within the overall strategy of Al Qaeda. One key Salafi-Jihadist scholar, Youssef al-Ayeri, argued in several influential writings posted on the Internet that Muslims have much at stake in Iraq. They were required to resist the occupation in Iraq not only because of the need to defend an Arab country but because Iraq was one link in the chain of attacks by the infidel West that would follow. Thus, if mujahideen failed to achieve victory in Iraq, they would also fail in defending future aggressions.[118]

Over the course of the insurgency, Iraq has also been mentioned more and more often as the ideal birthplace for the longed-for caliphate. In a letter written by Al Qaeda deputy leader Zawahiri to Zarqawi that was intercepted in July 2005, Zawahiri laid out the strategy clearly. Following the expulsion of the American forces from Iraq, in the second stage the mujahideen should "establish an Islamic authority or amirate, then develop it and support it until it achieves the level of a caliphate over as much territory as you can to spread its power in Iraq." In the following stages, the caliphate should be extended to "secular countries neighboring Iraq," followed by the fourth stage, namely "the clash with Israel."[119]

This transnational goal that supersedes limited, local objectives, such as to oust an occupation force, is reflected in the rhetoric of all Salafi-Jihadist groups. In the words of the commander of the Salafi-Jihadist Ansar al-Sunna Group, "the task [of jihad] is great and the issue momentous and concerns the fate of a nation and the aim does not end with the expulsion of the occupier and weakening him with inflicted wounds, but with the establishment of Allah's religion and the imposition of Muslim law to govern this Muslim land."[120]

As argued in previous chapters, Salafi-Jihadist ideology is particularly prone to violence, and in its most extreme form it even legitimizes the killing of Muslims if it serves a larger goal. In May 2005 an audiotape believed to be from

Zarqawi appeared in which the terrorist mastermind defended the killing of Muslims. "The shedding of Muslim blood . . . is allowed in order to avoid the greater evil of disrupting jihad," the voice said. In the tape, the speaker also defended the use of SMs, saying that "killing of infidels by any method including martyrdom operations has been sanctified by many scholars even if it meant killing innocent Muslims."[121]

Salafi-Jihadist ideology also has an endemic religious quarrel with the Shia, most strikingly expressed by members of AQI. In mid-January 2004 American officials obtained a detailed proposal believed to be from Zarqawi, directed at senior leaders of Al Qaeda. In the seventeen-page letter, found on a CD seized in a Baghdad safe house, Zarqawi asked the Al Qaeda leadership for help in waging a "sectarian war" in Iraq. Zarqawi said the extremists failed to mobilize sufficient support inside Iraq and failed in routing the U.S. forces. The document suggested that a counterattack be waged against the Shia community in Iraq, a step that would rally Sunni Arabs to the religious extremists. "The solution, and only God knows, is that we need to bring the Shia into the battle," the letter read. "It is the only way to prolong the duration of the fight between the infidels and us. If we succeed in dragging them into a sectarian war, this will awaken the sleepy Sunnis who are fearful of destruction and death" at the hands of the Shia.[122] Zarqawi promised the Al Qaeda leaders that "if you agree with it, and are convinced of the idea of killing the perverse sects, we stand ready as an army for you to work under your guidance and yield to your command."[123] In future letters, Zarqawi confirmed his repugnance for the Shia. In a letter to bin Laden dated June 15, 2004, for instance, Zarqawi referred to the Shia as "the lurking serpent, the cunning and vicious scorpion, the waylaying enemy, and the deadly poison."[124]

Given this high level of dehumanization, the extent of violence, including SMs, aimed at the Shia is hardly surprising.[125] While anti-Shia violence in Iraq is certainly in part instrumental, in the sense that it is designed to frighten Sunnis into adopting Salafi-Jihadist tenets, the origin of the hatred between the Sunni Salafi-Jihadists and Shia has deeper, doctrinal foundations. Shiism, which was borne out of the succession crisis that followed the death of the Prophet Muhammad in 632, implies a challenge to the idea that there can be one Sunni caliphate —a core tenet of Salafism.

The Salafi-Jihadist movement manages to attract a growing number of individuals to its side because its groups have managed to convince many young Muslims that the United States invasion is an attack on Islam. Under the principle of *fard ayn*, any attack on Islam must be repelled by waging a defensive jihad against the aggressor. This defensive jihad requires the individual participation of each and every Muslim in the struggle. Rhetorically, Salafi-Jihadists connect the invasion of Iraq with other perceived attacks against Muslims, including those in Palestine, Chechnya, Kashmir, Bosnia, and other places.

The influence of the Salafi Jihad also extends to groups that do not formally identify themselves as Salafists. Insurgency videos, for instance, often show the mujahideen in traditional Salafi dress code, such as Sarawil pants, which had virtually disappeared in Iraq. Moreover, Salafis reportedly played an inspirational role in the initial phase of the insurgency by posing as early Muslim warriors, duplicating their garbs and religious practices and exhibiting traditional, quasi-martial values. Insurgents have produced a lengthy, powerful video on this theme, which mixes contemporary footage of combat in Iraq with pictures from classical movies on the early ages of Islam.[126]

Most important perhaps, Salafi Jihad resonates because it provides relatively easy answers to complex questions. It also offers guidelines and recommendations that are relatively straightforward and can be followed by anyone who so wishes. It is thus a potentially inclusive ideology, if one is willing to pay the ultimate price. As a report on the insurgency suggests, Salafism benefits from the strength of weak ties, that is, from its ability to bind together people who may share little else:

> On the one hand, requirements for being a "good Muslim" (and the best of Muslims) are simple and easily met, since fighting a jihad satisfies the obligations of a pious life. On the other hand, because the focus is on duplicating the personal behavior and moral code of early Muslims, Salafism is an essentially apolitical doctrine and therefore avoids potentially divisive issues.[127]

Conclusion

Biographies of suicide bombers and a review of published accounts examined in this chapter show that suicide bombers in Iraq come from a variety of backgrounds. Suicide attackers who have perpetrated attacks in Iraq between 2003 and 2007 are largely foreigners, and of those, the single largest group consists of Saudis. Iraqis form a minority of suicide attackers, but there are some indications that their number is rising. Suicide bombers are both male and female, and some come from poorer backgrounds, while others left promising careers to join the jihad. Some were single, while others were married with children.

As far as individual motivations are concerned, the biographies examined here suggest that suicide attackers act in the name of the defense of Islam in the face of what is clearly perceived as a U.S.-led attack on their religion. SMs create a balance of terror that seeks to give the United States a taste of its own medicine. They are a mechanism that helps undo what is frequently cited as the humiliating subjugation of Muslims on the part of the United States, and the West in general. The struggle against this humiliation restores honor and dignity to the suicide bomber and his larger community and avenges those members of the community who sense an injustice that is not necessarily personally but often vicariously experienced. The attempt to restore honor may be coupled with more personal motivations, especially the desire to purify oneself from real or perceived sins that the suicide bomber has committed. In some cases, the suicide attacker appears influenced by a desire to reap additional benefits in paradise.

Of the groups that have perpetrated SMs, the majority are clearly Salafi-Jihadist in character. Organizational motivations and goals to engage in SMs, which are distinct from individual motivations, include the larger, strategic benefits and the more operational, tactical benefits of this modus operandi that allow the terrorists and insurgents to achieve maximum effectiveness at a relatively low cost. In the case of Salafi-Jihadist groups, SMs are also employed because martyrdom for the sake of God is elevated as the ultimate sacrifice a Muslim can make for the sake of the *umma*. SMs are also believed to be the best means to bring about the goal of ending Western occupation and establishing the caliphate. They are an integral part of the two main strategies to bring about this aim, namely the delegitimization of the Iraqi government (installed with American help) and the creation of ethnic tensions in Iraq.

Groups recruit mostly young Muslims to their ranks to carry out these SMs. They make extensive use of incitement and conspiracy theories to demonize their enemy while shaming potential recruits into action. They appeal to the honor and dignity of Muslims to defend their brothers (and especially their sisters), and they produce examples of "heroic" martyrs in order to convince additional Muslims to follow their lead.

Salafi-Jihadist doctrine has intensified in the course of the insurgency and increasingly dominates the rhetoric and behavior of the groups that plan and execute SMs. Salafi-Jihadist ideology aims to delegitimize the Iraqi regime, which is considered an apostate puppet of the West. It uses several mechanisms of delegitimization, including the process of *takfir*—the labeling of all those in disagreement with Salafi-Jihadist tenets as infidels—against Muslims and non-Muslims alike. For Salafi-Jihadist groups, bringing about an end to the occupation is merely the first stage in a larger project aimed at establishing a transnational Islamic caliphate ruled according to rigid fundamentalist Salafist principles.

In the context of the Iraqi insurgency, Salafi Jihad has been able to dominate other ideologies due to several factors. Salafi-Jihadist strategists and adherents have turned out to be far more Internet-savvy than their Baathist or tribal counterparts. Second, doctrinally, the U.S. invasion of Iraq neatly fits the principle of *fard ayn*. Salafi-Jihadists had a relatively easy time presenting the American occupation of Iraq as an attack on Islam, making the defense of Islam a rallying cry that was answered by Muslims in many countries. Finally, Salafi Jihad is an inherently attractive ideology to disillusioned young Muslims (and increasingly to converts to Islam) who appear to seek a sense of purpose in life as well as a sense of belonging. Salafi Jihad offers easy answers based on a simplistic, parsimonious division of the world into good and evil. In extolling jihad for the sake of God, it offers a sense of purpose. In its appeal to contribute to the well-being of the *umma*, it offers a sense of belonging to a larger, imagined community.

Conclusion

The vast majority of studies on suicide terrorism to date understandably focused on Hizballah, the LTTE, Hamas, the PFLP, Fatah, and the PKK—the groups responsible for the bulk of suicide attacks in the quarter century since 1981, when the modern phenomenon of suicide terrorism began. Although these groups continue to be fervent enemies of Israel, Sri Lanka, and Turkey, and most continue to plot violent attacks against their foes, the success rate of these groups' suicide missions has drastically declined in recent years.

Especially since 9/11, SMs by Al Qaeda, its affiliates, and other Salafi-Jihadist groups have risen exponentially, far outnumbering the attacks conducted by the previously dominant groups. Suicide attacks by Al Qaeda and its associates also target far more countries than have other groups before, and its attacks are more deadly. For these reasons, suicide attacks by Al Qaeda and its associated movements are the new epicenter of this deadly phenomenon.

Today's main theaters of the most deadly suicide attacks are no longer Tel Aviv, Beirut, or Colombo, but places like Algiers, Amman, Baghdad, Casablanca, Kabul, London, New York, and Rawalpindi. More suicide attacks have occurred in Iraq between 2003 and 2007 than have taken place since 1981 in all other countries combined. Afghanistan, Algeria, and Pakistan have joined Iraq as new hotbeds of terrorist and insurgent activity in recent years, quickly replacing Israel, Sri Lanka, and Lebanon as the leading arenas of SMs. The unprecedented transformations in the employment of SMs in the past decade indicate that the globalization of suicide attacks is a direct result of the rise of Al Qaeda as a global terrorist outfit and the growing appeal of its guiding ideology, the Salafi Jihad.

The Globalization of Suicide Missions

The vantage point for this book is the global rise of suicide attacks, the existence of which was demonstrated in chapter 1 using empirical data from 1,269 attacks between 1981 and April 2007. The rise of Al Qaeda and its guiding ideology are at the root of the globalization of SMs. Both Al Qaeda and Salafi-Jihadist ideology place utmost importance on the two core elements of the globalization of suicide attacks—the element of suicide operations, and the globalization of its actions. To that end, chapters 2 to 4 have provided ample evidence of the relationship between Al Qaeda and Salafi Jihad on the one hand and suicide attacks and global action on the other.

Suicide attacks have been Al Qaeda's preferred modus operandi since the second half of the 1990s. The group's intimate link with suicide operations is a consequence of both their tactical benefits and, more importantly, their symbolic value as a testament to the group's determination. Their intent is to help inspire many young Muslims to Al Qaeda's cause and to create such an intense amount of fear that the enemy's resolve is gradually weakened and discord is sowed among its ranks. More than any other terrorist outfit, Al Qaeda turned the individual duty for sacrifice into its formative ethos and managed to sustain this cult of martyrdom over a long period of time.

Al Qaeda has also, from the very outset, defined itself and behaved as a global actor, which over the course of time helped spread the tactic of suicide missions to more than thirty countries. Three reasons affected Al Qaeda's decision to become a terrorist entity of global dimensions. The first reason lies in Al Qaeda's core doctrine. Formulated by bin Laden's mentor Abdullah Azzam, the original plan for Al Qaeda envisioned that the group would develop into the vanguard of an international fighting force of global reach that would come to the aid of Muslims wherever they were in need. The second reason lies in the physical diffusion of Arab fighters from Afghanistan to other countries. Some of these Afghan Arabs had participated, albeit poorly, in the fight against the Soviets. Most fighters, however, trained in Al Qaeda–linked camps between 1996 and 2001, where most received instruction in insurgency, while a smaller, select group was trained as a terrorist cadre. From Afghanistan, these foreign fighters then returned to their host countries, to Western Europe and other regions, or remained in Afghanistan. The third reason affecting the group's decision to become a global terrorist actor was its deliberate change in strategy in the mid-1990s entailing a shift away from attacking the near enemy, that is, "un-Islamic" Arab and Muslim regimes, toward a strategy of attacking the far enemy, namely, the United States and its Western allies.

The conclusion is inescapable that Al Qaeda has successfully implemented its vision to become an actor with a global scope. In the aftermath of the attacks of 9/11, Al Qaeda has become the undisputed vanguard of a global jihad movement. Although weakened, the group has—within a few years of its forced exit from

Afghanistan—been able to reconstitute itself in the Pashtun-dominated region along the Afghan-Pakistan border.

Salafi-Jihadist ideology, meanwhile, has provided the much needed theological, religious, and moral justification for the employment of Al-Qaeda's SMs. The justification of this tactic distinguishes Salafi-Jihadists from most Muslims and even from most mainstream Salafists, who advocate a nonviolent call to Islam in order to spread their faith. Salafi-Jihadists regard "martyrdom operations," as the tactic is called in their ideological vernacular, as the ultimate form of devotion to God. Salafi-Jihadists extrapolate verses from the Quran and other holy Islamic texts in a highly selective fashion to provide justifications for a tactic that is inherently un-Islamic, inasmuch as suicide is expressly forbidden in Islam (as it is in the other monotheistic faiths). Ironically, it was the earlier, relatively widespread justification of suicide attacks against Israel among many Islamic scholars that paved the way for the eventual justification of suicide attacks even against fellow Muslims. The latter—especially the Shia, but also Sunnis who do not adopt the Salafi-Jihadist *Weltanschauung*—are simply described as infidels or apostates. These labels have done much to contribute to the downward spiral of suicidal violence that has killed far more Muslims than Westerners during the 1990s and, thus far, the 2000s.

Empirical analysis presented here provides firm evidence that Salafi-Jihadist organizations have become the predominant employers of this tactic. This fact is all the more worrisome because Salafi-Jihadist groups conduct far more lethal SMs than groups adhering to other ideologies.

How and why is the Salafi Jihad global in its call and aspirations? The Salafi Jihad is a religious ideology that, similar to other ideologies, attempts, at least in theory, to appeal to a broad audience. Its transnational appeal derives from its ability to offer an analysis and a vision that is seemingly inclusive. The Salafi Jihad purports to act on behalf of the entire *umma*, the global community of Muslim believers. The Internet plays a critical role in enabling the Salafi Jihad to spread this ideology to a vast number of potential recruits on a scale heretofore unseen.

Case Study Findings

Chapters 5 to 7 have offered discussions of more than a dozen countries where Salafi-Jihadist groups have conducted suicide attacks—specifically, Afghanistan, Algeria, Chechnya, Egypt, Indonesia, Jordan, Morocco, Pakistan, Saudi Arabia, Turkey, and Uzbekistan; the United Kingdom, with particular attention given to the 7/7 bombings; and Iraq, where the vast majority of SMs since 2003 have taken place. The conclusions drawn from the analysis of these cases are categorized into findings on the individual and organizational levels.

The Individual Level

This study has examined a number of biographies and wills of actual and would-be bombers, while keeping in mind the methodological problems related to the use of statements and other writings attributed to suicide attackers and the relatively small number of statements and wills identified compared with the total number of individuals who have conducted suicide attacks to date. Although these issues reduce the confidence level of the present findings to some extent, and render the findings regarding individual suicide attackers suggestive rather than conclusive, several trends surrounding suicide bombers nevertheless crystallize.

IDEOLOGY

Many bombers examined in this book appear to have been strongly influenced by Salafi-Jihadist ideology. According to their wills, their farewell videos, and reports from friends and family members, many of the suicide bombers echo the doctrines of Salafi Jihad. They adopt the general worldview offered by this ideology; the same diagnostic about the reasons for Islam's relative decline; the belief that Islam is attacked by an evil coalition; and the argument that their personal participation in martyrdom operations is the ultimate proof of their religious devotion. They have internalized Al Qaeda's and its Salafi-Jihadist allies' broad conception of the enemy as being composed not only of Westerners in general, Christians, and Jews, but also of those Muslims whose beliefs and practices do not meet the standards set by Salafi-Jihadists. They also buy into the Salafi-Jihadist belief that martyrdom is the ultimate form of waging jihad.

Though ideology matters a great deal for the rising global appeal of Salafi-Jihadist suicide bombers, there is no evidence—and no attempt to argue—that ideology is the cause of suicide attacks per se. The causes of suicide attacks are complex and must be found in the interplay of personal motivations, strategic and tactical objectives of the sponsoring groups, and the larger societal and structural factors affecting the bomber and the group. In addition, ideology is acquired by individuals for reasons having to do with emotions and beliefs—a complex process whose examination exceeds the scope of this book.

If ideology is not the cause of suicide attacks per se, then what is its role? This study suggests that ideology plays an important role in that it helps reduce the suicide attacker's reservations about perpetrating the act of killing and dying. Specifically, ideology fills two roles: it helps the suicide bomber justify the act, and it helps the suicide attacker to morally disengage himself from his act and from the victim.

Justifying the Act. Ideology helps the suicide attacker justify the deed by articulating why this act is called for and why every "true" Muslim must be willing to participate in it. The ideology describes—and statements by suicide bombers reflect—the need to defend Islam from attack as an individual duty for each and every Muslim; the participation in jihad as the ultimate proof of one's worthiness as a Muslim; and the failure to participate in jihad as an act of heresy.

Ideology shapes the mental framework of the suicide attacker by constantly repeating the West's real or perceived infractions against Islam. These infractions appear particularly grave to some Muslims because Salafi-Jihadists tend to employ conspiracy theories to further incite fear and hatred of the West. These conspiracy theories may involve a gross exaggeration of real infractions (e.g., accusing the United States of killing many more civilians in a military operation than have actually been killed), or a fabrication of lies (e.g., accusing the White House or Mossad of being behind 9/11). These conspiracy theories are often designed to deflect blame from Muslims (e.g., blaming the West, as opposed to Osama bin Laden, for 9/11), thus portraying Muslims as victims. This ongoing victimization of Muslims—a key Salafi-Jihadist strategy of indoctrination—has created a siege mentality among its adherents, who have accepted the notion that they are constantly under attack and subject to humiliation.

Moral Disengagement. Ideology is also a key tool used to morally disengage suicide attackers from their deeds, as well as from their victims. Processes of moral disengagement, for instance, often involve the creation of ingroups and outgroups. Salafi-Jihadist ideology helps to create this dichotomy of good-versus-evil by dividing the world between true Muslims and *kuffar*, or infidels. Dehumanization of the enemy is another mechanism of moral disengagement. From the perspective of the Salafi Jihad, the West, Christians, Jews, and the Shia are regarded as defiled, degenerate, bereft of any sense of decency, unjust, and cruel.

MOTIVATIONS

The second major finding concerns the individual bombers' motivations. The cases examined here strongly suggest that individual suicide bombers reach a decision to commit an SM for different reasons. Any attempt to explain the motivations of individual bombers using monocausal explanations is hence doomed to fail. Suicide bombers are also likely to be influenced by several motivations at the same time. The cases studied here suggest that four central motivations, which can be mutually reinforcing, are particularly salient among globalized suicide attackers: revenge, humiliation, commitment, and rewards.

Revenge. Statements and wills of the bombers examined in chapters 5 to 7 reflect an intense desire to exact revenge upon the enemy by inflicting upon him the same pain that he has allegedly inflicted on the bomber's brethren. An intense anger, and hatred of local Arab and Muslim regimes, the United States, Jews, and the Shia, who are believed to have formed an evil coalition against Islam, can be heard time and again, and many attacks are justified as direct acts of vengeance against these groups. Revenge, which may be heightened by humiliation or a crisis of identity, is perhaps the single most important motive for a person to become a suicide bomber.

Humiliation. Based on the statements by suicide bombers examined here, there are strong indications that many of them volunteer to perpetrate a suicide attack in order to restore their honor and, by extension, the honor of an Islam that they believe to have been subjected to repeated humiliation by the West over centuries and up to the present. There seem to be two levels in which humiliation affects human bombs, namely on a collective and on a personal level.

On a collective level, Osama bin Laden and other leaders of Al Qaeda are relatively successful in portraying local struggles of Muslims as part and parcel of a larger, global struggle between Muslims and infidels. By suggesting to Muslims in Afghanistan, Iraq, or Saudi Arabia that they are being ruled by apostate, pro-American regimes that are mere puppets of the West, and that their own alleged misery is the same plight that Muslims endure in other places like Palestine, bin Laden delocalizes smaller conflicts and in actuality helps portray local struggles as part of a broader clash of civilizations. Al Qaeda tries to convince Muslims that their humiliation occurs on the collective level—a result of centuries of anti-Muslim policies enacted by a conspiracy against Islam. To prove their point, Al Qaeda and its associated movements disseminate videos that depict the asymmetries that Muslims face in battles against the infidel armies, or that portray smiling Western leaders, often accompanied by apostate Arab and Muslim leaders, suggesting that they are all in a conspiracy, plotting additional crimes against the true followers of Muhammad.

Humiliation, however, also works on a more personal level. Many Muslims feel a growing sense that they are personally impotent in the face of the wholesale denigration of Muslims by an evil West. Groups employing suicide bombings exploit these feelings, suggesting time and again that conducting a suicide bombing is an act of heroism and manliness. Appeals to ordinary Muslims to "act like men" are evidenced in repeated claims on the part of the organization that Western countries dishonor Muslim women. These claims are intended to heighten the sense of urgency and shame that helps convince many young Muslims to seek violent action against the perpetrators.

Commitment. A strong commitment to the cell or larger group appears as a frequent motive for suicide attackers. Commitment to one's kin, a small social group, or larger community—which in some cases may be explained by primordial bonds—is intensified, in the case of globalized suicide attacks, by a shared sense of victimization. The Internet plays a crucial role in providing a sense of brotherhood, a sense of solidarity, belonging, pride, and empowerment to suicide bombers. It is partly as a result of the Internet that the new pattern of globalized suicide attacks exhibits a large number of cases where grievances are vicariously rather than personally experienced. Occupation, therefore, must not have been personally experienced by a suicide bomber in order for him or her to feel humiliated enough to seek such drastic action.

Cases discussed in chapters 5 to 7 suggest that a strong commitment is also felt toward family and friends or at the level of the small group. Several suicide bombers were brothers and sisters, including members of the 9/11 cell and suicide bombers in Morocco and Uzbekistan. Others were friends before deciding to become suicide bombers or were from the same neighborhood and likely knew each other, including suicide bombers in Afghanistan, Morocco, Pakistan, Saudi Arabia, Turkey, and the United Kingdom and many of the suicide bombers who have arrived in Iraq. As the case of the London bombers showed, the small group formed by Mohammed Siddique Khan was likely radicalized not only by attending training camps in Al Qaeda but also by spending much time together engaging in activities that strengthened their mutual bond and resolve.

Rewards. Statements and wills examined in this book strongly suggest that suicide bombers believe that by becoming a martyr, they will reap a number of benefits. They firmly believe that the act of martyrdom is a service to God and pleasing to him. Because of their willingness to sacrifice their lives in the service of God, they believe that he rewards the martyr by washing away all of the martyr's sins. Several biographies examined here suggested the use of a martyrdom operation as a mechanism for self-purification. The belief that martyrdom erases all one's sins in one fell swoop may help explain why a number of suicide bombers had criminal backgrounds.

Furthermore, the martyr believes that he will end up in paradise, where he will enjoy the benefits retained for martyrs, especially a reserved space in heaven for scores of family members as well as the services of beautiful women. Although the possibility of sexual motivations driving male suicide attackers is dismissed by some researchers, statements made by the bombers, as evidenced here, are replete with references to the women of paradise. While this fact, in itself, does not prove that suicide bombers die and kill for the hope of sexual pleasure, it is nevertheless clear that sponsoring groups continuously promise these rewards to would-be bombers. It is fair to assume that these groups would not consistently preach the rewards of paradise if they did not believe that these promises resonate at some level with would-be bombers. That said, there is no evidence suggesting that the expectation of such personal benefits is either a necessary or sufficient factor for a person to become a suicide bomber.

LACK OF A GENERAL PROFILE OF THE SUICIDE BOMBER

A third finding of the cases on the individual level confirms the conclusions of previous studies, namely that no general profile of suicide bombers can be established. Although most suicide attackers tend to be young (in their twenties) and male, there are quite a few exceptions even to these trends. Suicide attackers have been male or female, younger or older, richer or poorer, single or married (some with children), employed or unemployed. Some suicide attackers have engaged in petty crime, while others have not. Some appear to have had a difficult childhood, while others have grown up under seemingly solid circumstances. In sum, the finding of the official government account of the London bombings, which has found the four July 7, 2005, London bombers to be "largely unexceptional," appears to apply to suicide attackers at large.

Importantly, many of the suicide bombers examined here do not have a religious background. While it would be foolish to deny that most suicide attackers, certainly since 9/11, kill and die in the name of Islam, it would be equally wrong to neglect the fact that many suicide bombers have not been brought up in religious families. Several suicide bombers have converted to Islam from Christianity. Even some of the Muslim bombers can be said to have undergone a conversion of sorts from traditional (even "secular") Islam to Salafi Jihad in the years before executing an attack. This transformation is akin to a conversion to a born-again Muslim, complete with profound changes in behavior and lifestyle. It is hence wrong to assume that Islam per se is the root cause of suicide terrorism—a nonsensical assumption in any case, given the many examples of suicide attacks perpetrated by non-Muslim individuals and non-Muslim and even secular organizations. This finding hence underscores the fact that the Salafi-Jihadist ideology must be distinguished from the religion of Islam.

The Organizational Level

At the organizational level, tactical and strategic factors have led the groups under examination, many of whom have had an association with Al Qaeda or been otherwise influenced by Salafi-Jihadist ideology, to perpetrate suicide attacks. The evidence examined here—which ranges from written statements by the leadership of the groups, including books, papers, and other writings, to video recordings that may recruit members, claim responsibilities for attacks, record wills of suicide bombers, and issue statements by group leadership—suggests a number of conclusions about the groups that are planning and perpetrating globalized suicide attacks.

TACTICS

Tactical advantages of suicide attacks are of equal importance to Al Qaeda and its affiliates as they have been to groups that employed this tactic before the emergence of Al Qaeda. Thus, tactical benefits as a cause for suicide missions are one of the most striking continuities since 1981. Suicide operations are cost-effective, highly lethal, and the most accurate weapons available. Their use requires little planning, yet suicide attacks are among the most shocking and awe-inspiring tactics possible. Just like traditional groups employing suicide attacks, contemporary Salafi-Jihadist groups do not shy away from acknowledging the tactical value of these attacks, as many examples, from statements by bin Laden to Zawahiri to Zarqawi, have shown.

STRATEGY

The second finding relates to the strategy of suicide attacks. Unlike tactical benefits, which are universally important for all groups employing SMs, strategic reasons for the use of SMs differ significantly. In particular, there are stark contrasts between the traditional pattern of SMs of the 1980s and 1990s, and the globalized pattern of the past decade. The cases examined here show that most contemporary campaigns of SMs are designed to undermine the stability of a regime that the perpetrating groups deem illegitimate. In Afghanistan, Algeria, Egypt, Iraq, Morocco, Pakistan, Saudi Arabia, and Uzbekistan, local groups, joined in some cases by foreign entities, have targeted their own regimes, charging them with acting in an "un-Islamic" fashion. In Algeria, Egypt, Indonesia, Iraq, Jordan, Morocco, Pakistan, Turkey, and Uzbekistan, SMs have also targeted the tourist industry as well as international organizations such as the UN. The majority of contemporary groups employing suicide attacks have also assumed radically anti-Semitic positions. In a number of countries, including Egypt, Jordan, Kenya, Morocco, Tunisia, Turkey, and Uzbekistan, these groups have targeted (or attempted to target) institutions affiliated with Jews or Israel. Although these attacks could be understood merely as attacks against foreigners or outside organizations, in reality Salafi-Jihadist groups carrying out these attacks believe that they kill several birds with one stone. Not only do they punish the infidel foreigners and organizations that have helped humiliate Islam, but attacks against these institutions also help undermine stability in the country where the attacks are taking place. Jews are, together with the United States, at the very top of the list of enemies of the Salafi Jihad, and hence attacks against Jewish institutions are, in these groups' calculations, always worthwhile. They are also an integral part of the heritage of Salafi-Jihadist ideology, given the many examples of anti-Jewish resentment in Hassan al-Banna's and Sayyed Qutb's writings.

In reality, however, Salafi-Jihadists make few distinctions between their targets, be they the UN, tourists, government officials, or Jews. All of these targets are perceived as bastions of the infidel, and attacks against any of them serve the cause of the grand struggle against the enemies of Islam.

This is in marked contrast to the target patterns of non-Salafi-Jihadist groups that have conducted suicide attacks during the 1980s and most of the 1990s. Those groups, such as the LTTE, Hamas, the PKK, or Hizballah, had a relatively narrow conception of the enemy. These groups may have also considered their enemy government illegitimate, but that was not the stated reason why groups employed suicide attacks. Traditionally, groups conducted SMs mostly as a strategy to end a foreign occupation, establish a national homeland, or both.

In the cases under review, SMs occurred in many countries that were not occupied by any objective standard. Algeria, Egypt, Jordan, Morocco, Pakistan, Saudi Arabia, Turkey, and Uzbekistan, for example, are not occupied by a foreign army. Occupation, of course, plays a role in suicide attacks today, but Salafi-Jihadists have a far more abstract conception of occupation. It is no longer necessary for foreign troops to be present in a country in order for that country to be perceived as occupied, though such a foreign presence certainly helps. More important is the perception that a given regime is complicit in the attempted subjugation and humiliation of Muslims, which renders the country occupied in a more indirect way. In the eyes of Salafi-Jihadists, regimes in Algeria, Jordan,

Morocco, and Pakistan that entertain relations with the United States, and may even provide open or tacit support for U.S. actions in the Middle East, are as deserving of punishment as are Western infidel countries themselves because they are perceived to be puppets of the United States and its allies, and are hence "de facto occupied." One of the implications is that, in the event of a total U.S. withdrawal from the region, some Salafi-Jihadists may be assuaged. However, the vast majority will continue to find evidence of foreign occupation even if not a single Western soldier is left in the Middle East. In reality, short of a replacement of all Middle Eastern regimes by Salafi-Jihadists, the latter will continue to claim that the region is occupied.

Traditionally, countries targeted by SMs were attacked by groups who adhered to a different religion or belonged to a different ethnic group—be it the Sinhalese, Jews, or Turks. Many of today's groups, however, have replaced these narrower distinctions with a much broader dividing line. In their mind-set, this is no longer a war of individual ethnic groups or states but a cosmic war in which true Muslim believers (read: Salafi-Jihadists) are pitted against infidels and apostates. Fighting the nonbelievers using the most efficient means necessary is the true strategy of global jihadists.

THE ROLE OF AL QAEDA

The third finding on the group level concerns the various groups' links to Al Qaeda. The extent of the various groups' ties to the Al Qaeda core leadership varies from case to case. Some of the groups discussed in chapters 5 to 7 have gone as far as swearing loyalty to Osama bin Laden and are now known as Al Qaeda in the Islamic Maghreb, Al Qaeda in the Arabian Peninsula, or Al Qaeda in Iraq. Other groups, such as the Moroccan Islamic Combatant Group, Jemaah Islamiyah, the Taliban, or the Islamic Jihad Group, are affiliates of Al Qaeda. The status of still others, such as the group responsible for attacks on tourist sites in Egypt, remains unclear, but it is likely that, at the very least, these groups are inspired by Al Qaeda's message.

In fact, all groups examined in chapters 5 to 7 are, at the very least, strongly influenced by the strategic message relayed by Al Qaeda's core leadership (especially Osama bin Laden and Ayman al-Zawahiri). This is in stark contrast to groups such as the LTTE, PKK, Hizballah, and the various Palestinian organizations—groups that have been categorized here as traditional groups—that are not influenced or inspired by Al Qaeda's strategic message.[1]

The influence of Al Qaeda and the adoption of Salafi-Jihadist ideology also affect how these groups recruit, indoctrinate, and incite new adherents. Ideology enables individuals to perpetrate the act of killing and dying by helping to articulate the justification for the act and by helping the suicide attacker to morally disengage from his act and from the victim. In supplying this ideology and otherwise strengthening the resolve of the suicide attacker—that is, through indoctrination and incitement—the group plays a crucial part in the process of readying the individual for the attack. The cases studied in this book have provided many examples of how these groups indoctrinate and incite members or potential recruits. They do so, inter alia, by extolling jihad as the most honorable way to fight; by appealing to young Muslims' honor, manhood, and thirst for revenge by mentioning, for example, that Muslim women have been dishonored; by shaming individuals to act by claiming that even old men and women have joined the jihad; by employing *takfir*, the process of labeling those who do not agree with them as heretics; and by helping the volunteers overcome their fear of death, by telling would-be bombers that the martyr's death is painless, that all of his sins will be washed away, or that he will enjoy the benefits of the hereafter.

Implications for Research on Suicide Attacks

This study has argued that the impact of Al Qaeda and the Salafi Jihad on the phenomenon of suicide attacks is so significant that they define a completely new pattern of this tactic. The globalized pattern of suicide attacks differs from the traditional, localized pattern in five important ways. The first is in the *type of conflict* in which the attacks occur. Whereas traditional, localized attacks tend to occur in long-standing, historical conflicts and within an identified conflict zone—such as the Israeli-Palestinian conflict or the Tamil-Sinhalese conflict in Sri Lanka—globalized suicide attacks, such as the attacks of 9/11, often occur outside recognized conflict zones and are not necessarily the result of a decade-long conflict between two nations.

The second difference concerns the *ideology of the groups* perpetrating these attacks. Whereas traditional suicide attacks have been employed by both religious and secular groups (e.g., the religious Hamas and the secular PKK), globalized suicide attacks are planned and executed by Salafi-Jihadist organizations.

The third distinction is the *geographic scope of actors*. Whereas localized suicide attacks have been executed mostly by subnational actors and executed close to home, today's globalized suicide attacks are planned and executed by transnational terrorist and insurgent networks and movements. Thus, they may not be planned in the country where they are executed; the suicide bombers may detonate themselves in countries in which they do not reside; and attacks may be executed outside of a traditional zone of conflict.

The fourth difference relates to the *conceptions of their targets*. Whereas traditional organizations such as Hizballah, the PKK, and the LTTE limit their targeting mostly to people and assets of a narrowly defined enemy state (i.e., Israel, Turkey, and Sri Lanka, respectively), many contemporary organizations conducting SMs have a far more broadly defined understanding of their enemy and regard not only their host countries as enemies, but also their allies, the West in general, and even Arab and Muslim countries that do not abide by the Salafi-Jihadists' understanding of how Muslims should conduct their lives. Al Qaeda in Iraq, for example, does not limit its attacks to Iraq but has also been responsible for suicide attacks in Jordan and possibly the United Kingdom.

A final variation is the vastly different *conceptions of their goals*. Whereas traditional organizations conducting SMs have narrowly defined goals, such as the establishment of a national homeland, globalized groups conducting SMs today may believe that they are engaged in a cosmic war of good versus evil. In this total war, jihad (understood in its militant form) is an individual and permanent obligation in defense of Islam. It must be fought when Islam is under attack, as it is perceived to be in Iraq, India, Israel, Afghanistan, Turkey, and many other countries. However, Salafi-Jihadists have a rather soft understanding of when Islam is under attack. Islam is under attack not only when a foreign army invades a Muslim country but increasingly when even the slightest infraction is perceived.

The implications of this important distinction for the study on terrorism is that it allows researchers to place existing explanations into the proper context, recognize some important limitations, and define some important new avenues of research. Take the explanation championed by Robert Pape. At first glance, his argument that suicide terrorism is a response to foreign occupation appears to have some merit, given the widespread use of suicide terrorism among communities vying for a national homeland, such as the Palestinians and Tamils. Upon closer inspection, however, suicide attacks increasingly occur in places where there is no discernible occupation. Drawing a theoretical distinction between different patterns of suicide attacks allows us to place the role of occupation in its proper context. Thus, foreign occupation is far more important in countries whose suicide attacks fall under the more traditional, localized pattern. It is less of a necessary factor in the globalized pattern associated with Salafi-Jihadist ideology because Salafi-Jihadist ideology regards even the smallest hint of Western influence as evidence of occupation.

Another explanation that the theoretical division into patterns of suicide attacks can help contextualize is the outbidding theory, which argues that suicide attacks are used by groups when they are in competition with others for the sympathies of a local population. That theory may have explained the adoption of suicide attacks in some cases, but there is less evidence of outbidding among many of the contemporary groups employing suicide attacks. Take the London bombings of July 7, 2005, for example. The outbidding theory is unable to explain the 7/7 bombings because they were the first suicide attacks in the United Kingdom. The group around Mohammed Siddique Khan had no other group to outbid because no other group had employed this tactic in the United Kingdom before. In addition, the London bombers hardly vied for the sympathies of the domestic population—on the contrary, they detested the local population to such an extent that they blew themselves up in its midst.

Future research on suicide missions would greatly benefit from studies attempting to shed additional light into the nature and causes of radicalization in small cells, the role of social networks in generating terrorism, and the impact of culture, ideology, religion, and nationalism on suicide attacks.[2] Understanding major conceptual differences between types of suicide attacks can help refine such research in the future.

Policy Implications

Most suicide attacks today are perpetrated by terrorist groups (as opposed to nation-states), and the majority of these groups adhere to a radical Salafi-Jihadist ideology. If this premise is accepted, then the United States and its allies are facing, first and foremost, an ideological enemy. Challenging that ideology is a crucial component of an overall counterterrorism strategy that has often been overlooked.

Before we consider the content of these challenges, however, it is important to state that no counterterrorism strategy can focus on one measure alone, even such an important measure as waging a battle against an ideology. The components of a national strategy to combat suicide missions must include the following measures:

1. *Analytical measures*, designed to understand and reduce the risk factors of terrorism and suicide attacks, such as humiliation
2. *Outreach efforts*, which consist of measures that help improve the quality of life, education, governance, and civil society in communities that produce terrorists

3. *Preventive and preemptive measures*, employed by the intelligence services of a given state to thwart terrorist attacks
4. *Bureaucratic streamlining*, focused in particular on improving the institutional coordination and information sharing within a given state
5. *International cooperation*, emphasizing information sharing between states
6. *Offensive action*, including covert action and military action where needed
7. *Defensive measures*, including the hardening of physical infrastructure
8. *Disruptive measures*, focusing on the disruption of terrorist financing and foreign travel of suspects
9. *Counter-organizational measures*, focusing on exploiting the internal, organizational quarrels within the enemy's ranks
10. *Law enforcement measures*, designed to apprehend terrorists and bring them to justice
11. *Consequence management*, designed to train security, evacuation, and medical personnel and other first responders to better deal with terrorist attacks after they occur
12. *Counterideological measures*

Challenging Salafi-Jihadist ideology, the twelfth critically important measure, is a monumental and highly complex task, and the battle of wills must be fought by those who have the most to lose from terrorism. In this struggle, the United States must take a secondary role. Because of the grave danger the Salafi Jihad poses to Muslims even more than to Westerners, the ideological challenge to the Salafi Jihad must come first and foremost from among nonviolent Salafists, Islamists, and moderate Muslims.

The United States and its allies can do little to influence what must primarily be an internal Muslim debate over the future of the Muslim community. It can, however, discreetly convey to moderate Muslims and nonviolent Salafists why waging this internal battle is so important, thus quietly supporting these communities without running the risk of exposing them as "lackeys of the West." As Muslims gear up for this debate, Western states can respectfully convey to moderate Muslims what most of them already know, namely that the credibility of the Salafi Jihad suffers from a fundamental contradiction: on the one hand, Salafi-Jihadists claim to act for the benefit of Muslims; on the other hand, however, Muslims suffer the consequences of Salafi-Jihadist ideology and terrorism more than any other group.

Moderate Muslims could employ many arguments to undermine Salafi-Jihadists, including the following:

- *Muslims are the primary victims of Salafi-Jihadist terrorism, including suicide attacks.* More Muslims than non-Muslims have died and been maimed by Salafi-Jihadist terror in the past three decades. In Algeria alone, perhaps 100,000 or more Muslim lives have been lost to brutal acts of violence committed in large part by the Salafi-Jihadist GIA. In Iraq, the theater of most suicide attacks that have taken place since 1981, far more Iraqi civilians than foreign military or foreign civilian personnel have been killed by suicide attacks. In Afghanistan, civilians are the prime victims of the growing number of suicide attacks, even if these attacks were aimed at the International Security Assistance Force (ISAF). In Pakistan, too, a growing number of highly lethal suicide attacks kill above all Pakistanis.
- *Salafi-Jihadists openly justify the killing of Muslims under a logic of "the ends justifying the means."* Innocent Muslims not only die as a by-product of war and insurgency waged by Salafi-Jihadists, but Salafi-Jihadists believe that Muslims are expendable because, as Salafi-Jihadists believe, Muslim blood is cheap. As Abu Musab al-Zarqawi, for example, has noted, "Admittedly, the killing of a number of Muslims whom it is forbidden to kill is undoubtedly a grave evil; however, it is permissible to commit this evil—indeed, it is even required—in order to ward off a greater evil, namely, the evil of suspending jihad."[3]
- *The practice of* takfir, *the labeling of fellow Muslims as kuffar or infidels, is dividing the Islamic community and runs the risk of creating a Muslim civil war.* The Algerian civil war of the 1990s has already put the devastating consequences of the practice of *takfir* on display. The use of this label has created serious tensions within the Islamic community, and it is used to justify scores of suicide bombings against Muslims in places like Afghanistan, Algeria, Iraq, Jordan, and Pakistan. Unless rejected completely by moderate Muslims, who form the vast majority in Islam, the logic of *takfir* will continue to lead the Islamic *umma* on a downward spiral of self-inflicted violence. Moderate Muslims should remind their coreligionists that wrongly accusing another Muslim of being an infidel is a major sin in Islam.
- *Suicide is forbidden in Islam.* Salafi-Jihadists justify suicide attacks, which they euphemistically label martyrdom operations, by saying that people who commit suicide do it for personal reasons, whereas martyrs sacrifice themselves for God and the larger community. Of course, it is impossible to prove what the real intent of the individual bomber is, but there is much evidence that suicide bombers choose to become human bombs for personal more than for altruistic reasons. The expectation of personal rewards, including the belief that through an act of martyrdom all of the martyr's sins are erased, is likely to play

a huge role. Moderate Muslims should also ask why Salafi-Jihadists accuse the West of hedonism ("We love death, while the West loves life"), but offer their martyrs promises of hedonistic pleasures in the afterlife.

- *Organizations are exploiting Muslims for their own ends.* Moderate Muslims and Salafis who do not support violence must be made aware that there is a growing body of indications that groups are exploiting young Muslims for their own ends. In Afghanistan and Iraq, there are more frequent reports that individuals have been forced to blow themselves up against their will. Others have been duped, detonating themselves without their knowledge. Reports cited in this book suggest that more and more children and, in the case of Afghanistan, mentally unstable individuals are used by Salafi-Jihadist organizations as cannon fodder.
- *Leaders of organizations planning suicide bombings act hypocritically.* Moderate Muslims must ask themselves why the leaders of the organizations who perpetrate suicide attacks rarely, if ever, conduct a suicide operation themselves. If self-sacrifice is the highest duty that a Muslim can show to God, as bin Laden and his cohorts claim, then why are these leaders not the first to conduct a suicide bombing themselves?
- *Many Salafi-Jihadist leaders lack religious authority.* Al Qaeda leaders often issue fatwas declaring war on their enemies or legitimating a certain tactic, but they oftentimes lack the formal schooling necessary, and hence the authority, to issue religious decrees. They often ignore other, more benevolent fatwas issued by individuals who are far more knowledgeable about Islam.
- *Salafi-Jihadists offer no attractive vision of the future.* Moderate Muslims should ask themselves and Salafi-Jihadists what life under the rule of Salafi-Jihadists would look like. They would find that life would look much like Afghanistan under Taliban rule. Salafi-Jihadists do not offer any concrete political program. They build their raison d'être around what they are against, not what they are for.

The battle against suicide attacks is unlikely to be won by exposing the inconsistencies of the Salafi Jihad alone, but doing so will be necessary to reduce the appeal of the ideology justifying the bulk of today's "martyrdom operations." Even the most efficient counterterrorism strategy, however, will not eliminate the threat posed by suicide attacks entirely. Complete victory in the improperly termed "war against terrorism" is unlikely because individuals and groups have been willing, using various justifications, to die and kill for a cause since biblical times. Countries affected by the horrendous consequences of suicide missions would therefore be wise to shift their focus away from an attempt to defeat suicide attacks and toward a more dedicated attempt to manage the problem more effectively. Progress in the struggle against suicide attacks will be more likely if our commitment to fight suicide attacks matches or exceeds the commitment of suicide bombers to inflict damage.

Ideological Affiliation of Groups That Have Conducted Suicide Attacks from 1981 to 2007

1. As-Sirat al Moustaqim[1]	Salafi-Jihadist[2]
2. Al Dawa[3]	Shia
3. Al Qaeda	Salafi-Jihadist
4. Al Qaeda in Iraq[4]	Salafi-Jihadist
5. Amal	Shia
6. Ansar Allah	Shia
7. Ansar al-Sunna[5]	Salafi-Jihadist
8. Arab Resistance Movement	Unknown
9. Armed Islamic Group (GIA)[6]	Salafi-Jihadist
10. Army of the Levant[7]	Salafi-Jihadist
11. Chechen Separatists	Hybrid[8]
12. Chechen Separatists: Arbi Barayev[9]	Hybrid
13. Chechen Separatists: Karachaev Jamaat[10]	Unknown
14. Chechen Separatists: Ramzan Akhmadov[11]	Hybrid
15. Revolutionary People's Liberation Party/Front (DHKP/C)	Marxist
16. Fatah	Nationalist-separatist
17. Hamas[12]	Mainstream Islamist/nationalist-separatist[13]
18. Harkat-ul-Mujahideen[14]	Salafi-Jihadist
19. Hizballah	Shia
20. Hizb-ul-Mujahideen (HM)[15]	Salafi-Jihadist
21. Hizb-ut-Tahrir (HUT)[16]	Salafi-Jihadist
22. Islamic Army in Iraq[17]	Mainstream Islamist/nationalist-separatist
23. Islamic Movement of Uzbekistan (IMU)[18]	Salafi-Jihadist
24. Jaish-e-Muhammad (JEM)[19]	Salafi-Jihadist
25. Jamaat Jund-al-Sahaba[20]	Salafi-Jihadist
26. Jamatul Mujahedin Bangladesh (JMB)[21]	Salafi-Jihadist
27. Jemaah Islamiyah (JI)[22]	Salafi-Jihadist

28. Kashmir Separatists[23]	Hybrid
29. Kurdistan Workers Party (PKK)	Marxist/national-separatist
30. Lashkar-e-Jhangvi (LEJ)[24]	Salafi-Jihadist
31. Lashkar-e-Taiba (LET)[25]	Salafi-Jihadist
32. Lebanese Liberation Organization[26]	Unknown
33. Liberation Tigers of Tamil Eelam (LTTE)	Nationalist-separatist
34. Moroccan Islamic Combatant Group (GICM)[27]	Salafi-Jihadist
35. Mujahideen Shura Council[28]	Salafi-Jihadist
36. Palestinian Islamic Jihad	Mainstream Islamist/nationalist-separatist
37. Popular Front for the Liberation of Palestine (PFLP)	Marxist/national-separatist
38. Riyad as-Saliheen Martyrs Brigade[29]	Hybrid
39. Saddam Loyalists	Nationalist-separatist
40. Syrian Baath Organization	Nationalist-separatist
41. Syrian Social Nationalist Party	Marxist/national-separatist
42. Taliban[30]	Salafi-Jihadist
43. Victory and Jihad in Greater Syria[31]	Unknown

Notes to Appendix

1. Al-Assirat al-Moustaquim is the cell responsible for the Casablanca bombings. It is sometimes referred to as Salafia Jihadiya. A panel of eight experts at the Rand Corporation concluded that Salafia Jihadiya has "internalized the Al Qaeda worldview of Global Jihad." The panel consisted of Angel Rabasa, Peter Chalk, Kim Cragin, Sara A. Daly, Heather S. Gregg, Theodore W. Karasik, Kevin A. O'Brien, and William Rosenau. See Rabasa et al., *Beyond Al-Qaeda, Part I*, xxii, 2, 79. See also "Group Profile: Salafia Jihadia," *Terrorism Knowledge Base*. Available at www.tkb.org/Group.jsp?groupID=4257, last accessed 23 November 2006.

2. Salafi-Jihadist groups have been coded as such if any of the following applies: Membership of and/or adherence to Al Qaeda is reflected in the group's name (an example includes group 4); the group has "internalized the worldview of Al Qaeda and global jihad" (groups 4, 18, 23, 24, 27, 30, 31, and 34); the group is known to engage in *takfir* (group 9); or the group is devoted to the use of violence to overthrow an existing Islamic regime or regimes with the aim to create a transnational caliphate in its stead (groups 21, 26, 35, and 38).

3. According to the National Security Studies Center at Haifa University, a group called Al Dawa conducted at least three suicide attacks in Kuwait between 1983 and 1985. The Terrorism Knowledge Base identifies the group as Hizballah, a Shiite organization.

4. A panel of eight experts concluded that Tanzim Qaidat al-Jihad fi Bilad al-Rafidayn (Al Qaeda in Iraq) has "internalized the Al Qaeda worldview of Global Jihad." The report labels this group the "Al-Zarqawi network." Rabasa et al., *Beyond Al-Qaeda, Part I*, xxii, 2, 79.

5. According to the Terrorism Knowledge Base, Ansar al-Sunna (Followers of the Tradition) is an Iraqi Jihadist group, dedicated to the establishment of an Islamic state based on Sharia in Iraq, which it aims to achieve by the defeat of coalition forces and foreign occupation. The

group believes that jihad in Iraq has become obligatory for Muslims." See "Group Profile: Ansar Al-Sunnah Army," *Terrorism Knowledge Base*. Available at www.tkb.org/Group.jsp?groupID= 3921, last accessed 23 November 2006. On Ansar al-Sunna's Salafi roots, see also Hafez, "Suicide Terrorism in Iraq"; International Crisis Group, "In Their Own Words"; and Eisenstadt and White, "Assessing Iraq's Sunni Arab Insurgency."

6. The GIA engages in *takfir*. See Rabasa et al., *Beyond Al-Qaeda, Part II*, 28.

7. A group named the Army of the Levant (Jund al-Sham) took responsibility for the 19 March 2005 bombing of a theater in Doha, Qatar, that is near a British school and is popular among Westerners. The name has been claimed by several Sunni Islamic extremist entities, all or none of which may be tied together. "Although the connection between any or all of the Jund al-Sham entities is unclear, they all (save for the final group that may exist in name only) continue to clash with security elements and rival factions in their respective areas of operation in order to achieve the unified purpose of replacing what they view as misguided forms of Islam and governmental rule with their vision of a traditional Islamic caliphate extending across the Levant. Likewise, whether or not they are directly descended from Zarqawi's original band of fighters they represent a continued threat to the security of the Levant region in which al-Qaeda's presence is weaker, thereby fulfilling the purpose envisioned by Zarqawi's group. Like many second- and third-tier Islamic extremist entities, the Jund al-Sham organizations are believed to be incorporated, however loosely, under the greater al-Qaeda umbrella and therefore may be expected to remain active in various forms and guises throughout the region." See "Group Profile: Jund Al-Sham," *Terrorism Knowledge Base*. Available at www.tkb.org/Group .jsp?groupID=4503, last accessed 23 November 2006.

8. Hybrid organizations are defined here as organizations that are composed of members who have adopted a Salafi-Jihadist ideology as well as members who appear not to have adopted Salafi-Jihadist ideology but seem to be motivated primarily by ethnonationalist and separatist reasons. In actuality, of course, most Salafi-Jihadist groups are hybrids of one form or another, but there is nevertheless a difference between groups that have officially adopted an Al Qaeda worldview of global jihad (which are coded as Salafi-Jihadist), and hybrid groups that appear to be composed only in part of a membership that has adopted Salafi-Jihadist principles.

9. According to the Haifa/University of Texas at Austin database, on 7 June 2000, a truck bomb driven by two Chechen suicide bombers, one male and one female, exploded in Alkhan Yurt after it broke through a fence and stopped outside a building where an OMON (Special Forces Police) unit was housed. Chechen separatists under the leadership of Arbi Barayev, who are also known as the Special Purpose Islamic Regiment (SPIR), claimed responsibility. According to the Terrorism Knowledge Base, the primary objective of SPIR is the liberation of Chechnya and the formation of an independent Chechen state. "To achieve this goal, Barayev forged alliances with other prominent Chechen resistance organizations as well as foreign Islamic groups. After the start of the second Russo-Chechen War in 1999, SPIR greatly expanded its operations and became a significant force against Russian federal forces. It was also at this time that the first Islamic militants began entering Chechnya to take up the 'cause' against the Russian infidel. These 'mujahideen' offered connections to terrorist financers beyond Russia's borders. However, the Islamic fighters held larger aspirations than creating a Chechen state; they promoted a more radical strain of Islam and a desire to install a fundamentalist Islamic republic governed by Sharia law in Chechnya. Yet conventional wisdom holds that Chechen

terrorists, such as Arbi Barayev, tolerated the religious zealotry in order to take advantage of the funding and fighters provided by Islamic terrorist organizations. As the conflict continued, many observers noted that SPIR and other groups were actually integrating Islamic goals into their primary objectives, alongside Chechen independence." See "Group Profile: Special Purpose Islamic Regiment (SPIR)," *Terrorism Knowledge Base*. Available at www.tkb.org/Group.jsp?groupID=3732, last accessed 25 November 2006.

10. According to the dataset of the National Security Studies Center, Haifa University, on 24 March 2001, Chechen separatists under the leadership of Karachaev sent three suicide bombers to an area near the Russian border with Chechnya, where they detonated themselves in coordinated separate incidents, killing 20 and wounding about 140. The specific purpose of the attack remains unknown. No additional information was available about the group.

11. The Chechen separatist group around Ramzan Akhmadov was responsible for six suicide attacks in June and July 2000. While not enough information is available to determine whether the group is Salafi-Jihadist in character, Akhmadov was known as a radical Islamist and was likely influenced by Wahhabism. Like other Chechen terrorist groups, it is likely that this group comprised both Salafi-Jihadists and more nationalist elements.

12. Although Hamas's origins go back to the Muslim Brotherhood, its primary goal is the defeat of Israel. Hamas has resisted the adoption of Al Qaeda's doctrine of global jihad, and it does not engage in *takfir*. For example, in an open letter published in *Newsweek*, Mohammed Abu Tir, a key Hamas official who was assigned a second-place listing by the Hamas during the 2006 general elections in the Palestinian Authority, wrote: "The West has nothing to fear from Hamas. . . . Hamas deals only with the Israeli occupation. We are not Al Qaeda." See Mohammed Abu Tir, "Open Letter: Just Be Fair with Us," *Newsweek International*, 6 February 2006. Its unwillingness to adopt Al Qaeda's worldview of global jihad has elicited several heated exchanges between Al Qaeda's deputy leader, Ayman al-Zawahiri, and the Hamas leadership. Zawahiri has appealed to Hamas—and the Muslim Brotherhood, for that matter—not to participate in the democratic process. Participation in the democratic process is the major point of contention between Salafi-Jihadists and mainstream Islamist groups tied to the Muslim Brotherhood because the former believe power derived from the electorate rather than from God to be heretical. For additional information, see Paz, "The Islamic Debate over Democracy," and Ulph, "Al Zawahiri Takes Hamas to Task."

13. Groups coded here as Islamist are mainstream Islamist groups such as those affiliated with the Muslim Brotherhood, for example, Hamas or Palestinian Islamic Jihad. These groups differ from Salafi-Jihadist groups in that they participate in the political process—something that Salafi-Jihadist groups consider heretical because all power must derive from God, not from the electorate. In addition, mainstream Islamist groups do not engage in *takfir*—the labeling of other Muslims as *kufr*, or heretics. Inasmuch as most of the groups in this category are tied to the Muslim Brotherhood, they may be labeled as Salafi. However, as argued in chapter 3, a clear distinction must be drawn between mainstream Salafism and Salafi-Jihadism.

14. A panel of eight experts concluded that "Harakat-ul-Mujahideen (Kashmir)" has "pledged allegiance to Bin Laden" and "internalized the Al Qaeda worldview of Global Jihad." Rabasa et al., *Beyond Al-Qaeda, Part I*, xxii, 2, 79.

15. Although Hizb-ul-Mujahideen has ties with Salafi-Jihadist groups, including Lashkar-e-Taiba, its primary focus is the liberation of Kashmir and its accession to Pakistan. See "Group

Profile: Hizbul Mujahideen (HM)," *Terrorism Knowledge Base*. Available at www.tkb.org/Group.jsp?groupID=52, last accessed 23 November 2006. It is also tied to Jamaat-i-Islami, the mainstream Islamist party, and the equivalent of the Muslim Brotherhood in Pakistan.

16. According to the National Security Studies Center database, Hizb-ut-Tahrir was responsible for a suicide attack at the entrance to a children's clothing store in the local market in Tashkent, Uzbekistan, on 29 March 2004. According to the Web site Global Security.org, Hizb-ut-Tahrir al-Islami (Islamic Party of Liberation) is "a radical Islamic political movement that seeks 'implementation of pure Islamic doctrine' and the creation of an Islamic caliphate in Central Asia. . . . Its basic aim was struggle with infidels and the organization of a universal caliphate embracing all Islamic countries. . . . The political struggle is manifested in the struggle against the disbelieving imperialists, to deliver the Ummah from their domination and to liberate her from their influence by uprooting their intellectual, cultural, political, economic and military roots from all of the Muslim countries. The political struggle also appears in challenging the rulers, revealing their treasons and conspiracies against the Ummah, and by taking them to task and changing them if they denied the rights of the Ummah, or refrained from performing their duties towards her, or ignored any matter of her affairs, or violated the laws of Islam. . . . Unlike more traditional Islamic parties, it is supranational and refuses to be involved in local politics. . . . In 1999, the group was blamed for a series of bomb attacks in the Uzbekistan capital, Tashkent. It is believed by some to clandestinely fund and provide logistical support to a wide range of terrorist operations in Central Asia, and elsewhere, although attacks may be carried out in the names of local groups." See "Hizb Ut-Tahrir Al-Islami (Islamic Party of Liberation)," *GlobalSecurity.org*. Available at www.globalsecurity.org/military/world/para/hizb-ut-tahrir.htm, last accessed 25 November 2006.

17. The Terrorism Knowledge Base does not provide sufficient information to determine whether the Islamic Army in Iraq is a Salafi-Jihadist organization. According to Mohammed Hafez, the Islamic Army in Iraq is both nationalist and Islamist in character.

18. A panel of eight experts concluded that the Islamist Movement of Uzbekistan (IMU) has "internalized the Al Qaeda worldview of Global Jihad." Rabasa et al., *Beyond Al-Qaeda, Part I*, xxii, 2, 79.

19. A panel of eight experts concluded that Jaish-e-Muhammad has "internalized the Al Qaeda worldview of Global Jihad." Ibid.

20. According to the Terrorism Knowledge Base, Jamaat Jund-al-Sahaba (Soldiers of the Prophet's Companions) is a Sunni extremist organization responsible for two high-profile attacks on Shia targets in Iraq. The group has major grievances with Shia Muslims, who they believe to have a disproportionate amount of power in the newly created Iraqi government and security force. The group reflects Salafi-Jihadist doctrine by arguing that it seeks to defend Sunnis from what it sees as a corruption of true Islamic doctrine. A secondary goal of the Soldiers of the Prophet's Companions is to expel the "Jews and Crusaders" from Muslim territory. See "Group Profile: Soldiers of the Prophet's Companion," *Terrorism Knowledge Base*. Available at www.tkb.org/Group.jsp?groupID=4499, last accessed 1 December 2007. According to the SITE Institute, the group refers in its statements to Shias as "wicked people of the infidels and crusaders"—terms that are signature labels used by Salafi-Jihadists. See "Jamaat Jund Al-Sahaba Issues Warning to Those Who Disgrace Sunni Mosques," *SITE Institute*, 24 March 2005.

21. According to the Terrorism Knowledge Base, "Jamatul Mujahedin Bangladesh (JMB) is a

terrorist group dedicated to removing the country's secular government and imposing a Taliban inspired Islamic theocracy in its place. In addition to calling for an Islamic state based on Sharia law, JMB has denounced the American led invasion of Iraq, warning President Bush and British Prime Minister Blair to leave all Muslim countries." See "Group Profile: Jamatul Mujahedin Bangladesh (JMB)," *Terrorism Knowledge Base*. Available at www.tkb.org/Group.jsp?groupID=4497, last accessed 23 November 2006.

22. A panel of eight experts concluded that Jemaah Islamiyah has "internalized the Al Qaeda worldview of Global Jihad." Rabasa et al., *Beyond Al-Qaeda, Part I*, xxii, 2, 79.

23. A panel of eight experts concluded that Lashkar-e-Taiba, Jaish-e-Muhammad, and Harkat-ul-Mujahideen, the three major Kashmir separatist groups, have "internalized the Al Qaeda worldview of Global Jihad." Ibid., xxii, 2, 79.

24. A panel of eight experts concluded that Lashkar-e-Jhangvi has "internalized the Al Qaeda worldview of Global Jihad." Ibid., xxii, 2, 79.

25. A panel of eight experts concluded that Lashkar-e-Taiba has "internalized the Al Qaeda worldview of Global Jihad." Ibid., xxii, 2, 79.

26. On 11 November 1987, a female suicide bomber detonated 12 pounds of explosives packed in a briefcase at Beirut airport. The victims were friends and relatives seeing off passengers leaving on flights to the Gulf. On 14 November 1987, a female suicide bomber detonated two pounds of explosives connected to a nail-filled grenade concealed in a box of chocolates in the lobby of the American University hospital in West Beirut. According to the National Security Studies Center Database of Haifa University, the Lebanese Liberation Army claimed responsibility, but no solid information on the ideology of this group is available. Given the use of female suicide bombers, however, it is unlikely that the group was a Salafi-Jihadist group.

27. A panel of eight experts concluded that the Moroccan Islamic Combatant Group (GICM) has "internalized the Al Qaeda worldview of Global Jihad." Rabasa et al., *Beyond Al-Qaeda, Part I*, xxii, 2, 79. For additional information on the GICM's Salafi-Jihadist character, see Alonso and Rey, "The Evolution of Jihadist Terrorism in Morocco."

28. The Mujahideen Shura Council is the primary Salafi-Jihadist grouping in Iraq today and consists of six Sunni insurgent groups, including Al Qaeda in Iraq. Its stated goal is to manage "the struggle in the battle of confrontation to ward off the invading infidels and their apostate stooges." See "Group Profile: Mujahideen Shura Council," *Terrorism Knowledge Base*. Available at www.tkb.org/Group.jsp?groupID=4575; see also Tanzim Qaidat al-Jihad fi Bilad al-Rafidayn and Al Tawhid wal Jihad.

29. According to the Terrorism Knowledge Base, "the Riyad us-Saliheyn Martyrs Brigade is a relatively young terrorist organization, dedicated to the creation of an independent Islamic republic in Chechnya (and other primarily Muslim parts of Russia such as Dagestan, Kabardino-Balkaria, Ingushetia, Ossetia and Tataria)." The group, whose name translates to "requirements for getting into paradise," espouses radical Islamic doctrine (Wahabbism) and is believed to have strong ties to Al-Qaeda. However, most experts agree that the primary inspiration behind Riyad's activities is a desire for the independence of "Chechen lands," rather than religious zealotry. "Group Profile: Riyad Us-Saliheyn Martyrs' Brigade," *Terrorism Knowledge Base*. Available at http://www.tkb.org/Group.jsp?groupID=3673, last accessed 23 November 2006.

30. Although the Taliban's Deobandi roots are not congruent with Salafi-Jihadist ideology, the Taliban's ideology shares many common traits with the Salafi Jihad.

31. This previously unknown group claimed responsibility for the killing of Lebanese prime minister Rafiq Hariri on 14 February 2005. At the time of this writing, no additional information about this group was available. The investigation into the killing of Hariri was ongoing. For information on the attack being most likely a suicide attack, see "UN Probe into Murder of Former Lebanese Leader Nears Sensitive Stage—Inquiry Chief."

Introduction

1. The attack that resulted in the death of Bhutto consisted of a shooting, followed by a suicide bombing. The exact cause of Bhutto's death remains in dispute.

2. Although the Madrid train bombings of 11 March 2004 were not a suicide mission as defined in this book, seven of the bombing suspects detonated themselves weeks later in the Madrid suburb of Leganes, as Spanish special forces were about to storm their apartment. See Alonso and Reinares, "Maghreb Immigrants Becoming Suicide Terrorists."

3. Pape, *Dying to Win*, 6.

4. The dataset has been made available to me courtesy of Ami Pedahzur and Arie Perliger. I am grateful to them and to the National Security Studies Center researchers. For questions and queries on specific data points, please contact the author.

5. This section is derived from Moghadam, "Defining Suicide Terrorism."

6. For an extensive discussion of terrorism, see Schmid and Jongman, *Political Terrorism*; Laqueur, *Terrorism*; and Hoffman, *Inside Terrorism* (2006).

7. For a useful synopsis, see Hoffman, *Inside Terrorism* (1998), 13–44.

8. Some scholars regard suicide terrorism as a self-standing phenomenon that can be studied separately from terrorism in general. Robert Pape, for example, argues that " 'ordinary,' nonsuicide terrorism is significantly different [from suicide terrorism]." Pape, *Dying to Win*, 9. The present study does not agree with this premise and instead concurs that, although ordinary terrorism and suicide terrorism share many characteristics in common, the main exception is the "motive of individual self-sacrifice and martyrdom." See Crenshaw, " 'Suicide' Terrorism in Comparative Perspective," 21, 25.

9. This is not to say that terrorism has not been used as a tool by states. State terror has been inherent in the consolidation and maintenance of power by a large number of states, particularly dictatorships, most notoriously visible perhaps during Nazi Germany and the Soviet Union under Stalin. However, the literature generally refers to state-based terrorism as *terror*, and reserves the word *terrorism* for the tactic used by nonstate actors.

10. There is no universally accepted definition of terrorism, and not all definitions of terrorism define an act of terrorism as an attack on noncombatants or civilians. Some of the more frequently cited definitions, however, do. The U.S. State Department, for example, defines

terrorism as "premeditated, politically motivated violence perpetrated against noncombatant targets by subnational groups or clandestine agents, usually intended to influence an audience." Noncombatants include both civilians as well as military personnel who at the time of the incident are unarmed and/or not on duty. See U.S. Department of State, *Patterns of Global Terrorism, 2003*, xii. For a definition of terrorism that does not include a reference to noncombatants, see Hoffman, *Inside Terrorism*, 43.

11. Maris, Berman, and Silverman, *Comprehensive Textbook of Suicidology*, 31.

12. See Merari, "The Readiness to Kill and Die: Suicidal Terrorism in the Middle East," 196, and Moghadam, "Palestinian Suicide Terrorism in the Second Intifada," 68–69.

13. See, for example, Schweitzer, "Suicide Terrorism: Development and Main Characteristics," 78; Crenshaw, " 'Suicide' Terrorism in Comparative Perspective," 21; and Ganor, "Suicide Attacks in Israel," 78.

14. Maris, Berman, and Silverman, *Comprehensive Textbook of Suicidology*, 4.

15. Silke, "The Role of Suicide in Politics, Conflict, and Terrorism," 37.

16. Ibid., 38.

17. Lamont-Brown, *Kamikaze: Japan's Suicide Samurai*, 20.

18. On self-immolations, see especially Biggs, "Dying without Killing: Self-Immolations, 1963–2002."

19. Pedahzur, Perliger, and Weinberg, "Altruism and Fatalism."

20. Laqueur, *No End to War*, 73.

21. Ibid.

22. Ibid., 74.

23. Ibid., 76.

24. Ibid., 74–75.

25. Judges 16:26–30 (King James Version).

26. Lewis, *The Assassins*, 134.

27. Ibid., 4.

28. Ibid., 127.

29. Ibid., 131.

30. The Assassins did not call themselves Assassins, but *fedai*, which can roughly be translated as "devotee."

31. Lewis, *The Assassins*, 12.

32. Dale, "Religious Suicide in Islamic Asia: Anticolonial Terrorism in India, Indonesia, and the Philippines."

33. Ibid., 46–47.

34. Ibid., 48.

35. C. A. Majul, *Muslims in the Philippines* (Quezon: Asian Center, 1973), 392. Quoted in ibid., 51.

36. Majul, *Muslims in the Philippines*, 356. In ibid., 52.

37. Ibid., 56.

38. See Kalyvas and Sánchez-Cuenca, "Killing without Dying: The Absence of Suicide Missions," 221–22.

39. Geifman, *Thou Shalt Kill*, 132.

40. Hill, "Kamikaze," 5.

41. Ibid., 5–8.

42. Ibid.

43. Ibid., 1.

44. B. Smith, "Kamikaze—und der Westen."

45. Hill, "Kamikaze," 42.

46. "Geheimdienst Lehnte Selbstmordanschlag auf Hitler Ab."

47. Weinberg, "Suicide Terrorism for Secular Causes," 116–17. See also Hosmer, *Viet Cong Repression and Its Implications for the Future*, 53–56.

48. Weinberg, "Suicide Terrorism for Secular Causes," 117.

49. Capt. John Scire (U.S. Army ret.), e-mail message to Leonard Weinberg, 21 June 2005. Quoted in ibid., 118.

50. Ibid., 119.

51. Reuter, *My Life Is a Weapon*, 42.

52. The following section borrows heavily from Moghadam, "Mayhem, Myths, and Martyrdom: The Shia Conception of Jihad."

53. Armstrong, *Islam: A Short History*, 35–36.

54. Kramer, "Introduction," 2.

55. Richard, *Shiite Islam: Polity, Ideology, and Creed*, 29.

56. Kermani, *Dynamit des Geistes*, 12.

57. Pinault, *The Shiites: Ritual and Popular Piety in a Muslim Community*, 6.

58. Kramer, "Introduction," 2.

59. See especially Abedi and Legenhausen, *Jihad and Shahadat*; and Moghadam, "Mayhem, Myths, and Martyrdom: The Shia Conception of Jihad," 125–43.

60. Reuter, *My Life Is a Weapon*, 36.

61. Khosrokhavar, *Suicide Bombers*, 77.

62. Taheri, *Holy Terror*, 81.

63. Ibid., 82.

64. Shay, *The Shahids: Islam and Suicide Attacks*, 42. Robert Pape's data cite more than forty suicide attacks by Hizballah. However, it appears that many suicide attacks included in Pape's database that he cites as executed by Hizballah were actually perpetrated by other organizations.

65. McDonnell, "The World; Argentina Alleges Iran Ordered Attacks," 15; and "Argentina Seeks Arrest of Iran's Ex-Leader in 1994 Bombing Inquiry," 5.

66. Kramer, "The Moral Logic of Hizballah."

67. Shay, *The Shahids: Islam and Suicide Attacks*, 48–49.

68. Taheri, *Holy Terror*, 126–29.

69. Hussain's nephew Qasim, who also fell in Karbala, died shortly before his wedding. His wedding tent became the repository of his dead body, which then turned into a custom whereby mourners put a miniature version of the traditional Iranian wedding table with mirrors and candles in the display cabinets above the graves of unmarried men killed in war. See Reuter, *My Life Is a Weapon*, 48–49.

70. Ibid., 65–66.

71. Kramer, *Arab Awakening and Islamic Revival*, 225.

72. Hoffman and McCormick, "Terrorism, Signaling, and Suicide Attack," 259.

73. Ibid., 256. This number differs from the ninety-nine attacks listed in the National Security Studies Center database, but is a more likely figure. For a discussion of these numbers, see Hoffman and McCormick, "Terrorism, Signaling, and Suicide Attack," 275, n. 52. See also Hopgood, "Tamil Tigers, 1987–2002," 53–55.

74. Pedahzur, *Suicide Terrorism*, 72.

75. Hopgood, "Tamil Tigers, 1987–2002," 59.

76. Schalk, "Resistance and Martyrdom in the Process of State Formation of Tamil Eelam." Available at www.tamilnation.org/ideology/schalkthiyagam.htm, accessed 4 June 2008.

77. Hopgood, "Tamil Tigers, 1987–2002," 52.

78. Pedahzur, *Suicide Terrorism*, 72–73, 79–80.

79. Ibid., 55.

80. National Security Studies Center Database, University of Haifa.

81. "Suicide Bombing Terrorism during the Current Israeli-Palestinian Confrontation (September 2000–December 2005)," 2, 5. Available at www.intelligence.org.il/eng/eng_n/pdf/suicide_terrorism_ae.pdf, last accessed 28 April 2006.

82. Ibid., 6.

83. For additional details on these organizations, see Moghadam, "Palestinian Suicide Terrorism in the Second Intifada," 77–83.

84. Bloom, *Dying to Kill*.

85. Pedahzur, *Suicide Terrorism*, 64.

86. Moghadam, "Palestinian Suicide Terrorism in the Second Intifada," 82.

87. See Moghadam, "Suicide Terrorism, Occupation, and the Globalization of Martyrdom." Based on data provided in Pape, *Dying to Win*.

88. "Suicide Bombing Terrorism during the Current Israeli-Palestinian Confrontation (September 2000–December 2005)," 18–19, 22.

89. Moghadam, "Suicide Bombings in the Israeli-Palestinian Conflict," 11.

90. "Profile of a Suicide Bomber: Single Male, Average Age—21."

91. Trounson and Wilkinson, "After the Attack."

92. Guttman, "The Bomber Next Door," 5B.

93. Greenberg, "A Family Is Left 'Sad and Happy' by a Violent Death," A16.

94. Erlanger, "In Most Cases, Israel Thwarts Suicide Attacks without a Shot," 13.

95. Pedahzur, *Suicide Terrorism*, 89.

96. Pape, *Dying to Win*, 163.

97. Pedahzur, *Suicide Terrorism*, 90.

98. Bloom, *Dying to Kill*, 112.

99. Pedahzur, *Suicide Terrorism*, 90.

100. Moghadam, "Palestinian Suicide Terrorism in the Second Intifada"; Hafez, *Manufacturing Human Bombs*; Moghadam, "The Roots of Suicide Terrorism: A Multi-Causal Approach; Hafez, "Rationality, Culture, and Structure in the Making of Suicide Bombers."

101. Crenshaw, "The Causes of Terrorism," 380. See also Long, *The Anatomy of Terrorism*. For an overview of studies on terrorism using with a multicausal approach, see Moghadam, "The Roots of Suicide Terrorism: A Multi-Causal Approach."

102. Moghadam, "Palestinian Suicide Terrorism in the Second Intifada."

103. See, for example, Lachkar, "The Psychological Make-Up of a Suicide Bomber"; Lester, Yang, and Lindsay, "Suicide Bombers: Are Psychological Profiles Possible?"; Sarraj, "Suicide Bombers: Dignity, Despair, and the Need of Hope"; Berko, *The Path to Paradise.*

104. See Pedahzur, Perliger, and Weinberg, "Altruism and Fatalism."

105. McCauley and Segal, "Social Psychology of Terrorist Groups."

106. Victoroff, "The Mind of the Terrorist."

107. See, for example, Speckhard and Akhmedova, "Black Widows: The Chechen Female Suicide Terrorists."

108. For an application of humiliation-revenge theory, see especially Juergensmeyer, *Terror in the Mind of God,* and Stern, *Terror in the Name of God.*

109. Shaul Kimhi and Shmuel Even, "Who Are the Palestinian Suicide Bombers?"

110. Ibid.; Pedahzur, *Suicide Terrorism.*

111. Pedahzur, *Suicide Terrorism.*

112. Hafez, "Manufacturing Human Bombs: Strategy, Culture, and Conflict in the Making of Palestinian Suicide Bombers," 18–19.

113. Juergensmeyer, *Terror in the Mind of God*; Hassan, "An Arsenal of Believers"; Moghadam, "Palestinian Suicide Terrorism in the Second Intifada."

114. Bruce Bueno de Mesquita, for example, argues that suicide bombers are "young men with no economic prospects and little education. There is a rational expectation on the part of suicide bombers that they are providing for their families." Quoted in Bloom, *Dying to Kill,* 35.

115. See especially Stern, *Terror in the Name of God,* 189, 216.

116. Moghadam, "Palestinian Suicide Terrorism in the Second Intifada."

117. Sprinzak, "Rational Fanatics"; Moghadam, "Palestinian Suicide Terrorism in the Second Intifada"; Bloom, *Dying to Kill*; Pape, *Dying to Win*; Pedahzur, *Suicide Terrorism.*

118. Very few exceptions of individuals acting entirely on their own exist; examples include the "Unabomber," Theodore Kaczynski, as well as fifteen-year-old Charles Bishop, who crashed a light plane into the twenty-eighth floor of the Bank of America Plaza in Tampa, Florida, on 5 January 2002.

119. Crenshaw, "An Organizational Approach to the Analysis of Political Terrorism"; Crenshaw, "Theories of Terrorism: Instrumental and Organizational Approaches"; Crenshaw, "The Logic of Terrorism: Terrorist Behavior as a Product of Strategic Choice."

120. On the organizational striving for survival and maintenance, see Wilson, *Political Organizations,* and Crenshaw, "An Organizational Approach to the Analysis of Political Terrorism."

121. Pape, *Dying to Win,* 61. Others have challenged this contention by arguing that Pape overstates the degree of "success" of suicide terrorism. See Moghadam, "Suicide Terrorism, Occupation, and the Globalization of Martyrdom."

122. Al-Zawahiri, *Knights under the Prophet's Banner,* part 11. Published in eleven parts by Al-Sharq al-Awsat. Available at FBIS-NES-2002-0108, Document ID GMP20020108000197.

123. Kydd and Walter, "Sabotaging the Peace"; Hafez, *Suicide Bombers in Iraq.*

124. Brym and Araj, "Suicide Bombing as Strategy and Interaction."

125. Ibid.

126. Hoffman and McCormick, "Terrorism, Signaling, and Suicide Attack."

127. See, for example, Richburg, "Suicide Bomb Survivors Face Worlds Blown Apart," A15, and Harel, "Suicide Attacks Frighten Israelis More Than Scuds."

128. Holmes, "Al-Qaeda, September 11, 2001," 162.

129. Dolnik, "Die and Let Die."

130. Sprinzak, "Rational Fanatics"; Ganor, "Suicide Attacks in Israel"; Cronin, "Terrorism and Suicide Attacks."

131. Krueger and Maleckova, "Education, Poverty, Political Violence, and Terrorism"; Piazza, "Rooted in Poverty?"; Abadie, "Poverty, Political Freedom, and the Roots of Terrorism."

132. See Moghadam, *The Roots of Terrorism.*

133. Pape, *Dying to Win*, 23.

134. Atran, "The Moral Logic and Growth of Martyrdom"; Moghadam, "Suicide Terrorism, Occupation, and the Globalization of Martyrdom."

135. Khashan, "Collective Palestinian Frustration and Suicide Bombing."

136. Moghadam, "Suicide Terrorism, Occupation, and the Globalization of Martyrdom."

137. For a thorough critique of Robert Pape's book *Dying to Win*, see ibid. This section incorporates elements from this review article.

138. Pape, *Dying to Win*, 23.

139. Ibid., 46.

140. American commanders in Iraq say that foreigners make up more than 90% of the suicide bombers. See Filkins, "Foreign Fighters Captured in Iraq Come from 27, Mostly Arab, Lands," 8; Paz, "Arab Volunteers Killed in Iraq"; Obaid and Cordesman, "Saudi Militants in Iraq."

141. Pape, *Dying to Win.*

142. "Text of Fatwa Urging Jihad Against Americans," *Al-Quds al-Arabi* (London), 23 February 1998. Quoted in Blanchard, "Al Qaeda: Statements and Evolving Ideology," 3.

143. Speech by Osama bin Laden broadcast on Al-Jazeera Satellite Channel Television on 3 November 2001. The date of the speech is unknown. Quoted in "Bin Laden Rails against Crusaders and UN." Available at http://news.bbc.co.uk/1/hi/world/monitoring/media_reports/1636782.stm, last accessed 5 November 2005.

144. Statement by Usama bin Ladin," *Waqiaah*, 26 October 2002. Quoted in Anonymous, *Imperial Hubris*, 154.

145. See, for example, Sageman, *Understanding Terror Networks*, 3–17.

146. Pape, *Dying to Win*, 16.

147. Hoffman, *Inside Terrorism* (2006), chap. 4.

148. I thank Bruce Hoffman for this point.

149. Pape, *Dying to Win*, 17.

150. Hafez, *Suicide Bombers in Iraq*; International Crisis Group, "In Their Own Words."

151. Bloom, *Dying to Kill*, 78.

152. Bloom, "Palestinian Suicide Bombing."

153. See assessment by Ely Karmon, as quoted in Dickey, "Inside Suicide, Inc.," 26.

154. Kramer, "Sacrifice and Fratricide in Shiite Lebanon."

155. Bloom apparently recognizes this problem and does not argue that outbidding has been a factor in the adoption of suicide attacks by the LTTE. See Bloom, *Dying to Kill*, 71.

156. Ibid., 67.

One • The Global Proliferation of Suicide Missions

1. Although suicide attacks have occurred prior to 1981, this year marks the beginning of the modern phenomenon of suicide attacks with the attack on the Iraqi embassy in Beirut.

2. The dataset has been compiled by the National Security Studies Center at the University of Haifa, Israel. At the time of this writing, the dataset was last updated on 5 April 2007. I am indebted to Ami Pedahzur and Arie Perliger for granting me access to this database.

3. Indeed, if trends that began in the first three months and five days of 2007 continue, the projected number of suicide attacks by the end of 2007 would be 673.

4. These attacks, which killed between 100 and 150 people, took place on 28 February in Hilla; on 23 May in Baghdad; on 16 July in Musayyib; and on 14 September in Iraq.

5. This, however, is not the only possible conclusion. Another explanation could be that countries targeted by suicide attacks have learned to better cope with these attacks by adopting measures that have reduced the potency of this tactic. Yet another possible explanation could be that, increasingly, suicide bombers are more interested in dying than in killing.

6. Gunaratna, *Inside Al Qaeda*, 11.

7. Burke, *Al-Qaeda: The True Story of Radical Islam*, 290.

8. National Commission on Terrorist Attacks upon the United States, Statement of Marc Sageman; Gerges, *The Far Enemy*.

9. Wiktorowicz, "Anatomy of the Salafi Movement."

10. A similar categorization of the functions of ideology is used in Ball and Dagger, *Political Ideologies and the Democratic Ideal*.

11. Flood, *Political* Myth, 20.

12. Lawrence, *Defenders of God*, 77.

13. Holmes, "Al-Qaeda, September 11, 2001," 170.

14. Lawrence, *Defenders of God*, 79.

15. Ibid.

16. Adams, *The Logic of Political Belief*, 86–87.

17. Lawrence, *Defenders of God*, 97.

18. On women, see, for example, Rotella, "European Women Join Ranks of Jihadis," and Knop, "The Female Jihad."

19. See, for example, Kepel, *Jihad: The Trail of Political Islam*; Roy, *Globalized Islam*; U.S. Congress, House, Testimony of Steven Simon; Stemmann, "Middle East Salafism's Influence and the Radicalization of Muslim Communities in Europe."

20. Kepel, *Jihad: The Trail of Political Islam*; Roy, *Globalized Islam*; Haahr, "Emerging Terrorist Trends in Spain's Moroccan Communities"; Siegel, "Radical Islam and the French Muslim Prison Population"; Vidino, "The Danger of Homegrown Terrorism to Scandinavia"; Europol, "EU Terrorism Situation and Trend Report 2007 Te-Sat"; Haahr, "Italy's Underground Islamist Network"; Kulish, "New Terrorism Case Confirms That Denmark Is a Target," 8.

21. On the Middle East, see, for example, Sageman, *Understanding Terror Networks*.

22. See, for example, Valiyev, "The Rise of Salafi Islam in Azerbaijan."

23. See especially International Crisis Group, "Indonesia Backgrounder."

24. Farah, "Salafists, China, and West Africa's Growing Anarchy." Available at www.strategy

center.net/research/pubID.55/pub_detail.asp#/, last accessed 1 December 2006. See also the "Islam in Africa" Project of the Project for the Research of Islamist Movements (E-Prism). Available at www.e-prism.org/.

25. The origins and doctrine of Salafi Jihad are described in detail in chapter 5.

26. Mainstream Islamist groups differ from Salafi-Jihadist groups in that they participate in the political process—something that Salafi-Jihadist groups consider heretical because all power must derive from God, not from the electorate. See the appendix and chapter 3 for additional explanations.

27. Salafi-Jihadists, all of whom are Sunnis, consider the Shia stream of Islam to be heretical.

28. Hybrid groups are composed of both Salafi-Jihadist elements and non-Salafi-Jihadist elements. For additional explanations, see the appendix.

29. The dataset in fact lists fifty-three groups. However, I have grouped several organizations into a larger category. Thus, for example, the dataset listed Fatah, Fatah Tanzim, and the Al-Aqsa Martyrs Brigade as separate organizations. Because they are all part of Fatah, I have consolidated them to one organization. Similarly, Harkat-ul-Mujahideen and Harkat-ul-Mujahideen al-Almi (a subfaction of the former) were grouped together into Harkat-ul-Mujahideen.

30. The assessment that a group has "internalized the worldview of Al Qaeda and global jihad" is based on the best judgment of a group of eight terrorism experts at the Rand Corporation. See Rabasa et al., *Beyond Al-Qaeda, Part 1*; Rabasa et al., *Beyond Al-Qaeda, Part 2*.

31. This excludes groups such as Hamas, which engages primarily in violence against Israel, a non-Muslim state, but has generally avoided systematic attacks against the Palestinian Authority (prior to Hamas electoral victory in 2006) for fear of sparking a civil war. The Gamaa al-Islamiyya is not included in this list because it has all but relinquished violence against the Egyptian regime.

32. The practice of *takfir* is reserved to Salafi-Jihadist groups, which is why they are sometimes also referred to as *takfiris*.

33. MIPT integrates data from the Rand Terrorism Chronology and Rand-MIPT Terrorism Incident databases; the Terrorism Indictment database; and IDF International's research on terrorist organizations. For more information, visit www.tkb/org/.

34. Rabasa et al., *Beyond Al-Qaeda, Part 1*; Rabasa et al., *Beyond Al-Qaeda, Part 2*.

35. On Iraq, see International Crisis Group, "In Their Own Words," and Hafez, *Suicide Bombers in Iraq*. On Afghanistan, see UNAMA, "Suicide Attacks in Afghanistan (2001–2007)." For a discussion of the Taliban's Salafi-Jihadist character, see chapter 5 and the appendix.

36. The Ansar al-Sunna Group was formerly known as the Ansar al-Sunna Army.

37. See chapters 6 and 7, respectively, for details on the Salafi-Jihadist character of organizations conducting suicide attacks in Afghanistan and Iraq.

38. Pape, *Dying to Win*.

39. Yoram Schweitzer, e-mail communication with the author, 19 November 2006.

40. Pedahzur, *Suicide Terrorism*, 167–68.

41. For additional information, see chapter 6.

42. Michael Roberts, e-mail communication with the author, 20 November 2006; Stephen Hopgood, e-mail communication with the author, 24 November 2006.

43. Stephen Hopgood, e-mail communication with the author, 24 November 2006.

44. Hizballah is believed to have staged two attacks in Argentina: the 17 March 1992 suicide car bombing of the Israeli Embassy in Buenos Aires, which killed 29 people and injured more than 250; and the 18 July 1994 suicide car bombing of the Jewish Community Center (AMIA) building in Buenos Aires, that killed more than 80 people and wounded some 300.

45. On 21 May 1991, for example, a Tamil Tiger suicide bomber killed Indian prime minister Rajiv Gandhi in the Indian city of Madras.

46. Michael Roberts, e-mail communication with the author, 20 November 2006; Stephen Hopgood, e-mail communication with the author, 24 November 2006.

47. Stephen Hopgood, e-mail communication with the author, 24 November 2006.

48. Myers, "Suicide Strike," 4.

49. Schiff, "Islamization in Europe."

50. According to a Department of Defense News Briefing with Colonel Sean MacFarland, Commander of the First Brigade Combat Team, First Armored Division stationed in Ramadi, Iraq, "[foreign fighters] are very few in number, although as far as we can tell, they constitute about 100 percent of the suicide bombers." Quoted in Brookings Institution, "Iraq Index," 13 November 2006, 18. See also comments by Major Gen. Rick Lynch, who stated on 1 December 2005 that "at least 96 percent of suicide bombers [in Iraq] are not Iraqis." Tomlinson, "US General: Suicide and Car Bomb Attacks Down in Iraq."

51. Whitlock, "Amman Bombings Reflect Zarqawi's Growing Reach," A1.

52. Gall, "Afghan Attacks, Tied to Taliban, Point to Pakistan," 1.

53. This discussion is captured, for example, in Anonymous, *Imperial Hubris*.

54. "Al-Zawahiri in Two Recent Messages: 'Iran Stabbed a Knife into the Back of the Islamic Nation'; Urges Hamas to Declare Commitment to Restoring the Caliphate."

55. Craig Whitlock, "Al-Qaeda's Far-Reaching New Partner," A1.

56. Haahr, "GSPC Joins Al-Qaeda and France Becomes Top Enemy."

57. Rabasa et al., *Beyond Al-Qaeda, Part I*, xii, 22.

58. Gambill, "The Libyan Islamic Fighting Group (LIFG)."

59. Benjamin and Weimann, "What the Terrorists Have in Mind," 21.

Two • Al Qaeda and the Primacy of Suicide Attacks

1. Kepel, *Jihad: The Trail of Political Islam*, 139. Wahhabism and the Muslim Brotherhood are both discussed in chapter 3.

2. For biographies of Osama bin Laden, see especially Bergen, *Holy War, Inc.*; Bergen, *The Osama Bin Laden I Know*; and Wright, *The Looming Tower*.

3. Wright, *The Looming Tower*, 127.

4. Abdullah Azzam, "The Solid Base," quoted in Paz, "The Brotherhood of Global Jihad," 16–21, appendix 1. Available on line at www.e-prism.org, last accessed 14 August 2006.

5. Wright, *The Looming Tower*, 152–53.

6. Ibid., 153, 163.

7. Quoted in Burke, *Al-Qaeda: The True Story of Radical Islam*, 73.

8. Compare Anonymous, *Through Our Enemies' Eyes*, 102–3.

9. Wright, *The Looming Tower*, 192.

10. Quoted in National Commission on Terrorist Attacks upon the United States, *The 9/11 Commission Report*, 67.

11. Ibid.

12. Chivers and Rhode, "Turning out Guerrillas and Terrorists to Wage a Holy War," A1.

13. Ibid.

14. Ibid.

15. Gunaratna, *Inside Al Qaeda*, 72–73.

16. Al-Zawahiri, *Knights under the Prophet's Banner*, part 11.

17. Rhode and Chivers, "Qaeda's Grocery Lists and Manuals of Killing," A1.

18. Ibid.

19. Chivers and Rhode, "Turning out Guerrillas and Terrorists to Wage a Holy War," A1.

20. Wright, *The Looming Tower*, 340–41.

21. Gunaratna, *Inside Al Qaeda*, 59.

22. For an example of a contract, see "Document Afgp-2002-600045," in *Harmony Document Series* (Undated). Available on line at www.ctc.usma.edu/aq/AFGP-2002-600045-Trans.pdf, last accessed 1 August 2006.

23. National Commission on Terrorist Attacks upon the United States, *The 9/11 Commission Report*, 67.

24. Gunaratna, *Inside Al Qaeda*, 57–58; National Commission on Terrorist Attacks upon the United States, *The 9/11 Commission Report*, 56. For a detailed description of the committees, see "Document Afgp-2002-000078," in *Harmony Document Series* (Undated), available on line at www.ctc.usma.edu/aq/AFGP-2002-000078-Trans.pdf, last accessed 1 August 2006.

25. Egyptians in senior positions included Zawahiri; Muhammad Atef (Abu Hafs al-Masri), Al Qaeda's operational commander; Atef's successor, Saif al-Adel; Abu Ubaidah al-Banshiri, Al Qaeda's field commander responsible for the development of the group's African foothold; and Abu al-Walid al-Masri, an important theoretician.

26. Many of these documents have been made available through the Combating Terrorism Center (CTC) at the United States Military Academy at West Point, New York. The documents are available at www.ctc.usma.edu/harmony_docs.asp, last accessed 20 August 2006.

27. For Al Qaeda's bylaws, see "Document Afgp-2002-600048," in *Harmony Document Series* (Undated). Available at www.ctc.usma.edu/aq/AFGP-2002-600048-Trans.pdf, last accessed 1 August 2006.

28. "World Islamic Front Statement of Jihad against Jews and Crusaders," 23 February 1998. Available at www.fas.org/irp/world/para/docs/980223-fatwa.htm, last accessed 20 August 2006.

29. Bin Laden interview published on the Ummat Web site, 28 September 2001. Quoted in Scheuer, "Toronto, London, and the Jihadi Spring: Bin Laden as Successful Instigator."

30. "World Islamic Front Statement of Jihad against Jews and Crusaders," 23 February 1998.

31. Taysir Aluni interview with Osama bin Laden. Quoted in Wright, *The Looming Tower*, 238.

32. Al-Zawahiri, *Knights under the Prophet's Banner*, part 11.

33. "Bin Laden's Fatwa," 8 August 1996. Available at www.pbs.org/newshour/terrorism/international/fatwa_1996.html, last accessed 23 November 2007.

34. Al-Zawahiri, *Knights under the Prophet's Banner*, part 11.

35. Husayn, *Al-Zarqawi: The Second Generation of Al-Qaida*, part 8.

36. See "Document Afgp-2002-600048," *Harmony Document Series.*

37. Anonymous, *Through Our Enemies' Eyes*, 171.

38. Quoted in Daly and Ulph, "How and Why: The 9-11 Attacks on America."

39. Al-Zawahiri, *Knights under the Prophet's Banner*, part 11.

40. Quoted in Anonymous, *Through Our Enemies' Eyes*, xviii.

41. "The Full Version of Osama Bin Laden's Speech."

42. "Newly-Released Video of Al-Qaeda's Deputy Leader Ayman Al-Zawahiri's Interview to Al-Sahab TV."

43. Quoted in Scheuer, "Zawahiri: Foreshadowing Attacks on Israel and America?"

44. Al-Zawahiri, *Knights under the Prophet's Banner*, part 7.

45. Quoted in Scheuer, "Osama Bin Laden: Taking Stock of the 'Zionist-Crusader War.'"

46. Al-Zawahiri, *Knights under the Prophet's Banner*, part 7.

47. Ibid., part 7.

48. Ibid., part 10.

49. Scheuer, "Zawahiri: Foreshadowing Attacks on Israel and America?"

50. Husayn, *Al-Zarqawi: The Second Generation of Al-Qaida*, part 8.

51. Anonymous, *Through Our Enemies' Eyes*, 46–47.

52. Daly and Ulph, "How and Why: The 9-11 Attacks on America."

53. Ulph, "Al Qaeda Commentaries on Ramadan, Iraq, and the Jihad."

54. Husayn, *Al-Zarqawi: The Second Generation of Al-Qaida*, part 8.

55. "The Full Version of Osama Bin Laden's Speech."

56. "Qaeda Video Calls for Attacks on Gulf Oil Plants."

57. Husayn, *Al-Zarqawi: The Second Generation of Al-Qaida*, part 8.

58. Anonymous, *Through Our Enemies' Eyes*, 49–50.

59. "Osama Bin Laden: 'Today There Is a Conflict between World Heresy under the Leadership of America on the One Hand and the Islamic Nation with the Mujahideen in Its Vanguard on the Other.'"

60. In March 2008, for example, Zawahiri referred to the United Nations as "an enemy of Islam and Muslims. It is the one which codified and legitimized the setting up of the state of Israel and its taking over of the Muslims' land." "Al-Qaeda Deputy: UN Enemy of Islam," AlJazeera.net, 3 April 2008, http://english.aljazeera.net/News/aspx/print.htm, last accessed 8 April 2008.

61. Al-Zawahiri, *Knights under the Prophet's Banner*, part 11.

62. "Pakistan Interviews Bin Laden." Quoted in Blanchard, "Al Qaeda: Statements and Evolving Ideology," 3.

63. "A New Bin Laden Speech."

64. Al-Zawahiri, *Knights under the Prophet's Banner*, part 11.

65. Scheuer, "'The Pious Caliphate Will Start from Afghanistan': Is Al-Qaeda's Long-Held Afghan Strategy Now Unfolding?"; Scheuer, "Osama Bin Laden: Taking Stock of the 'Zionist-Crusader War.'"

66. Reuven Paz, interview with the author, Washington, DC, 17 July 2006.

67. Wright, *The Looming Tower*, 122.

68. For a good overview of Azzam's martyrology, see Cook, *Understanding Jihad*, 153–57.

69. Burke, *Al-Qaeda: The True Story of Radical Islam*, 74.

70. Available at www.islamicawakening.org/viewarticle.php?articleID=1012&, last accessed 15 August 2006.

71. Wright, *The Looming Tower*, 125.

72. Gerges, *The Far Enemy*, 142–43.

73. Wright, *The Looming Tower*, 248–49.

74. "Bin Laden's Fatwa," 8 August 1996.

75. Chivers and Rhode, "Turning out Guerrillas and Terrorists to Wage a Holy War," A1.

76. National Commission on Terrorist Attacks upon the United States, *The 9/11 Commission Report*, 234.

77. Ibid.

78. Ibid., 232.

79. Ibid., 235.

80. Schweitzer and Goldstein Ferber, "Al Qaeda and the Internationalization of Suicide Terrorism," 41.

81. Ibid., 45.

82. Quoted in Bruce Hoffman, "Al Qaeda, Trends in Terrorism, and Future Potentialities," 436–37.

83. Wright, *The Looming Tower*, 124.

84. Quoted in Blanchard, "Al Qaeda: Statements and Evolving Ideology," 10.

85. "Al-Qaeda Film on the First Anniversary of the London Bombings."

86. National Commission on Terrorist Attacks upon the United States, *The 9/11 Commission Report*, 61.

87. Ibid., 153.

88. Al-Zawahiri, *Knights under the Prophet's Banner*, part 11.

89. Ibid.

90. Ibid. The book was serialized in the London-based magazine *Al-Sharq al-Awsat* between 2 and 10 December 2001, and translated by the Foreign Broadcast Information Service (FBIS), FBIS-NES-2001-1202.

91. Daly and Ulph, "How and Why: The 9-11 Attacks on America."

92. Ibid.

93. National Commission on Terrorist Attacks upon the United States, *The 9/11 Commission Report*, 251.

94. Al Qaeda may have been involved in the funding, planning, or execution of additional suicide attacks during this period and after, although its involvement has not been proved conclusively.

95. This list does not include attempted suicide attacks, such as that of "shoe bomber" Richard Reid, nor is it argued here that the list is exhaustive. However, for these six attacks, Al Qaeda's central role has been established to more certain degrees than their role in other attacks discussed in chapter 5.

96. Bergen, *Holy War, Inc.*, 120.

97. Anonymous, *Through Our Enemies' Eyes*, 200.

98. National Commission on Terrorist Attacks upon the United States, *The 9/11 Commission Report*, 69.

99. Schweitzer and Ferber, "Al Qaeda and the Internationalization of Suicide Terrorism," 54.

100. Ibid.

101. National Commission on Terrorist Attacks upon the United States, *The 9/11 Commission Report*, 149.

102. Ibid., 190.

103. Ibid., 152.

104. Ibid., 153.

105. Ibid.; see also Wright, *The Looming Tower*.

106. National Commission on Terrorist Attacks upon the United States, *The 9/11 Commission Report*, 153. For more on the Bojinka Plot, see Brzezinski, "Bust and Boom," W9.

107. National Commission on Terrorist Attacks upon the United States, *The 9/11 Commission Report*, 153.

108. Ibid., 154.

109. Ibid., 160.

110. Ibid., 165.

111. Sageman, *Understanding Terror Networks*, 107.

112. National Commission on Terrorist Attacks upon the United States, *The 9/11 Commission Report*, 166–67.

113. On the importance of friendship and kinship ties for the global jihad, see Sageman, *Understanding Terror Networks*.

114. National Commission on Terrorist Attacks upon the United States, *The 9/11 Commission Report*, 161.

115. Sageman, *Understanding Terror Networks*, 104.

116. National Commission on Terrorist Attacks upon the United States, *The 9/11 Commission Report*. 163.

117. Sageman, *Understanding Terror Networks*, 105.

118. National Commission on Terrorist Attacks upon the United States, *The 9/11 Commission Report*, 164.

119. Ibid., 231–32.

120. Ibid., 233.

121. Ibid., 236–37.

122. Ibid., 147.

123. Frantz and Butler, "Germans Lay out Early Qaeda Ties to 9/11 Hijackers," A1.

124. Schweitzer and Ferber, "Al Qaeda and the Internationalization of Suicide Terrorism," 58–59.

125. Hedges, "Tunisian Killed in Synagogue Blast Was Unlikely Convert to Militancy," 22.

126. Schweitzer and Ferber, "Al Qaeda and the Internationalization of Suicide Terrorism," 60.

Three • Salafi Jihad and the Veneration of Martyrdom

1. Roy, *Globalized Islam*, 235.

2. Husayn, *Al-Zarqawi: The Second Generation of Al-Qaida*, part 4.

3. Reuven Paz, e-mail communication with the author, 18 August 2006.

4. Stanley, "Understanding the Origins of Wahhabism and Salafism."

5. Wiktorowicz, "Anatomy of the Salafi Movement," 212.

6. Roy refers to them as neofundamentalists because, arguing that contemporary fundamentalism, unlike the traditional one, is coping with the deterritorialization of Islam. Roy, *Globalized Islam*, 234.

7. See, for example, ibid., 236. Reuven Paz, too, refers to Wahhabis as one branch of Salafism. Reuven Paz, e-mail communication with the author, 18 August 2006.

8. Wahhabis are against the veneration of individuals, because only God must be obeyed. Hence, they do not like to call themselves Wahhabis, which would suggest that they follow an individual—Muhammad ibn Abd al-Wahhab—rather than only God.

9. Wiktorowicz, "Anatomy of the Salafi Movement," 209.

10. Paz, "Programmed Terrorists: An Analysis of the Letter Left Behind by the September 11 Hijackers."

11. Wiktorowicz, "Anatomy of the Salafi Movement," 210–11.

12. Roy, *Globalized Islam*.

13. Ibid., 244.

14. Sageman, *Understanding Terror Networks*, 4.

15. The names of the factions are adopted from Wiktorowicz. Needless to say, these divisions are parsimonious, and the Salafi movement is far more complex and divided than indicated here. However, Wiktorowicz's distinction remains the most useful effort to date to clarify the broader trends within Salafism. See Wiktorowicz, "Anatomy of the Salafi Movement."

16. Ibid., 220.

17. Reuven Paz, e-mail communication with the author, 18 August 2006.

18. For more on the Sahwa, see Jones, "The Clerics, the Sahwa, and the Saudi State."

19. Reuven Paz, e-mail communication with the author, 18 August 2006.

20. Sayyed Qutb will be discussed in the following section.

21. Lia, "'Destructive Doctrinarians': Abu Musab Al-Suri's Critique of the Salafis in the Jihadi Current."

22. Wiktorowicz, "A Genealogy of Radical Islam."

23. Bar, "Jihad Ideology in Light of Contemporary Fatwas."

24. Kharajites were members of a sect in Islam that had seceded from the followers of Ali because of their belief that the Shia were exceedingly willing to compromise with Muawiya, then the governor of Damascus, who competed with Ali over the rightful succession of the caliphate.

25. Sageman, *Understanding Terror Networks*, 14.

26. For examples of such hadiths, see Wiktorowicz, "A Genealogy of Radical Islam," 77.

27. Ibid., 86–87.

28. Ibid., 87.

29. Bar, "Jihad Ideology in Light of Contemporary Fatwas," 10–11.

30. Quoted in Scheuer, "Osama Bin Laden: Taking Stock of the 'Zionist-Crusader War.'"

31. I thank Reuven Paz for this point.

32. Wiktorowicz, "A Genealogy of Radical Islam," 90.

33. "Tape Justifies Killing Innocent Muslims." Available at www.cnn.com/2005/WORLD/meast/05/18/iraq.main/, last accessed 15 August 2006.

34. Bar cites a fatwa by 'Abu Ruqaiya' in *Nida ul-Islam*, December–January 1996–97. See Bar, "Jihad Ideology in Light of Contemporary Fatwas," 18, n. 38.

35. Reuven Paz, interview with the author, Washington, DC, 17 July 2006.

36. For a recent justification of suicide attacks against Israelis, see the comments of Sheikh Gamal al-Bana. "Syrian-British Islamist Sheikh Omar Bakri, Shi'ite Liberal Intellectual Diyaa Al-Musawi, and Egyptian Intellectual Sheikh Gamal Al-Bana Debate the Meaning of Jihad on New TV."

37. Wiktorowicz, "A Genealogy of Radical Islam," 92.

38. Quoted in Hoffman, "The Logic of Suicide Terrorism."

39. Abu Ayman al-Hilali, Adhwa 'hawla al-irhab al-Suhyuni waturuq mukafahatihi. Placed on www.aloswa.org/in early May 2002. Cited in Paz, "Qaidat Al-Jihad."

40. Tyler and Van Natta, "Militants in Europe Openly Call for Jihad and the Rule of Islam," A1.

41. Al-Muhajiroun was disbanded in October 2004, when it was replaced by two successor groups, the Saviour Sect and Al-Ghurabaa. The British government banned these two offshoots in July 2006.

42. Quoted in Tyler and Van Natta, "Militants in Europe Openly Call for Jihad and the Rule of Islam," A1.

43. Moghadam, "Suicide Bombings in the Israeli-Palestinian Conflict," 24.

44. Rapoport, "Sacred Terror: A Contemporary Example from Islam," 117–18.

45. For an elaborate discussion on suicide in Islam, see Rosenthal, "On Suicide in Islam."

46. Wiktorowicz, "A Genealogy of Radical Islam," 93.

47. Ibid., 78.

48. Ibid., 81.

49. Benjamin and Simon, *The Age of Sacred Terror*, 55.

50. Ibid., 57.

51. Ibid., 59.

52. Sageman, *Understanding Terror Networks*, 14.

53. Ibid., 12.

54. Benjamin and Simon, *The Age of Sacred Terror*, 66–68.

55. Al-Zawahiri, *Knights under the Prophet's Banner*, part 3.

56. Mohammed Abd-al-Salam Faraj, *The Neglected Duty*. Quoted in Sageman, *Understanding Terror Networks*, 15.

57. Paz, "Sawt Al-Jihad."

58. For Maqdisi's description of his relationship with Abu Musab al-Zarqawi, see Husayn, *Al-Zarqawi: The Second Generation of Al-Qaida*.

59. Paz, "Global Jihad and the United States."

60. Paz, "Sawt Al-Jihad," 2, 6.

61. Paz, "The Impact of the War in Iraq on Islamist Groups and the Culture of Global Jihad," 4.

62. Taheri, "The World Watches as Iraq Becomes a Litmus Test of Democratic Success."

63. Paz, "Islamic Legitimacy for the London Bombings," 1–2.

64. Ibid.

65. Zambelis, "Al-Hakaima Positions Himself for Key Role in the Global Salafi Jihad."

66. The book has been translated by Will McCants and can be accessed at the Web site of the Combating Terrorism Center at West Point, http://ctc.usma.edu/publications/naji.asp, last accessed 6 December 2007. For a discussion of the importance of Naji, see also Brachman and McCants, "Stealing Al-Qaida's Playbook."

67. Whitlock, "Architect of New War on the West."

68. Al-Shishani, "Abu Musab Al-Suri and the Third Generation of Salafi-Jihadists."

69. Ulph, "Setmariam Nasar: Background on Al-Qaeda's Arrested Strategist."

70. Ibid.

71. Brynjar Lia, "Al-Suri's Doctrines for Decentralized Jihadi Training—Part I."

72. Lia, " 'Destructive Doctrinarians': Abu Musab Al-Suri's Critique of the Salafis in the Jihadi Current."

73. McCants, "Militant Ideology Atlas"; Heffelfinger, "Kuwaiti Cleric Hamid Al-Ali."

74. Paz, "Hasan Al-Qaed (Abu Yahya Al-Libi) on Jihadi Terrorism against Muslims in Muslim Countries."

75. Kepel, *Jihad: The Trail of Political Islam*, 42.

76. Ibid., 67.

77. Ibid.

78. Roy, *Globalized Islam*, 4.

79. Ibid., 5.

80. Ibid., 20.

81. Examples for the rejection of local Islams and certain traditions can be found in Saudi Arabia, for example, where Wahhabis (a form of Salafism) resist the celebration of the Prophet Muhammad's birthday and the veneration of his shrine, as well as local, pagan traditions. Examples can also be found in the activities of the Taliban or by Salafi-Jihadist insurgents in Iraq, who attempted to suppress Sufi traditions.

82. Roy prefers to call this form of re-Islamization neofundamentalism rather than Salafism.

83. Roy, *Globalized Islam*, 258.

84. Ibid., 19.

85. Ibid., 159–60.

86. Ibid., 152.

87. Holmes, "Al-Qaeda, September 11, 2001," 153.

88. Khosrokhavar, *Suicide Bombers*, 156.

89. Ibid., 152.

90. Friedman, *The World Is Flat*, 400.

91. This section incorporates material from Moghadam, *The Roots of Terrorism*, chap. 4.

92. Paz, "The Brotherhood of Global Jihad," 2.

93. Khosrokhavar, *Suicide Bombers*, 155.

94. Ibid.

95. Friedman, *The World Is Flat*, 397.

96. See, for example, Arquilla and Ronfeldt, *The Advent of Netwar*; Arquilla and Ronfeldt,

Networks and Netwars; Sageman, *Understanding Terror Networks*; and Jackson, "Groups, Networks, or Movements."

97. Radu, "London 7/7 and Its Impact." Available at www.fpri.org, last accessed 6 December 2006.

98. Friedman, *The World Is Flat*, 392.

99. Tarrow, *The New Transnational Activism*.

100. Ibid., 7.

101. David E. Kaplan, "The Saudi Connection," 18.

102. 2002 United Nations Security Council Report, cited in ibid.

103. The Muslim World League had branches in about thirty countries in the mid-1990s, Al-Haramain had fifty, and the International Islamic Relief Organization as many as ninety. Ibid.

104. Reuven Paz, e-mail communication with author, 18 August 2006.

105. Paz, "The Brotherhood of Global Jihad," 9.

106. Stern, "How America Created a Terrorist Haven," 21. In 2006, a classified National Intelligence Estimate report said that Iraq helped spawn a new generation of Islamic radicalism. See DeYoung, "Spy Agencies Say Iraq War Hurting U.S. Terror Fight," A1.

107. Paz, "The Impact of the War in Iraq on the Global Jihad," 39.

108. Nesser, "Jihadism in Western Europe after the Invasion of Iraq," 337–38.

109. Timmerman, "This Man Wants You Dead."

110. National Commission on Terrorist Attacks upon the United States, *The 9/11 Commission Report*, 67.

Four • From Al Qaeda to Global Jihad

1. Clarke et al., *Defeating the Jihadists*, 12.

2. Despite Al Qaeda's official name change, I will continue to refer to the group as Al Qaeda because it is under this name that the group is universally known. On Al Qaeda's merger with the EIJ and the change of names, see, for example, Paz, "Qaidat Al-Jihad."

3. Anonymous, *Through Our Enemies' Eyes*, 137–41.

4. National Commission on Terrorist Attacks upon the United States, *The 9/11 Commission Report*, 58.

5. On the jihad in Bosnia, see Kepel, *Jihad: The Trail of Political Islam*, and Kohlmann, *Al-Qaida's Jihad in Europe*.

6. Sageman, *Understanding Terror Networks*, 41.

7. Ibid., 44–45.

8. Gerges, *The Far Enemy*, 65.

9. Anonymous, *Through Our Enemies' Eyes*, 172–73.

10. Paz, "From Riyadh 1995 to Sinai 2004."

11. Burke, *Al-Qaeda: The True Story of Radical Islam*, 165.

12. Al-Zawahiri, *Knights under the Prophet's Banner*, part 11.

13. Ibid.

14. Sageman, *Understanding Terror Networks*, 45.

15. "Bin Laden's Fatwa," 8 August 1996. The full text of the declaration of war can be found on the Web site of the Public Broadcasting Service, www.pbs.org/newshour/terrorism/international/fatwa_1996.html, last accessed 21 August 2006.

16. Orbach, "Usama Bin Ladin and Al-Qaida: Origins and Doctrines," 59–60.

17. "World Islamic Front Statement of Jihad against Jews and Crusaders," 23 February 1998.

18. Orbach, "Usama Bin Ladin and Al-Qaida: Origins and Doctrines," 60.

19. Burke, *Al-Qaeda: The True Story of Radical Islam*, 261.

20. Rhode and Chivers, "Qaeda's Grocery Lists and Manuals of Killing," A1.

21. For example, at a speech in Johnstown, Pennsylvania, on 9 September 2004, President Bush said that "more than three-quarters of Al Qaeda's key members and associates have been brought to justice." Quoted in Risen, "In Tape, Top Aide to Bin Laden Vows New Strikes at U.S.," 10.

22. The plots included a plan disrupted in late 2001 to attack several embassies and other targets in Singapore using simultaneous truck bombs, and the planned suicide boat attack in May 2002 against U.S. and British warships in the Straits of Gibraltar. See "Interrogation of Suspect Reveals New Details of Singapore Plot" and Burke, *Al-Qaeda: The True Story of Radical Islam*, 264.

23. See, for example, Priest and Schmidt, "Al Qaeda's Top Primed to Collapse, U.S. Says," A1.

24. Paz, "The Brotherhood of Global Jihad," 14.

25. Paz, "Global Jihad and the European Arena," 1. Available at www.e-prism.org/, last accessed 6 December 2006.

26. Paz, "The Brotherhood of Global Jihad," 1.

27. See Rotella, "Terrorism Suspects Traced to Iran"; Clarke et al., *Defeating the Jihadists*, 14. On Iranian support to Al Qaeda, see also National Commission on Terrorist Attacks upon the United States, *The 9/11 Commission Report*, 61, 240–41; and Meyer, "Some U.S. Officials Fear Iran Is Helping Al Qaeda."

28. Anonymous, *Imperial Hubris*, 64–65. See also Rhode and Risen, "A Hostile Land Foils the Quest for Bin Laden," 1.

29. Burke, *Al-Qaeda: The True Story of Radical Islam*, 264.

30. Ibid.

31. Husayn, *Al-Zarqawi: The Second Generation of Al-Qaida*, part 8.

32. Windrem, "The Frightening Evolution of Al-Qaida," Available on line at www.msnbc.msn.com/id/8307333, last accessed 1 August 2006.

33. Gorka, "Al Qaeda's Next Generation"; McElroy, "U.S. Forces Hunt Down Al-Qaeda in Sudan," 26.

34. Johnston and Van Natta, "U.S. Officials See Signs of a Revived Al Qaeda," 1.

35. Waldman and Masood, "Elaborate Qaeda Network Hid 2 Captives in Pakistan," 10; Waldman and Lipton, "Rounding up Qaeda Suspects," 12.

36. Johnston and Sanger, "New Leaders Are Emerging for Al Qaeda," A1.

37. Hoffman, "Al Qaeda, Trends in Terrorism, and Future Potentialities: An Assessment," 434.

38. Stern, "The Protean Enemy."

39. Ibid. See also Stern, *Terror in the Name of God*, 237–80.

40. Hoffman, "Al Qaeda, Trends in Terrorism, and Future Potentialities: An Assessment," 435.

41. Burke, "Think Again: Al Qaeda."

42. U.S. Congress, Senate, Statement by the Director of National Intelligence, John D. Negroponte.

43. Ibid.

44. Ibid.

45. Ibid.

46. Shrader, "Negroponte: Al-Qaida the Biggest Threat."

47. Scheuer, "Al-Qaeda and Algeria's GSPC."

48. Paz, "Qaidat Al-Jihad: Moving Forward or Backward?"; Hoffman, "Remember Al Qaeda? They're Baaack."

49. Yousafzai, Moreau, and Hosenball, "Al Qaeda's Western Recruits." On the likelihood of American recruits, see Mazzetti, "Intelligence Chief Says Al Qaeda Improves Ability to Strike in U.S.," 1.

50. Mazzetti and Rohde, "Al Qaeda's Leaders Rebuilding Networks," 1; Hsu and Pincus, "U.S. Warns of Stronger Al Qaeda," 1.

51. Riedel, "Al-Qaida's Resurgence in Pakistan."

52. See, for example, statements by Defense Intelligence Agency Director LTG Michael Maples, as quoted in "Al-Qaeda Rebuilding in Pakistan."

53. U.S. Congress, Senate, Testimony of Gen. Michael V. Hayden.

54. Whitlock, "The New Al Qaeda Central," A1.

55. U.S. Congress, Senate, Statement by the Director of National Intelligence, John D. Negroponte.

56. Such a strategy also crystallized from the writings of Abu Abdel Aziz, known as "Barbarossa," a Saudi who commanded the brigades of the Arab Jihadi volunteers in Bosnia, in an analysis of the bombings in London published on 7 July 2005 on a Jihadi Web site of a leading Saudi supporter of Al Qaeda. See Paz, "From Madrid to London: Al-Qaeda Exports the War in Iraq to Europe."

57. Bernstein, "Tape, Probably Bin Laden's, Offers 'Truce' to Europe."

58. Lia and Hegghammer, "Jihadi Strategic Studies."

59. Scheuer, "Zawahiri: Internationalizing Jihad, Uniting Muslims and Trumping Saudi Clerics."

60. Scheuer, "Al-Zawahiri's September 11 Video Hits Main Themes of Al-Qaeda."

61. Scheuer, "Latest Al-Zawahiri Tape Targets American Society."

62. Paz, "The 'Global Campaign against Aggression': The Supreme Council of Global Jihad."

63. Ulph, "Al-Qaeda TV, via the Web"; Musharbash, "Al-Qaida Startet Terror-TV."

64. Bakier, "Forum Users Improve Electronic Jihad Technology."

65. The figure is given by Gabriel Weimann, as quoted in Perelman, "A New, Younger Jihadi Threat Emerges."

66. "Letter from Al-Zawahiri to Al-Zarqawi." Available at the Web site of GlobalSecurity. See www.globalsecurity.org/security/library/report/2005/zawahiri-zarqawi-letter_9jul2005.htm, accessed 6 April, 2008.

67. Paz, "Qaidat Al-Jihad: Moving Forward or Backward?" 1.

68. See, for example, Weimann, *Terror on the Internet*, 118, and U.S. Congress, House, Testimony by Dr. Bruce Hoffman; Hunt, "Osama Bin Laden Fan Clubs, Jihad Recruiters, Build Online Communities," 4A.

69. Ulph, "A Guide to Jihad on the Web."

70. Bakier, "The New Issue of Technical Mujahid, a Training Manual for Jihadis."

71. Stenersen, "The Internet: A Virtual Training Camp?"

72. U.S. Congress, Senate, Testimony of Ltc Joseph H. Felter.

73. Ulph, "The Voice of Jihad Is Back."

74. Quoted in Friedman, *The World Is Flat*, 450.

75. Anonymous, *Imperial Hubris*, 81.

76. "A World Wide Web of Terror"; Krebs, "Three Worked the Web to Help Terrorists"; Musharbash, "37.000 Kreditkarten für 'Terrorist 007.' "

77. Kohlmann, "American Greases Al-Qaida Media Machine."

78. Whitlock, "The New Al Qaeda Central."

79. IntelCenter, 14 December 2007. Quoted in Scheuer, "Al-Qaeda at Year's End 2007: What Do the Facts Say?"

80. Rogan, "Dynamics of the Jihadi Online Media Campaign."

81. Ulph, "Al-Qaeda's Online Publications"; Scheuer, "Assessing London and Sharm Al-Sheikh."

82. Jaber, "Middle-Class Bombers Find DIY 'Martyr Belt' Online," Available at http://www.timesonline.co.uk/tol/news/uk/article544897.ece, last accessed 6 April 2008.

83. Stenersen, "The Internet: A Virtual Training Camp?"

84. Ibid.

85. Curiel, "Terror.Com," A1.

86. Coll and Glasser, "Terrorists Turn to the Web as Base of Operations," A1.

87. Eben Kaplan, "Terrorists and the Internet." Available at www.cfr.org/publication/10005/#5/, last accessed 11 December 2006.

88. Krebs, "Three Worked the Web to Help Terrorists," D1.

89. Friedman, *The World Is Flat*, 430.

90. Musharbash, "Wie Al-Qaida den Jahrestag der Anschläge Begeht."

91. Bakier, "Jihadis Provide Internet Training for Female Mujahideen."

92. Sageman, *Understanding Terror Networks*, 161.

93. Ibid., 162.

Five • Suicide Missions from Afghanistan to Uzbekistan

1. Numbers of suicide attacks in Afghanistan for 2004–6 are taken from a 2007 report by the United States Assistance Mission to Afghanistan. See UNAMA, "Suicide Attacks in Afghanistan (2001–2007)," 38. The figure for 2007 has been provided by Brian Williams. Brian G. Williams, e-mail communication with the author, 7 April 2008.

2. "Afghan Suicide Bombing Kills 17"; "Kabul Suicide Bomb Hits US Convoy."

3. Gall and Wafa, "Suicide Bomber Kills 16 in Kabul near Embassy," 1; Gall, "Suicide

Bomber Kills a Governor in Afghanistan," 1; "Canadians Die in Afghan Bombing"; Gall, "Attacks in Afghanistan Grow More Frequent and Lethal," 15.

4. Rahmani, "Afghan Authorities Apprehend Leaders of Kabul Suicide Cell."

5. *Afghan Islamic Press*, 7 October 2006. Quoted in Scheuer, "The West Is Running out of Time in Afghanistan."

6. Williams and Young, "Cheney Attack Reveals Taliban Suicide Bombing Patterns."

7. Baldauf, "Taliban Turn to Suicide Attacks," 1.

8. "Taliban Recruiting Hundreds of Suicide Bombers for Major Attack on NATO Forces in the Spring: Al Jazeera Reports."

9. "Taliban Boasts of 1000 Suicide Bombers."

10. The video is available on YouTube at www.youtube.com/watch?v=TwwiGXIhnKo, last accessed 16 November 2007.

11. According to UNAMA, body-borne devices kill 5.95 victims per successful attacks, while vehicle-born devices kill an average of 3.89. UNAMA, "Suicide Attacks in Afghanistan (2001–2007)," 51.

12. Williams and Young, "Cheney Attack Reveals Taliban Suicide Bombing Patterns."

13. Williams, "The Taliban Fedayeen: The World's Worst Suicide Bombers?"

14. Ibid.

15. UNAMA, "Suicide Attacks in Afghanistan (2001–2007)," 75–77.

16. Ibid., 87–89.

17. Marzban, "The Foreign Makeup of Afghan Suicide Bombers."

18. Badkhen, "Foreign Jihadists Seen as Key to Spike in Afghan Attacks," A1.

19. Scheuer, "The West Is Running out of Time in Afghanistan."

20. Gebauer, Musharbash, and Stark, "Cüneyt C.—Der erste Selbstmordattentäter aus Deutschland?"

21. Gall, "Pakistan Link Seen in Afghan Suicide Attacks," 1.

22. Lamb, "NATO Chief Will Front Musharraf to Demand Taliban Leader Omar's Arrest," 9.

23. UNAMA, "Suicide Attacks in Afghanistan (2001–2007)," 83.

24. Kepel, *Jihad: The Trail of Political Islam*, 235.

25. Scheuer, "Al-Qaeda's New Leader in Afghanistan: A Profile of Abu Al-Yazid."

26. Rahmani, "Combating the Ideology of Suicide Terrorism in Afghanistan."

27. Karzai, "Afghanistan and the Logic of Suicide Terrorism."

28. "A Video Produced by Al-Sahab Media Depicting a Suicide Bomber's Will and Operation Targeting American Forces in Kabul, Afghanistan."

29. Rahmani, "Combating the Ideology of Suicide Terrorism in Afghanistan."

30. Craig S. Smith, "2 Bombs Set by Unit of Al Qaeda Kill 23 in Algeria," 10.

31. Cruickshank, "Al-Qaida's Expanding Franchise."

32. Bennhold, "Privation and Despair Colored an Algiers Bomber's Life," 3.

33. Kepel, *Jihad: The Trail of Political Islam*, 261–63.

34. Ibid., 273.

35. Haahr, "GSPC Joins Al-Qaeda and France Becomes Top Enemy."

36. Ibid.

37. Siegel, "AQIM Renews Its Threats against France."

38. Black, "AQIM Employs Martyrdom Operations in Algeria."

39. Whitlock, "From Iraq to Algeria, Al-Qaeda's Long Reach," A7.

40. Craig S. Smith, "North Africa Feared as Staging Ground for Terror," 1; Siegel, "AQIM Renews Its Threats against France."

41. Felter and Fishman, *Al-Qaida's Foreign Fighters in Iraq: A First Look at the Sinjar Records.*

42. Cruickshank, "Al-Qaida's Expanding Franchise."

43. Black, "The Ideological Struggle over Al-Qaeda's Suicide Tactics in Algeria."

44. Paz, "Suicide Terrorist Operations in Chechnya."

45. Billingsley, "Chechen Rebels Hone Tactics for Long Haul."

46. Quoted in Paz, "Suicide Terrorist Operations in Chechnya."

47. Wines, "19 Die as Suicide Bomber Destroys Bus near Chechnya," A1.

48. The numbers here are based not on the National Security Studies Center database, but on data provided in Speckhard and Ahkmedova, "The Making of a Martyr." On the theater takeover, see especially Speckhard et al., "Research Note: Observations of Suicidal Terrorists in Action."

49. Vidino, "The Arab Foreign Fighters and the Sacralization of the Chechen Conflict," 1.

50. Trenin, Malashenko, and Lieven, *Russia's Restless Frontier.*

51. Vidino, "The Arab Foreign Fighters and the Sacralization of the Chechen Conflict," 2.

52. Speckhard and Ahkmedova, "The Making of a Martyr," 445.

53. Ibid.

54. Riebling and Eddy, "Jihad@work: Behind the Moscow Theater Attack." Available at www.nationalreview.com/comment/comment-riebling102402.asp, last accessed 21 September 2006.

55. Trenin, Malashenko, and Lieven, *Russia's Restless Frontier*, 94.

56. Gutman and Keinon, "IDF Concludes Sinai Rescue Operation."

57. Schiff, "Analysis: Dahab Terror Attack Indicative of Egypt's Failure."

58. "Egypt Suicide Bombers Were Bedouin Islamists."

59. Sweilam, "Egyptians Kill Three Bombing Suspects"; "Egypt Names Islamist Group Suspected of Sinai Attacks."

60. "Sinai Bombers Sentenced to Death."

61. Paz, "From Riyadh 1995 to Sinai 2004."

62. Slackman, "Out of Desert Poverty, a Caldron of Rage in the Sinai," 6.

63. See also Karmon, "Egypt as a New Front of Al Qaeda." Available at www.ict.org.il/articles/articledet.cfm?articleid=565, last accessed 26 September 2006.

64. Magouirk, Atran, and Sageman, "Connecting Terrorist Networks," 6–7.

65. Schweitzer and Ferber, "Al Qaeda and the Internationalization of Suicide Terrorism."

66. Schweitzer, "Global Jihad as Reaction to American Policy."

67. "Bali Attack 'Targeted Australians.' "

68. Cindy Wockner, "Bombers' Jail Rant."

69. Bradsher, "Indonesia Bombing Kills at Least 10 in Midday Attack," 1.

70. Magouirk, Atran, and Sageman, "Connecting Terrorist Networks," 9.

71. Bonner and Perlez, "Macabre Clues Advance Inquiry in Bali Attacks," 1.

72. Bonner, "A Terrorist Strike in Bali, Choreographed for the Bombers on a Plotter's Computer," 6.

73. Research conducted for this section was made possible thanks to the generous support from the Jebsen Center for Counter-Terrorism Studies at The Fletcher School at Tufts University.

74. Slackman and Mekhennet, "Jordan Says Bombing Suspect Aimed to Avenge Brother," 3.

75. Husseini, "Witness Gives Testimony on Discovery of Explosives Belt"; Ahmad Kurayshan, "State Security Directs Charges of Terrorist Plotting and Possession of Explosive Charges."

76. Husseini, "Sajida Pleads 'Not Guilty' in Terror Trial; Court Says No to Psychiatric Evaluation."

77. Kurayshan, "State Security Directs Charges of Terrorist Plotting and Possession of Explosive Charges."

78. Powell, "A War without Borders," 48.

79. "Osama Bin Laden: 'Today There Is a Conflict between World Heresy under the Leadership of America on the One Hand and the Islamic Nation with the Mujahideen in Its Vanguard on the Other."

80. Levitt and Sawyer, "Zarqawi's Jordanian Agenda."

81. Fuad Husayn, interview with the author, Amman, Jordan, 7 June 2006.

82. Ulph, "Al-Qaeda in Iraq Takes Credit for the Amman Bombings."

83. "Al-Qaeda Explains Amman Bombings."

84. Ibid.

85. Ibid.

86. Ibid.

87. Al-Shishani, "Salafi-Jihadists in Jordan: From Prison Riots to Suicide Operation Cells."

88. Husseini, "Jordan Charges Five Iraqis, Two Others with Terror Conspiracy."

89. "Jordan's 9/11: Dealing with Jihadi Islamism," 8.

90. Abdullah Abu Rumman, interview with International Crisis Group. In ibid., 4.

91. Husayn, *Al-Zarqawi: The Second Generation of Al-Qaida*, part 1.

92. Ibid.

93. Maqdisi was subsequently rearrested and released several times. As of April 2008, he was out of prison.

94. See Maqdisi's testimony in ibid., parts 6–7. See also Paz, "Islamic Legitimacy for the London Bombings."

95. Omestad, "The Casbah Connection."

96. Ibid.

97. Schweitzer and Ferber, "Al Qaeda and the Internationalization of Suicide Terrorism," 68.

98. Alonso and Rey, "The Evolution of Jihadist Terrorism in Morocco."

99. Whitlock, "Suicide Bombers Strike N. Africa Again," A19.

100. Whitlock, "In Morocco's 'Chemist,' a Glimpse of Al-Qaeda."

101. Ibid.

102. Whitlock, "Odyssey of an Al Qaeda Operative," A1.

103. Perelman, "A New, Younger Jihadi Threat Emerges."

104. Alonso and Rey, "The Evolution of Jihadist Terrorism in Morocco."

105. Alonso and Reinares, "Maghreb Immigrants Becoming Suicide Terrorists."

106. Haahr, "The Growth of Militant Islamist Micro-Diaspora Communities: Observations from Spain," 15–16.

107. Felter and Fishman, *Al Qaida's Foreign Fighters in Iraq*, 19.

108. Alonso and Rey, "The Evolution of Jihadist Terrorism in Morocco."

109. Ibid., 574.

110. Syed, "56 Suicide Attacks Occurred since 2002"; Abbas, "A Profile of Tehrik-i-Taliban Pakistan," 1.

111. Gannon, "Pakistan Suicide Bomber Kills 15," 24.

112. Syed, "56 Suicide Attacks Occurred since 2002."

113. Kepel, *Jihad: The Trail of Political Islam*, 223–25.

114. Ramachandran, "Killers Turn to Suicide."

115. Oxford, "Pakistan Grapples with Menace of Suicide Bombers."

116. Ramachandran, "Killers Turn to Suicide."

117. Dugger, "Group in Pakistan Is Blamed by India for Suicide Raid," 1.

118. Pennington, "Musharraf Survives Another Suicide Attack," A20.

119. Bokhari, "Pakistan PM-Elect Survives Suicide Attack," 8.

120. Gall, "Local Pakistani Militants Boost Qaeda Threat."

121. Quoted in Burke, "The New Taliban," 31.

122. Moreau, "Where the Jihad Lives Now."

123. Burke, "The New Taliban," 31.

124. Moreau, "Where the Jihad Lives Now," 34.

125. Laabs and Rotella, "Terrorists in Training Are Going to Pakistan."

126. Burke, "The New Taliban."

127. Mazzetti, "CIA Sees Qaeda Link in the Death of Bhutto," 8.

128. Gall, "Islamic Militants' New Front: Pakistan."

129. Gall, "Local Pakistani Militants Boost Qaeda Threat."

130. Gall, "Islamic Militants' New Front: Pakistan."

131. Abbas, "A Profile of Tehrik-i-Taliban Pakistan"; Ali, "Baitullah Mehsud—The Taliban's New Leader in Pakistan."

132. Latif, "The Land of an Eye for an Eye."

133. Gall and Masood, "Suicide Bomber Kills 42 Soldiers at Pakistan Training Site," 24.

134. Quoted in Gall, "Local Pakistani Militants Boost Qaeda Threat."

135. Musharbash, "Die Pakistan-Connection." Available at www.spiegel.de/panorama/0,1518,431334,00.html, last accessed 28 September 2006.

136. Schweitzer and Ferber, "Al Qaeda and the Internationalization of Suicide Terrorism," 70–71.

137. Quoted in ibid., 71.

138. Whitlock, "Al Qaeda Shifts Its Strategy in Saudi Arabia," 28.

139. "Car Bombers Target Saudi Security Units"; MacFarquhar, "Suicide Bomber Attacks Saudi Arabia's Interior Ministry," 8.

140. Specifically, bin Laden called for attacks against oil facilities in a December 2004 audio message, which was followed by Zawahiri in the autumn of 2005. See Henderson, "Al-Qaeda

Attack on Abqaiq: The Vulnerability of Saudi Oil." Available at www.washingtoninstitute.org/, last accessed 20 September 2006.

141. Husain, Al-Khobar, and Conradi, "Al-Qaeda Pledges War on Saudi Oil Plants."

142. Shihri and Michael, "Foiled Plot Mirrored 9/11 Attack."

143. Hegghammer, "Terrorist Recruitment and Radicalization in Saudi Arabia."

144. Schweitzer and Ferber, "Al Qaeda and the Internationalization of Suicide Terrorism," 72. See also Whitlock, "Al Qaeda Shifts Its Strategy in Saudi Arabia," 28.

145. "*Blood That Will Not Have Flown in Vain*—a Video Presentation of the Martyrs of Saudi Arabia, Issued by Al-Qaeda in Saudi Arabia."

146. Stenersen, "The Internet: A Virtual Training Camp?"

147. Hegghammer, "Terrorist Recruitment and Radicalization in Saudi Arabia," 49.

148. Ibid., 52.

149. Vick, "Al-Qaeda's Hand in Istanbul Plot," A1.

150. Ibid.

151. Williams and Altindag, "El Kaide Turka."

152. Former Turkish counterterrorism official, interview with the author, Istanbul, Turkey, 10 June 2005.

153. Ibid.

154. Vick, "Al-Qaeda's Hand in Istanbul Plot."

155. Williams and Altindag, "El Kaide Turka."

156. Vick, "Al-Qaeda's Hand in Istanbul Plot."

157. Karl Vick, "A Bomb-Builder, 'out of the Shadow.' "

158. Vick, "Al-Qaeda's Hand in Istanbul Plot."

159. "Seven Jailed for Turkey Bombing."

160. Hyland, "New Arrests Show Turkey as a Recruiting Ground for Islamist Militants."

161. "Islamic Jihad Group (Uzbekistan)." Available at www.tkb.org, last accessed 10 November 2006.

162. Knop, "The Female Jihad: Al Qaeda's Women."

Six • The United Kingdom and the 7/7 Bombings

1. Although the main focus of this chapter is on the 7/7 bombings, other staged and attempted suicide attacks by British bombers, as well as by non-British bombers against British targets, are also discussed in the final part of the chapter.

2. "Report of the Official Account of the Bombings in London on 7th July 2005," 24.

3. Tumelty, "An In-Depth Look at the London Bombers."

4. "Report of the Official Account of the Bombings in London on 7th July 2005," 13.

5. Malik, "My Brother the Bomber."

6. Ibid.

7. Ibid.

8. "Report of the Official Account of the Bombings in London on 7th July 2005," 14.

9. Alvarez, "Lives of Three Men Offer Little to Explain Attacks."

10. Raghavan, "Friends Describe Bomber's Political, Religious Evolution."

11. "Report of the Official Account of the Bombings in London on 7th July 2005," 15.

12. Chamberlain, "Attacker 'Was Recruited' at Terror Group's Religious School," 2.
13. Alvarez, "New Muslim at 15, Terror Suspect at 19," 8.
14. Ibid.
15. "Report of the Official Account of the Bombings in London on 7th July 2005," 18.
16. Alvarez, "Lives of Three Men Offer Little to Explain Attacks," 13.
17. "Report of the Official Account of the Bombings in London on 7th July 2005," 14.
18. Tumelty, "An In-Depth Look at the London Bombers."
19. "Report of the Official Account of the Bombings in London on 7th July 2005," 15.
20. Ibid., 24.
21. Waldman, "Seething Unease Shaped British Bombers' Newfound Zeal," 1.
22. Ibid.
23. "Muslim Americans: Middle Class and Mostly Mainstream," 3.
24. "Al-Qaeda Film on the First Anniversary of the London Bombings."
25. "The Complete Al-Qaeda Video on the London July 7th Blast." Transcript of Mohammed Siddique Khan's statements by the author.
26. "Al-Qaeda Film on the First Anniversary of the London Bombings."
27. "The Complete Al-Qaeda Video on the London July 7th Blast."
28. "Al-Qaeda Film on the First Anniversary of the London Bombings."
29. Norton-Taylor, "Iraq War 'Motivated London Bombers.' "
30. "Security, Terrorism, and the UK."
31. "The Complete Al-Qaeda Video on the London July 7th Blast."
32. Ibid.
33. Ibid.
34. Ibid.
35. Ibid.
36. Ibid.
37. "Al-Qaeda Film on the First Anniversary of the London Bombings."
38. "Report of the Official Account of the Bombings in London on 7th July 2005," 4.
39. Bandura, "Mechanisms of Moral Disengagement."
40. "Focus: Undercover in the Academy of Hatred."
41. Ibid.
42. Raghavan, "Friends Describe Bomber's Political, Religious Evolution," A16.
43. Ibid.
44. Hussain, "Focus: Undercover on Planet Beeston."
45. "Al-Qaeda Film on the First Anniversary of the London Bombings."
46. "The Complete Al-Qaeda Video on the London July 7th Blast."
47. Ibid.
48. Ibid.
49. Additional information on Al-Muhajiroun appears later in this chapter.
50. "Focus: Undercover in the Academy of Hatred."
51. On the psychological effects of the London bombings, see especially "Report of the 7 July Review Committee." Available at http://news.bbc.co.uk/2/shared/bsp/hi/pdfs/05_06_06_london_bombing.pdf, last accessed 9 August 2006.
52. Tumelty, "An In-Depth Look at the London Bombers."

53. "Report of the Official Account of the Bombings in London on 7th July 2005," 21.

54. Ibid., 20.

55. Ibid., 21.

56. "The Complete Al-Qaeda Video on the London July 7th Blast."

57. Bergen, "Al-Qaeda, Still in Business," B1.

58. Ibid.

59. Corera, "Were Bombers Linked to Al-Qaeda?"

60. "Report of the Official Account of the Bombings in London on 7th July 2005," 27.

61. "Al-Qaeda Film on the First Anniversary of the London Bombings."

62. Glees, "Campus Jihad," A15.

63. O'Neill, Reid, and Evans, "7/7 'Mastermind' Is Seized in Iraq."

64. Quoted in Scheuer, "The London Bombings."

65. Ibid.

66. "New Al-Jazeera Videos."

67. Ibid.

68. Ibid.

69. "*The First Anniversary of the Bombings in London*—a Video Presentation by as-Sahab Featuring Speeches from Shehzad Tanweer, Azzam the American, and Al-Qaeda Leadership."

70. "Al-Qaeda Film on the First Anniversary of the London Bombings."

71. Sageman, *Understanding Terror Networks*, 110.

72. Ibid., 169.

73. Ibid., 113.

74. "Report of the Official Account of the Bombings in London on 7th July 2005," 16.

75. "Report into the London Terrorist Attacks on 7 July 2005," 12.

76. Coll and Glasser, "In London, Islamic Radicals Found a Heaven," A1.

77. Ibid.

78. Katz and Kern, "Center of the Jihadist World; They Call It Londonistan for a Reason."

79. Gibson, "New Recruits; Why Did Quiet, Well-Liked British Men Travel to Israel to Become Suicide Bombers?"

80. Sciolino and Van Natta, "For a Decade, London Thrived as a Busy Crossroads of Terror," A1.

81. Coll and Glasser, "In London, Islamic Radicals Found a Heaven," A1.

82. O'Neill and McGrory, "Abu Hamza and the 7/7 Bombers," A1.

83. Coll and Glasser, "In London, Islamic Radicals Found a Heaven," A1.

84. "Police Found Weapons at Finsbury Park Mosque."

85. The term Londonistan was first coined by French officials dissatisfied with the British government's inability to extradite an Algerian who had been charged in France with financing a series of attacks on the public transportation system in Paris in 1995. See Caldwell, "After Londonistan," 42.

86. Radu, "London 7/7 and Its Impact."

87. "Terrorist Threat to UK—MI5 Chief's Full Speech."

88. O'Neill and McGrory, "9/11 Prisoners Reveal British Terror Targets."

89. Gibson, "New Recruits; Why Did Quiet, Well-Liked British Men Travel to Israel to Become Suicide Bombers?"

90. Ibid.

91. Cowell, "Zeal for Suicide Bombing Reaches British Midlands," 6.

92. Malik, "My Brother the Bomber."

93. Caldwell, "After Londonistan," 42.

94. Winnett and Leppard, "Leaked No. 10 Dossier Reveals Al-Qaeda's British Recruits."

95. Tait and MacAskill, "Iranian Group Seeks British Suicide Bombers," 1.

96. Cowell, "Britain Says Two Dozen Major Terrorist Conspiracies Are under Investigation," 8.

97. "Terrorist Threat to UK—MI5 Chief's Full Speech."

98. Scheuer, "Al-Qaeda at Year's End 2007."

99. Stringer, "7 Convicted in Muslim Terror Camps in UK"; Scheuer, "Is Global Jihad a Fading Phenomenon?"

100. "Six Accused of London Bomb Plot."

101. For more on the Bojinka plot, see National Commission on Terrorist Attacks upon the United States, *The 9/11 Commission Report*, and Brzezinski, "Bust and Boom," W9.

102. "Terror Police Find 'Martyr Tapes' "; "Q&A: UK Aircraft Bombplot," available on line at http://news.bbc.co.uk/2/hi/uk_news/4778889.stm, last accessed 13 August 2006.

103. The trial of the Heathrow plotters is still ongoing at the time of this writing.

104. Scheuer, "The London Plot: A Tactical Victory in an Eroding Strategic Environment."

105. "Al Qaeda Plotter Jailed for Life."

106. Sciolino and Grey, "British Terror Trial Traces a Path to Militant Islam," 1; "Fertiliser Plot Leader Was Son of Wealthy Businessman."

107. Woolcock, "How Police and MI5 Foiled 'Britain's 9/11.' "

108. Naughton, "Five Given Life for Fertiliser Bomb Terror Plot."

109. Bonner, Perlez, and Schmitt, "British Inquiry of Failed Plots Points to Iraq's Qaeda Group."

110. Sageman, *Understanding Terror Networks*, 135.

111. "Terrorist Threat to UK—MI5 Chief's Full Speech."

112. Prior to the attack of September 11, 2001, Britain arrested or extradited relatively few radical Islamists, although it monitored many of them.

Seven • The Rise of Suicide Attacks in Iraq

1. The total number of suicide attacks between 1981 and April 2007 was 1,269, of which 628 attacks occurred in Iraq, and 641 in other countries. Unless stated otherwise, statistics on suicide attacks on Iraq are taken from the University of Haifa's Suicide Terrorism database. There is no doubt that the actual number of suicide attacks in Iraq is even higher than the number stated here. The University of Haifa's Suicide Terrorism Database lists only confirmed suicide bombings, and likely does not include many suicide attacks in Iraq that are not reported in the press, or that are not reported with sufficient detail.

2. "Television Stations Carry Images of Suicide Bombers."

3. Burns, "5 Bomb Attacks Kill 26 as Vote by Iraqis Nears," 1.

4. Jaff and Worth, "Blast Kills 122 at Iraqi Clinic in Attack on Security Recruits," 1.

5. Semple, "Iraqis Stunned by the Violence of a Bombing," 1.

6. Cloud, "Insurgents Using Bigger, More Lethal Bombs, U.S. Officers Say," 9.

7. Khalil, "Iraq's Sufi Community Shaken by Deadly Attack."

8. On 17 September 2006, for instance, at least ten suicide attacks occurred in a single day. "U.S.: Iraq Suicide Attacks Rising during Ramadan"; Al-Ansary and Adeeb, "Most Tribes in Anbar Agree to Unite against Insurgents."

9. On 5 January 2006, suicide bombers killed at least 130 people, mostly Shias, in the Shii holy city of Karbala and Ramadi. On 7 April 2006, three suicide bombers, including one woman, detonated themselves in the historic Baratha Mosque in northern Baghdad, and on 18 July 2006, a suicide car bomber killed at least 53 people and wounded more than 100 in the holy Shii city of Kufa by driving into a crowd of laborers. These attacks were symptomatic of scores of other high-profile attacks against Shias.

10. 5 April 2007 is the cutoff date for data that was available from the University of Haifa's database. It is, again, important to note that the actual number of suicide attacks is likely much higher. According to a U.S. Defense Department official quoted in *Newsweek*, for example, there were 540 suicide attacks between 1 January and 30 June 2007, killing thousands of Iraqis. See Nordland and Dehghanpisheh, "Surge of Suicide Bombers," 30.

11. Alissa J. Rubin, "70 Killed in Wave of Revenge in Northern Iraq," 16.

12. See the Iraq Index at The Web site of the Brookings Institution for up to date numbers on the composition of the Iraqi insurgency. Available at www.brookings.edu/fp/saban/iraq/index.pdf, last accessed 17 October 2006. See also for example, Quinn and Shrader, "Foreigners Blamed for Iraq Suicide Attacks."

13. Partlow, "An Uphill Battle to Stop Fighters at Border," A12.

14. In February 2006, for example, Director of National Intelligence John Negroponte confirmed that "extreme Sunni jihadist elements, a subset of which are foreign fighters, constitute a small minority of the overall insurgency, but their use of high-profile suicide attacks gives them a disproportionate impact." U.S. Congress, Senate, Statement by the Director of National Intelligence, John D. Negroponte. For statements that foreigners are the dominant perpetrators of suicide attacks issued in 2005, see, for example, Glasser, "Martyrs in Iraq Mostly Saudis; Web Sites Track Suicide Bombings," A1; Quinn and Shrader, "Foreigners Blamed for Iraq Suicide Attacks"; and Filkins, "Foreign Fighters Captured in Iraq Come from 27, Mostly Arab, Lands," 8.

15. Paz, "Arab Volunteers Killed in Iraq: An Analysis."

16. Al-Shishani, "The Salafi-Jihadist Movement in Iraq."

17. McDonnell and Rotella, "Making Bombers in Iraq."

18. Quinn and Shrader, "Foreigners Blamed for Iraq Suicide Attacks."

19. Ulph, "New Brigade for 'Iraqi' Suicide Bombers."

20. Miller and Marshall, "More Iraqis Lured to Al Qaeda Group."

21. Hafez, "Suicide Terrorism in Iraq," 557–59.

22. Abdul-Ahad, "Outside Iraq but Deep in the Fight," A1.

23. Paz, "Arab Volunteers Killed in Iraq: An Analysis."

24. Ibid. On the importance of kinship ties, see especially Sageman, *Understanding Terror Networks*, 112–13, and Pedahzur and Perliger, "The Changing Nature of Suicide Attacks."

25. Al-Shishani, "The Salafi-Jihadist Movement in Iraq."

26. Quinn and Shrader, "Foreigners Blamed for Iraq Suicide Attacks."

27. Schmitt, "U.S. And Allies Capture More Foreign Fighters," 8.

28. "Iraq Bomber Was 'Belgian Woman.' "

29. Dickey, "Women of Al Qaeda."

30. Felter and Fishman, *Al-Qaida's Foreign Fighters in Iraq*, 9.

31. I thank Rita Katz and the SITE Institute for providing me with most of the following biographies. The biographies are available to subscribers at www.siteinstitute.org/.

32. Musharbash, "Der Cyber-Friedhof der Dschihadis."

33. Ibid.

34. Musharbash, "Er war Schöner als der Mond."

35. The author watched the majority of the videos that are cited in this chapter. I thank the SITE Institute for making these videos available to me.

36. "*The Battle of the Captured Sheikh, Dr. Omar Abdul Rahman*."

37. "From the Biographies of the Prominent Martyrs of Al-Qaeda in Iraq, Sayf Al-Ummah."

38. "From the Biographies of the Prominent Martyrs of Al-Qaeda in Iraq, Abu Umayr Al-Suri."

39. "Jihadist Forum Provides Biography of a Suicide Bomber in Iraq, Abu Osman Al-Yamani."

40. "From the Biographies of the Prominent Martyrs of Al-Qaeda in Iraq, Abu Maaz Al-Janoubi."

41. "*Fatimah's Fiancé*—Video of a Suicide Car Bombing on a Combined Checkpoint of American Soldiers and Iraqi National Guards by the Muhahideen Shura Council."

42. Mary Habeck, "Knowing the Enemy: Jihadist Ideology and the War on Terror," lecture at the MIT Security Studies Program's Wednesday Seminar Series, Massachusetts Institute of Technology, Cambridge, Massachusetts, 15 February 2006.

43. Glasser, "Martyrs in Iraq Mostly Saudis," A1.

44. Ghosh, "Inside the Mind of an Iraqi Suicide Bomber," 22.

45. Ibid.

46. MacFarquhar, "Lebanese Would-Be Suicide Bomber Tells How Volunteers Are Waging Jihad in Iraq," 11.

47. Filkins, "Qaeda Video Vows Iraq Defeat for 'Crusader' U.S.," A1.

48. Abdul-Ahad, "In Hideout, Foreign Arabs Share Vision of 'Martyrdom,' " A1.

49. Knickmeyer, "They Came Here to Die," A1.

50. Musharbash, "Terroristen Benutzen Zehnjaehrigen als Selbstmordattentaeter."

51. Semple, "Iraq Bombers Blow up 2 Children Used as Decoys."

52. Abu-Nasr, "Saudi Turns His Back on Jihad."

53. Nordlan, Masland, and Dickey, "Unmasking the Insurgents," 20.

54. See the Brookings Institution, "Iraq Index," and Eisenstadt and White, "Assessing Iraq's Sunni Arab Insurgency."

55. Eisenstadt and White doubt that Saddam Hussein planned to lead a postwar resistance movement. Joe Klein argues that Saddam had planned the insurgency from the outset. Eisenstadt and White, "Assessing Iraq's Sunni Arab Insurgency"; Klein, "Saddam's Revenge," 44.

56. International Crisis Group, "In Their Own Words," 5.

57. Eisenstadt and White, "Assessing Iraq's Sunni Arab Insurgency," 3.

58. Osman, "What Do the Insurgents Want?" B1.

59. Eisenstadt and White, "Assessing Iraq's Sunni Arab Insurgency," 13.

60. Gambill, "Abu Musab Al-Zarqawi: A Biographical Sketch"; Husayn, *Al-Zarqawi: The Second Generation of Al-Qaida.*

61. AQI is sometimes also referred to as Al Qaeda in Mesopotamia and Al Qaeda in the Land of the Two Rivers.

62. International Crisis Group, "In Their Own Words," 2.

63. Yousafzai and Moreau, "Terror Broker," 56.

64. Hafez, "Suicide Terrorism in Iraq."

65. Paz, "Zarqawi's Strategy in Iraq—Is There a New Al-Qaeda?," 2–3. See also Ulph, "Al-Zarqawi as Master Strategist in Iraq, Rising Leader of the Global Jihad."

66. Salafi-Jihadists use several derogatory terms for Shiis, including the label "Alqamis." Muayyed al-Din ibn al-Alqami was a Shii minister of the last Sunni caliphate during the Abbasid Empire. During the Mongol occupation of Baghdad in the thirteenth century, he was accused of assisting the Mongol army under Hulagu and thus of committing high treason. For Sunnis, the term Alqami became henceforth a synonym for Shii treason.

67. Katz, "The Coming New Wave of Jihad." The other members of the council are Jaysh al-Taifa al-Mansura, Ansar al-Tawhid, Al-Ghuraba, Al-Jihad al-Islami, and Al-Ahwal. See Ulph, "Al-Zarqawi's Group under Pressure and Seeking Allies."

68. Hazan, "Sunni Jihad Groups Rise up against Al-Qaeda in Iraq."

69. Khalil, "The Islamic State of Iraq Launches"; Parker, "Insurgents Report a Split with Al Qaeda in Iraq."

70. Khalil, "Divisions within the Iraqi Insurgency."

71. Bakier, "Al-Qaeda Adapts Its Methods in Iraq as Part of a Global Strategy"; Hafez, "Al-Qaida Losing Ground in Iraq."

72. Rubin, "Ansar Al-Sunna: Iraq's New Terrorist Threat."

73. Rageh, "Ansar Al-Sunnah Army Gains Clout in Iraq."

74. International Crisis Group, "In Their Own Words," 2.

75. Filkins, "Profusion of Rebel Groups Helps Them Survive in Iraq," A1.

76. Hafez, "Suicide Terrorism in Iraq"; Hafez, *Suicide Bombers in Iraq.*

77. Hafez, "Suicide Terrorism in Iraq," 533.

78. Ibid., 535.

79. Nordland, Masland, and Dickey, "Unmasking the Insurgents," 20.

80. Semple, "Bombers Strike Baghdad Hotels," A1.

81. See also Moghadam, "The Chlorine Gas Attacks in Iraq and the Specter of Suicide Attacks with CBRN Weapons." Available at http://counterterrorismblog.org/2007/03/the_chlorine_gas_attacks_in_ir.php, last accessed 24 November 2007.

82. In his "Mini-Manual of the Urban Guerrilla," Carlos Marighella suggested just such a strategy. For a copy of the manual, see the appendix in Moss, *Urban Guerrilla.*

83. Georgy, "Iraq Insurgency More Sophisticated-U.S. Intelligence."

84. Semple, "Iraqis Stunned by the Violence of a Bombing," 1; Ghosh, "Professor of Death," 44.

85. "Iraq: Suicide Attacks." Available at www.cfr.org/pub8286/lionel_beehner/iraq_suicide_attacks.php, last accessed 21 August 2005.

86. Musharbash, "Reiseführer für Terror-Touristen."

87. U.S. ambassador to Iraq Zalmay Khalilzad said in a speech on 1 August 2005 that "Iran is working along two contradictory tracks. On the one hand, Tehran works with the new Iraq; on the other there is movement across its borders of people and material used in violent acts against Iraq." See Ridolfo, "Iraq: U.S. Ambassador Announces Seven-Point Plan for Country."

88. Ibid.

89. Risen and Sanger, "Border Clashes as U.S. Pressures Syria over Iraq," 1.

90. Pleming, "Us Tells Syria to Stop Bombers Crossing into Iraq."

91. MacFarquhar, "Lebanese Would-be Suicide Bomber Tells How Volunteers Are Waging Jihad in Iraq," 11.

92. Beeston and Hider, "Following the Trail of Death."

93. Ibid.

94. Burns, "Iraq's Ho Chi Minh Trail," 1.

95. Ibid.

96. MacFarquhar, "Lebanese Would-be Suicide Bomber Tells How Volunteers Are Waging Jihad in Iraq," 11.

97. Ghosh, "Inside the Mind of an Iraqi Suicide Bomber," 22.

98. Ghosh, "Professor of Death," 44.

99. Mekhennet and Moss, "In Jihadist Heaven, a Goal: To Kill and Die in Iraq."

100. The videos have been made available to the author courtesy of the SITE Institute.

101. "Leader of Al-Qaeda in Iraq Al-Zarqawi Declares 'Total War' on Shiites."

102. "*The Battle of the Captured Sheikh, Dr. Omar Abdul Rahman*."

103. "Leader of Al-Qaeda in Iraq Al-Zarqawi Declares 'Total War' on Shiites."

104. "A Video Will of a Suicide Bomber from Al-Qaeda in Iraq, and His Operation on an American Checkpoint in Al-Fallujah."

105. "*The Battle of the Captured Sheikh, Dr. Omar Abdul Rahman*."

106. "The Complete Video Presentation of the Abu Anas Al-Shami Attack at Abu Ghraib Prison by Al-Qaeda in Iraq."

107. "Al-Qaeda in Iraq Issues Video of the Oldest Suicide Bomber."

108. "Jaish Ansar Al-Sunnah Insurgency Group in Iraq Releases Detailed Communiqué and Video."

109. The article was translated by the Middle East Media Research Institute (MEMRI). See "The Iraqi Al-Qaida Organization: A Self-Portrait."

110. Hafez, "Suicide Terrorism in Iraq," 536.

111. International Crisis Group, "In Their Own Words," i.

112. Ibid., 7.

113. Ibid., 10.

114. Paz, "The Impact of the War in Iraq on the Global Jihad," 44.

115. International Crisis Group, "In Their Own Words," 7, n. 49.

116. Quoted in Ulph, "Al-Zarqawi as Master Strategist in Iraq, Rising Leader of the Global Jihad."

117. Al-Shishani, "Al-Zarqawi's Rise to Power."

118. Paz, "The Impact of the War in Iraq on the Global Jihad."

119. The original Arabic version and a translated copy of the letter, which is dated 9 July

2005, were available on the Web site of the Director of National Intelligence in 2005. See www.dni.gov/release_letter_101105.html, last accessed 24 November 2005.

120. Quoted in Hafez, "Suicide Terrorism in Iraq," 536–37.

121. "Tape Justifies Killing Innocent Muslims."

Available at www.cnn.com/2005/WORLD/meast/05/18/iraq.main, last accessed 18 October 2006.

122. Filkins, "U.S. Says Files Seek Qaeda Aid in Iraq Conflict," 1.

123. Ibid.

124. Quoted in Scheuer, "Coalition Warfare, Part II."

125. Studies of aggression have confirmed that it is easier to mistreat people once they are dehumanized. See, for example, Bandura, "Mechanisms of Moral Disengagement," 181.

126. International Crisis Group, "In Their Own Words," 11.

127. Ibid.

Conclusion

1. On the contrary, even Islamic groups like Hamas, which I have labeled a mainstream Islamist group, fiercely resist joining Al Qaeda's global jihadist call. As a result, it has drawn heavy criticism especially on the part of Ayman al-Zawahiri. See, for example, Ulph, "Al Zawahiri Takes Hamas to Task"; "Al-Zawahiri in Two Recent Messages."

2. For an excellent discussion on new agendas for research on suicide attacks, see Crenshaw, "Explaining Suicide Terrorism: A Review Essay."

3. Quoted in "Jihad and Terrorism Studies."

BIBLIOGRAPHY

Abadie, Alberto. "Poverty, Political Freedom, and the Roots of Terrorism." *NBER Working Paper No. 10859*. Cambridge, MA: National Bureau of Economic Research, October 2004.

Abbas, Hassan. "A Profile of Tehrik-i-Taliban Pakistan." *CTC Sentinel* 1, no. 2 (January 2008): 1.

Abdul-Ahad, Ghaith. "In Hideout, Foreign Arabs Share Vision of 'Martyrdom.'" *Washington Post*, 9 November 2004, A1.

——. "Outside Iraq but Deep in the Fight." *Washington Post*, 8 June 2005, A1.

Abedi, Mehdi, and Gary Legenhausen, eds. *Jihad and Shahadat: Struggle and Martyrdom in Islam*. Houston, TX: Institute for Research and Islamic Studies, 1986.

Abu-Nasr, Donna. "Saudi Turns His Back on Jihad." *Washington Post*, 28 July 2007.

Abu Tir, Mohammed. "Open Letter: Just Be Fair with Us." *Newsweek International*, 6 February 2006.

Adams, Ian. *The Logic of Political Belief: A Philosophical Analysis of Ideology*. New York: Harvester Wheatsheaf, 1989.

"Afghan Suicide Bombing Kills 17." *BBC News*, 28 August 2006.

Al-Ansary, Khalid, and Ali Adeeb. "Most Tribes in Anbar Agree to Unite against Insurgents." *New York Times*, 18 September 2006.

"Al-Qaeda Explains Amman Bombings." *MEMRI Special Dispatch Series* No. 1043 (8 December 2005).

"Al-Qaeda Film on the First Anniversary of the London Bombings Features Messages by Bomber Shehzad Tanweer, American Al-Qaeda Member Adam Gadahn and Al-Qaeda Leader Ayman Al-Zawahiri." *MEMRI TV Monitor Project* Clip No. 1186 (6 July 2006).

"Al-Qaeda in Iraq Issues Video of the Oldest Suicide Bomber, Claims Responsibility for Ongoing Battles in Al-Ramadi, and Announces Fighting Those Who Refuse 'Allah's Law.'" *SITE Institute*, 12 August 2005.

"Al Qaeda Plotter Jailed for Life." *BBC News*, 7 November 2006.

"Al-Qaeda Rebuilding in Pakistan." *BBC News*, 14 January 2007.

Al-Shishani, Murad. "Abu Musab Al-Suri and the Third Generation of Salafi-Jihadists." *Terrorism Monitor* 3, no. 16 (11 August 2005).

——. "Al-Zarqawi's Rise to Power: Analyzing Tactics and Targets." *Terrorism Monitor* 3, no. 22 (17 November 2005).

——. "The Salafi-Jihadist Movement in Iraq: Recruitment Methods and Arab Volunteers." *Terrorism Monitor* 3, no. 23 (2 December 2005).

——. "Salafi-Jihadists in Jordan: From Prison Riots to Suicide Operation Cells." *Terrorism Focus* 3, no. 9 (7 March 2006).

Al-Zawahiri, Ayman. *Knights under the Prophet's Banner*. London: Al-Sharq al-Awsat, 2001.

"Al-Zawahiri in Two Recent Messages: 'Iran Stabbed a Knife into the Back of the Islamic Nation'; Urges Hamas to Declare Commitment to Restoring the Caliphate." *MEMRI Special Dispatch Series* No. 1787 (18 December 2007).

Ali, Imtiaz. "Baitullah Mehsud—The Taliban's New Leader in Pakistan." *Terrorism Focus* Vol. 5, no. 1 (8 January 2008).

Alonso, Rogelio, and Fernando Reinares. "Maghreb Immigrants Becoming Suicide Terrorists: A Case Study on Religious Radicalization Processes in Spain." In *Root Causes of Suicide Terrorism: The Globalization of Martyrdom*, edited by Ami Pedahzur, 179–97. New York: Routledge, 2006.

Alonso, Rogelio, and Marcos Garcia Rey. "The Evolution of Jihadist Terrorism in Morocco." *Terrorism and Political Violence* 19 (2007): 571–92.

Alvarez, Lizette. "Lives of Three Men Offer Little to Explain Attacks." *New York Times*, 14 July 2005, 13.

——. "New Muslim at 15, Terror Suspect at 19." *New York Times*, 18 July 2005, 8.

Anonymous. *Imperial Hubris: Why the West Is Losing the War on Terror*. Washington, DC: Brassey's, 2004.

——. *Through Our Enemies' Eyes: Osama Bin Laden, Radical Islam, and the Future of America*. Washington, DC: Brassey's, 2003.

"Argentina Seeks Arrest of Iran's Ex-Leader in 1994 Bombing Inquiry." *New York Times*, 10 November 2006, 5.

Armstrong, Karen. *Islam: A Short History*. New York: Random House, 2002.

Arquilla, John, and David F. Ronfeldt. *The Advent of Netwar*. Santa Monica, CA: Rand, 1996.

——. *Networks and Netwars: The Future of Terror, Crime, and Militancy*. Santa Monica, CA: Rand, 2001.

Atran, Scott. "The Moral Logic and Growth of Martyrdom." *Washington Quarterly* 29, no. 2 (Spring 2006): 127–47.

Badkhen, Anna. "Foreign Jihadists Seen as Key to Spike in Afghan Attacks." *San Francisco Chronicle*, 25 September 2006, A1.

Bakier, Abdul Hameed. "Al-Qaeda Adapts Its Methods in Iraq as Part of a Global Strategy." *Terrorism Monitor* 5, no. 24 (20 December 2007).

——. "Forum Users Improve Electronic Jihad Technology." *Terrorism Focus* 4, no. 20 (26 June 2007).

——. "Jihadis Provide Internet Training for Female Mujahideen." *Terrorism Focus* 3, no. 40 (17 October 2006).

——. "The New Issue of Technical Mujahid, a Training Manual for Jihadis." *Terrorism Monitor* 5, no. 6 (29 March 2007).

Baldauf, Scott. "Taliban Turn to Suicide Attacks." *Christian Science Monitor*, 3 February 2006, 1.

"Bali Attack 'Targeted Australians.'" *BBC News*, 10 February 2003.

Ball, Terence, and Richard Dagger. *Political Ideologies and the Democratic Ideal*. 3rd ed. New York: Longman, 1999.

Bandura, Albert. "Mechanisms of Moral Disengagement." In *Origins of Terrorism: Psychologies, Ideologies, Theologies, States of Mind*, edited by Walter Reich, 161–91. Washington, DC: Woodrow Wilson Center Press, 1998.

Bar, Shmuel. *Jihad Ideology in Light of Contemporary Fatwas*. Research Monographs on the Muslim World. Center on Islam, Democracy, and the Future of the Muslim World. Washington, DC: Hudson Institute, September 2006.

"*The Battle of the Captured Sheikh, Dr. Omar Abdul Rahman*—a Film by Al-Qaeda in Iraq Depicting the Preparation, Suicide Bombers' Farewells, and Executing of an Operation Targeting Al-Hamra Hotel in Baghdad." *SITE Institute*, 12 January 2006.

Beeston, Richard, and James Hider. "Following the Trail of Death: How Foreigners Flock to Join Holy War." *Times Online* (London), 25 June 2005.

Benjamin, Daniel, and Steven Simon. *The Age of Sacred Terror*. New York: Random House, 2002.

Benjamin, Daniel, and Gabriel Weimann. "What the Terrorists Have in Mind." *New York Times*, 27 October 2004.

Bennhold, Katrin. "Privation and Despair Colored an Algiers Bomber's Life." *New York Times*, 14 December 2007.

Bergen, Peter L. "Al-Qaeda, Still in Business." *Washington Post*, 2 July 2006, B1.

——. *Holy War, Inc.: Inside the Secret World of Osama Bin Laden*. New York: Touchstone, 2002.

——. *The Osama Bin Laden I Know: An Oral History of Al-Qaeda's Leader*. New York: Free Press, 2006.

Berko, Anat. *The Path to Paradise: The Inner World of Suicide Bombers and Their Dispatchers*. Westport, CT: Praeger Security International, 2007.

Bernstein, Richard. "Tape, Probably Bin Laden's, Offers 'Truce' to Europe." *New York Times*, 16 April 2004, 3.

Biggs, Michael. "Dying without Killing: Self-Immolations, 1963–2002." In *Making Sense of Suicide Missions*, edited by Diego Gambetta, 173–208. Oxford: Oxford University Press, 2005.

Billingsley, Dodge. "Chechen Rebels Hone Tactics for Long Haul." *Jane's Intelligence Review* 13, no. 2 (1 February 2001).

"Bin Laden's Fatwa." 8 August 1996. Available online at www.pbs.org/newshour/terrorism/international/fatwa—1996.html, accessed 8 April 2008.

"Bin Laden Rails against Crusaders and UN." *BBC News*, 3 November 2001.

Black, Andrew. "AQIM Employs Martyrdom Operations in Algeria." *Terrorism Focus* 4, no. 29 (18 September 2007).

——. "The Ideological Struggle over Al-Qaeda's Suicide Tactics in Algeria." *Terrorism Monitor* 6, no. 3 (7 February 2008).

Blanchard, Christopher M. "Al Qaeda: Statements and Evolving Ideology." In *CRS Report for Congress RL32759*, 1–16. Washington, DC: Congressional Research Service, Library of Congress, 2005.

"Blood That Will Not Have Flown in Vain—a Video Presentation of the Martyrs of Saudi Arabia, Issued by Al-Qaeda in Saudi Arabia." *SITE Institute*, 28 April 2006.

Bloom, Mia M. *Dying to Kill: The Allure of Suicide Terror*. New York: Columbia University Press, 2005.

——. "Palestinian Suicide Bombing: Public Support, Market Share and Outbidding." *Political Science Quarterly* 119, no. 1 (Spring 2004): 61–88.

Bokhari, Farhan. "Pakistan PM-Elect Survives Suicide Attack." *Financial Times*, 31 July 2004, 8.

Bonner, Raymond. "A Terrorist Strike in Bali, Choreographed for the Bombers on a Plotter's Computer." *New York Times*, 3 July 2006.

Bonner, Raymond, and Jane Perlez. "Macabre Clues Advance Inquiry in Bali Attacks." *New York Times*, 3 October 2005, 1.

Bonner, Raymond, Jane Perlez, and Eric Schmitt. "British Inquiry of Failed Plots Points to Iraq's Qaeda Group." *New York Times*, 14 December 2007.

Brachman, Jarret M., and William F. McCants. "Stealing Al-Qaida's Playbook." *CTC Report*, 1–25. West Point, NY: Combating Terrorism Center, January 2006.

Bradsher, Keith. "Indonesia Bombing Kills at Least 10 in Midday Attack." *New York Times*, 6 August 2003, 1.

Brookings Institution. "Iraq Index: Tracking Variables of Reconstruction and Security in Post-Saddam Iraq," edited by Michael O'Hanlon and Nina Kamp, 1–57. Washington, DC: Brookings Institution, 2006.

Brym, Robert J., and Bader Araj. "Suicide Bombing as Strategy and Interaction: The Case of the Second Intifada." *Social Forces* 84, no. 4 (June 2006): 1969–86.

Brzezinski, Matthew. "Bust and Boom." *Washington Post*, 30 December 2001, W9.

Burke, Jason. *Al-Qaeda: The True Story of Radical Islam*. London: I. B. Tauris, 2004.

——. "The New Taliban." *Observer*, 14 October 2007.

——. "Think Again: Al Qaeda." *Foreign Policy*, May–June 2004.

Burns, John F. "5 Bomb Attacks Kill 26 as Vote by Iraqis Nears." *New York Times*, 20 January 2005, 1.

——. "Iraq's Ho Chi Minh Trail." *New York Times*, 5 June 2005, 1.

Caldwell, Christopher. "After Londonistan." *New York Times Magazine*, 25 June 2006, 42.

"Canadians Die in Afghan Bombing." *BBC News*, 18 September 2006.

"Car Bombers Target Saudi Security Units." *Washington Post*, 30 December 2004, A16.

Chamberlain, Gethin. "Attacker 'Was Recruited' at Terror Group's Religious School." *Scotsman*, 14 July 2005.

Chivers, C. J., and David Rhode. "Turning out Guerrillas and Terrorists to Wage a Holy War." *New York Times*, 18 March 2002, A1.

Clarke, Richard A., Glenn P. Aga, Roger W. Cressey, Stephen E. Flynn, Blake W. Mobley, Eric Rosenbach, Steven Simon, William F. Wechsler, and Lee S. Wolosky. *Defeating the Jihadists: A Blueprint for Action: Report of a Task Force Chaired by Richard Clarke*. New York: Century Foundation Press, 2004.

Cloud, David S. "Insurgents Using Bigger, More Lethal Bombs, U.S. Officers Say." *New York Times*, 4 August 2005, 9.

Coll, Steve, and Susan B. Glasser. "In London, Islamic Radicals Found a Heaven." *Washington Post*, 10 July 2005, A1.

"The Complete Al-Qaeda Video on the London July 7th Blast, Released on the Internet by Al-Sahab." *SITE Institute*, 7 November 2005.

"The Complete Video Presentation of the Abu Anas Al-Shami Attack at Abu Ghraib Prison by Al-Qaeda in Iraq." *SITE Institute*, 9 February 2006.

Cook, David. *Understanding Jihad*. Berkeley: University of California Press, 2005.

Corera, Gordon. "Were Bombers Linked to Al-Qaeda?" *BBC News*, 6 July 2006.

Cowell, Alan. "Britain Says Two Dozen Major Terrorist Conspiracies Are under Investigation." *New York Times*, 14 August 2006, 8.

——. "Zeal for Suicide Bombing Reaches British Midlands." *New York Times*, 2 May 2003.

Crenshaw, Martha. "The Causes of Terrorism." *Comparative Politics* 13, no. 4 (July 1981): 379–99.

——. "Explaining Suicide Terrorism: A Review Essay." *Security Studies* 16, no. 1 (January–March 2007): 133–62.

——. "The Logic of Terrorism: Terrorist Behavior as a Product of Strategic Choice." In *Origins of Terrorism: Psychologies, Ideologies, Theologies, States of Mind*, edited by Walter Reich, 7–24. Washington, DC: Woodrow Wilson Center Press, 1998.

——. "An Organizational Approach to the Analysis of Political Terrorism." *Orbis* 29, no. 4 (Fall 1985): 465–89.

——. " 'Suicide' Terrorism in Comparative Perspective." In *Countering Suicide Terrorism*, edited by International Policy Institute for Counter-Terrorism (ICT), 21–29. Herzliyya, Israel: ICT, 2001.

——. "Theories of Terrorism: Instrumental and Organizational Approaches." In *Inside Terrorist Organizations*, edited by David C. Rapoport, 44–62. New York: Frank Cass, 1988.

Cronin, Audrey Kurth. "Terrorism and Suicide Attacks." *CRS Report for Congress RL32058*, 1–22. Washington, DC: Congressional Research Service, Library of Congress 2003.

Cruickshank, Paul. "Al-Qaida's Expanding Franchise." *Guardian Online*, 12 December 2007.

Curiel, Jonathan. "Terror.Com." *San Francisco Chronicle*, 10 July 2005, A1.

Dale, Stephen Frederic. "Religious Suicide in Islamic Asia: Anticolonial Terrorism in India, Indonesia, and the Philippines." *Journal of Conflict Resolution* 32, no. 1 (March 1988): 37–59.

Daly, John C. K., and Stephen Ulph. "How and Why: The 9-11 Attacks on America." *Spotlight on Terror* 1, no. 2 (22 December 2003).

DeYoung, Karen. "Spy Agencies Say Iraq War Hurting U.S. Terror Fight." *Washington Post*, 24 September 2006, A1.

Dickey, Christopher. "Inside Suicide, Inc." *Newsweek*, 15 April 2002, 26–32.

——. "Women of Al Qaeda." *Newsweek*, 12 December 2005.

"Document Afgp-2002-600045." In *Harmony Document Series*, undated.

"Document Afgp-2002-600048." In *Harmony Document Series*, undated.

"Document Afgp-2002-000078." In *Harmony Document Series*, undated.

Dolnik, Adam. "Die and Let Die: Exploring Links between Suicide Terrorism and Terrorist Use of Chemical, Biological, Radiological, and Nuclear Weapons." *Studies in Conflict and Terrorism* 26, no. 1 (2003): 17–35.

Dugger, Celia W. "Group in Pakistan Is Blamed by India for Suicide Raid." *New York Times*, 15 December 2001, 1.

"Egypt Names Islamist Group Suspected of Sinai Attacks." Agence France Press, 26 March 2006.

"Egypt Suicide Bombers Were Bedouin Islamists." Agence France Press, 3 September 2005.

Eisenstadt, Michael, and Jeffrey White. "Assessing Iraq's Sunni Arab Insurgency." *Policy Focus No. 50*. Washington, DC: Washington Institute for Near East Policy, December 2005.

Erlanger, Steven. "In Most Cases, Israel Thwarts Suicide Attacks without a Shot." *New York Times*, 25 July 2005.

Europol. "EU Terrorism Situation and Trend Report 2007 Te-Sat." The Hague, Netherlands: Europol, March 2007.

Farah, Douglas. "Salafists, China, and West Africa's Growing Anarchy." *International Assessment and Strategy Center*, 7 December 2004.

"*Fatimah's Fiancé*—a Video of a Suicide Car Bombing on a Combined Checkpoint of American Soldiers and Iraqi National Guards by the Muhahideen Shura Council." *SITE Institute*, 13 February 2006.

Felter, Joseph, and Brian Fishman. *Al-Qaida's Foreign Fighters in Iraq: A First Look at the Sinjar Records*. West Point, NY: U.S. Military Academy, December 2007.

"Fertiliser Plot Leader Was Son of Wealthy Businessman." *Times Online*, 30 April 2007.

Filkins, Dexter. "Foreign Fighters Captured in Iraq Come from 27, Mostly Arab, Lands." *New York Times*, 21 October 2005, 8.

——. "Profusion of Rebel Groups Helps Them Survive in Iraq." *New York Times*, 2 December 2005.

——. "Qaeda Video Vows Iraq Defeat for 'Crusader' U.S." *New York Times*, 26 April 2006.

——. "U.S. Says Files Seek Qaeda Aid in Iraq Conflict." *New York Times*, 9 February 2004, 1.

"*The First Anniversary of the Bombings in London*—a Video Presentation by as-Sahab Featuring Speeches from Shehzad Tanweer, Azzam the American, and Al-Qaeda Leadership." *SITE Institute*, 7 July 2006.

Flood, Christopher G. *Political Myth: A Theoretical Introduction*. New York: Garland, 1996.

"Focus: Undercover in the Academy of Hatred." *Sunday Times* (London), 7 August 2005.

Frantz, Douglas, and Desmond Butler. "Germans Lay out Early Qaeda Ties to 9/11 Hijackers." *New York Times*, 24 August 2002, A1.

Friedman, Thomas L. *The World Is Flat: A Brief History of the Twenty-First Century*. New York: Farrar, Straus and Giroux, 2005.

"From the Biographies of the Prominent Martyrs of Al-Qaeda in Iraq, Abu Maaz Al-Janoubi." *SITE Institute*, 5 April 2006.

"From the Biographies of the Prominent Martyrs of Al-Qaeda in Iraq, Abu Umayr Al-Suri." *SITE Institute*, 17 November 2005.

"From the Biographies of the Prominent Martyrs of Al-Qaeda in Iraq, Sayf Al-Ummah." *SITE Institute*, 9 January 2006.

"The Full Version of Osama Bin Laden's Speech." *MEMRI Special Dispatch Series* No. 811 (5 November 2004).

Gall, Carlotta. "Afghan Attacks, Tied to Taliban, Point to Pakistan." *New York Times*, 12 February 2006, 1.

——. "Attacks in Afghanistan Grow More Frequent and Lethal." *New York Times*, 27 September 2006, 15.

——. "Islamic Militants' New Front: Pakistan." *New York Times*, 15 March 2007.

——. "Local Pakistani Militants Boost Qaeda Threat." *New York Times*, 30 December 2007.

——. "Pakistan Link Seen in Afghan Suicide Attacks." *New York Times*, 14 November 2006, 1.

——. "Suicide Bomber Kills a Governor in Afghanistan." *New York Times*, 11 September 2006, 1.

Gall, Carlotta, and Salman Masood. "Suicide Bomber Kills 42 Soldiers at Pakistan Training Site." *New York Times*, 9 November 2006.

Gall, Carlotta, and Abdul Waheed Wafa. "Suicide Bomber Kills 16 in Kabul near Embassy." *New York Times*, 9 September 2006, 1.

Gambill, Gary. "Abu Musab Al-Zarqawi: A Biographical Sketch." *Terrorism Monitor* 2, no. 24 (16 December 2004).

——. "The Libyan Islamic Fighting Group (LIFG)." *Terrorism Monitor* 3, no. 6 (24 March 2005).

Gannon, Kathy. "Pakistan Suicide Bomber Kills 15; Blast Rocks Egyptian Embassy." *Chicago Sun-Times*, 20 November 1995, 24.

Ganor, Boaz. "Suicide Attacks in Israel." In *Countering Suicide Terrorism*, edited by International Policy Institute for Counter-Terrorism (ICT), 140–54. Herzliyya, Israel: ICT, 2001.

Gebauer, Matthias, Yassin Musharbash, and Holger Stark. "Cüneyt C.—Der erste Selbstmordattentäter aus Deutschland?" *Spiegel Online*, 15 March 2008.

"Geheimdienst lehnte Selbstmordanschlag auf Hitler Ab." *Spiegel Online*, 9 January 2007.

Geifman, Anna. *Thou Shalt Kill: Revolutionary Terrorism in Russia, 1894–1917*. Princeton, NJ: Princeton University Press, 1993.

Georgy, Michael. "Iraq Insurgency More Sophisticated-U.S. Intelligence." Reuters, 29 May 2005.

Gerges, Fawaz A. *The Far Enemy: Why Jihad Went Global*. Cambridge: Cambridge University Press, 2005.

Ghosh, Aparisim. "Inside the Mind of an Iraqi Suicide Bomber." *Time*, 4 July 2005, 22.

——. "Professor of Death." *Time*, 24 October 2005.

Gibson, Helen. "New Recruits; Why Did Quiet, Well-Liked British Men Travel to Israel to Become Suicide Bombers?" *TIME Europe*, 12 May 2003.

Glasser, Susan B. "Martyrs in Iraq Mostly Saudis; Web Sites Track Suicide Bombings." *Washington Post*, 15 May 2005, A1.

Glees, Anthony. "Campus Jihad." *Wall Street Journal*, 23 October 2006.

"Global Unease with Major World Powers. 47 Nation Pew Global Attitudes Survey." In *The Pew Global Attitudes Project*, 133. Washington, DC: Pew Research Center, 2007.

Gorka, Sebastian. "Al Qaeda's Next Generation." *Terrorism Monitor* 2, no. 15 (29 July 2004).

Greenberg, Joel. "A Family Is Left 'Sad and Happy' by a Violent Death." *New York Times*, 7 December 2001, A13.

"Group Profile: Ansar Al-Sunnah Army." *Terrorism Knowledge Base*.

"Group Profile: Hizbul Mujahideen (HM)." *Terrorism Knowledge Base*.

"Group Profile: Jamatul Mujahedin Bangladesh (JMB)." *Terrorism Knowledge Base*.

"Group Profile: Jund Al-Sham." *Terrorism Knowledge Base*.

"Group Profile: Mujahideen Shura Council." *Terrorism Knowledge Base*.

"Group Profile: Riyad Us-Saliheyn Martyrs' Brigade." *Terrorism Knowledge Base*.

"Group Profile: Salafia Jihadia." *Terrorism Knowledge Base*.

"Group Profile: Soldiers of the Prophet's Companion." *Terrorism Knowledge Base*.

"Group Profile: Special Purpose Islamic Regiment (SPIR)." *Terrorism Knowledge Base*.

Gunaratna, Rohan. *Inside Al Qaeda: Global Network of Terror*. New York: Columbia University Press, 2002.

Gutman, Matthew. "The Bomber Next Door." *Jerusalem Post*, 14 September 2001, 5B.

Gutman, Matthew, and Herb Keinon. "IDF Concludes Sinai Rescue Operation. 13 Israelis among 32 Bombing Victims." *Jerusalem Post*, 11 October 2004, 1.

Haahr, Kathryn. "Emerging Terrorist Trends in Spain's Moroccan Communities." *Terrorism Monitor* 4, no. 9 (4 May 2006).

——. "The Growth of Militant Islamist Micro-Diaspora Communities: Observations from Spain." *CTC Sentinel* 1, no. 4 (March 2008): 15–18.

——. "GSPC Joins Al-Qaeda and France Becomes Top Enemy." *Terrorism Focus* 3, no. 37 (26 September 2006).

——. "Italy's Underground Islamist Network." *Terrorism Monitor* 5, no. 16 (16 August 2007).

Hafez, Mohammed M. "Al-Qaida Losing Ground in Iraq." *CTC Sentinel* 1, no. 1 (December 2007): 6–8.

——. "Manufacturing Human Bombs: Strategy, Culture, and Conflict in the Making of Palestinian Suicide Bombers." Revised paper submitted to the United States Institute of Peace for publication in the Peaceworks series, Version 2, 4 April 2005.

——. *Manufacturing Human Bombs: The Making of Palestinian Suicide Bombers*. Washington, DC: United States Institute of Peace Press, 2006.

——. "Rationality, Culture, and Structure in the Making of Suicide Bombers: A Preliminary Theoretical Synthesis and Illustrative Case Study." *Studies in Conflict and Terrorism* 29, no. 3 (April–May 2006): 165–85.

——. *Suicide Bombers in Iraq: The Strategy and Ideology of Martyrdom*. Washington, DC: United States Institute of Peace Press, 2007.

——. "Suicide Terrorism in Iraq: A Preliminary Assessment of the Quantitative Data and Documentary Evidence." *Studies in Conflict and Terrorism* 29, no. 6 (September 2006): 531–60.

Harel, Amos. "Suicide Attacks Frighten Israelis More Than Scuds." *Haaretz*, 13 February 2003.

Hassan, Nasra. "An Arsenal of Believers: Talking to the 'Human Bombs.'" *New Yorker* 77, no. 36 (2001): 36–41.

Hazan, D. "Sunni Jihad Groups Rise Up against Al-Qaeda in Iraq." *MEMRI Special Dispatch Series* No. 336 (22 March 2007).

Hedges, Chris. "Tunisian Killed in Synagogue Blast Was Unlikely Convert to Militancy." *New York Times*, 9 June 2002, 22.

Heffelfinger, Chris. "Kuwaiti Cleric Hamid Al-Ali: The Bridge between Ideology and Action." *Terrorism Monitor* 5, no. 8 (26 April 2007).

Hegghammer, Thomas. "Terrorist Recruitment and Radicalization in Saudi Arabia." *Middle East Policy* 13, no. 4 (Winter 2006): 39–60.

Henderson, Simon. "Al-Qaeda Attack on Abqaiq: The Vulnerability of Saudi Oil." *PolicyWatch* No. 1082 (28 February 2006).

Hill, Peter. "Kamikaze, 1943–5." In *Making Sense of Suicide Missions*, edited by Diego Gambetta, 1–42. Oxford: Oxford University Press, 2005.

"Hizb Ut-Tahrir Al-Islami (Islamic Party of Liberation)." *GlobalSecurity.org*. Accessed 8 April 2008.

Hoffman, Bruce. "Al Qaeda, Trends in Terrorism, and Future Potentialities: An Assessment." *Studies in Conflict and Terrorism* 26, no. 6 (November–December 2003): 429–42.

——. *Inside Terrorism*. New York: Columbia University Press, 1998.

——. *Inside Terrorism*. Revised and expanded ed. New York: Columbia University Press, 2006.

——. "The Logic of Suicide Terrorism." *Atlantic Monthly*, June 2003, 40–47.

——. "Remember Al Qaeda? They're Baaack." *Los Angeles Times*, 20 February 2007.

Hoffman, Bruce, and Gordon H. McCormick. "Terrorism, Signaling, and Suicide Attack." *Studies in Conflict and Terrorism* 27, no. 4 (July–August 2004): 243–81.

Holmes, Stephen. "Al-Qaeda, September 11, 2001." In *Making Sense of Suicide Missions*, edited by Diego Gambetta, 131–72. Oxford: Oxford University Press, 2005.

Hopgood, Stephen. "Tamil Tigers, 1987–2002." In *Making Sense of Suicide Missions*, edited by Diego Gambetta, 43–76. Oxford: Oxford University Press, 2005.

Hosmer, Stephen T. *Viet Cong Repression and Its Implications for the Future*. Lexington, MA: Heath Lexington Books, 1970.

Hsu, Spencer S., and Walter Pincus. "U.S. Warns of Stronger Al Qaeda." *Washington Post*, 12 July 2007, 1.

Hunt, Kasie. "Osama Bin Laden Fan Clubs, Jihad Recruiters, Build Online Communities." *USA Today*, 9 March 2006, 4A.

Husain, Syed Rashid, Al-Khobar, and Peter Conradi. "Al-Qaeda Pledges War on Saudi Oil Plants." *Sunday Times*, 26 February 2006.

Husayn, Fuad. *Al-Zarqawi: The Second Generation of Al-Qaida*. London: Published in Arabic in 15 Parts by *Al-Quds al-Arabi*; translation by Foreign Broadcast Information Service, 2005.

Hussain, Ali. "Focus: Undercover on Planet Beeston." *Sunday Times*, 2 July 2006.

Husseini, Rana. "Jordan Charges Five Iraqis, Two Others with Terror Conspiracy." *Jordan Times*, 7 June 2006.

——. "Sajida Pleads 'Not Guilty' in Terror Trial; Court Says No to Psychiatric Evaluation." *Jordan Times*, 16 May 2006.

——. "Witness Gives Testimony on Discovery of Explosives Belt." *Jordan Times*, 6 June 2006.

Hyland, Frank. "New Arrests Show Turkey as a Recruiting Ground for Islamist Militants." *Terrorism Focus* 4, no. 18 (12 June 2007).

International Crisis Group. "In Their Own Words: Reading the Iraqi Insurgency." *ICG Middle East Report No. 50*. Brussels: International Crisis Group, 15 February 2006.

——. "Indonesia Backgrounder: Why Salafism and Terrorism Mostly Don't Mix." *Asia Report No. 83*, 1–59. Brussels: International Crisis Group, 13 September 2004.

"Interrogation of Suspect Reveals New Details of Singapore Plot." *International Policy Institute for Counter-Terrorism*, 19 December 2002.

"Iraq Bomber Was 'Belgian Woman.'" *BBC News*, 30 November 2005.

"The Iraqi Al-Qaida Organization: A Self-Portrait." *MEMRI Special Dispatch Series* No. 884 (24 March 2005).

"Iraq: Suicide Attacks." *Council on Foreign Relations*, 1 August 2005.

"Islamic Jihad Group (Uzbekistan)." *Terrorism Knowledge Base*.

Jaber, Hala. "Middle-Class Bombers Find DIY 'Martyr Belt' Online." *Times Online*, 17 July 2005.

Jackson, Brian A. "Groups, Networks, or Movements: A Command-and-Control-Driven Approach to Classifying Terrorist Organizations and Its Application to Al Qaeda." *Studies in Conflict and Terrorism* 29, no. 3 (April–May 2006): 241–62.

Jaff, Warzer, and Robert F. Worth. "Blast Kills 122 at Iraqi Clinic in Attack on Security Recruits." *New York Times*, 1 March 2005.

"Jaish Ansar Al-Sunnah Insurgency Group in Iraq Releases Detailed Communiqué and Video on Their Attack against the US Base in Mosul." *SITE Institute*, undated.

"Jamaat Jund Al-Sahaba Issues Warning to Those Who Disgrace Sunni Mosques." *SITE Institute*, 24 March 2005.

"Jihad and Terrorism Studies." *MEMRI Special Dispatch Series* No. 917 (7 June 2005).

"Jihadist Forum Provides Biography of a Suicide Bomber in Iraq, Abu Osman Al-Yamani." *SITE Institute*, 18 April 2006.

Johnston, David, and David E. Sanger. "New Leaders Are Emerging for Al Qaeda." *New York Times*, 10 August 2004, A1.

Johnston, David, and Don Van Natta Jr. "U.S. Officials See Signs of a Revived Al Qaeda." *New York Times*, 17 May 2003, 1.

Jones, Toby Craig. "The Clerics, the Sahwa, and the Saudi State." *Strategic Insights* 4, no. 3 (March 2005).

"Jordan's 9/11: Dealing with Jihadi Islamism." *ICG Middle East Report No. 47*, 1–28. Brussels: International Crisis Group, 2005.

Juergensmeyer, Mark. *Terror in the Mind of God: The Global Rise of Religious Violence*. Berkeley: University of California Press, 2001.

"Kabul Suicide Bomb Hits US Convoy." *BBC News*, 8 September 2006.

Kalyvas, Stathis, and Ignacio Sánchez-Cuenca. "Killing without Dying: The Absence of Suicide Missions." In *Making Sense of Suicide Missions*, edited by Diego Gambetta, 209–32. Oxford: Oxford University Press, 2005.

Kaplan, David E. "The Saudi Connection: How Billions in Oil Money Spawned a Global Terror Network." *U.S. News & World Report*, 15 December 2003.

Kaplan, Eben. "Terrorists and the Internet." *Council on Foreign Relations Backgrounder*, 12 May 2006.

Karmon, Ely. "Egypt as a New Front of Al Qaeda." *International Policy Institute for Counter-Terrorism (ICT)*, 5 May 2006.

Karzai, Hekmat. "Afghanistan and the Logic of Suicide Terrorism." *IDSS Commentaries* 20 (27 March 2006).

Katz, Rita. "The Coming New Wave of Jihad." *Boston Globe*, 13 March 2006.

Katz, Rita, and Michael Kern. "Center of the Jihadist World; They Call It Londonistan for a Reason." *National Review Online*, 11 July 2005.

Kepel, Gilles. *Jihad: The Trail of Political Islam*. Cambridge, MA: Harvard University Press, 2002.

Kermani, Navid. *Dynamit des Geistes: Martyrium, Islam, und Nihilismus*. Göttingen: Wallstein Verlag, 2002.

Khalil, Ashraf. "Iraq's Sufi Community Shaken by Deadly Attack." *Los Angeles Times*, 5 June 2005.

Khalil, Lydia. "Divisions within the Iraqi Insurgency." *Terrorism Monitor* 5, no. 7 (12 April 2007).

——. "The Islamic State of Iraq Launches." *Terrorism Focus* 4, no. 7 (27 March 2007).

Khashan, Hilal. "Collective Palestinian Frustration and Suicide Bombing." *Third World Quarterly* 24, no. 6 (2003): 1049–67.

Khosrokhavar, Farhad. *Suicide Bombers: Allah's New Martyrs*. Translated by David Macey. London: Pluto, 2005.

Kimhi, Shaul, and Shmuel Even. "Who Are the Palestinian Suicide Bombers?" *Terrorism and Political Violence* 16, no. 4 (Winter 2004): 815–40.

Klein, Joe. "Saddam's Revenge." *Time*, 26 September 2005, 44.

Knickmeyer, Ellen. "They Came Here to Die." *Washington Post*, 11 May 2005, A1.

Knop, Katharina von. "The Female Jihad: Al Qaeda's Women." *Studies in Conflict and Terrorism* 30, no. 5 (May 2007): 397–414.

Kohlmann, Evan. *Al-Qaida's Jihad in Europe: The Afghan-Bosnian Network*. New York: Berg, 2004.

——. "American Greases Al-Qaida Media Machine." *NBC News*, 14 July 2006.

Kramer, Martin. *Arab Awakening and Islamic Revival: The Politics of Ideas in the Middle East*. New Brunswick, NJ: Transaction, 1996.

——. "Introduction." In *Shiism, Resistance, and Revolution*, edited by Martin Kramer, 1–18. Boulder: Westview Press, 1987.

——. "The Moral Logic of Hizballah." In *Origins of Terrorism: Psychologies, Ideologies, Theologies, States of Mind*, edited by Walter Reich, 131–57. Washington, DC: Woodrow Wilson Center Press, 1998.

——. "Sacrifice and Fratricide in Shiite Lebanon." *Terrorism and Political Violence* 3, no. 3 (Winter 1991): 30–47.

Krebs, Brian. "Three Worked the Web to Help Terrorists." *Washington Post*, 6 July 2007.

Krueger, Alan B., and Jitka Maleckova. "Education, Poverty, Political Violence, and Terrorism: Is There a Causal Connection?" *NBER Working Paper No. 9074*, 1–47. Cambridge, MA: National Bureau of Economic Research, July 2002.

Kulish, Nicholas. "New Terrorism Case Confirms That Denmark Is a Target." *New York Times*, 17 September 2007.

Kurayshan, Ahmad. "State Security Directs Charges of Terrorist Plotting and Possession of Explosive Charges." *Al-Ra'y*, 16 March 2006.

Kydd, Andrew, and Barbara F. Walter. "Sabotaging the Peace: The Politics of Extremist Violence." *International Organization* 56, no. 2 (2002): 263–96.

Laabs, Dirk, and Sebastian Rotella. "Terrorists in Training Are Going to Pakistan." *Los Angeles Times*, 14 October 2007.

Lachkar, Joan. "The Psychological Make-Up of a Suicide Bomber." *Journal of Psychohistory* 29, no. 4 (Spring 2002): 349–67.

Lamb, Christina. "NATO Chief Will Front Musharraf to Demand Taliban Leader Omar's Arrest." Agence France Press, 9 October 2006, 9.

Lamont-Brown, Raymond. *Kamikaze: Japan's Suicide Samurai*. London: Cassell, 1997.

Laqueur, Walter. *No End to War: Terrorism in the Twenty-First Century*. New York: Continuum, 2003.

——. *Terrorism*. Boston: Little Brown, 1977.

Latif, Aamir. "The Land of an Eye for an Eye." *U.S. News & World Report*, 19 August 2007.

Lawrence, Bruce B. *Defenders of God: The Fundamentalist Revolt against the Modern Age*. Edited by Frederick M. Denny. Studies in Comparative Religion. Columbia, SC: University of South Carolina Press, 1995.

"Leader of Al-Qaeda in Iraq Al-Zarqawi Declares 'Total War' on Shiites That the Sunni Women of Tel Afar Had 'Their Wombs Filled with the Sperm of the Crusaders.'" *MEMRI Special Dispatch Series* No. 987 (16 September 2005).

Lester, David, Bijou Yang, and Mark Lindsay. "Suicide Bombers: Are Psychological Profiles Possible?" *Studies in Conflict and Terrorism* 27, no. 4 (July–August 2004): 283–95.

"Letter from Al-Zawahiri to Al-Zarqawi." Available at the Web site of GlobalSecurity.

Levitt, Matthew, and Julie Sawyer. "Zarqawi's Jordanian Agenda." *Terrorism Monitor* 2, no. 24 (16 December 2004).

Lewis, Bernard. *The Assassins: A Radical Sect in Islam*. New York: Oxford University Press, 1987.

Lia, Brynjar. "Al-Suri's Doctrines for Decentralized Jihadi Training—Part I." *Terrorism Monitor* 5, no. 1 (18 January 2007).

——. *"Destructive Doctrinarians": Abu Musab Al-Suri's Critique of the Salafis in the Jihadi Current*. Kjeller, Norway: Norwegian Defence Research Establishment, 2007.

Lia, Brynjar, and Thomas Hegghammer. "Jihadi Strategic Studies: The Alleged Al Qaida Policy Study Preceding the Madrid Bombings." *Studies in Conflict and Terrorism* 27, no. 5 (September–October 2004): 355–75.

Long, David E. *The Anatomy of Terrorism*. New York: Free Press, 1990.

MacFarquhar, Neil. "Lebanese Would-Be Suicide Bomber Tells How Volunteers Are Waging Jihad in Iraq." *New York Times*, 2 November 2004, 11.

——. "Suicide Bomber Attacks Saudi Arabia's Interior Ministry." *New York Times*, 30 December 2004, 8.

Magouirk, Justin, Scott Atran, and Marc Sageman. "Connecting Terrorist Networks." *Studies in Conflict and Terrorism* 31, no. 1 (January 2008): 1–16.

Malik, Shiv. "My Brother the Bomber." *Prospect Magazine*, June 2007.

Maris, Ronald W., Alan L. Berman, and Morton M. Silverman, eds. *Comprehensive Textbook of Suicidology*. New York: Guilford Press, 2000.

Marzban, Omid. "The Foreign Makeup of Afghan Suicide Bombers." *Terrorism Focus* 3, no. 7 (21 February 2007).

Mazzetti, Mark. "Intelligence Chief Says Al Qaeda Improves Ability to Strike in U.S." *New York Times*, 6 February 2008.

——. "CIA sees Qaeda Link in the Death of Bhutto." *New York Times*, 19 January 2008, 8.

Mazzetti, Mark, and David Rohde. "Al Qaeda's Leaders Rebuilding Networks." *International Herald Tribune*, 20 February 2007, 1.

McCants, William F. "Militant Ideology Atlas." West Point, NY: Combating Terrorism Center, November 2006.

McCauley, Clark R., and M. E. Segal. "Social Psychology of Terrorist Groups." In *Group Processes and Intergroup Relations: Review of Personality and Social Psychology*, edited by C. Hendrick, 231–56. Newbury Park: Sage, 1987.

McDonnell, Patrick J. "The World; Argentina Alleges Iran Ordered Attacks." *Los Angeles Times*, 26 October 2006, 5.

McDonnell, Patrick J., and Sebastian Rotella. "Making Bombers in Iraq." *Los Angeles Times*, 29 February 2004.

McElroy, Damien. "US Forces Hunt Down Al-Qaeda in Sudan." *Sunday Telegraph*, 1 August 2004, 26.

Mekhennet, Souad, and Michael Moss. "In Jihadist Heaven, a Goal: To Kill and Die in Iraq." *New York Times*, 4 May 2007.

Merari, Ariel. "The Readiness to Kill and Die: Suicidal Terrorism in the Middle East." In *Origins of Terrorism: Psychologies, Ideologies, Theologies, States of Mind*, edited by Walter Reich, 192–207. Washington, DC: Woodrow Wilson Center Press, 1998.

Meyer, Josh. "Some U.S. Officials Fear Iran Is Helping Al Qaeda." *Los Angeles Times*, 21 March 2006.

Miller, Greg, and Tyler Marshall. "More Iraqis Lured to Al Qaeda Group." *Los Angeles Times*, 16 September 2005.

Moghadam, Assaf. "The Chlorine Gas Attacks in Iraq and the Specter of Suicide Attacks with CBRN Weapons." *Counterterrorism Blog* (19 March 2007).

——. "Defining Suicide Terrorism." In *Root Causes of Suicide Terrorism: The Globalization of Martyrdom*, edited by Ami Pedahzur, 13–24. New York: Routledge, 2006.

——. "Mayhem, Myths, and Martyrdom: The Shia Conception of Jihad." *Terrorism and Political Violence* 19, no. 1 (Spring 2007): 125–43.

——. "Palestinian Suicide Terrorism in the Second Intifada: Motivations and Organizational Aspects." *Studies in Conflict and Terrorism* 26, no. 2 (2003): 65–92.

——. "The Roots of Suicide Terrorism: A Multi-causal Approach." In *Root Causes of Suicide Terrorism: The Globalization of Martyrdom*, edited by Ami Pedahzur, 81–107. New York: Routledge, 2006.

——. *The Roots of Terrorism*. New York: Chelsea House, 2006.

——. "Suicide Bombings in the Israeli-Palestinian Conflict: A Conceptual Framework." Herzliyya, Israel: Project for the Research of Islamist Movements (PRISM), May 2002.

——. "Suicide Terrorism, Occupation, and the Globalization of Martyrdom: A Critique of 'Dying to Win.'" *Studies in Conflict and Terrorism* 29, no. 8 (December 2006): 707–29.

Moreau, Ron. "Where the Jihad Lives Now." *Newsweek*, 29 October 2007.

Moss, Robert. *Urban Guerrilla Warfare*. London: International Institute for Strategic Studies, 1971.

Musharbash, Yassin. "37.000 Kreditkarten für 'Terrorist 007.'" *Spiegel Online*, 26 July 2007.

——. "Al-Qaida Startet Terror-TV." *Spiegel Online*, 7 October 2005.

——. "Der Cyber-Friedhof der Dschihadis." *Spiegel Online*, 25 October 2005.

——. "Die Pakistan-Connection." *Spiegel Online*, 11 August 2006.

——. "Er war schöner als der Mond." *Spiegel Online*, 25 October 2005.

——. "Reiseführer für Terror-Touristen." *Spiegel Online*, 25 July 2005.

——. "Terroristen benutzen Zehnjaehrigen als Selbstmordattentaeter." *Spiegel Online*, 12 November 2007.

——. "Wie Al-Qaida den Jahrestag der Anschläge Begeht." *Spiegel Online*, 11 September 2006.

"Muslim Americans: Middle Class and Mostly Mainstream." Washington, DC: Pew Research Center, 2007.

Myers, Steven Lee. "Suicide Strike; with Bombing, Iraqis Escalate Guerrilla Tactics and Show New Danger on Front Lines." *New York Times*, 30 March 2003, 4.

National Commission on Terrorist Attacks upon the United States. *The 9/11 Commission Report: Final Report of the National Commission on Terrorist Attacks upon the United States*. New York: Norton, 2004.

——. Statement of Marc Sageman to the National Commission on Terrorist Attacks upon the United States, 9 July 2003.

Naughton, Philippe. "Five Given Life for Fertiliser Bomb Terror Plot." *Times Online*, 30 April 2007.

Nesser, Petter. "Jihadism in Western Europe after the Invasion of Iraq: Tracing Motivational Influences from the Iraq War on Jihadist Terrorism in Western Europe." *Studies in Conflict and Terrorism* 29, no. 4 (June 2006): 323–42.

"New Al-Jazeera Videos: London Suicide Bomber before 'Entering Gardens of Paradise,' and Ayman Al-Zawahiri's Threats of More Bombings in the West." *MEMRI Special Dispatch Series* No. 979 (3 September 2005).

"A New Bin Laden Speech." *MEMRI Special Dispatch Series* No. 539 (18 July 2003).

"Newly-Released Video of Al-Qaeda's Deputy Leader Ayman Al-Zawahiri's Interview to Al-Sahab TV." *MEMRI Special Dispatch Series* No. 1044 (8 December 2005).

Nordland, Rod, and Babak Dehghanpisheh. "Surge of Suicide Bombers." *Newsweek*, 13 August 2007.

Nordland, Rod, Tom Masland, and Christopher Dickey. "Unmasking the Insurgents." *Newsweek*, 7 February 2005, 20.

Norton-Taylor, Richard. "Iraq War 'Motivated London Bombers.'" *Guardian*, 3 April 2006.

Obaid, Nawaf, and Anthony Cordesman. *Saudi Militants in Iraq: Assessment and Kingdom's Response*. Center for Strategic and International Studies, September 2005.

O'Neill, Sean, and Daniel McGrory. "9/11 Prisoners Reveal British Terror Targets." *Times Online*, 8 September 2006.

——. "Abu Hamza and the 7/7 Bombers." *Times* (London), 8 February 2006.

O'Neill, Sean, Tom Reid, and Michael Evans. "7/7 'Mastermind' Is Seized in Iraq." *Times*, 28 April 2007.

Omestad, Thomas. "The Casbah Connection: Why Morocco Is Producing Some of the World's Most Feared Terrorists." *U.S. News & World Report*, 9 May 2005, 20–33.

Oppel, Richard A., Jr. "Foreign Fighters in Iraq Are Tied to Allies of U.S." *New York Times*, 22 November 2007.

Orbach, Benjamin. "Usama Bin Ladin and Al-Qaida: Origins and Doctrines." *Middle East Review of International Affairs (MERIA)* 5, no. 4 (December 2001): 54–68.

"Osama Bin Laden: 'Today There Is a Conflict between World Heresy under the Leadership of America on the One Hand and the Islamic Nation with the Mujahideen in Its Vanguard on the Other.'" *MEMRI Special Dispatch Series* No. 838 (30 December 2004).

Osman, Hiwa. "What Do the Insurgents Want? Different Visions, Same Bloody Tactics." *Washington Post*, 8 May 2005, B1.

Oxford, Esther. "Pakistan Grapples with Menace of Suicide Bombers." *Independent*, 30 November 2000, 18.

Pape, Robert A. *Dying to Win: The Strategic Logic of Suicide Terrorism*. New York: Random House, 2005.

Parker, Ned. "Insurgents Report a Split with Al Qaeda in Iraq." *Los Angeles Times*, 27 March 2007.

Partlow, Joshua. "An Uphill Battle to Stop Fighters at Border." *Washington Post*, 5 May 2007.

Paz, Reuven. "Arab Volunteers Killed in Iraq: An Analysis." *PRISM Occasional Papers* 3, no. 1 (March 2005): 1–7.

——. "The Brotherhood of Global Jihad." *Project for the Research of Islamist Movement (PRISM)* (October 2001): 1–27.

——. "From Madrid to London: Al-Qaeda Exports the War in Iraq to Europe." *PRISM Occasional Papers* 3, no. 3 (July 2005): 1–7.

——. "From Riyadh 1995 to Sinai 2004: The Return of Al-Qaeda to the Arab Homeland." *PRISM Occasional Papers* 2, no. 3 (October 2004): 1–9.

——. "The 'Global Campaign against Aggression': The Supreme Council of Global Jihad." *PRISM Occasional Papers* 1, no. 6 (May 2003): 1–5.

——. "Global Jihad and the European Arena." Paper presented at the International Conference on Intelligence and Terrorism, Priverno, Italy, 15–18 May 2002.

——. "Global Jihad and the United States: Interpretation of the New World Order of Usama Bin Ladin." *PRISM Series of Global Jihad* 1, no. 1 (March 2003): 1–8.

——. "Hasan Al-Qaed (Abu Yahya Al-Libi) on Jihadi Terrorism against Muslims in Muslim Countries." *PRISM Occasional Papers* 5, no. 2 (August 2007): 1–7.

——. "The Impact of the War in Iraq on Islamist Groups and the Culture of Global Jihad." Paper presented at the International Conference on the Impact of Global Terrorism, International Policy Institute for Counter-Terrorism, Herzliyya, Israel, 11–14 September 2004.

——. "The Impact of the War in Iraq on the Global Jihad." *Current Trends in Islamist Ideology* 1 (2005): 39–49.

——. "The Islamic Debate over Democracy: Jihadi-Salafi Responses to Hamas' Victory in the Palestinian Elections." *PRISM Occasional Papers* 4, no. 1 (January 2006): 1–9.

——. "Islamic Legitimacy for the London Bombings." *PRISM Occasional Papers* 3, no. 4 (July 2005): 1–8.

——. "Programmed Terrorists: An Analysis of the Letter Left Behind by the September 11 Hijackers." *International Policy Institute for Counter-Terrorism (ICT)*, 13 December 2001.

——. "Qaidat Al-Jihad: Moving Forward or Backward? The Algerian GSPC Joins Al Qaeda." *PRISM Occasional Papers* 4, no. 5 (September 2006): 1–10.

——. "Qaidat Al-Jihad: A New Name on the Road to Palestine." *International Policy Institute for Counter-Terrorism (ICT)*, 7 May 200, 1–7.

——. "Sawt Al-Jihad: New Indoctrination of Qaidat Al-Jihad." *PRISM Occasional Papers* 1, no. 8 (October 2003): 1–7.

——. "Suicide Terrorist Operations in Chechnya: An Escalation of the Islamist Struggle." *International Policy Institute for Counter-Terrorism (ICT)*, 20 June 2000.

——. "Zarqawi's Strategy in Iraq—Is There a New Al-Qaeda?" *PRISM Occasional Papers* 3, no. 5 (August 2005): 1–5.

Pedahzur, Ami. *Suicide Terrorism*. Cambridge: Polity, 2005.

Pedahzur, Ami, and Arie Perliger. "The Changing Nature of Suicide Attacks: A Social Network Perspective." *Social Forces* 84 (June 2006): 1987–2008.

Pedahzur, Ami, Arie Perliger, and Leonard Weinberg. "Altruism and Fatalism: The Characteristics of Palestinian Suicide Terrorists." *Deviant Behavior* 24, no. 4 (July-August 2003): 405–23.

Pennington, Matthew. "Musharraf Survives Another Suicide Attack." *Gazette*, 26 December 2003, A20.

Perelman, Marc. "A New, Younger Jihadi Threat Emerges." *Christian Science Monitor*, 28 December 2007.

Piazza, James. "Rooted in Poverty? Terrorism, Poor Economic Development and Social Cleavages." *Terrorism and Political Violence* 18, no. 1 (Spring 2006): 159–78.

Pinault, David. *The Shiites: Ritual and Popular Piety in a Muslim Community*. New York: St. Martin's Press, 1992.

Pleming, Sue. "US Tells Syria to Stop Bombers Crossing into Iraq." Reuters, 27 March 2007.

"Police Found Weapons at Finsbury Park Mosque." *Times Online* (London), 7 February 2006.

Powell, Bill. "A War without Borders." *Time*, 21 November 2005.

Priest, Dana, and Susan Schmidt. "Al Qaeda's Top Primed to Collapse, U.S. Says." *Washington Post*, 16 March 2003, A1.

"Profile of a Suicide Bomber: Single Male, Average Age—21." *Haaretz*, 24 August 2001.

"Q&A: UK Aircraft Bombplot." *BBC News*, 12 August 2006.

"Qaeda Video Calls for Attacks on Gulf Oil Plants." Associated Press, 7 December 2005.

Quinn, Patrick, and Katherine Shrader. "Foreigners Blamed for Iraq Suicide Attacks." Associated Press, 1 July 2005.

Rabasa, Angel, Peter Chalk, Kim Cragin, Sara A. Daly, Heather A. Gregg, Theodore W. Karasik, Kevin A. O'Brien, and William Rosenau. *Beyond Al-Qaeda, Part 1: The Global Jihadist Movement*. Santa Monica, CA: RAND, 2006.

——. *Beyond Al-Qaeda, Part 2: The Outer Rings of the Terrorist Universe*. Santa Monica, CA: RAND, 2006.

Radu, Michael. "London 7/7 and Its Impact." *Foreign Policy Research Institute (FPRI) E-Notes* 6, no. 5 (July 2005).

Rageh, Rawya. "Ansar Al-Sunnah Army Gains Clout in Iraq." Associated Press, 25 December 2004.

Raghavan, Sudarsan. "Friends Describe Bomber's Political, Religious Evolution." *Washington Post*, 29 July 2005, A16.

Rahmani, Waliullah. "Afghan Authorities Apprehend Leaders of Kabul Suicide Cell." *Terrorism Focus* 3, no. 39 (10 October 2006).

——. "Combating the Ideology of Suicide Terrorism in Afghanistan." *Terrorism Monitor* 4, no. 21 (2 November 2006).

Ramachandran, Sudha. "Killers Turn to Suicide." *Asia Times*, 15 October 2004.

Rapoport, David C. "Sacred Terror: A Contemporary Example from Islam." In *Origins of Terrorism: Psychologies, Ideologies, Theologies, States of Mind*, edited by Walter Reich, 103–30. Washington, DC: Woodrow Wilson Center Press, 1998.

"Report into the London Terrorist Attacks on 7 July 2005." Intelligence and Security Committee, May 2006.

"Report of the 7 July Review Committee." London: London Assembly, June 2006.

"Report of the Official Account of the Bombings in London on 7th July 2005." House of Commons, 11 May 2006.

Reuter, Christoph. *My Life Is a Weapon: A Modern History of Suicide Bombing*. Princeton, NJ: Princeton University Press, 2004.

Rhode, David, and C. J. Chivers. "Qaeda's Grocery Lists and Manuals of Killing." *New York Times*, 17 March 2002, A1.

Rhode, David, and James Risen. "A Hostile Land Foils the Quest for Bin Laden." *New York Times*, 13 December 2004, 1.

Richard, Yann. *Shiite Islam: Polity, Ideology, and Creed*. Oxford: Blackwell, 1995.

Richburg, Keith B. "Suicide Bomb Survivors Face Worlds Blown Apart." *Washington Post*, 31 January 2004, 15.

Ridolfo, Kathleen. "Iraq: U.S. Ambassador Announces Seven-Point Plan for Country." *Radio Free Europe/Radio Liberty*, 2 August 2005.

Riebling, Mark, and R. P. Eddy. "Jihad@work: Behind the Moscow Theater Attack." *National Review Online* (24 October 2002).

Riedel, Bruce. "Al-Qaida's Resurgence in Pakistan." *CTC Sentinel* 1, no. 1 (December 2007): 8–10.

Risen, James. "In Tape, Top Aide to Bin Laden Vows New Strikes at U.S." *New York Times*, 10 September 2004, 10.

Risen, James, and David E. Sanger. "Border Clashes as U.S. Pressures Syria over Iraq." *New York Times*, 15 October 2005, 1.

Rogan, Hanna. "Dynamics of the Jihadi Online Media Campaign." Kjeller, Norway: Norwegian Defence Research Establishment, 2007.

Rosenthal, Franz. "On Suicide in Islam." *Journal of the American Oriental Society* 66, no. 3 (July–September 1946): 239–59.

Rotella, Sebastian. "European Women Join Ranks of Jihadis." *Los Angeles Times*, 10 January 2006.

———. "Terrorism Suspects Traced to Iran." *Los Angeles Times*, 1 August 2004.

Roy, Olivier. *Globalized Islam: The Search for a New Ummah*. New York: Columbia University Press, 2004.

Rubin, Alissa J. "70 Killed in Wave of Revenge in Northern Iraq." *New York Times*, 29 March 2007.

Rubin, Michael. "Ansar Al-Sunna: Iraq's New Terrorist Threat." *Middle East Intelligence Bulletin* 6, no. 5 (May 2004).

Sageman, Marc. *Understanding Terror Networks*. Philadelphia: University of Pennsylvania Press, 2004.

Sarraj, Eyad. "Suicide Bombers: Dignity, Despair, and the Need of Hope." *Journal of Palestine Studies* 31, no. 4 (Summer 2004): 71–76.

Schalk, Peter. "Resistance and Martyrdom in the Process of State Formation of Tamil Eelam."

Scheuer, Michael. "Al-Qaeda and Algeria's GSPC: Part of a Much Bigger Picture." *Terrorism Focus* 4, no. 8 (3 April 2007).

———. "Al-Qaeda at Year's End 2007: What Do the Facts Say?" *Terrorism Focus* 4, no. 42 (19 December 2007).

———. "Al-Qaeda's New Leader in Afghanistan: A Profile of Abu Al-Yazid." *Terrorism Focus* 4, no. 21 (3 July 2007).

———. "Al-Zawahiri's September 11 Video Hits Main Themes of Al-Qaeda." *Terrorism Focus* 3, no. 36 (19 September 2006).

———. "Assessing London and Sharm Al-Sheikh: The Role of the Internet Intelligence and Urban Warfare Training." *Terrorism Focus* 2, no. 15 (5 August 2005).

———. "Coalition Warfare, Part II: How Zarqawi Fits into Bin Laden's World Front." *Terrorism Focus* 2, no. 8 (28 April 2005).

———. "Is Global Jihad a Fading Phenomenon?" *Terrorism Focus* 5, no. 13 (1 April 2008).

———. "Latest Al-Zawahiri Tape Targets American Society." *Terrorism Focus* 4, no. 13 (8 May 2007).

———. "The London Bombings: For Al-Qaeda, Steady as She Goes." *Terrorism Focus* 2, no. 14 (22 July 2005): 5–8.

———. "The London Plot: A Tactical Victory in an Eroding Strategic Environment." *Terrorism Focus* 3, no. 32 (15 August 2006).

———. "Osama Bin Laden: Taking Stock of the 'Zionist-Crusader War.' " *Terrorism Focus* 3, no. 16 (25 April 2006).

———. " 'The Pious Caliphate Will Start from Afghanistan': Is Al-Qaeda's Long-Held Afghan Strategy Now Unfolding?" *Terrorism Focus* 2, no. 12 (24 June 2005).

———. "Toronto, London, and the Jihadi Spring: Bin Laden as Successful Instigator." *Terrorism Focus* 3, no. 22 (6 June 2006).

———. "The West Is Running Out of Time in Afghanistan." *Terrorism Focus* 3, no. 40 (17 October 2006).

———. "Zawahiri: Foreshadowing Attacks on Israel and America?" *Terrorism Focus* 3, no. 2 (18 January 2006).

———. "Zawahiri: Internationalizing Jihad, Uniting Muslims and Trumping Saudi Clerics." *Terrorism Focus* 3, no. 30 (1 August 2006).

Schiff, Zeev. "Analysis: Dahab Terror Attack Indicative of Egypt's Failure." *Haaretz*, 25 April 2006.

———. "Islamization in Europe." *Haaretz*, 11 November 2005.

Schmid, Alex P., and A. J. Jongman. *Political Terrorism: A Research Guide to Concepts, Theories, Data Bases, and Literature*. New Brunswick, NJ: Transaction, 1984.

Schmitt, Eric. "U.S. and Allies Capture More Foreign Fighters." *New York Times*, 19 June 2005, 8.

Schweitzer, Yoram. "Global Jihad as Reaction to American Policy: A Dangerous Delusion." *Tel Aviv Notes* No. 118 (9 December 2004).

———. "Suicide Terrorism: Development and Main Characteristics." In *Countering Suicide Terrorism*, edited by International Policy Institute for Counter-Terrorism (ICT), 77–88. Herzliyya, Israel: ICT, 2001.

Schweitzer, Yoram, and Sari Goldstein Ferber. "Al Qaeda and the Internationalization of Suicide Terrorism." In *Jaffee Center for Strategic Studies Memorandum No. 78*, 1–94. Tel Aviv, Israel, 2005.

Sciolino, Elaine, and Stephen Grey. "British Terror Trial Traces a Path to Militant Islam." *New York Times*, 26 November 2006, 1.

Sciolino, Elaine, and Don Van Natta Jr. "For a Decade, London Thrived as a Busy Crossroads of Terror." *New York Times*, 10 July 2005.

"Security, Terrorism, and the UK." In *ISP/NSC Briefing Paper 05/01*, 1–8. London: Economic & Social Research Council, Chatham House, July 2005.

Semple, Kirk. "Bombers Strike Baghdad Hotels." *New York Times*, 25 October 2005, A1.

———. "Iraq Bombers Blow up 2 Children Used as Decoys." *New York Times*, 21 March 2007.

———. "Iraqis Stunned by the Violence of a Bombing." *New York Times*, 18 July 2005, 1.

"Seven Jailed for Turkey Bombing." *BBC News*, 17 February 2007.

Shay, Shaul. *The Shahids: Islam and Suicide Attacks*. New Brunswick, NJ: Transaction Publishers, 2004.

Shihri, Abdullah, and Maggie Michael. "Foiled Plot Mirrored 9/11 Attack." Associated Press, 28 April 2007.

Shrader, Katherine. "Negroponte: Al-Qaida the Biggest Threat." Associated Press, 12 January 2007.

Siegel, Pascale Combelles. "AQIM Renews Its Threats against France." *Terrorism Focus* 4, no. 26 (7 August 2007).

——. "Radical Islam and the French Muslim Prison Population." *Terrorism Monitor* 4, no. 15 (27 July 2006).

Silke, Andrew. "The Role of Suicide in Politics, Conflict, and Terrorism." *Terrorism and Political Violence* 18, no. 1 (Spring 2006): 35–46.

"Sinai Bombers Sentenced to Death." *BBC News*, 30 November 2006.

"Six Accused of London Bomb Plot." *BBC News*, 15 January 2006.

Slackman, Michael. "Out of Desert Poverty, a Caldron of Rage in the Sinai." *New York Times*, 7 May 2006, 6.

Slackman, Michael, and Souad Mekhennet. "Jordan Says Bombing Suspect Aimed to Avenge Brother." *New York Times*, 15 November 2005.

Smith, Barry. "Kamikaze—und der Westen." In *Terror und der Krieg gegen ihn: Öffentliche Reflexionen*, edited by G. Meggle, 107–18. Paderborn, Germany: Mentis, 2003.

Smith, Craig S. "2 Bombs Set by Unit of Al Qaeda Kill 23 in Algeria." *New York Times*, 12 April 2007.

——. "North Africa Feared as Staging Ground for Terror." *New York Times*, 20 February 2007.

Speckhard, Anne, and Khapta Akhmedova. "Black Widows: The Chechen Female Suicide Terrorists." In *Female Suicide Bombers: Dying for Equality?*, edited by Yoram Schweitzer, 63–80. Tel Aviv: Jaffee Center for Strategic Studies, 2006.

——. "The Making of a Martyr: Chechen Suicide Terrorism." *Studies in Conflict and Terrorism* 29, no. 5 (July–August 2006): 429–92.

Speckhard, Anne, Nadejda Tarabrina, Valery Krasnov, and Khapta Akhmedova. "Research Note: Observations of Suicidal Terrorists in Action." *Terrorism and Political Violence* 16, no. 2 (2004): 305–27.

Sprinzak, Ehud. "Rational Fanatics." *Foreign Policy*, September–October 2000, 66–73.

Stanley, Trevor. "Understanding the Origins of Wahhabism and Salafism." *Terrorism Monitor* 3, no. 14 (15 July 2005).

Stemmann, Juan José Escobar. "Middle East Salafism's Influence and the Radicalization of Muslim Communities in Europe." *Middle East Review of International Affairs* 10, no. 3 (September 2006): 1–14.

Stenersen, Anne. "The Internet: A Virtual Training Camp?" Kjeller, Norway: Norwegian Defence Research Establishment, 2007.

Stern, Jessica. "How America Created a Terrorist Haven." *New York Times*, 20 August 2003, 21.

——. "The Protean Enemy." *Foreign Affairs* 82, no. 4 (July–August 2003): 27–40.

——. *Terror in the Name of God: Why Religious Militants Kill*. New York: Ecco/Harper Collins, 2003.

Stringer, David. "7 Convicted in Muslim Terror Camps in UK." *Associated Press*, 27 February 2008.

"Suicide Bombing Terrorism during the Current Israeli-Palestinian Confrontation (September 2000–December 2005)." Intelligence and Terrorism Information Center at the Center for Special Studies (C.S.S), 2006.

Sweilam, Ashraf. "Egyptians Kill Three Bombing Suspects." Associated Press, 21 November 2005.

Syed, Azaz. "56 Suicide Attacks Occurred since 2002." *Daily Times*, 22 October 2007.

"Syrian-British Islamist Sheikh Omar Bakri, Shiite Liberal Intellectual Diyaa Al-Musawi, and Egyptian Intellectual Sheikh Gamal Al-Bana Debate the Meaning of Jihad on New TV." *MEMRI Special Dispatch—Jihad & Terrorism Studies Project* 1529 (30 March 2007).

Taheri, Amir. *Holy Terror: Inside the World of Islamic Terrorism*. Bethesda, MD: Adler & Adler, 1987.

——. "The World Watches as Iraq Becomes a Litmus Test of Democratic Success." *Times* (London), 16 August 2005.

Tait, Robert, and Ewen MacAskill. "Iranian Group Seeks British Suicide Bombers." *Guardian*, 19 April 2006, 1.

"Taliban Boasts of 1000 Suicide Bombers." *The Herald*, 2 March 2007.

"Taliban Recruiting Hundreds of Suicide Bombers for Major Attack on NATO Forces in the Spring: Al Jazeera Reports." *MEMRI Special Dispatch Series—Afghanistan/Jihad & Terrorism* No. 1473 (23 February 2007).

"Tape Justifies Killing Innocent Muslims." *CNN.com*, 19 May 2005.

Tarrow, Sidney. *The New Transnational Activism*. Cambridge: Cambridge University Press, 2005.

"Television Stations Carry Images of Suicide Bombers." Associated Press, 4 April 2003.

"Terror Police Find 'Martyr Tapes.'" *BBC News*, 19 August 2006.

"Terrorist Threat to UK—MI5 Chief's Full Speech." *Times Online*, 10 November 2006.

Timmerman, Kenneth. "This Man Wants You Dead." *Readers' Digest*, July 1997, 50–57.

Tomlinson, Chris. "US General: Suicide and Car Bomb Attacks Down in Iraq." Associated Press, 1 December 2005.

Trenin, Dmitri V., Aleksei V. Malashenko, and Anatol Lieven. *Russia's Restless Frontier: The Chechnya Factor in Post-Soviet Russia*. Washington, DC: Carnegie Endowment for International Peace, 2004.

Trounson, Rebecca, and Tracy Wilkinson. "After the Attack." *Los Angeles Times*, 20 September 2001, A15.

Tumelty, Paul. "An In-Depth Look at the London Bombers." *Terrorism Monitor* 3, no. 15 (28 July 2005): 1–4.

Tyler, Patrick E., and Don Van Natta Jr. "Militants in Europe Openly Call for Jihad and the Rule of Islam." *New York Times*, 26 April 2004, A1.

Ulph, Stephen. "Al Qaeda Commentaries on Ramadan, Iraq, and the Jihad." *Terrorism Focus* 1, no. 6 (15 October 2004).

——. "Al-Qaeda in Iraq Takes Credit for the Amman Bombings." *Terrorism Focus* 2, no. 21 (14 November 2005).

——. "Al-Qaeda TV, via the Web." *Terrorism Focus* 2, no. 18 (4 October 2005).

——. "Al-Qaeda's Online Publications." *Terrorism Focus* 1, no. 5 (1 October 2004).

——. "Al-Zarqawi's Group under Pressure and Seeking Allies." *Terrorism Focus* 3, no. 2 (18 January 2006).

——. "Al-Zarqawi as Master Strategist in Iraq, Rising Leader of the Global Jihad." *Terrorism Focus* 2, no. 20 (31 October 2005).

——. "Al Zawahiri Takes Hamas to Task." *Terrorism Focus* 3, no. 9 (7 March 2006).

——. "A Guide to Jihad on the Web." *Terrorism Focus* 2, no. 7 (31 March 2005).

——. "New Brigade for 'Iraqi' Suicide Bombers." *Terrorism Focus* 2, no. 12 (24 June 2005).

——. "Setmariam Nasar: Background on Al-Qaeda's Arrested Strategist." *Terrorism Focus* 3, no. 12 (28 March 2006).

——. "The Voice of Jihad Is Back." *Terrorism Focus* 2, no. 8 (28 April 2005).

UNAMA. "Suicide Attacks in Afghanistan (2001–2007)." New York: United Nations Assistance Mission to Afghanistan, 2007.

"UN Probe into Murder of Former Lebanese Leader Nears Sensitive Stage—Inquiry Chief." *United Nations News Centre*, 18 December 2006.

U.S. Congress. House. Committee on International Relations. Testimony of Steven Simon before the House of Representatives' Committee on International Relations, Subcommittee on the Middle East and Central Asia. "Is There a Clash of Civilizations? Islam, Democracy, and U.S. Middle East and Central Asia Policy." 109th Cong., 2nd sess., 14 September 2006.

——. Permanent Select Committee on Intelligence. Testimony by Dr. Bruce Hoffman Presented to the House Permanent Select Committee on Intelligence. 109th Cong., 2nd sess., 4 May 2006.

U.S. Congress. Senate. Armed Services Committee. Testimony of Gen. Michael V. Hayden to the Senate Armed Services Committee on "The Current Situation in Iraq and Afghanistan." 109th Cong., 2nd sess., 15 November 2006.

——. Committee on Homeland Security and Government Affairs. Testimony of Ltc. Joseph H. Felter before the Senate Committee on Homeland Security and Governmental Affairs. "The Internet: A Portal to Violent Islamist Extremism." 110th Cong., 1st sess., 3 May 2007.

——. Select Committee on Intelligence. Statement by the Director of National Intelligence, John D. Negroponte, to the Senate Select Committee on Intelligence. 109th Cong., 2nd sess., 2 February 2006.

U.S. Department of State. *Patterns of Global Terrorism, 2003*. Washington, DC : U.S. Department of State, 2004.

"U.S.: Iraq Suicide Attacks Rising during Ramadan." *CNN.com*, 27 September 2006.

Valiyev, Anar. "The Rise of Salafi Islam in Azerbaijan." *Terrorism Monitor* 3, no. 13 (1 July 2005).

Vick, Karl. "Al-Qaeda's Hand in Istanbul Plot." *Washington Post*, 13 February 2007.

——. "A Bomb-Builder, 'out of the Shadow.' " *Washington Post*, 6 February 2006, A1.

Victoroff, Jeff. "The Mind of the Terrorist: A Review and Critique of Psychological Approaches." *Journal of Conflict Resolution* 49, no. 1 (February 2005): 3–42.

"A Video Produced by Al-Sahab Media Depicting a Suicide Bomber's Will and Operation Targeting American Forces in Kabul, Afghanistan." *SITE Institute*, 30 January 2006.

"A Video Will of a Suicide Bomber from Al-Qaeda in Iraq, and His Operation on an American Checkpoint in Al-Fallujah." *SITE Institute*, 21 July 2005.

Vidino, Lorenzo. "The Arab Foreign Fighters and the Sacralization of the Chechen Conflict." *Al Nakhlah* 4, no. 1 (Spring 2006): 1–11.

——. "The Danger of Homegrown Terrorism to Scandinavia." *Terrorism Monitor* 4, no. 20 (19 October 2006).

Waldman, Amy. "Seething Unease Shaped British Bombers' Newfound Zeal." *New York Times*, 31 July 2005, 1.

Waldman, Amy, and Eric Lipton. "Rounding Up Qaeda Suspects: New Cooperation, New Tensions, New Questions." *New York Times*, 17 August 2004, 12.

Waldman, Amy, and Salman Masood. "Elaborate Qaeda Network Hid 2 Captives in Pakistan." *New York Times*, 3 August 2004, 10.

Weimann, Gabriel. *Terror on the Internet: The New Arena, the New Challenges*. Washington, DC: United States Institute of Peace Press, 2006.

Weinberg, Leonard. "Suicide Terrorism for Secular Causes." In *Root Causes of Suicide Terrorism: Globalization of Martyrdom*, edited by Ami Pedahzur, 108–21. London: Routledge, 2006.

Whitlock, Craig. "Al-Qaeda's Far-Reaching New Partner: Salafist Group Finds Limited Appeal in Its Native Algeria." *Washington Post*, 5 October 2006, A1.

——. "Al Qaeda Shifts Its Strategy in Saudi Arabia." *Washington Post*, 19 December 2004, 28.

——. "Amman Bombings Reflect Zarqawi's Growing Reach." *Washington Post*, 13 November 2005, A1.

——. "Architect of New War on the West." *Washington Post*, 23 May 2006, A1.

——. "From Iraq to Algeria, Al-Qaeda's Long Reach." *Washington Post*, 30 May 2007.

——. "In Morocco's 'Chemist,' a Glimpse of Al-Qaeda." *Washington Post*, 7 July 2007.

——. "The New Al Qaeda Central." *Washington Post*, 9 September 2007.

——. "Odyssey of an Al Qaeda Operative." *Washington Post*, 2 May 2005, A1.

——. "Suicide Bombers Strike N. Africa Again." *Washington Post*, 15 April 2007, A19.

Wiktorowicz, Quintan. "Anatomy of the Salafi Movement." *Studies in Conflict and Terrorism* 29, no. 3 (April–May 2006): 207–39.

——. "A Genealogy of Radical Islam." *Studies in Conflict and Terrorism* 28, no. 2 (March–April 2005): 75–97.

Williams, Brian Glyn. "The Taliban Fedayeen: The World's Worst Suicide Bombers?" *Terrorism Monitor* 5, no. 14 (19 July 2007).

Williams, Brian Glyn, and Feyza Altindag. "El Kaide Turka: Tracing an Al-Qaeda Sprinter Cell." *Terrorism Monitor* 2, no. 22 (18 November 2004).

Williams, Brian Glyn, and Cathy Young. "Cheney Attack Reveals Taliban Suicide Bombing Patterns." *Terrorism Monitor* 5, no. 4 (1 March 2007).

Wilson, James Q. *Political Organizations*. New York: Basic Books, 1973.

Windrem, Robert. "The Frightening Evolution of Al-Qaida." *MSNBC.com*, 24 June 2005.

Wines, Michael. "19 Die as Suicide Bomber Destroys Bus near Chechnya." *New York Times*, 6 June 2003.

Winnett, Robert, and David Leppard. "Leaked No. 10 Dossier Reveals Al-Qaeda's British Recruits." *Times* (London), 10 July 2005.

Wockner, Cindy. "Bombers' Jail Rant." *Herald Sun*, 7 October 2007.

Woolcock, Nicola. "How Police and MI5 Foiled 'Britain's 9/11.'" *Times Online*, 30 April 2007.

"World Islamic Front Statement of Jihad against Jews and Crusaders." 23 February 1998. Available online at the Web site of the Federation of American Scientists, http://www.fas.org/irp/world/para/docs/980223-fatwa.htm, last accessed 8 April 2008.

"A World Wide Web of Terror." *Economist*, 12 July 2007.

Wright, Lawrence. *The Looming Tower: Al-Qaeda and the Road to 9/11*. New York: Vintage Books, 2007.

Yousafzai, Sami, and Ron Moreau. "Terror Broker." *Newsweek*, 11 April 2005, 56.

Yousafzai, Sami, Ron Moreau, and Mark Hosenball. "Al Qaeda's Western Recruits." *Newsweek*, 1 January 2007.

Zambelis, Chris. "Al-Hakaima Positions Himself for Key Role in the Global Salafi Jihad." *Terrorism Focus* 3, no. 41 (24 October 2004).

INDEX